LITERARY MODERNISM AND MUSICAL AESTHETICS

Pater, Pound, Joyce, and Stein

This book examines the theory and the practice of music, in relation to the writing of four major modernist figures: Walter Pater,
Ezra Pound, James Joyce, and Gertrude Stein. Brad Bucknell
argues that in the nineteenth century, music was often invoked as
the paradigm of transcendent art. For the modernists, however, late
nineteenth-century debates about music's powerful, but non-
referential ability to make meaning became a significant focus for
their written work. Bucknell examines modernist writers' relationship and engagement with music – from theories about music and
musical–literary relations to the composition of music and libretti
– to show how music actually became another complex trope
deployed in modernism's justification of its own aesthetic practice.
Bucknell's study investigates how music, as a discrete artistic mode
of expression, and a recurring theme in the work of these four
writers, reveals the intricate and varied nature of the modernist
project.

BRAD BUCKNELL is Assistant Professor at the University of
Alberta. He has been a studio musician, a songwriter, a singer, and
a band leader – all before gaining a Ph.D. in English at the
University of Toronto. He has published on the figure of Salome,
on Pater, on African-American literary theory, and on T. S. Eliot.

LITERARY MODERNISM AND MUSICAL AESTHETICS

Pater, Pound, Joyce, and Stein

BRAD BUCKNELL

University of Alberta

CAMBRIDGE
UNIVERSITY PRESS

PUBLISHED BY THE PRESS SYNDICATE OF THE UNIVERSITY OF CAMBRIDGE
The Pitt Building, Trumpington Street, Cambridge, United Kingdom

CAMBRIDGE UNIVERSITY PRESS
The Edinburgh Building, Cambridge CB2 2RU, UK
40 West 20th Street, New York, NY 10011–4211, USA
477 Williamstown Road, Port Melbourne, VIC 3207, Australia
Ruiz de Alarcón 13, 28014 Madrid, Spain
Dock House, The Waterfront, Cape Town 8001, South Africa

http://www.cambridge.org

First published 2001

Printed in the United Kingdom at the University Press, Cambridge

Typeface Baskerville MT 11/12.5 pt.   *System* QuarkXPress™   [SE]

A catalogue record for this book is available from the British Library

ISBN 0 521 66028 9 hardback

To Harold and Lucille Bucknell, with love and gratitude

Contents

Illustrations

Acknowledgments

The familiar formula for thanking those who have contributed to the good parts of your writing, yet relieving them of responsibility for the bad, remains in use here. I have many to thank.

First, I must thank my parents, Harold and Lucille, who have encouraged and supported me throughout the course of the writing of this book. This book is dedicated to them, with love. I would also like to thank my brother, Barry, and my sister, Barbara, and their families, for their good humor and sincere interest over the years.

I must give special thanks to Linda Hutcheon, who at every stage, and in every way, was supportive and enthusiastic. Her intelligence and patience have made all the difference to me, and I offer her my warmest thanks. J. E. Chamberlin read this closely and with an acute and intelligent eye when it was still a thesis. For his time, suggestions, and expansive view of modernity, I am grateful. Deborah Esch and Robert Morgan offered crucial insights into some of the philosophical and musical issues here, and their suggestions came at important moments in the progress of the work. One of the most important teachers, and friends, I have remains Fred Radford, who stirred an early interest in Joyce, and who throughout his career has shown humanity, integrity, intelligence – and great style. I thank him warmly.

Thanks, too, to my teachers, both at the University of Toronto and the University of Alberta: Professors Shirley Rose, S. C. Neuman, R. R. Wilson, Linda Woodbridge, Brian Corman, and Mieke Bal, who have all, in some very important ways, contributed to this work. I must also thank Jennifer Levine and Julian Patrick of the Literary Studies Program at the University of Toronto for allowing me to work with them, and for their generous support.

Many friends have sustained me over the years. Many have read parts of this book, and made comments of great value to me. Suzanne Matheson, Alex McKay, Claudia Clausius, Wyman Herendeen, and the ever witty and precise Colin Atkinson are the best of readers, and the most graceful of friends. Tom Dilworth remains remarkably himself, and that is a blessing. Edward Patterson, Joanne McDowell and Rod Williams have shown ongoing support and interest. So too have Paul Endo and Michael Trussler, two people who have offered the best of friendship, and the best of their considerable intelligence and acumen. Special thanks also to Ashraf H. A. Rushdy, who enthusiastically read parts of the thesis, and who supported my endeavors. To Jeanne Perreault I will always be grateful. Sumita Lall and Wendy Foster helped in the preparation of the manuscript. I have a special affection for them. Karen Clavelle helped with the bibliography, and I thank her here. Many thanks to Elsie Hepburn, my voice teacher, for many years of friendship and instruction.

Special thanks go to my editor, Ray Ryan, and to his assistants, Nikki Burton and Rachel De Wachter for their enduring support and patience. I thank them warmly here. Many thanks, too, to Lesley Atkin for all her assistance in copy editing and to Carol Berger for her fine work on the index. Many thanks to Karl Howe for seeing this through the press.

My thanks to the Social Sciences and Humanities Research Council of Canada for a postdoctoral fellowship which allowed me to do the initial work on Stein. The Bienecke Rare Books and Manuscripts Library at Yale has kindly helped me with the reproductions from Pound's *Le Testament de François Villon*. The Estate of Ezra Pound has graciously allowed me to reproduce pages of the opera. G. Schirmer Inc. has kindly allowed me to reproduce sections of the piano-vocal score of *Four Saints in Three Acts*. Thanks too to the Universities of Manitoba, Windsor, and Alberta whose start up funds have helped in the completion of this book. I am grateful to my colleagues at the University of Manitoba for their support, and especially to David Arnason who supported me so strongly.

Finally, Christine Wiesenthal has made the making of this book real, possible, worthwhile. In silent places, I could always hear her voice. For her intelligence, endurance, and love I give the deepest thanks of all.

Introduction

This book traces certain threads in the relations between music and literature during the modernist period. I will take up here the issue of music, literature, and modernism as a matrix of aesthetic and epistemological ideas variously approached, and just as variously resolved by four significant figures in literary modernism: Walter Pater, Ezra Pound, James Joyce, and Gertrude Stein. These writers are devising and executing their own separate approaches to literature at a time when "music" for many writers refers obliquely to an art which transcends referential or lexical meaning, and which has the power of some kind of excessive, yet essential, element to which the literary may point, but which it can never fully encompass.

The notion that music offers artists of various media a model for some deeper significance, some sense of a non-material harmony and coherence is indeed a very old one. Moreover, the tension residing in the need for a style, or a particular kind of practice of an art, which can point beyond itself to a level of meaning or coherence which is not merely discursive or rhetorical is not new either. But modernism (and perhaps postmodernism in a different way) seems particularly concerned with the invention of new techniques, new methods of showing meaning in the hope of making meaning new as well. Seen in this context, music, or the idea of "music," may be (perhaps too quickly) associated with modernism's elitism, its striving for the recondite through recondite means. In part, I choose the authors I do because, especially in the cases of Pound, Joyce, and Stein, there are perhaps no modernists who better represent the varieties of stylistic and formal difficulty which so identify the movement. From one point of view, these writers represent a kind of conventional notion of "high" modernity; they also in different ways participate in very complex relationships with music or ideas about the aesthetic potential of music, especially in so far as music has to do with temporality. Pater enters my discussion not so much for his stylistic innovations as for his attempt to take on the epistemological problems which art presents and his attempt to resolve these issues through the use of music as the paradigm of all art. More significantly, it is Pater's paradoxical use of the temporal art of music to accomplish his apparently transcendent task which I believe resonates in various ways, and at various levels, in the texts of the later authors. Indeed, it is Pater who so clearly articulates the scene of the modernist difficulty of style and form in his sense of the work of art as the difficult, and potentially obscure, interface of parallel interiorities – that of the artist, that of the viewer/reader/listener.

That music should enter into modernist justifications for innovation in writing is not surprising given the increasingly prominent idea of music's expressive, and specifically non-linguistic, power, an idea which grew steadily in the nineteenth century. Alex Aaronson points to the desire of many twentieth-century novelists to adopt an idea of music as that which transcends thought and logical or rational structuring.[1] The issue then becomes one of shaping a linguistic and formal design for the novel, in particular, which can achieve results similarly transcendant to those supposedly attained by music. While noting that no single model of musical patterning evolves in the novel which can capture this depth, Aaronson points out that the formal experimentation that novelists develop usually revolves around attempts to represent consciousness and to portray non-verbal awareness by verbal means:

> The concern with musical form and content on the part of such different novelists as Proust, Forster, Virginia Woolf and Thomas Mann, in the first half of the twentieth century is no coincidence . . . All of them alike turned to the musical experience as embodying a primordial vision of human life expressed through rhythm or melody, pitch or volume, concord or discord. In their search for a faithful representation of the inwardness of experience, be it through individual consciousness or through the awareness of social identity, they discovered in music a metaphor of harmonious coexistence.[2]

Precisely what Aaronson means by "harmonious coexistence" is unclear. Even among those authors Aaronson himself lists, music is not always used to portray typical notions of "harmoniousness": one need only think of Adrien Leverkuhn's diabolical musical experiment (modeled, significantly enough, on Schoenberg's twelve-tone technique) in Mann's *Doctor Faustus* or Woolf's socially complex representation of popular music in *Between the Acts* to recognize that inward harmony is not the only thing the moderns sought from music.

Still, the basic point Aaronson makes is valid: in a kind of strange recuperation of a romantic belief in the expressive potential of music and in its capacity to go beyond the mere rationality of language, many moderns do indeed turn to music in their search for a form to represent both conscious and unconscious levels of emotion. The attempt to claim music as a model for inwardness is part of a musical–expressivist aesthetic paradigm that had grown on many fronts in the nineteenth century.[3] As such, the move toward music seems part of a tension within modernism itself which seeks both to abolish and preserve its romantic past at one and the same time. But the very notion of the inward, of subjective consciousness *and* the problem of what might constitute a representation of it are not simple things to separate. Indeed, how can one be sure that the very forms of representation are not *creating* the inwardness they claim to portray? Though it may be unspoken, such an anxiety is, I believe, operative beneath the constantly revised poetics of someone like Ezra Pound. In his ongoing attempts to devise a program for the way in which poetry should make meaning, Pound exemplifies the anxious and perhaps infirm relationship between style and expression, between the object perceived and the making of its meaning. Such a tension suggests the possibility that many moderns are simultaneously trying to reshape the idea of inwardness and the forms that could represent it. Music is therefore not simply linked as a metaphorical solution to the representation of consciousness, rather it becomes part of the larger question of the problem of representation in modernism itself.

Michael Levenson, examining the shift in Pound's aesthetic from imagism to vorticism, discusses this very problem of the tension between the sensibilities of the artist's ego and the representation of this significant inwardness. Levenson notes Pound's shifting claims between 1912, the year he invented the term "imagism," and 1915, the period of extreme vorticism. Pound wants simultaneously to link "poetry to psychology and individual consciousness."[4] Levenson continues: "For Pound, then, the art-work is a formal structure whose components nevertheless are essentially psychological constituents: energy, emotion, idea."[5] The tension here is between a romantic notion of the artist's ego as a place of "original" perception and energetic creation, and the technique of the poem as a somehow objective and detached presentation of the "truth" of these inner perceptions:

Insofar as the movement [Vorticism] celebrates "pure form," then it appears to overturn wholly distinct human will, and to mark a break with a romantic aesthetic. But insofar as its basis remains the freedom of the artist and the absolute priority of personal vision, then it remains only as an extreme romantic individualism . . . Pure form was a goal; individual will was its underpinning.[6]

My examination of Pound's conception of the relations between music and poetry in chapter two will show that he is straining to bridge the space between inside and outside, between the poetic object and the artist's interior through the idea of music. As we will see, Pound's use of music is part of his overall revisionary project and as such participates in its larger aesthetic and political contradictions.

I do not propose here a musical–literary aesthetics of modernism, nor do I wish to attempt an exhaustive accounting of all possible modernist authors and their relations to music.[7] What I want to do is examine a certain strain of literary and musical relations which exists in modernism, and which is a crucial part of modernism's self-divided nature. I choose then in Pound, Joyce, and Stein three of the century's most significant literary innovators, but they are also three whose literary and musical sensibilities are, as indeed are their literary approaches, truly unique. What interests me about these authors is the different ways in which music, or ideas about music, are articulated in their literary works, and further, just how they in their various ways are trying to deal with the tension between interiority and artistic form in relation to notions of music.

In order to show the variety of possible "modernist" responses as these relate to the issue of music and literature, this book is framed in a very specific way. The discussion of Mallarmé, Wagner and Pater which opens the book is meant not merely to outline the decadent/symbolist inheritance of high modernism. Rather, I turn to this territory in order to discover why and how the question of musical–literary relations becomes so significant to writers after Wagner (and this Wagnerian influence can be seen among writers everywhere in Europe, not just those in Mallarmé's France and Pater's England). The struggle between Mallarmé and Wagner for the supremacy of the Book against the musical *Gesamstkunstwerk* may seem a rather elitist squabble between high-flying aesthetes. But, of course, such a view is not quite accurate. Wagner's preeminence in cultural circles in the second half of the nineteenth century cannot be rivaled by Mallarmé's much more localized and circumscribed fame. Moreover, if Wagner was a major figure in values of high nineteenth-century art, one must remember that he was also extremely *popular*, something which Mallarmé never was (still isn't), and never aspired to be.

What Mallarmé contests with Wagner is the notion of *total expressivity* that the conception of the *Gesamstkunstwerk* proposes. He wishes to reclaim a kind of mystery or secretiveness that Wagner would prefer to overcome through the performance of total art. For Wagner, there is clearly the sense that outside and inside can be made congruous, that the vagaries of day-to-day expression or communication, be it in music, language, or gesture, could be purged of imprecision in the great work and could then set forth the emotional, intellectual and *national* essence of Germany – Wagner's Germany, anyway.

Mallarmé is much less sure (and perhaps more consistent in his thinking) when considering whether or not the totality of an art work can be anything like fully expressive. In this, Mallarmé could not be less Wagnerian. Wagner linked music and emotions firmly together; the inside could be made manifest in the non-lexical domain of music. Mallarmé retreats from such revelation, seeing music's very non-lexicality, its obscurity, as the paradigm for the untranslatable surface/core of the artwork. I slash together the words "surface/core" for a reason. Surface and depth, outside and inside, become *undifferentiated* in Mallarmé's aesthetic, whereas in Wagner's they are meant to be *united*. For Mallarmé, outside and inside become hard surfaces of possibilities of greater interpretive depth; where to stop becomes undecidable.

What Mallarmé points to is the very fact that in *any* work of art, occurring at any moment in time, depth (and its associated terms such as emotion, expressivity, feeling) relies firmly on the experience of the surface of the work.[8] Wagner could see a possible fusion here between surface and depth and a concomitant concordance between the artist's interior and the technique of expressing that interiority. Mallarmé moves this interiority paradoxically into the work itself using music as a *spatial* metaphor for the combining of surface and depth in the strange object of the Book. The gesture is significant especially when we keep in mind the modernist struggle to place the interior of the artist and the object of art in some necessary relationship. None of the writers I discuss here, with the exception of Pater, would see themselves as inheritors of a symbolist aesthetic; nevertheless it is evident that Mallarmé and Wagner define a polarity in the conception of the possibility of expression itself. Mallarmé's ironic appropriation of the idea of music and his repositioning of it in "the Book" exposes a desire for congruence between work and expression that is both longed for, and yet unattainable. Both this desire for congruence *and* the unattainability of it are worked out in various ways in relation to music in Pater, Pound, Joyce, and Stein.

Pater's connection to this aesthetic debate refocuses it on somewhat more clearly epistemological grounds. Pater's very notion of music as the

paradigm for all art ironically occurs in *The Renaissance*, a book primarily concerned with painting and sculpture. Arts traditionally assigned
respectively to space (visual art) and time (music) are here, if not exactly
brought together, at least significantly counterpoised through the very
articulation of the problem of knowledge that Pater raises in the
Conclusion of the book. What he makes explicit there is precisely the
difficulty of being able to *know* and then *express* anything. Mallarmé preferred to take Wagner's notion of the fullness of expressivity and cast a
shadow of mystery back across the light of full expression of either the
human interior or the work of art. Pater allows the problems of knowing
and of interiority to rest uneasily but necessarily beside the problem of
expression: what *can* one know about the thing outside of oneself,
whether that thing is another person, an object in the natural world, or,
indeed, a work of art – spatial or temporal? If figures such as Mallarmé
and Pater are commonly associated with foreshadowing modernism's
emphasis on consciousness, they must also be connected with the immediate *irony* of *presenting* or *re-presenting* this consciousness, of attempting to
put it "out there" again as the possibility for some kind of aesthetic inter-
subjective connection.

Music comes into the strain of modernism I am following here as an
articulation precisely of the problem of this inter-subjective possibility.
Pound could not see the irony of this; Joyce could; Stein (neither modernist nor postmodernist in any easy terms) seems not to have cared.
Pound's connection to music is long and complex. He was reviewer,
concert organizer, aesthetician, and composer. There is, as I hope to
show, something consistently "Poundian" about his performance in all
of these guises. Pound's relationship to music in any of these areas is of
a piece with his conception of art, and especially his theories of poetry.
However much Pound may try to disparage so much of the nineteenth-
century's poetic legacy (Romantic, Victorian and decadent alike), he is
nevertheless bound to it in several ways. The very notion of the concreteness of the image, or, less clearly, the vortex, is Pound's attempt to
break through the possible solipsism of decadent/symbolist creation, to
set the poet back into the world of concrete things and, indeed, to establish the poet as a maker whose constructions are continuous with that
first world. But, of course, this could not be enough. If poetry is to have
social, political, economic, national, and international importance then
the poet's position (as it was for the Romantics) must itself be elevated.
Moreover, the poetic world created by the now *acknowledged* legislator of
mankind cannot really just make the poetic world simply as concrete as

the "real" one. Poetic concreteness must cross subjective boundaries by mystical reverberation and non-linear interrelationship. For Pound, music enters here as the figuration of temporal non-linearity. Music, for Pound, extends beyond the mere possibility of sonorous likeness between music as heard and poetry spoken or written. Pound seeks from music a means of reconciling and justifying his own poetic technique. He uses music to suggest that poetry is not *merely* technique, but rather that it can and should be part of an almost mystical reconciliation of spatial and temporal dimensions. But with so personal a sense of tradition, so arcane a practice of technique, Pound runs into the very problem that Mallarmé held up to Wagner's image of the *Gesamstkunstwerk*; the inside may be only one artist's inside and all that exists to make this manifest is the very *technical* virtuosity which can only be used teleologically to prove the original, and originary, inwardness. Expression, however you assume it to be figured, leads back to the need for the surface, and no surface, not even one as heavily laden, as indirect and potentially rich as Pound's, can guarantee the inter-subjective, mystical moment.

Joyce never let go of the irony of the paradox of depth and surface, and his technical virtuosity from the middle of *Ulysses* to the end of *Finnegans Wake* will not let us forget this. The "Sirens" chapter of *Ulysses* is his most talked about piece of "musical" writing. Formally, however, despite Joyce's own contentions, the chapter is not strictly a fugue or a *fuga per canonem*. The contrapuntal dimension of the text is largely a matter of representing the goings on in various narrative spaces within the Ormond bar and across Dublin as Blazes Boylan makes his way to Molly Bloom. The "musicality" of the writing exists in Joyce's method of parodying musical–poetic expressivity. The border between interiority and outward expression is blurred in "Sirens" to such a point that the very notion of a self existing outside or separate from the communal codes of expression and understanding of that self is cast into doubt through Joyce's representation of music.

Joyce and Pound split over "Sirens". Pound apparently did not like the growing prominence of Leopold Bloom, nor, it seems, Joyce's less than reverent musical linguistic practice. The division is instructive. Pound looked to music for a model of deep symbolic reverberation, for a non-lexical and potentially mystical justification for his increasingly non-linear poetic practice. Joyce, in contrast, seems to cast doubt upon the whole issue of expression and self-expression by highlighting a technical linguistic practice which links the representation of inside and outside so closely together, and in so intimate an association with music as a *social* phenomenon, that the possibility of mystical depth becomes somewhat flattened against a wall of social interpretive practice. Pound, in fact, seems to want to reconcile the Mallarmé–Wagner opposition; he seeks a kind of elevation of poetic practice to something like the scale of total art while trying to preserve the non-linguistic, non-rational associations which can cut across the image or vortex (as in Mallarmé's Book). Joyce plays more toward the ironic pole, using the non-linear sensibilities of writing and its potential associations with the expressivity of music to construct a narrative–musical scene into which the aesthetic expression of the inward shifts perilously close to becoming the overpopulated space of public cliché. His radiantly playful style moves counter to the notion of "serious" expression and feeling, and the mystical possibilities of non-linear interconnection become a kind of ironic field of narrative spatial coincidence ruled over by the parodic representations of the all-pervasive narrator.

Stein is perhaps the most unique instance of literary–musical relations taken up here. *Four Saints in Three Acts: An Opera To Be Sung*, while written specifically as an opera libretto, participates in Stein's general and ongoing experimentation with language and temporality. Stein spoke of *Four Saints* (and most critics have followed her example) as a "landscape," a kind of writing intended to reduce the difference between the viewer's experience of the object of art (be it painting, poem, opera, etc.) and that of its creator. The appeal to temporal coincidence requires a disruption in the flow of events; there is no history – symbolic, cultural, national, or religious – which can organize the presentation of events, or which can reintegrate these disparate appearances of objects and events on some deeper symbolic level. In this regard, Stein resists some of the usual mythological or psychological justifications of modernism. For Stein, perception, knowledge and the way these two combine in aesthetic experience, all exist on a flat plane of immediacy. Yet, since this is an opera, the *ideal* existence of this work must be in *physical* space. Much of the opera *Four Saints* resists both narrative linearity and symbolic recuperation – which makes it all the more interesting in its contrast to Virgil Thomson's very tonal, very traditional score. It is then, more than curious that Thomson should take an interest in a writer so vigorously devoted to disparaging tradition and the history of cause and effect that literary tradition might impose upon her – curious and profoundly ironic. Thomson's score dances around Stein's language, shifting it apparently in every direction of goal-oriented movement that tonal music can supply, yet he moves it not at all. Nor does he really want to. Stein's language and Thomson's score form a superbly ironic icon of the original "struggle" between Mallarmé and Wagner: Stein's book (literally) offers few means of entry, few ways of transforming itself into something other than what it is. It remains at play in its own apparently enigmatic interrelationships, contrasting, making and remaking itself, stopping, but not ending. Thomson's score, on the other hand, alludes to the momentous; it son-orously brings forth the tender, the boisterous, the whole repertoire of tonal music's images of expression. But, unlike Wagner's *Gesamstkunstwerk*, this tonality, much simpler than Wagner's, finds no secure interior to express; its performance remains adjacent to the lan-guage, facilitating its enunciation, and its enactment, but never break-ing its surface. The music's appeal is to an interiority which the language does not possess. The Stein–Thomson collaboration then, may return us to the place that we began, but perhaps with a difference. The collaborative irony of music and language becomes not a place of conflict, but rather of unresolveable conciliation. Book and music form two contrasting images which interpenetrate but do not change each other. Indeed, in the opera, there is almost a kind of Lacanian reversal, whereby Thomson's music seems to take on a kind of symbolic order-ing function, while Stein's libretto keeps suggesting imaginary identifi-cations which never seem to solidify. Even more significant, however, is the peculiar return to history and the social which the opera suggests. Though the work seems to resist history (as fact, as linear narrative of causes and effects), it nevertheless is marked, as we will see, by a distinct historicity written nowhere in words or music.[9]

It is, then, Walter Pater who, I believe, articulates the problem of expressing the inward, as the moderns will inherit it, in his observations on music in *The Renaissance*. These statements, in conjunction with the epistemological problems that he outlines in the Conclusion to the book, elaborately link the issues of inwardness, music, and artistic form. In so doing, Pater also reintroduces the issue of temporality precisely into the problematic of defining an aesthetic paradigm. The dimension of time will become central to Pound's use of music in his own revised poetics. It is, moreover, Pound who articulates the problem of musical–literary inwardness most clearly; it is Joyce who parodies it most concisely; and it is Stein who will return to the whole issue with the very notion of the inward turned out. The text below is an exploration, then, of a certain complex terrain wherein concepts about music, musical practice itself, and literary modernity enter into relation. The results of these interactions are by no means uniform. Clearly, though, the notion that music could offer literary modernism a paradigm which could span the gap between form and transcendence is not the case. If anything, what might unite my reading of these various modernist texts is the fact that in one way or another, music – either the concept or the practice of it – tends to underscore, and in some cases reinforce, the supplementary character of the modernist literary project itself with its desire for the absolute congruence between form and the transcendence of form. What follows in the chapters below is an examination of some of the ways that modernism's "musical" desire has manifested itself.

CHAPTER ONE

Preliminaries: of music and modernism

In the 1920s, while English modernism was at its peak, Paul Valéry reflected back on the symbolist movement, the time of his own birth as a poet, and the source of great influence on many writers at work in the twenties. Valéry describes the shock, and the affront, felt by those earlier poets when exposed to the music of Wagner and Berlioz, how these poets "came away from concerts overwhelmed," "as though transported to the seventh heaven by some cruel favor . . ." In Valéry's telling, the preeminence of the poets, "their immemorial possession of the lyre,"[1] was seriously in danger. It was as though someone had invented a poetic wheel beyond their imagining, as though someone had set loose some new aesthetic force, in the face of which their own grand poetic project seemed to pale. Valéry's description seems to require such an apocalyptic reading. But this "discovery" of music was not the end of the poetic world. It was, rather, the inspiration for the making of a new one:

. . . we were nourished on music, and our literary minds dreamed only of extracting from language the same effects, almost, as were produced on our nervous systems by sound alone.

Valéry credits this musical nurturance with the refocusing of poetic effort, now with an emphasis on "the many-sided nature" of language. For many writers of this period, "[e]verything was an allusion; nothing confined merely to being; in those kingdoms adorned with mirrors, everything thought; or at least everything seemed to think . . ."[2] All is not only allusion but, in a way, illusion; everything *seemed* to think. The task was to rejuvenate appearances, in fact, to *make* appear a renewed sense of the depth of writing; and, significantly, one of the causes of this rejuvenation was music.

Valéry's image of the mirrors of language echoes backward and forward in time. Backward, not only to his own beginnings in Symbolism, but also to Nietzsche and his version of the world as held together, not by the necessity of some underlying principle of reality, but rather by a will to power over reality. As Sandford Schwartz puts it,

Will to power is the production of forms that express no underlying unity, the perpetual creation of new modes of life that manifest no universal principle, the ceaseless play of differences without ultimate identity.[3]

In the Nietzschean scheme, the production of forms, artistic or otherwise, guarantees no coherence other than that which can be imposed from without. Everything that "seemed to think," that alludes to thought, composes its own depth. "All art is at once surface and symbol," writes Wilde in the Preface to *Dorian Grey*, a book where the inside of the character is turned out, and where the sacrifice to the illusion – and allusion – of beauty turns to excessive proportions. A somewhat younger Nietzsche was aware of the necessity of, and the cost of, such illusions. In *The Birth of Tragedy*, subtitled, *Out of the Spirit of Music*, he gives a version of the Greek Apollinian world of the "*principium individuationis*,"[4] "which always must first overthrow . . . an abysmal and terrifying view of the world and the keenest susceptibility to suffering through recourse to the most forceful and pleasureable illusions." Culture, in its self-conscious phase, creates deliberately. Apollo, resisting the terror that sits upon humanity "in the midst of a world of torments" brings the "wisdom of *illusion*."[5] And Apollo is one of the gods of music.

Valéry's words also point forward to Borges, representative of a later, or "post"-modernity, who, with a similar sense of the troubling conflict between surface and depth, has a character relate one of the sayings of a fictional Uqbar heresiarch: "mirrors and copulation are abominable, because they increase the number of men."[6] Image and reality are conflated: in the story, the image or at least the imaginary world of Uqbar eventually becomes reality. Perhaps modernity, early or late, shares the same problem of legitimation, the same difficulty in making artistic surfaces that offer no security of a depth based on the premises of some "truth" that lies beyond the text itself. The crucial difference lies in the early modernist attempt at the recuperation of depth, in its reinstatement of an underlying unity, or unities, of very complex kinds. Hence, the focus in so much early twentieth-century literature on subjective experience (even as Hulme and Pound expounded versions of the necessary return to concreteness in poetry and in art generally), both conscious and unconscious. Hence, too, the use of mythic structures or historical intertexts as methods of focusing and organizing writing, and the increasing complexity – and necessity of being able to follow – a wider range of intertextual citations and models.

Modris Eksteins notes the conflicting reports that surround the tumultuous opening night of Stravinsky's *Le Sacre du printemps* in Paris, May, 1913:

> . . . that opening night of *Le Sacre* represents a milestone in the development of "modernism," modernism as above all a culture of the sensational event, through which art and life both become a matter of energy and are fused as one.[7]

This fusion occurs, according to Eksteins, in the breakdown of boundaries between ballet and audience. "The audience," in its tumult of derision and approbation, "was as much a part of this performance as the corps de ballet." But, aside from this appearance of art as the struggle of the new or shocking against the conventional, the other struggle that lies beneath the event is the seeming impossibility of telling fact from fiction. The reports on the opening night are, as Eksteins amply shows, far from consistent: Carl Van Vechten seems to conflate his several viewings of the ballet into a "first night recollection"; Gertrude Stein suggests that she was there on the first night, but she was not.[8] The occasion of the first night of *Le Sacre* may represent the birth of modern art as confrontation, and, indeed, the collapse of distinctions between world and work, but it also seems to point to the emphasis on, and the difficulty in ascertaining the objective truth of, subjective responses. Interpreting the event is in some sense more important than the event itself, and we see that even the "inside" offers no certainty, no stronghold of experience, or culture, or history – no certainty other than, perhaps, the importance of subjective response itself. As Eksteins' description of this event makes clear, however, some response is necessary, even if it is illusory – perhaps especially if it is illusory. Indeed, it is possible to see that part of the urge of modernity is to make a virtue, or even a necessity, of illusion. Many years before *Le Sacre*, Baudelaire had noted the necessity of illusion in his discussion of the dandy. He claimed that dandyism is "a kind of cult of the ego . . . which can even survive what are called illusions."[9]

To make an apparent continuity with the past, to make an illusion through allusion, to make everything appear "to think" of a *true* history, of a *true* shared tradition, even while perhaps not quite believing it can be done – the position of the early modern is, in part, the proposition of making connections, within the present and in relation to the past, that are both tenuous and necessary.

Critics have often pointed out that this kind of apocalyptic view of modernism is simply inaccurate. Harold Bloom, for instance, maintains that there is a distinct continuity between what we call modernism and the earlier "high" romanticism of the turn of the eighteenth century. The continuity lies precisely in the intense value placed on the imagination which romanticism developed and of which modernism is but a continuation: "The Romantic movement is from nature to the imagination's freedom (sometimes a reluctant freedom), and the imagination's freedom is frequently purgatorial, redemptive in direction but destructive of the social sense."[10] Such a reading of the connection between romanticism and modernism may offer an explanation of modernism's continuing interest in, and exploration of, the subjective and imaginative realm; it may give a heritage to the exalted status of art and of the alienated artist so prevalent in modernist literature; and, too, it may suggest clear precedents for the experimentation in artistic forms that is a continuing part of twentieth-century literature. Frank Kermode agrees with Bloom's sentiment that the new is not really so new. He suggests that the apocalyptic claims of both early modernism and "neo-modernism" (what we might call today the postmodern) have their beginnings in earlier romantic conceptions of art. Rather than seeing these versions of modernisms as radical breaks with the past, Kermode says that the urge to be radically new is itself part of an ongoing history: "What subverts form is 'an effort essentially formal'; and the sense of standing at an end of time, which is so often invoked as an explanation of difference, is in fact evidence of similarity."[11] Both Bloom and Kermode are perhaps echoing (with significant differences) the earlier work of Edmund Wilson who suggested in 1931 that "the movement of which in our own day we are witnessing the mature development is not merely a degeneration or an elaboration of Romanticism, but rather a counterpart to it, a second flood of the same tide."[12]

But Wilson, reading backward in literary history in the midst of the second tide, seems less ready to foreclose the possibilities of distinctive differences between the modern and the romantic. Articulating as he does in *Axel's Castle* the more immediate influence of the symbolists, Wilson is at pains to note that repetition of romantic tendencies does not constitute only an identity with the first-wave of romanticism, but too, some necessary distinctions. Wilson acknowledges that in several ways the symbolists recuperated different strands of English and American influence. He notes the knowledge of English which Mallarmé and

Verlaine possessed; the presence of such Americans as Stuart Merrill and Francis Vielé-Griffin within symbolist circles; and most of all, the influence of Edgar Allen Poe. Poe's appeal to the French, according to Wilson, rests largely in his interest in establishing a self-conscious theory of art.[13] Wilson also suggests that Poe's emphasis on the vague yet powerful effects of music becomes important to the symbolists, especially Baudelaire and Mallarmé. Of particular significance here is Poe's sense of the distinction between poetry and "Truth," a distinction in which music plays an important role. As Poe says in "The Poetic Principle," "[t]he demands of Truth are severe. She has no sympathy with the myrtle. All *that* which is so indispensable in Song is precisely all *that* with which *she* [Truth] has nothing to do." The opposition between Truth and poetry places the two, it seems, in the position of requiring different criteria for justification. The aspirations of poetry and music go beyond the prosaic demands of Truth, and aspire not to "the Beauty before us," but to "the Beauty above." Both leave us with a deferred sense of this transcendence, and with an "impatient sorrow at our inability to grasp *now*, wholly, here on earth, once and for ever, those divine and rapturous joys of which *through* the poem, or *through* the music, we attain to but brief and indeterminate glimpses."[14]

Though Poe's separation of art and its transcendent trajectory from the quotidian places him clearly in a romantic vein, it seems that there is here a more marked separation of work and world than other romantic writers would maintain. The pursuit of a "purer" beauty is loose here; the artist as the unacknowledged legislator of mankind seems to fall away and is replaced by the artist as one who ignores the social purpose of art. Imagination turns not only from nature, but from the world of social intercourse.

It is easy to see that with some adjustments Poe's separation of poetry and Truth could be given a more "art for art's sake" interpretation. Moreover, it is implicit here that Poe's sense of how poetry and music work is through a powerful suggestiveness of the unattainable – through allusions, perhaps, to an illusory and unachievable realm of significance. As he says at the end of "The Philosophy of Composition," along with a "complexity" of design, a work of art must contain "some amount of suggestiveness – some under-current, however indefinite, of meaning . . ." This is achieved, in Poe's view, not by waiting for the muse to descend, but rather, as he emphasizes throughout the essay, by the meticulous, even "mathematical"[15] attention to the structuring of the work; that is, by the scrupulous working of its surface.

As Jean Pierrot points out, this concern with technical perfection is one of the major strains of influence that Poe inspires in the symbolists.[16] But we must note that the pursuit of such precision affords the poet no guarantee of achieving the "divine rapturous joys" to which one aspires. The symbolists may be attracted to Poe for his emphasis upon technique; at the same time, however, they inherit this very doubt in the ability of technique and artifice to accomplish any transcendent task.

Poe's discussion of the necessary suggestiveness of art points especially to Mallarmé, who, as we will see later in this chapter, picks up on this aspect of music which Poe sees as crucial to the production of poetry. However, part of Mallarmé's view of the music of poetry involves the accentuation of the artificial and intricate construction of poetic language to such an extreme that both the "transcendent" elements *and* the objects of the ordinary world seem lost within the web of allusions and mirrors. Mallarmé is not interested, as Wordsworth might say, in a language really used by men, or even a selection of such a language. He is instead emphasizing the language of "the sensations and emotions of the individual" poet, to the point where "making poetry [becomes] so much a private concern of the poet's that it turn[s] out to be incommunicable to the reader." Wilson continues with an echo of Mallarmé himself: "To intimate things rather than state them plainly was thus one of the primary aims of the Symbolists."[17] But some critics suggest that the process of intimation is part of Mallarmé's use of the "chance" element of reference and is thus a kind of parodic *intrusion* of the subjective poetic voice, a refinement of its presence even as it disappears into obscurity. The point is not that communication fails or turns simply to solipsism, but rather that, as Kathleen Staudt says, "[t]he poet's mission" is "to enable [the] mysterious dimension of language itself to emerge, by discovering new relationships among pure signs." Such a project may fail – just as Poe's project fails – since there is perhaps no escaping the referential, or "chance" dimensions of language.[18] Still, the fact that reference or mimesis needs to be overcome is the unusual point here. In Mallarmé's scheme, reference is an arbitrary weight placed upon language's potential, and this seems to overturn or reverse a certain sense of the need of many romantics to ensure the reader's understanding and ability to follow the voice of the poem.[19]

In part, of course, this notion of reference as chance is of a piece with Mallarmé's broader, more elitist concern with reforming and "saving" language from the influence of newspapers and popular forms of writing.[20] Such an attempt to maintain the distinction between "high" and "low" art forms is also part of the modernist inheritance, as is (though in many and varied ways) the Mallarméan sense of the spiritual and formal poetic–musical text. At the same time, a desire to maintain such distinctions also forms part of modernism's dislike of modernity and modernization, of its reaction against technological production and other manifestations in the material, and increasingly materialist, world. Some of Mallarmé's ideas do bear a strong resemblance to the sense of cultural hierarchy which pervades the thought of a figure like Yeats, or, in a much more idiosyncratic, and truly fascist way, Pound. Moreover, to the degree that Mallarmé's use of music falls in line with a certain idealism in aesthetic thought concerning music in the nineteenth century, we could also say that music lends itself to the larger discourse of art as an entity separate from the world of more material social concerns. As I hope to show especially in my discussion of Joyce, this last point is not necessarily the case. As well, I believe that Mallarmé's counter-reading of Wagnerian aesthetics will prove a much more ironic idealism than it may first appear, or than usual readings of Mallarmé's aestheticism have hitherto suggested.

However, to the extent that music is the inspiration for this turn in Mallarmé toward hermeticism in poetic language, it leads language away from more common forms of reference and expression. According to some commentators of the time, artificiality is one of the common properties that language and music share. Eduard Hanslick, music critic and aesthetician, points this out in 1854 in his *On the Musically Beautiful*: "Language is an artifact in exactly the same sense as music, in that neither has its prototype in external nature, but both have come into being gradually, and both must be learned." But Hanslick also maintains that the referential element of language creates a profound distinction between the two arts: "The essential difference is that in speech the sound is only a sign, that is, a means to an end which is entirely distinct from that means, while in music the sound is an object, i.e. it appears to us as an end in itself."[21] Hanslick determines the distinction between language and music based on the mere instrumentality of language – a distinction which probably few poets, even those before Mallarmé, would have allowed to stand. Mallarmé, however, connects the two arts precisely along the axis of artifice, and in doing so, hopes to resist poetry's lexical restrictions. Artifice is an operation of the text, a delineation of its functioning, indeed, part of its quasi-organic and mystical status. It is part of its structuration of time and space, not simply part of its static structure.

The resistance to lexicality, and indeed, to syntactic, syntagmatic, and even narrative linearity and causality, will appear in different forms in the "musical" experiments of the moderns I discuss here – though I would not claim that all formal disruptions considered "spatial" or non-linear are necessarily "musical." However, in Mallarmé's work music does seem to be a model for the "spatialization" of the text. (The best example in Mallarmé might be something like *Un Coup de Dés*.) That space should be used to "musicalize," and as such, to *figure time* in texts should not be so surprising since any strict opposition between poetry and music as temporal arts and the spatial arts of painting and sculpture would be false.[22] Mallarmé's own pursuit of the spatialized musical text is a sign of the text's artificiality, and artificiality is meant to be its own spiritual reward in Mallarmé. We see this in his sense of the Book as a spiritual artifact, and, too, in his notion of the poverty of language which only poetry, and its arbitrary relations as sustained in a book, can redeem. All this gives poetry the sense of a second, and perhaps redeemed nature, where no chance is allowed. Poetry saves language from its failure to identify with nature by turning back from nature toward language. If poetry, at least for Mallarmé, states little in specific terms, it nevertheless runs less risk of repeating such a failure of identification with some "objective" realm since it asks little of that realm in the first place. In Mallarmé's "Crisis in Poetry," we come upon what may be the source of Valéry's reminiscences about symbolism. In this essay, Mallarmé states that "allusion is sufficient," and he goes on to describe the "chimera" of interrelations that constitute the Book, that artifact of musicalized language:

The inner structures of a book of verse must be inborn; in this way, chance will be eliminated and the poet will be absent. From each theme, itself predestined, a given harmony will be born somewhere in the parts of the total poem and take its proper place within the volume; because, for every sound, there is an echo. Motifs of like pattern will move in balance from point to point. There will be none of the sublime incoherence found in the page-settings of the Romantics, none of the artificial unity that used to be based on the square measurements of the book. Everything will be hesitation, disposition of parts, their alternations and relationships – all this contributing to the rhythmic totality, which is the very silence of the poem, in its blank spaces, as that silence is translated by each structural element in its own way.[23]

It seems that the removal of chance, or the imperfect, in language depends on the removal of any conventional notions of the poet as the ground of romantic expression. Moreover, the articulation of this removal, placed as it is within a discussion of poetry as the "true source of Music,"[24] seems to undermine the expressivist sense of music so common in nineteenth-century writing about music. The opposition between Mallarmé's musical poetics and the expressivist view of music as articulated by Richard Wagner will be discussed at some length below. For now, however, I want to pursue some of the ramifications of this passage.

If the poet's interiority is no longer offered as the guarantee of poetic depth, then any such depth remains in the layered surfaces of the artifact, the book, and the book is thus the emblem of the interplay of surface and depth: it compiles in one place and at one time a collection of writings. Since the time of Lessing's *Laocoön*, if not before, writing has been viewed as an art of time. And music, as Stravinsky says, repeating an age-old view, "is a chronologic art."[25] But what is interesting in this passage by Mallarmé is the way it combines images of music in both spatial and temporal ways. He writes: "a given harmony will be somewhere in the parts of the total poem"; "Motifs of like pattern in balance from point to point"; "Everything will be hesitation, disposition of parts, their alternation and relationship." His musical poetics does not lead to the direct presentation, or apprehension, of the "thing," either subjective or objective; nor does it accept a strict temporality of language. Rather, the poem becomes its own "thing," a composition that sustains itself through the rigorous temporal and spatial interrelationship of language become material. It is significant, I think, that Mallarmé borrows the spatial metaphors for the workings of poetry from music, that other art of time.

Mallarmé, through the emphasis of the artifice of music seems to call down an older (though here more paradoxical) sense of the sacredness of music. But ironically, the music is inscribed in the silences of the text; the "rhythmic totality" resides in the "very silence of the poem," the written object existing in the spatial confines of the text points to its blank spaces as entry points for time – that is, *for time as deferred space*, as the potential, perhaps even unattainable, revelation of the *fullness* of harmony. The space–time cross over here is ironically positioned; Mallarmé uses a negative dimension of the poem – its "very silence," its "blank spaces" – to save the musical poem from the "sublime incoherence" and "artificial unity" of page settings; the "silence"/space is to be "translated by each structural element in its own way." Thus, the formal properties become at once a means to design the space where they do not exist, their blanks, their silences. Nevertheless, these formal adumbrations enter as properties of *completeness*. Space/silence allows for the future retrieval of meaning, later on, somewhere else, in some other way; indeed, perhaps by some as yet unknown means. "[S]tructural elements" offer the means for this completeness, but point to silence, space, futurity, an almost indeterminate blend of diachronic and synchronic alternations. This "dispositional" poetic does not clearly lead to the end of reference in the pursuit of some transcendent ideal; rather, as Peter Dayan suggests, "[t]he implication is always present, in the poet's dispositional argument, that poetry is not music, that sound does not give direct access to the ideal, and that no structure in itself can install the ideal in poetry."[26] No structure, and I would add, no property, not even reference, lexicality, mimesis. If "poetry is not music," and music not sufficiently itself until it becomes music, then where is "the ideal"? Even as Mallarmé posits it, it seems to disappear: perhaps it can be stated, but not acheived, glimpsed, as Poe might say, but not attained in this realm.

MUSIC AS AESTHETIC PARADIGM

The Mallarméan irony has a parallel in the history of nineteenth-century music aesthetics. Music seems to offer a more dubious or duplicitous epistemological and aesthetic ideal even as it attains its status in the nineteenth century as the ideal art form. A certain fear of music has always both accompanied and resisted claims about music's potential universal emotional power. Where Pythagoras could see a rational and semi-mystical order of things with which music was in accord (indeed, music was seen as part of the basis of this order), Plato feared that music could also be the cause of irrationality and disorder; later, where many saw the birth and growth of opera as a potential expansion of musical expressivity, others, such as Dryden, felt that the language of their libretti was cramped almost to irrational drivel by the necessities of developments in music's own "rhetoric." And while composers (Liszt, Berlioz, Wagner) would attempt totally to revitalize or destroy classical forms and harmony for the purposes of expanded "expressivity," they were also intensely interested in corralling their experiments through the use of musical "programs," or narrative/musical devices such as the leitmotif. For as "high" as music might lead, a sense of vertigo has also followed close behind. The possibilities for musical meaning which stem from the very nature of its purported inclinations toward transcendence would seem to be accompanied by a concomitant fear of excess. It is precisely this tension that concerns me here.

Philosophers such as Kant and Hegel, while acknowledging music's emotional power, maintain reservations about music and its particularly ambiguous properties of expression, and they do so at a time when music itself is gaining ground as the art of arts. Kant, in the *Critique of Judgement*, is deeply ambivalent about the place of music. He says that "although it speaks by means of mere sensations without concepts, and so does not, like poetry, leave anything over for reflection, it yet moves the mind in a greater variety of ways and more intensely, although only transitorily." This transitoriness proves to be music's undoing in Kant's scheme, for though music may be a kind of "universal language of sensations intelligible to every man," Kant measures "the worth of the beautiful arts by the culture they supply to the mind and take as a standard the expansion of the faculties which must concur in the judgement for cognition . . ." Hence, music must have the "lowest place" among such arts because "it merely plays with sensations."[27]

Hegel has perhaps more respect for and understanding of music and its processes. He points out that musical notes "in themselves are an ensemble of differences and may be separated and combined in the most varied sorts of direct harmonies, essential oppositions, contradictions and modulations." The movement of such combining and recombining could fruitfully correspond to the "inner nature of this or that subject-matter," so that "such note relationships . . . provide the animated expression of what is present in the spirit as a specific content." But he also warns (especially in the case of instrumental music) of the potential for music to wander off into a practice of mere indulgence:

Indeed, in the series of the developments of the kinds of instrumental music the composer's own caprice becomes the untrammelled master along with, in contrast to the fixed course of melodic expression and the content of music as an accompaniment, its fancies, conceits, interruptions, ingenious freaks, deceptive agitations, surprising turns, leaps and flashes, eccentricities, and extraordinary effects.[28]

If music has powerful capacities for expression of the inward, these powers must be contained since they are subject, quite easily it seems, to the abuses of potential triviality. Significantly, the "subject," taken in the sense of the trace of the composer's own egoistic presence, can disrupt the manifestation of Spirit. Hence, music's non-referential expression requires a certain scrutiny; the subject, in Hegel, cannot be trusted absolutely. As we will see, the need for such containment is very much a concern even for so convinced an "expressivist" as Wagner.

Schopenhauer marks an important turn in the aesthetic attitude toward music in his suggestion of music's transcendent powers. For

Schopenhauer, music, unlike the other arts, "is not an image of phenomena, or, more correctly, of the adequate objectification of the Will, but a direct image of the Will itself." The other arts represent the Will only indirectly through the presentation of "individual objects" which are representations of the ideas, and the ideas themselves are already objectifications of the Will. The Will, for Schopenhauer, is the ultimate reality, the principle of desire that lies behind the ideas and which precedes their particular manifestation in individual objects. Music's power rests in its capacity to grasp the "inner essence"[29] of things, and is thus "far more powerful and penetrates far more deeply than . . . the other arts." Schopenhauer admits that the ideas and music are analogous since both offer extensive variability in their respective means of differentiation and manifestation of the Will: "The inexhaustibility in differentiating melodic possibilities corresponds to nature's inexhaustibility in differentiating individuals, physiognomies and careers." But this is only an analogy, for music

does not express this or that particular joy, but anxiety, pain, horror, jubilation, happiness, contentment *in themselves*, to a certain extent in the abstract, unaccompanied by any incidentals and thus by any self interest. And yet we understand them completely in this quintessential form.[30]

Any strictly imitative (i.e. onomatopoeic) uses of music are therefore to be "condemned outright." And even when music is used in conjunction with "images from life," such as in pantomime, opera, or song, we must recognize that there is no necessary connection between the verbal or visual presentation and the music itself. Such individual images stand in relation to music "only in the same relationship as any given example does to a universal concept: in the distinctness of phenomenal reality they represent what music represents in the universal terms of form alone."[31]

Schopenhauer's notion of music as the direct representation of the Will presents perhaps more problems than it solves. The Will is no Elysium to which the appreciative listener can ascend and contemplate the purity of aesthetic beauty. It is a place of desire, of tumult and uncertainty. As Carl Dahlhaus points out, for Schopenhauer, the ultimate reality of the Will has little in common with Platonic ideas of the "Good," but is rather a "a blind tangled will and urge, exhausting itself in alternation between the unrest and pain of want and the boredom of achieved peace." If music has the ability to represent and to act directly on the listener's emotions, then it is "more a disgrace than an excellence.

Without Schopenhauer's having made this explicit, it is only consistent with his metaphysics."[32]

Whether or not we agree that the Will so conceived is more a matter of "disgrace" than excellence, what is clear is that even with the idea of music's inwardness secured, this inwardness itself is of a difficult nature, contradictory in its energies, excessive in its demands. Music may risk, at the moment of its ascension above the other arts, not triviality, as in Hegel's scheme, but an inwardness without boundaries, a kind of internal universe of chaos. Moreover, even if one were to accept this idea of music as a transparent image of the Will, the problem still arises for both listener and composer as to the precise means by which such an image is to be made. A will to transcendence may overleap the fact of music as artifice, and in a sense, render the issue of musical artifice itself as transparent – in a way, a non-issue.

Still, for all the tensions that might surround music and its expressive capacities, the notion of "absolute music" as the ideal art form remained dominant in the first half of the nineteenth century. By "absolute music" I mean not only music without programs or words or other extramusical devices and reference points, but, in the romantic ideal, music removed from mundane affects and purposes, and which is instead a "revelation of the absolute, specifically because it 'dissolves' itself from the sensual, and finally from the affective sphere."

It is "absolute" then in its separation from any non-musical support, and, more significantly, in its ability to express the sublime or inexpressible. Carl Dahlhaus, in a discussion of the aesthetics of Wilhelm Wackenroder and Ludwig Tieck, points to a very significant shift in the perception of instrumental music occurring at the end of the eighteenth century. Noting that Wackenroder and Tieck frame their new aesthetic on categories found in the ongoing "*Querelle des anciens et des modernes*," Dahlhaus points out that

In a sudden reversal of esthetic judgement, "harmonic," "artificial" music, music dissolved from language and even from expression of affections (i.e., the absolute instrumental music despised by Rousseau) had appeared as the "true" music; "indeterminacy" of content was no longer judged a deficiency but rather a hallmark of the "sublime" style, and distancing from the simple "language of the heart" was perceived as an intimation of the "infinite" rather than as a flight into empty abstraction.[33]

The remarkable thing here is the exoneration of artifice, the sense that the human musical construction may lead to the sublime not merely to the self-indulgent. Moreover, precisely what Kant and Hegel fear about music – its indeterminacy, its non-lexicality – becomes here the most convincing feature of its spiritual or sublime nature. As we have already seen, this respect for artifice will also be part of Hanslick's position on music more than fifty years after Tieck and Wackenroder.

Thus, behind the prevalent nineteenth-century conception of music as the highest of art forms, possessing, as Pater contended, an exquisite balance between "form and content" there also lurks the sense that the realm toward which music tends may also be one of disturbing plenitude or excess.[34] Music supplies a formal ideal, a sense of art's potential integrity which suggests that the aesthetic object can mark out a space beyond the quotidian. But music might also suggest that once one is beyond or outside the everyday there may be no necessary order. Music may be too much, and, at the same time, too little. Music, or the idea of music can be seen, then, as a *less* than ideal paradigm of art, an ambiguous position which I believe it remains for many writers of the twentieth century.

It is possible, then, to see part of the problematic of modernity, at least as it is articulated through the idea of music from the late nineteenth century on, in terms of a kind of supplementarity, a kind of simultaneous excess and depletion that exists as a necessary element in our (most current) outbreak of modernity. I have in mind Derrida's examination in *Of Grammatology* where, in his discussion of Rousseau and the problem of writing, he points out that "the concept of the supplement . . . harbors within itself two significations whose cohabitation is as strange as it is necessary." On the one hand, "[t]he supplement adds itself, it is a surplus, a plenitude enriching another plenitude . . ." But on the other hand, it "adds only to replace . . . It intervenes or insinuates itself *in-the-place-of*; it fills . . . As substitute . . . its place is assigned in the structure by the work of an emptiness."[35] Transposing Derrida's argument (not without some necessary violence) from the issue of writing to that of the idea of music as perfect expressive art, I want to suggest that music can be seen as the articulation of modernity's dis-ease. For many, music signifies the possibility of a kind of romantic transcendence, and is meant to display the potential space of the fullness of expressivity. As we will see at the beginning of the next section, for some (such as Liszt and Hoffmann) it is the very means to a kind of sublime space, to a plenitude where artifice seems to be done away with. But this is, paradoxically, precisely the moment where the elaboration of artifice reasserts itself, and, in effect, cancels out the moment of transcendence by virtue of music's own presence as one of the most highly artificial of the arts.

I will again turn to Mallarmé who best illustrates my point about supplementarity in his essay "Crisis in Poetry," where he makes use of "music" in the articulation of a curious idealism which coalesces around the idea of "the Book":

> . . . our present task, precisely (now that the great literary rhythms I spoke of are being broken up and scattered in a series of distinct and almost orchestrated shiverings), is to find a way of transposing the symphony to the Book: in short, to regain our rightful due. For, undeniably, the true source of Music must not be the elemental sound of brasses, strings, or wood winds, but the intellectual and written word in all its glory – Music of perfect fulness and clarity, the totality of universal relationships.[36]

The musical verbals ("orchestrated," "transposing") are common enough; they are often evident in descriptions of the supposed perfections of literary works. But in this passage, Mallarmé wants to have his ideal arts two ways at once. It is equally necessary to "transpose" the symphony to the Book, and to discover (or dislodge?) the "true source of music." But this true source resides already in "the intellectual and written word in all its glory." Music becomes Book, and yet "true" music is already the "written word." A figure (a quite conventional figure) of language reaching a musical apex is suddenly reversed when we discover that music at its truest is *already* the word.

In one way, Mallarmé's discussion seems to participate in a predictable decadent/symbolist dream: the issues under discussion have nothing "natural" about them. The perfection that is somehow due us comes about as the result of the intersection of two arts; or it might be more accurate to say two kinds of artifact: the symphony and the Book. The figures do not come from nature, but are part of the realm of human construction. In this regard we must also notice the levels of artificiality that play off between the art *form* (the symphony) and the object that may *contain* art (the Book, or that which could presumably contain both poem and/or symphony). For Mallarmé, the Book is no simple object capable of the dispersal of some singular text. Instead, the very "foldings of a book . . . have an almost religious significance" which "create depth and mystery." As the "tomb in miniature for our souls," the Book displaces the body, or, it seems, removes the soul *from* the body, placing that traditionally spiritual essence at some remove from its earthly home. But, (again) at the same time, the Book will fold back upon us until at some unknown point of apotheosis, "all earthly existence [will] ultimately be contained in a book." We are voided and refilled, or voided and encased (like some shell inside an empty room); in effect, we will transcend by not transcending, become "immortal for a brief hour, free of all reality" by virtue of the Book that will at once empty and recuperate "all *earthly* existence."[37] Symphony and Book, body and soul, real and artificial seem simultaneously disclaimed and reclaimed.

This perplexing movement and counter-movement can be seen as a kind of articulation of modernity itself, and music, as a kind of figure of the "art of arts," is perhaps one of the most fitting images for this process.

MUSIC AND THE POSSIBILITY OF SPEECH; POETRY AND THE
MUSIC OF SILENCE: THE END(S) OF WAGNERIAN ROMANTICISM
AND THE CURIOUS MAKING OF MALLARMÉ'S MUSICAL POETICS

The complex connections between music, writing, and modernity which Mallarmé exemplifies can be better understood in terms of the ideas on the relationship between music and language offered by one of the most influential composers of the nineteenth century, Richard Wagner. Wagner was a major influence on French writers and intellectuals for much of the later nineteenth century, even when, as Elwood Hartman notes, their knowledge, both of music in general and of Wagner's writings and musical works in particular, was often less than complete. Mallarmé, like many, had much to say about "the Master" and some of the issues that he raised, especially as they apply to poetic language. But it is Mallarmé's resistance to, and appropriation of, the idea of the totality of the Wagnerian expressive musical art which will be of most significance here. By the mid-nineteenth century, music is well established, especially in Germany, as the paradigmatic expressive art.[38] Seen within the larger context of romantic theories of art, music's preeminence, according to many, rests in its power to appeal beyond language and reason directly to the emotions. E. T. A. Hoffmann, for instance, claims that music is "the only genuinely romantic [art] – for its sole subject is the infinite." In Hoffmann's view, music's transcendent strength lies precisely in its lack of referential specificity: "music discloses to man an unknown realm, a world that has nothing in common with the external sensual world that surrounds him, a world in which he leaves behind him all definite feelings to surrender himself to an inexpressible longing."[39] Franz Liszt makes similar claims, stating that music's advantage over "most arts and especially . . . the art of words" is that it can "reproduce the impressions of [the] soul" by means of making "each inner impulse audible without the assistance of reason." Such are the heights achievable by music, that "[f]eeling itself lives and breathes in music without representational shell . . ."[40] The supremacy of feeling over thought (sound over word) is linked to a privileging of interiority where the "inside" is turned out, or "reproduced," to use Liszt's term. Some, however, like Wagner, while convinced of music's expressivity, were extremely concerned with *how* this interiority could be expressed, in other words, precisely with the poetic and symphonic means that constituted the interior's "representational shell."

Wagner's version of musical expressivity, like Hoffmann's and Liszt's, rests upon a distinction between feeling/sound and words/thought; and while it does seem true that Wagner, like the others, gives ascendency to music, he also attempts to construct within his notion of the *Gesamtkunstwerk*, or the "total artwork," a kind of equilibrium of music, word, and gesture. For Wagner, the state of both music (at least until Beethoven) and words is corrupted by the short-sighted demands of taste. Disgusted by pre-Beethoven "Italian operatic melody" and instrumental music in general, Wagner believed that until Beethoven, music had been brought "so low that novelty was all that wanton taste demanded, since last year's melody was already intolerable."[41] Similarly, the language of the contemporary world is also in a fallen state. The language of the present appeals only to the understanding; it is "a language whose usages and claims, based on the logic of the understanding, we must unconditionally obey . . ." Thus, "we cannot discourse on this language according to our innermost emotion . . . in *it* [i.e. modern language], we can only impart our emotions to the understanding, but not to the implicitly understanding feeling . . ."[42] Wagner finds the redemption of both music and language in the music of Beethoven, and especially in the final movement of the Ninth Symphony, where word and tone are reconciled in the "Song of Joy." Here is the clue to the art of the future, a *dramatic* art which exploits the potentials of tone and word. But here too is the tacit acknowledgement of music's limitations: though it seems to transcend the limits of language, it also appears to require language. The perfect art is not music freed from language, but rather, music bound to language.

Wagner outlines an elaborate interrelating of word and tone in his movement to rejuvenate drama. The poet must purge language of all its unnecessary weight and attempt to "raise" (note the ascension) language to "the *fullness* of a sensuous expression to rouse the feeling's interest." The sensuous appeal comes from a kind of rhythmic structuring of the poetic line, where emphatic words are properly "conditioned" by unemphatic words. Language moves still further toward the sensuous/expressive (past the constrictions of "state politics and religious dogmas") by attaining to the "sensuous substance of . . . *roots of speech*." "*Stabreim*" is the process of fitting together these roots based on affinities of meaning and consonantal (first and last) and vowel sounds organized in "sensuously cognizable resemblance."[43] Through the relationships of sound, concepts that are alike, or even akin in opposition, bridge the space between meaning and sound. Here language is returned to the senses, and thus, to the feelings:

From the instant of the musical intonation of the vowel in word speech, the feeling has become the appointed orderer of all further announcements to the senses, and henceforth musical feeling alone prescribes the choice and significance both of lesser tones and chief tones . . .[44]

When language has returned to tone speech, music then intervenes:

The unitarian expression of the poet most completely won, at last, in the ascension of his word verse into the melody of song; and the latter wins its unitarian expression, its unfailing operation on the feeling, through instinctively displaying to the senses the inner kinship of its tones.[45]

The sense that language is somehow redeemed in its ascension toward music clearly outlines language's inferiority, at least as a method of communicating to, and with, the emotions. At the same time, if language must work its way toward the feeling capacity of sound, musical sound must also slide toward speech. If music's necessity to move toward speech seems to undermine its supremacy, this movement is, in Wagner's terms, nonetheless, a requirement of the new dramatic art.

Music's organ of speech is the orchestra: "The orchestra indisputably possesses a *faculty of speech*, and the creations of modern instrumental music [i.e. Beethoven's] have disclosed it to us." Now, as if to repossess the power of tone speech that he has suggested the poet brings to the musician, Wagner performs a striking reversal, suggesting that the melody the poet has been at pains to create is *already* inhabited by music: "the melody which we have seen the poet inventing from out of the word verse was more a *discovered* one – as being conditioned by harmony – than one *invented* by him." Thus, "[b]efore the poet could find this melody, to his redemption, the musician had already conditioned it by his own-est powers . . ." To reinforce language's return to its secondary position in relation to music, Wagner attempts to illustrate his idea of orchestral speech through an analogy with the relationship between word speech, or spoken verse, and gesture. Essentially, the kind of emotional content/stimulus that word speech lacks is supplied to the eye by means of gesture, just as the orchestra, with all of its harmonic depth, provides for the ear the necessary emotional supplement that tone speech cannot deliver:

Now there comes the language of the orchestra, completely sundered from the word speech; and that tale of gesture's, which was unutterable in word-tone speech, the orchestra is just as able to impart to the ear as the gesture itself imparts it to the eye.[46]

Musical speech here comes closer to no speech at all. Instead, music is likened to the expressive presence of the body in gesture, the body turning its emotional inside, out.

However, the theoretical plot has thickened. Language, which is understood to be redeemed by an already present harmony, becomes part of the "speech" of the orchestra. In a way, it is cancelled out and then returned. But the ability of utterance which the orchestra has is, significantly, "the faculty of uttering the unspeakable." The unspeakable that the orchestra articulates is "not a thing unutterable per se, but merely unutterable through the organ of our understanding [i.e. through language]; thus not a mere fancy, but a reality . . ."[47] Wagner here is resorting to a figure of speech in order to mark the limitations *of* speech, the borderline of its own silence, *and* also to demarcate the place where musical speech intercedes. But his insistence that the orchestra's utterances are "not a mere fancy, but a reality" points up the strain of his figuration of speech as the image of non-speech. The struggle to delineate language's limitations seems to recall language, in the form of a kind of *non*-language, in the next instant.

What we witness here is not a theory wherein the component parts of the drama complement each other and coalesce, but rather one in which the limitations of each part must take on, and not take on, the traits of the other. Music is analogous to gesture in its emotional import, but both gesture and music hinge upon speech. Speech, it seems, requires both gesture and orchestra to complete its effect upon the emotions. But elsewhere, Wagner again seems to eschew the ascendency of music and returns to some sort of interdependence of words and music:

Let us not forget, however, that the orchestra's equalizing moments of expression are never to be determined *by the caprice of the musician*, as a random tricking out of sound, but *only by the poet's aim*. Should these "moments" utter anything not connected with the situation of the dramatis personae . . . then the unity of expression is itself disturbed by this departure from the content.

The struggle is given its clearest delineation in Wagner's working out of the dramatic implications of motif. He says that "[m]usic cannot think: but she can materialize thoughts . . .":

A musical motive (*Motiv*) can produce a definite impression on the feeling, inciting it to a function akin to thought, only when the emotion uttered in that motive has been definitely conditioned by a definite object, and proclaimed by a definite individual before our eyes.

Within the confines of the drama, music takes on a referential function. Supplied with the already present representational capacity of language, music can enter into the events of the narrative chain, and even cross outside their linear framework if it has already been properly conditioned by (i.e. associated with) language. It also conditions the next narrative moment which is "derived in turn from that earlier one."[48] Music seems to be filled, and then in turn, to fill, completing itself in a moment of reference to language, and to the action which language has incited.

Music (or gesture) is unable to utter its unutterable speech without the presence of speech itself, yet this fact must be hidden if the expressive supremacy of music is to be maintained, even though Wagner seems to fear (as did Hegel) that music can easily slide outside the proper frame of expression. If expression must control the drama, it must also be controlled, and language, annulled in its capacities of expression in relationship to music, must return to save music from its potential intractability.

Wagner's theoretical attempt to keep the expressive possibilities of the total art work alive while simultaneously trying to fend off ambiguity is a struggle which tries to maintain a hierarchy *and* perform a reconciliation among equals all at the same time. Music is enough, and yet not enough. Language is secondary, but also necessary, at times even more imperative to the expressive enterprise than music. The strain to create an art form of supreme expression forces music and language into an ambiguous, fluid relationship wherein the supposed intelligible plenitude of language must be refined by the direct emotional appeal (in a sense, the *greater* plenitude) of music, but where music must as well be guarded from its own lack of intelligiblity by a language moved toward its most musical/expressive pole. But an apparent symmetry of functions cannot hide the strain of the potential limitations of the component parts; the oscillation between plenitudes reiterates the strain of their respective limitations.

If Wagner's dream of the *Gestamtkunstwerk* alternately veils and reveals the supremacy of music, Mallarmé has his own dream of the total art work which both rejects and aspires to the supremacy of musical drama outlined in Wagner's theory. Mallarmé's appropriations from the realm of music take a decisive turn away from the notions of totality that we have seen in Wagner's theoretical struggle. Suzanne Bernard notes that Mallarmé and Wagner share certain views concerning the methods of poetic language. These involve connections between Mallarmé's use of alliteration and Wagner's concern with *Stabreim*, and the need to "condense," poetic language, as Wagner would say, to its essentials.[49] But Mallarmé's attack on everyday language differs from Wagner's in some significant ways. For Wagner, language's primary limitation lies in its appeal to the reason, and the idea of the *Stabreim*, the movement toward the sensual roots of language through the use of sound, is meant to redeem it. For Mallarmé, the imperfection of language lies also in the dissonance between sound and meaning, but this is part of the salvation of poetry. In "Crisis in Poetry" he says that "languages are imperfect because multiple; the supreme language is missing." The diversity of language renders the uttering of Truth itself impossible; such is "nature's law." Any given language enacts its sonorous imperfections all the time. Mallarmé notes that "compared to the opacity of *ombre*, the word *ténèbre* does not seem very dark; and how frustrating the perverseness and contradiction which lend dark tones to *jour*, bright tones to *nuit!*" However, it is precisely the failure of language to be "self-succeeding" in both meaning and sound which makes space for the poetic project. Rather than some kind of proposed return such as we see in Wagner, Mallarmé's project begins by stepping into the fallenness of language: "verse . . . in all its wisdom, atones for the sins of languages . . ." Language has its origin here, in the past, and at every moment of the discord between sound and meaning ("Arcane étrange . . . a jailli métrique aux temps incubatoires"[50]). There is no root, no foundation of secured sound and meaning to which the poet can return, and this is precisely the place of most opportunity; from here comes the potentiality for mystery.

Mallarmé points out that "[m]ystery is said to be Music's domain," but he says too that "the written word can also lay claim to it." But how? Especially if music possesses a "matchless efficacy, [which] we feel unable to translate . . . into any language save that of the listener's ideas. [Its] contact with our spirit is direct and fitting . . ." But here is the crucial turn. Poetry calls for its own claim to the "Ideal" in the same way that music does – by its *untranslatability*, in the silence of its "noiseless flight." Mallarmé opposes the "speech" of Wagner's verbal/orchestral art with the silent potentials, and mysteries, of the poetic *written* word: "Both Music and Lyric call for the previous discarding of the spoken word, of course, in order to prevent mere talking." "Mere talking" is the language required by those who wish for a "pedestrian clarity," full of "plagiarism" and "platitudes" (that is, readers of the newspaper as opposed to the Book).[51]

Mallarmé requires a conscious forgetfulness through which the poet can, in "reverence," "transform, through the miracle of infinity, [the letters of the alphabet] into some special language of his own . . . Through this initiative, or through their own virtual power, these divine characters will become a work of art." Mallarmé joins music and literature not so much at the level of their transcendence, but at the level of their obscurity, in precisely the place where they do not speak.[52] As Bernard points out, Mallarmé was well aware of the importance of silence in music, "et non seulment pour séparer des phrases ou pour marquer certain rythmes . . . mais pour nous laisser entendre ce qu'elle ne dit pas, ce que ne peut etre dit pas des sonorités matérielles . . ." The spoken and the unspoken, the heard and the unheard, in both music and literature, take their power from the work of "evocation, *allusion, suggestion*," from their own appearance and disappearance ("To create is to conceive an object in its fleeting moment, in its absence"). Hence, music and literature "constitute the moving facet – now looming toward obscurity, now glittering unconquerably – of that single, true phenomenon which I have called the Idea."[53] The Idea, however, is itself a place of mixed affinities, a sphere of silence and dubious plenitude. As Mallarmé says in a letter to Henri Cazalis (July 1866), "I have been on the purest glaciers of Esthetics; because after I had found Nothingness, I found Beauty."[54] Thus, the very foundation of the Mallarméan project, rather than assuming some kind of ideal of fulfillment, takes into account its own passing, and in doing so, it includes and subsumes music within an aesthetic of untranslatability.

Such an aesthetic might have less to do with what Mallarmé actually describes or refers to than with his method of resonant construction of the work. This is especially true if we consider his poetic enactment of silence in terms of his use of space, including the use of images of whiteness, or, indeed, the very blanks which "fill" his work, since such "blanks unfailingly return; before they were gratuitous; now they are essential; and now at last it is clear that nothing lies beyond; now silence is genuine and just."[55] I do not want to suggest, however, that a taxonomy of images of vacancy (a thematics) and/or an accounting or critical "measuring" of blank spaces can somehow adumbrate Mallarmé's unique musical poetics. Nor do I want to indicate that the Mallarméan text is merely "iconic." What I do want to suggest here is that Mallarmé's aesthetic of silence or the untranslatable, so marked by the weight of blanks and textual silences, is a process of the mobile interrelationship of possible meanings. As Derrida says, borrowing an image from Mallarmé himself, the process of Mallarmé's texts is "the very movement and structure of the fan-as-text, the deployment and retraction of all its valences; the spacing . . . *between* all these meaning-effects, with writing setting them up in relations of difference and resemblance."[56] The sense of "space" I am pointing to which most closely resembles Mallarmé's musical-poetics of silence has at least some figurative affinity with a kind of mobile "architectural" sensibility.

Suzanne Bernard discusses this "conception architecturale" in Mallarmé's work. By a "conception architecturale," Bernard means that Mallarmé is well aware that music not only takes place in time ("chaque son s'évanouit et disparait pour laisser la place à un autre"), but also, that these sounds take place within "un système de relations qui n'aura sa pleine existence qu'une fois l'œuvre entendue en son entier." Thus, from a certain point of view, both music and architecture can be considered non-representational, and hence, dependent upon structural relation-ships to achieve coherence.[57]

Seen in this way, an "architectural" conception of music comes closer to the way music is conceived by Wagner's rival, the critic and aesthetician Eduard Hanslick, who maintained that, instead of an emphasis on the emotions represented or aroused by music, the "content of music is tonally moving forms." For Hanslick, music achieves meaning through a self-consistency which is strictly musical or formal, rather than associational. Hanslick does in fact make an analogy between music and architecture: "Music consists of tonal sequences, tonal forms; these have no other content than themselves. They remind us once again of architecture and dancing which likewise bring us beautiful relationships without content."[58] It is the relationships among elements, rather than their referential capacity which informs the poem and/or the piece of music. Bernard notes that for Mallarmé one of the attractions to music is the sense of the multiplicity of possible relationships, both motivic and rhythmic, which the more complex musical forms such as the fugue and the symphony could achieve. Especially in terms of such works as *Un Coup de dés*, Bernard points out how

la structure de la fugue, aussi bien que celle de la symphonie, s'éloigne de la simple mélodie linéaire: nous avons ici affaire à des partitions construites dans les deux dimensions, horizontale et verticale; d'où une véritable «spatialisation» de la musique, et par suite une possibilité, pour l'écrit, d'imiter une telle structure.

An awareness of the horizontal and the vertical does seem to be a necessary aspect of the reading of *Un Coup de dés*, as Mallarmé himself points out in his introduction to the poem, and which the text itself bears out.[59]

But to leap too readily into the horizontal and the vertical movements of the Mallarméan text (these issues will return later on in the discussions of Pound and Joyce) is perhaps to bypass the still troubling issue of the "blanks" or silences that Mallarmé has adopted from music. Silence seems to be part of Mallarmé's rationale for linking the arts of music and literature. If, to a certain extent, the spatialization of the written text is one of its most profound means of elaborating its "musicality," we must still try to understand such a move within the context of the link between Beauty and "le Néant." The best way to accomplish this is to turn (or return) to Mallarmé's own reading of Wagner.

Mallarmé's two major pieces addressed to Wagner, the essay "Richard Wagner, rêverie d'un poète français" (1885) and the sonnet "Hommage (à Richard Wagner)" (1886), seem both to deify Wagner, and yet to delimit, or even undermine, his significance. Mallarmé sees through Wagner's attempt to use music as the sign of aesthetic unity, and thus, overlays his own aesthetic concepts of a crucial negativity that asserts and removes the fullness of the idea of the total art work. The very title of the earlier essay especially claims the presence of the Master (Wagner) as already part of the poet's own musing: Wagner, the recently dead god (in the sonnet, Mallarmé refers to Wagner as "Le dieu Richard Wagner"; the associations with Wagnerian dead gods are thick here) is paratactically joined to, and constituted by, the poet's "rêverie." Mallarmé continues this paratactic procedure to enlarge upon Wagner's significance, while at the same time binding and displacing it through the movement of this (day)dream.[60]

Early in the essay, it is Wagner who has usurped "the duty" of the poets with his new form of theatre. But later on, it becomes clear that, as remarkable as is his achievement in marrying ("il effectua l'hymen") the "mutually exclusive" arts of "intimate drama and ideal music," Mallarmé refers to this feat as an "harmonious *compromise*," suggesting less a truly new creation than a merely new theatre.[61] Moreover, when the successful drama has been accomplished, and the hero appears "in a distance which is filled with the mist of lamentations, victories, and joys" brought on by music, the effect is more of a *second* coming, or a re-presentation of the originary power of "Legend." Such fullness of presentation allows an ostensibly forgetful (i.e. unmindful of the fact that Wagnerian theatre is *still* theatre) Germanic people to "borrow sacred feelings from the past and look upon the secret of their origins, even as that secret is being acted out." But this will not do for the "strictly imaginative, abstract and therefore poetic French mind," which "shrinks back from Legend," preferring instead the "Fable, which lives virginally apart from all known places, times, and persons." For such a French (read "Mallarméan") mind, "[t]he hero must have no name . . .," and exist only in the "glance of the audience." The tenuous constitution of the nameless hero in the glance of the "silent audience" disintegrates the musical theatre of the presentation of origins, and reconstitutes an ephemeral "paradise on earth," a paradise of transience, indeed, the "Mystery" of the City.[62] If, for some, the "house of . . . Art" constructed by Wagner calls up the very god's existence (but which god – the hero with a name, or Wagner himself?), the scintillations of Mallarmé's art translate such orchestral completion back into silence:

. . . the orchestra, which just now demonstrated the god's existence, distills the very same immortal, inborn subtleties and splendors which live unsuspected in the midst of a silent audience.

"[L]'édifice" of Wagnerian art, in its fullness, is only a deceptive apex, existing but "half-way up the saintly mountain."[63] The struggle which underlies Mallarmé's reverie is more than the agon which arises between two artists vying for the supremacy of their respective arts; it is the juxtaposition of two different ideals of art, one Wagnerian, which gives a model of complete art, but which offers the problematic completion of a massive and breathtaking substitute, and the other Mallarméan, which is unattainable as edifice, but "complete" in its ephemerality, in the silence of its own passing.[64] Mallarmé thus attempts to forge a parodied aesthetic of fullness, an aesthetic which, as we shall see, traverses the writing of certain moderns again and again as they attempt to link their writing with "fullness" under the sponsorship of music.

Mallarmé works his poetics against Wagnerian expressivism and representation out of the need to create a poetics which could incorporate the "fallen" nature of language itself. As such, I would view Mallarmé's musical poetics not only as a part of modernism's formalist inheritance, and its tendency, in certain writers, toward hermeticism and perhaps unnecessary difficulty. Rather, I would maintain that Mallarmé paradoxically offers a model of anti-expressivism through the use of the art of music, that art which, from the late eighteenth century on, has been viewed as the most expressive. I would not say that modernism itself is anti-expressive. Nor do I believe that the writers whose work I take up in this study follow a strictly Mallarméan parodic expressivism in the practice of their particular writings. What I do believe is that, after the Mallarméan project, writers can no longer view music as the trope of a secure inwardness. As such, it can no longer be viewed as the art of transcendence, the art of an inscrutable completeness and presence of the inside. Music, as an art of both temporal and spatial dimensions, offers language no way out of its own sense of inadequacy, but rather, reinscribes the growing modernist concern with the reestablishment of depth at the same time as it offers another, uncertain, model for the making of surfaces.

If it is true that music, even after Mallarmé – either as an actual practice, or simply as an idea – offers writers a model of art which they can use to work out their own specific desires for a surface with depth, it is also the case, that after Mallarmé such a surface may have to be its own imperfect guarantee of that depth. In other words, poets and writers may call upon music as the most expressive of arts, but they can never do it with the same assurance.

Music becomes in a way then a kind of figure for modernism's supplemental struggle, its attempt to make a poetic tradition out of a new poetry itself: the new is both an aid to the construction of continuity and a substitute for that continuity. "Music" is perhaps an allusion to an illusion, and thus may be both a model for, and an emblem of, this struggle.

CHAPTER TWO

Walter Pater: music and the aesthetic resistance to history

Mallarmé's parodied aesthetic of fullness may at first sight seem to have little connection with Pater's famous claim that *"[a]ll art constantly aspires to the condition of music."* Pater's words are a kind of pithy (though not revolutionary) recasting of the musical romantic ideal of music's self-presence. If music has what all the other arts want – the complete unity of form and content – then Pater is merely following certain nineteenth-century doxa, placing the powerful, yet semantically ambivalent, art of music at the top of some implicit hierarchy of arts. Seen in this light, Pater's phrase seems merely to extend music's association with aestheticism and with later modernism's subjectivist project. Music ostensibly joins in the figuration of art's self-exile from the horizons of social and political contention – indeed, even from the realm of time and history as such.[1]

Such observations, though perhaps not without some truth, are at the same time too totalizing, too dismissive of the diversity of modernist thought and practice, and thus, prone to overlook the kinds of epistemological and representational anxieties which lie beneath the thought and texts of so many moderns. I think that the notion of the transcendent predilections of modernism can be contested with reference to one of its forerunners, Walter Pater, and in terms of some of his best-known statements on the ideal art of music.

It is clear from Pater's Conclusion to *The Renaissance*, and as well in his whole emphasis on "aesthetic criticism," that subjectivity is by no means a place of privileged knowledge or certainty. Although Pater may emphasize the importance of the subject in relation to history and aesthetic evaluation, he is not merely extending a late-romantic belief in the primacy of the poet or artist "self" as the ground of epistemological certainty. I will suggest here that with music, Pater figures a paradoxical idealization of art, precisely because of music's age-old association with time. In Pater's hands, music reintroduces the temporal into the very heart of the synchronic moment, and therefore links the limitations of the subject directly to the issues of artistic evaluation, history, and the provisionality of knowledge.

What may link Pater more firmly with Mallarmé's parodic aesthetic of musical fullness, and have implications for Pater's influence on modernism as well, lies in an exploration of the context of Pater's statements on music and what is implied in his aesthetic approach. Clive Scott's suggestion concerning Mallarmé's poetic project – that "[w]riting poetry becomes a means of activating what is missing"[2] – may also be true of Pater's critical project in *The Renaissance*. Disparaging a programmatic approach to aesthetic perception and to the writing of that perception, Pater develops a complex engagement with the aesthetic object, a doing and undoing which in a sense involves both the object and the perception of it in a profound and enigmatic interplay. Pater's ideas on music, as expressed in *The Renaissance*, are part of his overall epistemological and aesthetic exploration; indeed, as we will see later on, Pater's statements about music are part of what links him so strongly to the later modernist struggle with time and history. But in order to elaborate fully Pater's sense of "music," I must first give some detailed attention to the problems of knowledge and art with which he is concerned.

Perhaps what is "missing" in Pater is also what is at every moment present: the activity of a subject who rarely, if ever, claims the unity of an "I" who presides over the object it perceives – "music, poetry, artistic and accomplished forms of human life" – but which nevertheless at all times situates the object in relationship to itself. As Pater writes: "What is this song or picture, this engaging personality presented in life or in a book, to *me*?" Pater's idea of aesthetic criticism is intended to subvert the Arnoldian desire to "see the object as in itself it really is." Pater is attempting to work the desire for such immediacy into the much more limited space of the subjective response, and to make this place of necessary confinement into its own virtue. Music, or at least Pater's idea of music, will become part of his aesthetic exoneration of this space of subjective restriction.[3]

The emphasis on subjective response seems romantic enough, and it is so. But we must note the shift from objects of nature to objects of art – though this too has romantic precedents in Wordsworth's reflections on the painting of Peele Castle, or in Keats' revery on the Grecian urn. But Pater, insofar as he identifies himself as a "modern," does so by denying a singularity of value to any necessary connection between "life" and "art." He is largely uninterested in the Shelleyan idea of the poet who participates in "the eternal, the infinite and the one," or in Wordsworth's sense of poetry as "the first and last of all knowledge . . . as immortal as the heart of man," or in Arnold's attachment to "the traditional moral scheme," with no "desire to alter the traditional conceptions of right action and right feeling." Pater plays down any tendencies toward either romantic apotheosis, or nostalgic certitude, at least as these are solidified into some kind of programmatic method of perception, and, as Graham Hough puts it, "shows considerable willingness to involve himself in the flux."[4] As Pater himself says in *Appreciations*, "Modern thought is distinguished from ancient by its cultivation of the 'relative' spirit in place of the absolute . . . To the modern spirit nothing can be rightly known, except relatively and under conditions." The sense of the absoluteness of any kind of knowledge, be it visionary, or orthodox, is eroded in Pater. It is not that aesthetic schemes of transcendence or orthodoxy (or various combinations of both) disappear with the slow emergence of what we know as "modernism," rather what is at stake in Pater's aesthetic criticism, as it is submerged here in his words on modern relativism, is the sense that, in Barthes' words, "what modernity allows us to read is the plurality of modes of writing."[5]

Pater's aesthetic criticism and his sense of his own modernity are based upon the shifting ground of the quiet conflation of beauty and pleasure, especially as such pleasure pertains to the senses. This sensuous element figures into Pater's "antinomianism" or that "spirit of rebellion and revolt against the moral and religious ideas of the time" that Pater sees as part of the first bloom of the Renaissance within the Middle Ages, and that we must assume is an essential element of his own resistance to dogma which is present in the notion of aesthetic criticism. Maintaining a clearly anti-metaphysical stance, Pater claims that it is not his intention to find a "universal formula" for beauty, but rather "the formula which expresses most adequately this or that manifestation of it."[6] While such a position still assumes that there is something which can be called beauty, Pater is nevertheless refusing any predeterminations or absolute criteria for the beautiful, and instead, locating the struggle to determine what any given *moment* of beauty might be within the confines and limitations of a much less "universalized" idea of subjective space. Such provisionality relies upon a linking of synchronic and diachronic senses of experience which, throughout *The Renaissance*, works to resist any fixed or universal condition of knowledge. In the Preface to *The Renaissance*, he points out that it is the function of the aesthetic critic to distinguish, to analyse, and separate from its adjuncts, the virtue by which a picture, a landscape, a fair personality in life or in a book, produces this special impression of beauty or pleasure, to indicate what the source of that impression is, and under what conditions it is experienced.

The forms of nature, gathered together with those of human creation, are subject to analysis not by paradigm, but by the critic's predilection to beauty and pleasure. As Patricia Clements puts it, using Pater's own word, the ideal critic depends "not on a system but on a susceptibility."[7] Thus, for Pater, a study of the Renaissance is not merely, or even, the examination of a specific historical, cultural period, but is rather a *way* of assessing and creating in a certain manner, a manner in which the experiencing subject is central, but without centrality, dislodged from its programmatic moorings.

If one resists doctrines (moral, religious, aesthetic, or philosophical), the result may be a kind of isolation that suspends one over a potential abyss between the poles of subjective and objective knowledge. But I do not think that Pater's sense of isolation is mere solipsism – not even heroic solipsism. His resistance to romantic or "progressive" orthodoxies calls for a kind of relentless sensual examination. In his Conclusion to *The Renaissance*, Pater seems to suspend the individual between mere inclusion with the scattering forces of the physical world and a kind of impressionism of the "inward world" which allows for little, if any, certitude about the nature of our sensations.[8] Concerning the forces of the outside world, he says that

[l]ike the elements of which we are composed, the action of these forces extends beyond us; it rusts iron and ripens corn . . . That clear, perpetual outline of face and limb is but an image of ours, under which we group them – a design in a web, the actual threads of which pass out beyond it.

Turning to the processes of the inward world, he points out how reflection further reduces the "flood of external objects" into "a group of impressions" until "the whole scope of observation is dwarfed into the narrow chamber of the individual mind" which is itself "ringed round for each one of us by that wall of personality through which no real voice has pierced on its way to us." Thus, "all that is actual . . . [is] a single moment, gone while we try to apprehend it . . . ." This kind of suspension between the outward, perhaps even deterministic, forces of nature and the inward inability even to grasp our impressions fully (whether or not they supply us with any accurate information about the world) makes it seem inevitable that Pater would suggest that the only alternative is "[t]o burn always with this hard, gem-like flame, to maintain this ecstasy [i.e. the ecstacy of experience itself] . . ." Ian Fletcher is partially correct in saying that the "real message" of the Conclusion seems to be "that we should multiply and intensify our sensations at all cost," that the "excitement of experiencing" is the "one necessary thing."[9]

But this is not all. In the first paragraph of the Conclusion, Pater maintains a position of extreme conflation, suggesting that the sensory experience of the "delicious recoil from the flood of water in summer heat" can be reduced to "a combination of natural elements to which science gives their names . . ."[10] The irony here is that, if science is to explain all, it must first reduce everything to quantifiable elements, none of which explain the difference between "the delicious recoil" and the "combination of elements." The romantic idea of an atonement with nature becomes, in scientific terms, nothing but a desolate description of indifferent physical forces. The realm of sensory experience, so reduced to a scientific extreme, ruins the transcendent possibilities of subjective sensation. In the second paragraph an inversion of the first paragraph takes place, but this time the focus is the inward world. While each of us may be a "solitary prisoner" locked only in our "dream of a world," the "thick wall of personality" which imprisons us is not so immutable as it may at first seem. While we attempt to grasp the moment that continually dissipates, we find that "what is real in our life fines itself down," and we discover that the "thick wall" of personality *itself* is subject to the same forces of decomposition and recomposition:

To such a tremulous wisp constantly re-forming itself on the stream, to a single sharp impression, with a sense in it, a relic, more or less fleeting, of such moments gone by, what is real in our life fines itself down. It is this movement, with the passage and dissolution of impressions, images, sensations, that analysis leaves off – that continual vanishing away, that strange, perpetual, weaving and unweaving of ourselves.

It may be important to burn with a gem-like flame, but it is equally important to resist the formation of habits.[11] The intensification of experience comes out of the need for an isolated self to take on the fatality of its own re-composition and to do so at every moment. The subject that is returned in a backhanded fashion in the first paragraph is not merely reduced to isolation in the second, but also forced to live in a flux which proves the substantiality of the world "outside" even if one cannot claim to *know* it: it is there, whatever it is. Thus, in the second passage, the world of objects returns and at precisely the point where an exploration of the mind has been as reductively described as the forces of the outward world were in the first passage. We come to see in Pater a sense of subject/object relations that remains mobile, and which takes place upon the site of a subject that cannot form itself without the "world," and a world continually remade by the mobile subject.

Although she elaborates it somewhat differently, Carolyn Williams puts forth a similar reading of Pater's Conclusion. She notes the double metaphoric procedures of the first paragraph with its contradictory movement between "atomism" (the breakdown of reality into separable elements) and "inextricable interrelation" (disparate elements are involved in all processes). She also outlines a similar kind of doubling in the second paragraph where Pater constructs a vision of "solipsism" (nothing can get in or out of the mind) and "mania" (the mind can hold onto nothing it perceives). She concludes that

[t]he inevitability of material annihilation makes the self irrelevant; epistemo-logical nihilism makes the world of objects – and finally the mind itself – unknowable. Without at least a provisional outside, there is no inside; without solid objects, there can be no subject . . .

Williams sees Pater as a significant transitional figure, holding "simulta-neously [a] late romantic, late Victorian, and early modern position," within his "intensified awareness that the problem of 'objective' knowl-edge and the problem of 'subjectivity' are intractably one and the same problem." His position is not that of a "mere" aesthete passing onto the twentieth century an elitist sense of the primacy of art over "life," but rather that of a person embroiled in the scientific, philosophical prob-lems of his time, a time where neither romantic idealism nor renewed belief in progress (scientific or social) was wholly adequate.[12]

Pater's aestheticism cannot be denied, but it can no longer be seen as a kind of escape from a world we cannot know, or a mind we cannot control. The idea of art as escape seems to be behind Wolfgang Iser's view of Pater's aesthetics. Iser suggests that, for Pater, "Art composes experience anew, giving it a density that enables us to forget the otherwise destructive dimensions of time," thus "endow[ing] human existence with a seeming perfection which in reality it lacks." However, Pater's aestheticism is really less a method of escape than it is a means of coming to terms with the "real." His particular sense of the aesthetic maintains the problem of knowing the world and the past, but it does so in a manner removed from the solidity of paradigm. Iser himself points out that Pater's own attitude toward history varies greatly from those, such as Hegel and Darwin, who, in very different ways, conceive of history in teleological terms:

For both [Hegel and Darwin] the whole process of development is the expression and realization of a metahistorical idea. Hegel's eschatology and Darwin's "struggle to survive" impose a particular form on historical development, . . . [but for Pater] history is neither the sacrificial altar of the spirit, nor the survival of the fittest; it is the preserver of all that has been.

Pater makes this notion of history as preservation clear enough when he describes Pico Della Mirandola's humanism as "that belief . . . that nothing which has ever interested living men and women can wholly lose its vitality . . ."[13]

Pater's answer to the problem of history is, like his solution to the problem of epistemology, an "aesthetic" answer, and, as we will see, one in which the idea of music plays a crucial role. Pater's solution proposes a continual confrontation with the past within the present. It is in this confrontation that we recognize one of Pater's strongest connections to the twentieth century. Stephen Spender stated in the 1960s that the distinctive element of modernism, especially in the first three decades of the twentieth century, was "the tension between past and present, which could only be expressed in a revolutionary kind of art." The moderns, by which he means those we normally think of as "high" modernists (Joyce, Eliot, Pound, Lawrence, Woolf, but *not* Stein) attempt to take on "the *whole* experience of modern life." In the face of the "all-embracing fatality which is progress," the modern realizes a new "sensibility of style and form."[14] Lionel Trilling describes the confrontation between past and present in even more combative terms, saying that what defines modern literature is the "bitter line of hostility to civilization that runs through it." To be modern is to feel "the disenchantment of . . . culture with culture itself . . ."[15] Such a sense of confrontation, at least as it concerns early twentieth-century modernity, is easily discernible in Pound's attempts both to "Make It New" and, at the same time, forge a live tradition from literary histories as diverse as those which include the Provençal poets and Browning, Whitman, Chinese ideograms, and the Anglo-Saxons. Or we can see the same diversity of confrontation in Eliot's copious shoring of fragments in *The Wasteland.* Or, again, we might recall Woolf's "Mr. Bennett and Mrs. Brown," where the real point of the essay lies not so much in her apocalyptic pronouncement that "in or about December, 1910, human character changed," but rather in her sense that the novelists of the recent past (Bennett, Galsworthy, Wells) no longer offer a *form* that is capable of grasping Mrs. Brown, or "human nature." The idea of a linear causal progress in the novel is disrupted when she claims as her own models novelists such as

Sterne and Austen, for whom "everything was inside the book." The very diversity of "pasts" and traditions among various moderns suggests a lack of any simple sense of historical–literary development. Moreover, Woolf's claim that it is the *forms* of the past (at least the immediate past) which no longer serve the representation of "human nature," or her sense of a "new" reality, points toward a necessary and ongoing revitalization of both the literary past and *present* with the "form" or artifice of the literary text as the site of the reappropriation or recognition of the "real."[16]

The sense that writers of modernity share with Pater is that the past can be, and usually is, constructed creatively. Pater recognizes, as Hayden White says in another context, that "[t]he difference between a historical and a fictional account of the world is formal, not substantive; it resides in the relative weights given to the constructive elements in them . . ."[17] Temporality and facts are not done away with but are rather included within the aesthetic recreation of experience in the face of both the extant object of art, *and* the sense of its lost historical context.

This, at least in part, accounts for Pater's expansive sense of period, since he suggests a beginning to the Renaissance as far back as twelfth-century France ("Two Early French Stories") and a putative ending as late as the eighteenth century ("Winkelmann"). But even more than his broad sense of period, it is Pater's way of discussing both the art and people of the past that reveals his unique sense of historical and aesthetic concerns. In fact, I would suggest that what Pater is trying to inscribe in his aesthetic criticism is temporality itself: that is, he is figuring the very gap that time, as a kind of entropic or negative presence, leaves on the work of art – even as a subject, *itself* circumscribed by its own time and space, its own philosophical and scientific models of knowledge, approaches the work.

Pater suggests that his form of impressionism is a kind of distillation of the special "virtue" of the object, not unlike that of the chemist who "notes some natural element, for himself and for others." Seen in terms of our discussion of the Conclusion, the analogy seems a bit ironic – and at the expense of the chemist. Given Pater's sense of the provisionality of the subject in relation to experience, it is clear that he is including (very cryptically) the natural scientist within the mobile sense of self that the aesthetic critic is also forced to work within. Since, as Wolfgang Iser says, "impression[s] [are] in no way pure imagination, for [they depend] at least partly on elements that are outside the imagination." However, I disagree with Iser's sense that what Pater is "searching for in the impression is its basic constituent quality," or that which "enables it to defy time by freezing the transient into a permanent image," for, in Pater, no image truly coalesces into permanence, but instead always maintains its relationship to time.[18] "[O]ur only chance," says Pater, referring to the period given us between birth and death, "lies in expanding that interval, in getting as many pulsations as possible into the given time."[19] Pater's figure is commonplace, but it turns upon the ambiguity (or the fusion) in the word "interval" which applies both to time and space, and which resides in the temporal structure of the sentence between the spatial sense given in the word "expanding" and the sense of sequence (though not order) suggested by "pulsations." Pater's criticism aims at a kind of epiphanic intensity, but such moments are, to use Harold Bloom's word, "de-idealized," and what such de-idealization requires is a constant interchange between both synchronic and diachronic realms, a movement for which music will become the figure.

Such an interchange is implied in Pater's interest in both painting and poetry, arts that since the time of Lessing had been opposed to one another in terms of their respective relationships to space and time.[20] The book proper begins with a discussion of two medieval French stories, contains an examination of Michelangelo's *poetry* (a significant shift of emphasis here), the painting of Botticelli and Da Vinci, the poetry of Du Bellay, the thought and influence of the critic Winkelmann – all this aside from the aesthetic and epistemological significance of the Preface and the Conclusion. The variousness of approach is part of Pater's unique method of critical assessment of both art and history. Pater's ostensibly absolute epithet concerning music as the art of all arts, when seen within the context of his own critical enterprise, discloses a matrix of doing and undoing that connects the idea of music to matters central to the problem of modernity. His words suggest that music offers an ideal criterion for art, a place outside of the contingencies of history and literary tradition from which to make art new. At the same time, however, the critic or artist who would adopt such a desire to be new must deal with history and tradition, either in terms of what it means to "lose" the past by creating a break with it, or to situate one's present endeavor in some kind of relationship with those who have come before. The idea of music becomes joined with synchronic desire, ostensibly free of historical evolution. But at the same moment music is, either directly or indirectly, joined to history, as we shall see is especially the case in the essay on the school of Giorgione, the place in which Pater's most significant words about music occur. Temporality is figured *as* aesthetic contemplation and thus becomes an illusory and ironic synchronic revery.

"The School of Giorgione" opens with an argument that resists the unified aesthetic appraisal of the arts.[21] Pater says that "it is the mistake of much popular criticism to regard poetry, music, and painting . . . as but translations into different languages of one and the same fixed quantity of imaginative thought . . ." He is at pains to point out that "the sensuous material of each art brings with it a special phase or quality of beauty, untranslatable into the forms of any other . . ." "[T]rue aesthetic criticism" begins with such a distinction, and the distinction is crucial for Pater's next move, which is to locate what he feels is the art into which all other arts are commonly, albeit unconsciously, translated: poetry. He says of painting,

> To assume that all is mere technical acquirement in delineation or touch, working through and addressing itself to the intelligence, on the one side, or a merely poetical, or what may be called literary interest, addressed also to the pure intelligence, on the other; – this is the way of most spectators, and of many critics . . .

The point is to return to some kind of sensual aspect of the painting which "first of all [must] delight the sense." The senses, then, troubled as they are, must be foremost in the aesthetic experience: "In its primary aspect, a great picture has no more definite message for us than the accidental play of sunlight and shadow for a few moments on the wall or floor . . ."[22] This is not just an aestheticizing removal from the import or "meaning" of the object, but, in a sense, a re-temporalizing of it. Sensuous apprehension must occur first, an acknowledgment of the "untranslatable charm" of each particular medium of the arts. But this is then succeeded by the attempt to delineate the potentially poetic structure of the work: "this primary and essential condition fulfilled, we may trace the coming of poetry into painting, by fine gradations upward . . ." Pater's phrase about observing the coming of poetry into painting has a certain Dantean ring to it ("by fine gradations upward"). But there is no sense of a climax in Pater's scheme, even though one can conceivably ascend from the first hints of poetry in Japanese fan-painting to the full-blown article in the work of Titian.[23] Rising upward by fine gradations is tantamount to progression without end; the temporality of aesthetic apprehension as Pater is outlining it is veiled beneath a figure of ascent. Such a rise seems to take one not to a place of interpretive solidity, but rather into the parameters of another *art*. Presumably, the whole process would have to start again, in the case of painting, in terms of yet another art, and so on. The chain of deferral, rising or otherwise figured, seems potentially endless. The attempt to locate the untranslatable sensuous charm of each art which marks the first step of aesthetic criticism is meant, in fact, to give shape to the project of translating these arts – in a certain way – in terms of each other. The notion of the primacy of the sensuous here gives way to the need for a different kind of discourse, one with very little chance of completion.

While attempting to situate the arts in terms of their distinctiveness, Pater introduces the idea of the *Anders-streben*, that "striving after other-ness" which Pater defines as the tendency of each art to express "a partial alienation from its own limitations." Through such an alienation, the arts do not "supply the place of one another," but instead "recipro-cally . . . lend each other new force."[24] But all such striving after other-ness is subsumed under what Pater tellingly calls the "musical law": "all the arts in common aspir[e] towards the principle of music; music being the typical, or ideally consummate art, the object of the great *Anders-streben* of all art . . ."

Music arrives, it seems, to take the place of the "literary interests" that formerly lurked beneath aesthetic interpretation. But its appearance sets a horizon for interpretation which, by virtue of music's position as the "great *Anders-streben* of all art," is impossible to reach. The sense is clear in Pater's own words:

All art constantly aspires towards the condition of music. For while in all other kinds of art it is possible to distinguish the matter from the form, and the understanding can always make this distinction, yet it is the constant effort of art to obliterate it.[25]

Pater has reversed the Hegelian priority of poetry over music, and he has done so on exactly the same grounds that Hegel would have given eminence to poetry. Music lacks a clearly definable discursive level, and what would have led Hegel to fear the potential trivialization of music here leads Pater, like many romantic music critics before his time, to give it preeminence.

Indeed, a certain vagueness seems essential to Pater's sense of music as the paradigm of arts. "Form," as Pater uses the term, does not seem to be prescriptive, but pertains broadly to the method of manipulation of materials, or to some vague interface between technique and "the spirit[ ] of the handling." He says of lyric poetry, for instance, that it is the "highest and most complete form of poetry," because "in it we are least able to detach the matter from the form, without a deduction from the matter itself . . ." The perfection of lyric poetry thus lies in "a certain suppression or vagueness of mere subject, so that the meaning reaches us through ways not directly traceable by the understanding . . .". Such vagueness seems appropriate given the problematics of knowledge that are outlined in the "Conclusion." And by offering music as the art towards which all others aspire, Pater undermines the whole issue of transcendent desire, since music, even more than poetry, is associated with time. The ideal here, the moment of removal from time, or of escaping to renew it, is itself subject to time, not only in the sense of taking place within time, but also in its use of sequence and duration as structuring principles. Thus, not only is the ideal deferred, in that all arts must aspire to it, but the ideal *as an art* takes for one of its constituent principles the element of time.

The provisionality of the musical ideal is worked out indirectly in the rest of the Giorgione essay. Pater maintains the predominence of the sensuous element of art, claiming that the Venetian school to which Giorgione belongs never forgets "that painting must be before all things decorative, a thing for the eye." Moreover, for Pater, Giorgione proceeds to fulfill the next requirement: "in the subordination of mere subject to pictorial design, to the main purpose of a picture, he [Giorgione] is typical of that aspiration of all the arts towards music . . ." But, alas, for Pater, there are almost no Giorgiones left. He is wrong in this, as any Pater critic will point out. Nevertheless, he believes that there is only one extant Giorgione, and that the science employed to determine such things, "as in other instances, has not made the past more real for us, but assured us only that we possess less of it than we seemed to possess."[26] Science, as usual, disperses reality, dislodges it instead of solidifying it. Thus, with only a slim idea of the sensuous material of Giorgione, Pater seeks to establish the strain of the artist's influence.

Pater's task seems impossible, or at least highly "subjective" – and it is. But facts, like legends, can be subject to revision, to new histories which disintegrate the facts, or change their significance. In the one painting Pater believes to be authentic, the *Concert*, he finds the definitive traits of the artist: "The sudden act, the rapid transition of thought, the passing expression . . ." In words that echo his description of the *Mona Lisa*, he says that the defining character resides in the "wholly concrete moment – into which, however, all the motives, all the interests and effects of a long history, have condensed themselves, and . . . seem to absorb past and future in an intense consciousness of the present." The moment of Giorgione is found, but it is insufficient, for its characteristics are spread across time, and must therefore be discovered and rediscovered elsewhere, "out of all those fascinating works rightly or wrongly attributed to him; out of many copies from, or variations on him, by unknown or uncertain workmen, . . . out of the immediate impression he made upon his contemporaries . . ."[27] And we could add, in Pater's impressionistic recreation of the past as well.

The dispersed history of the school is signaled in the painting by the motion implied in the apparently static medium: the sudden act, the rapid transition of thought, the passing expression. They are refigured into one synchronic "musical" ideal, then lost in the temporality of a pervasive and barely traceable influence. As with Mallarmé's symphonic book, the moment of Giorgione's school is immediately lost even within the images which describe it. Aspiring to the condition of music for the one beholding the work of art is not to conquer time (even, as Eliot might say, *through* time), but to refigure its loss, its surety and its ephemerality. Just as Mallarmé's Book both fills us and voids us at the same time, so does the "condition" of music. It offers a discursive property, a rhetoric of apparent longing which cannot be fulfilled. Music, for Pater as for Mallarmé, figures an ideal even as it dissipates it, sets the stage as the mode of perception and even creation, even while placing an impossible evanescence at the center of this desire, or perception, or creation.

The *Concert* seems to offer an origin for the "School" of Giorgione's art, but it is based upon Pater's own recreation. The "School," like the "musical law," is an ideal into which time and difference are built. Music, in part, depends on time (though as I suggested in the last chapter, it is not strictly an art of time), on the passing of sounds, on the particularity of their duration even when placed in concurrent relationship with other sounds. Like the School of Giorgione, music is a dispersed ideal; its own status as an art of time – though it can be replayed and recalled – challenges the very idea of the stability of the aesthetic moment removed from, or solidifying, an instant of time. The Paterian notion of music implicates the temporal in the ideal, fashioning an aesthetics of the provisional out of the necessary recognition of historical and epistemological limitations. Seen in this way, Pater's "musical law" of art can be read as a means of marking out the parameters for a modernist aesthetics which resists transcendence and, instead, is always attempting to re-anchor itself (through the exploration of myth, of consciousness, of history) while simultaneously recognizing (or *not* recognizing, as in Pound's case) that no absolute can be attained. Pater's conception of "music," then, offers us yet another image of modernity's supplementary condition; it plays against itself as an image of fullness, and, as in Pater's retrospective creation of the School of Giorgione, it embodies the lack of completion which can only be compensated for, again and again.

CHAPTER THREE

The musical aesthetics of Ezra Pound: its sorts and conditions from imagism and vorticism to the Cantos

Ezra Pound may be among the least amenable figure to today's critical atmosphere – though his anti-materialism and, indeed, his anti-capitalism may often come nearer our hearts than we might like to admit. His sense, however, of how the modern world of capital and consumption might be resisted – his appeal to fascism as a means of political and social stability; his tendency to have many of his analyses of capitalist economics, especially in the form of "usury," collapse into an incoherent anti-Semitism – leave us rather colder today than generations of critics before the present. Many social, cultural, and literary critics might, with variations, agree with Pound's sense of the profound affect capitalism has had on the arts, say in his "Murder by Capital" from *The Criterion* of 1933. Few would probably nod at his contention near the end of the same piece that "Mussolini is the first head of state in our time to perceive and to proclaim *quality* as a dimension of national production." Even darker, though, is Pound's loyalty to fascism as an ideal *contra* capitalism and communism, especially as these are both, in his mind, linked to variant forms of Jewish "infection":[1] hence, Pound's take on the nature of communist Russia:

The basis of a state is its economic justice. It exists by texture. Communism with its dictatorship of the proletariat is merely barbarous and Hebrew, and it is on a level with primitive theocracies.

Elsewhere, in telling the tale of the bankrupt town of Wörgl which had begun to issue its own currency for local use, Pound says that it "sent shivers down the backs of all the lice of Europe, Rothschildian and others" when a note of the currency appeared in an Innsbruck bank: "The judaic–plutocratic monopoly had been infringed. Threats, fulminations, anathema!" Indeed, for Pound, it is "usury" – an exorbitant, and for Pound, Jewish-inspired rate of interest – which "ruined the Republic" of America.[2]

The scope and nature of Pound's fascism and anti-Semitism seem a disturbing and unnecessary development of his sense that poetry and art are not merely secondary attributes of a society, but central to its development. Donald Davie remarks that Pound's poetry and his fascism (and I would add, his anti-Semitism) "[represent] disastrously false judgement[s] made in the course of following through a conviction *not* self-evidently false – about there being a connection between the health of letters and the health of the commonweal." By 1938, however, in his *Guide to Kulchur*, Pound had taken his sense of the interconnection between the two so far as to maintain that "finer and future critics of art will be able to tell from the quality of a painting the degree of tolerance or intolerance of usury extant in the age and milieu that produced it."

It may now be impossible to separate Pound's poetic and aesthetic concerns from his politics, partly because they have been for so long held apart by critics, and partly because such a separation was untenable to Pound himself, as is evident both in the *Cantos* and in a great many of his other writings. Robert Casillo suggests that for Pound the definition of the Jews as other is required, since "without the arbitrary assignment of difference and confused otherness to this group . . . Pound would never be able to carry out, if only provisionally and questionably, his major project of calling things by their right names." As such, they are the "unrecognized double of the confusion and uncertainty"[3] which lie at the heart of Pound's political and aesthetic projects.

Pound's poetics and his theorizing about music and literature participate in the confusions and complexities of his larger cultural and social project. For what Pound seeks from his musical poetics, and indeed, from his sense of music, has much in common with what he seeks socially and poetically elsewhere: and that is a kind of essential hierarchical structure, a truth beyond the merely material or materialistic, yet a truth which is always manifest through concrete action or style: image, vortex, or ideogram. Pound reasserts the expressive depth of music, even as he wishes to reinstate the permanence of "the enduring constants in human composition,"[4] of hierarchies and order in the social world which would include art. But the protestations seem too loud, too fraught with the sense that perhaps no such orders are possible. Despite the confidence and even audacity of his statements on almost every subject he took up, Pound's sense of the immanence of non-material hierarchy leads to a kind of compulsive desire for control over the manifest: technique, form, the audible are all various means for making this *other* order appear. The loudness, the apparent thoroughness, the all-encompassing reach which

Pound extends in so many directions and with such prolific force, suggests, however, a strained anxiety about the possibility of ever elucidating the proof of such a fundamental plane; it is this very anxiety which lies beneath the contradictions, and which forces the ever more strenuous attempts to make that essential order a material and present fact.

I want here to see how music fits into Pound's broader aesthetic and social concerns, as far-reaching, and contradictory as these may be. Pound's fascism and anti-Semitism will form part of the necessary context of my discussion; much thorough commentary has recently dealt with these issues, and I will not recapitulate it here except where necessary. Insofar as pulling one thread is to tug upon the whole fabric of Pound's discourse, my discussion of his musical–literary relations must therefore be connected to his political and cultural concerns. But I am explicitly after a sense of his musical and literary projects here, in terms of both their profundity *and* their "confusion and uncertainty." I will trace Pound's conception of the relations between music and writing from his pre-imagist phase to the *Pisan Cantos* as this matrix forms itself into a kind of paradoxical ideogram – perhaps with only Pound at the center to authorize its validity. We will come, finally, to Pisa and to Pound's inscription, or really, his reinscription, of the bird-song of Jannequin while incarcerated for treason just after the war. In many ways, this last Pisan scene of Pound's writing will constitute an apt, if sorry, ideogram of Pound at work in the field of his own literary/musical and political contradictions.

THE CLAIMS FOR TECHNIQUE

Ezra Pound is usually remembered as one of this century's leading exponents of visual concreteness in poetry, an association which is reinforced by his relationship with, and writing upon, such visual artists as Wyndham Lewis and Henri Gaudier-Brzeska. But the emphasis on visuality, especially in Pound's theoretical statements on imagism and vorticism, overshadows his significant interest in the interstice between music and literature. Behind his desire to establish a poetics of concreteness, be it imagist, vorticist, ideogrammic, the importance of music in poetry stands always as an expressivist shadow. What I want first to explore here is the way in which music functions as a crucial element in Pound's project for the modernization of poetry and the arts in general. Pound's belief in the significance of music for poetry touches upon many issues that arose in the preceeding chapters. He begins with more or less predictable notions about the expressive musicality of poetic language. These ideas grow in complexity as his poetics increasingly concerns itself with simultaneity. His idea that the music of poetry is an essential element in achieving the congruence of word and emotion recalls Wagner's requirement that sound and sense be so balanced as to establish a precise rendering of emotion. Though Pound had little patience with the *symbolistes*, his desire to rejuvenate poetry through the "musicalization" of the poetic line reminds us of Mallarmé's idea of music as a poetic paradigm, and we may hear further Mallarméan overtones in Pound's conception of the fullness of silence in his theory of the "Great Bass." Finally, his emphasis on the concreteness of poetic language, and his growing use of poetic synchrony, move Pound into some of the issues of synchronic desire that were operant in Pater's elaboration of music as the paradigmatic art.

What is significant in Pound's claims about the necessity of the joining of music and poetry is his implicit and explicit interweaving of music into a theory of poetry which makes strong epistemological claims on the concreteness of words. Pound's notion of music forms part of the substructure of his attempt to make poetic language both concrete and spatial. The irony is that music, the supposed art of time, is brought most prominently into writing (another time-bound art) at the point of disruption or complication of the successive level of language. But, for Pound, this more "spatial" sense of language does not mean that we simply come to a place where we see or hear *through* the word, either to the thing itself, or to some sublime space marked out by language as symbol. What we have instead is the use of musical conceptions to complicate language and its process of linear representation. However, what exactly it is that *is* seen or heard as language *presents*, rather than *re*presents, the realm of Pound's artistic truth will remain a matter of some difficulty both for Pound and his readers.

Pound's thought on the relationship between music and writing is at the very center of the problem of coordinating the material practice of poetry – that is, technique – and its expressive dimensions. Marianne Korn points out that the early Pound "followed aesthetic principles which belonged to the mainstream of nineteenth-century poetry," extending back from Pater to the early romantics, and "ultimately [to] Longinus."[5] The Longinian influence is significant since it places so much emphasis on the force of inspiration and the scintillations of insight which occur within the poet–hero. Pound's romantic urges, while pervasive in his early career, never really disappear. But in his growing concern with technique, a concern in which music figures prominently, the conflict inherent in offering form as the guarantee of a subjective integrity is most dramatically played out.

In the series of essays called "I gather the limbs of osiris" (1911–1912), Pound clearly outlines his belief in the necessity of poetic technique. The "Osiris" essays are important because they contain some of Pound's earliest statements on the significance of music for poetry, especially as music might pertain to the issue of poetic technique. It is here that the struggle for a form that will justify itself begins to emerge within the context of a kind of Longinian attitude toward literary history: that is, literary history as the apprehension of the "luminous detail." In part, the idea of the luminous detail has to do with Pound's sense that the art of the past (the best art anyway) can have an immediate effect upon the modern reader. Scholarly study of this artist or of that art work is less important than the experience of the work itself. Pound maintains that "[a] few days in a good gallery are more illuminating than years would be if spent in reading a description of these pictures." Without direct experience, knowledge is "relegated to the specialist or to his shadow, the dilletante." He says that he himself is "more interested in the Arts than in the histories of this or that [art], for the Arts work on life as history works on the development of civilization and literature."[6] Pound does not outline exactly what the differences between "life" and "civilization and literature" are. Nor is it clear just what the difference is between "Art" and "literature" as Pound uses the terms here. Presumably, direct experience, or "life" is somehow truer, less mediated than the other category. "Art," too, would seem to have a less civilized, and therefore more accurate relationship to "life" than "literature" does. But though Pound seems to denigrate the present state of "civilization and literature," he surely has a certain investment in the traditions of both, no matter how much they may have degenerated. Perhaps the only way to explain the distinction Pound is trying to make here is to see the categories of "life" and "civilization and literature" as opposed attitudes toward experience – indeed, as opposed epistemological stances.

"The artist," says Pound, "seeks out the luminous detail and presents it. He does not comment. His work remains the permanent basis of psychology and metaphysics."[7] The luminous detail seems literally to impose itself on the audience (viewer, listener, reader). It crosses time, making historical development a secondary issue, and forces a kind of immediate contact that traditional ways of knowing, those of "civilization and literature," cannot do. This notion is strikingly Paterian, at least

in the sense that the perception of the luminous detail sounds very much like Pater's belief in the importance of the critic's personal response to the work of art as foremost in the assessment of the work. What is different is Pound's ostensible faith in the possibility of basing a literary history upon such a method. Pater cast his impressionistic technique within the parameters of a problematized subject position as outlined in his Conclusion to *The Renaissance*. But Pound seems to have fewer doubts about the possibility of direct apprehension of the artistic object; thus, he goes on to construct a version of the artistic past as eccentric as Pater's, but with much less anxiety about the problem of knowledge.

However, perhaps Pound's rhetoric of certainty misleads us. Peter Nicholls points toward a shared emphasis upon the visual in Pater and Pound, a shared sense of "the revelation of single numinous objects": ". . . Pater's handling of myths as visual images suggested a way of countering the modern tendency to abstraction, through a recovery of an original untainted concretness." At the same time, Nicholls suggests that Pound and Pater also feared the limitations of the forms of human art, and that "[a]lthough Pound defines his 'image' in more resolute terms [than Pater], his theory conceals a similar concern about the capacity of language to reduce *preconceptual totality* to a simple sign."[8] The point seems crucial to me: if, as Nicholls suggests, these writers are convinced of some kind of reality which is *preconceptually* whole, then entering into any kind of artistic production can only be a kind of necessary, if potentially reductive, second order of business. My suggestion throughout this chapter is that Pound becomes increasingly anxious about the possibility of such a preconceptual reality and that it may only be possible to posit such a space from the "simple sign[s]" themselves. Instead of the danger of a reduction of the first reality, the problem is really that these very signs – visual, poetic, musical – may in fact be *inventing* that "first" reality, and not merely obscuring or reducing it.

Pound points out that scholarship (by which he seems to mean historical scholarship) and new movements in literature err in "presenting all detail as if of equal import." It is Pound's mission to see that the "'new method'" of luminous detail will overcome such errors. Pound's "method" is a perhaps not so radical combination of synchronic and diachronic examination. He notes that "every masterpiece contains its laws within itself, self-sufficing to itself," but he goes on to say that "[b]efore we can discuss any possible 'laws of art' we must know, at least, a little of the various stages by which that art has grown from what it was to what it is." Luminous details seem to have histories. In fact, they are

both culminations *of* history, and a kind of break *with* history. In survey-
ing the writing of a period, Pound observes, one discovers that there are
both "'symptomatic'" and "'donative'" works. The symptomatic work
exemplifies what one would expect "in such and such a year and place."
But the donative draws the tradition into itself; it stands as a kind of culmination of the past and, at the same time, a break with it:

> . . . the 'donative' author seems to draw down into the art something which was
> not in the art of his predecessors. If he also draw [sic] from the air about him,
> he draws latent forces, or things present but unnoticed, or things perhaps taken
> for granted but never examined.[9]

Significantly, the donative artist may introduce new themes or subjects
into poetry, or, as we will see in a moment with the "musical" innovations of a poet like Arnaut Daniel, the poet can make some new contribution to form or technique.

One of the most significant consequences of Pound's theory of symptomatic and donative writers is the practical nature of the study
involved: the study of donative works may be put to use in the service of
educating the contemporary writer. As Korn points out, Pound's sense
of history is "synchronic, linguistic, [and] practical." Specific traditions
are less important than the effects that may be discerned by those who,
like Pound, are interested in good poetry right now. Hence, "fine poetry
may consist of elements that are or seem to be almost mutually exclusive," and part of Pound's purpose in the "Osiris" essays is to elaborate
through demonstration – as in the translation of the Old English "The
Seafarer" or the lyrics of Cavalcanti – or through explication – as in his
discussion of the important properties of Arnaut Daniel.[10]

The discussion of Daniel is important because in it we see Pound elaborating the significant connections between music and poetic technique.
Daniel's donation to and extention of his particular tradition are largely
technical. Through a new attention to the use of rhyme (not to the
"multiplicity" of rhymes, but to "their action the one upon the other") a
new "manner of writing in which each word . . . bear[s] some burden,
. . . make[s] some special contribution to the effect of the whole" comes
into being. The movement is away from the skillful performance of verse
convention and toward a self-justifying organicism, toward *mélos*, or the
"union of words, rhythm and music (i.e., that part of music which we do
not perceive as wed to rhythm)." Such improvements in style lead Daniel,
in Pound's view, inevitably to a more "accurate . . . observation of
Nature."[11] A refined technical practice seems to lead back to the world.

But, at the same time, the "world" seems to have more to do with the imagination of the poet than anything else. Pound's praise of Daniel's greater accuracy in the presentation of "Nature" suggests that some kind of "objective" reality can be better grasped by both poet and reader through a more rigorous poetic method. But in fact, Pound's conception of the practice of art here is expressive, not mimetic. He says unequivocally toward the end of the "Osiris" essays that "we are damned and clogged by the mimetic." The power of Homer, for instance, lies not in the accuracy of his descriptions of events, but rather in his grasp of "things severed from their attendent trivialities;" as such, Homer's poetry gains its power as "a work of imagination and not of observation." This ability to imbue the outer world with mystery is Homer's particular "*virtù*," or, in Pound's terms, the particular quality of "some one element which predominates [in the soul], which is in some peculiar and intense way the quality or *virtù* of the individual."[12] It is because of such *virtù* that true and distinctive works of art exist.

Pound works at securing the possible distance between the interiority of artistic virtue and the ocular – and aural – proof of technique. Technique must bear the weight of the distinctive expression of virtue: "technique is the means of conveying an exact impression of exactly what one means in such a way as to exhilarate." Moreover, technique becomes, in Pound's words, "the only gauge of a man's sincerity."[13] From here, Pound goes on to tie in the issue of technique with music. The first discussion of music in "Osiris" tells us little about the actual relations between the arts of poetry and music, but it does further reveal the connection Pound is trying to articulate between expression and technique.

In the section entitled "On Music," Pound sidesteps a discussion of the similarities and differences between the arts of music and literature and moves instead into a more specific handling of the ways in which poetry and music can be combined: as with his sense of history, Pound's explication of musical–literary relations shifts to the quasi-practical. On the whole, the section on music examines the consistent interplay between the rhythms of music and poetry. As we will see later, this emphasis on rhythm casts the manifest and the hidden aspects of the poem into a kind of absolute conjunction. But here too, in Pound's discussion of the setting of a poem to music, the poetry seems to get preference; indeed, it is not just the poetry or the metrics of the line with which the musician must be concerned, it is the "inner form," the special rhythm of the poetry to which the musician must attend:

Yet it is possible to set this rhythm in a musician's rhythm without, from the poet's feeling in the matter, harming it or even "altering it," which means altering the part of it to which he is sensitive; which means, again, that both poet and musician "feel around" the movement, "feel at it" from different angles.

The whole notion of "inner form" sounds rather like Wagner's notion of "*Stabreim*," and, as is the case with the setting of *Stabreim*, there is a sense in which the setting of "inner form" seems to be something different from the practice of good technique for both the musician who sets the line of poetry and the poet who invents it. The creation and setting of "inner form" do not involve the mere mastery of metrical systems, nor of systems of quantity; "inner form" is instead the very manifestation of "*virtù*," that unique and indefinable quality which in turn defines "the great masters of rhythm – Milton, Yeats, whoever you like . . ." In a sense, inner form seems to spring from technique, but must remain something which technique alone cannot secure. It is significant here that at the crucial moment where technique is meant to insure the inwardness of the gifted poet (and all this is plainly romantic enough), music – at least insofar as it concerns rhythm – enters as the sign of this distinctive interiority.

Pound asks, in the next section of the essays on "Pitch," if it is possible to have "in speech, as there is in music, 'tone-leading'." "What I want to get at is this: in the interpreting of the hidden melody of poetry into the more manifest melody of music, are there in the words themselves 'tone-leadings'?" Pound is after a sense of (tonal) music latent within the language, a sense of the movement between words and word sounds which would parallel the "necessary" movement from one pitch or chord construction to another in music (say from the fifth of the scale to the tonic): "Does, for instance, the voice really fall a little in speaking a vowel and a nasal, and is a ligature of two notes one half-tone lower than the other and the first very short, a correct musical interpretation of such a sound as 'son', 'un', 'cham'?"[14] In any strict sense this is probably not possible. Clearly, Pound believes there is such a thing as "tone-leading" in language, but he must avoid answering his own questions directly because if he tried, he would have to recognize that there are no standardized pitches in the English language as there are in music. Moreover, even the sound relationships between phonemic combinations are, or would be, difficult to standardize as well.

In another sense, however, there is a kind of poetic "tone-leading" which can be said to occur when works with strict metrical forms, with line lengths and rhyme schemes establish a kind of internal expectation

of sound and rhythm. But Pound wants to go beyond such formal prescriptions, and, as Korn points out, in Pound's notion of tone-leading,
the interdependence of sounds relies in part upon memory which is not
just linked to the expectation of a patterned scheme. Pound desires
instead "a system of overtones, cadences" which comprises a rhythmic
sonority in "the sense of a sequence of vowels and consonants with
rising and falling inflections." Pound says as much in "A Retrospect":
"There is, however, in the best verse a sort of residue of sound which
remains in the ear of the hearer and acts more or less as an organ-
base."[15] The absence of any clear definition of tone-leading in Pound's
"Osiris" essay, however, suggests that he does know the problems
involved in any strict musical analogy. Still, he desires this latent music,
this sonorous trace, born of technique, but extending beyond it.

You can see what Pound is after in some of the translations he includes
in the "Osiris" essays. Pound praises Daniel for his sense of "polyphonic
rhyme," which consists, as Hugh Kenner puts it, elaborating on Pound
himself, of a "polyphony, not of simultaneous elements which are
impossible in poetry, but of something chiming from something we
remember from earlier . . ."[16] A clear instance of such durational
harmony appears in Pound's translation of Daniel's "*Sols sui.*" Pound
maintains the elaborate use of seven different endings in each stanza
which are rhymed in successive stanzas:

> I only, and who elrische pain support
> Know out love's heart o'er borne by overlove,
> For my desire that is so firm and straight
> And unchanged since I found her in my sight
> And unturned since she came within my glance,
> That far from her my speech springs up aflame;
> Near her comes not. So press the words to arrest it.

Pound does not use the same sounds as in Daniel's original, but he tries
to be consistent with the original in terms of rhyme scheme and in the
use of internal echoing of sounds within stanzas. Thus, in Daniel's
second and third lines we hear the openness of the vowels: "*Al cor d'amor
sofren per sobramar, / Car mos volers es tant ferms et entier.*"[17] The open vowels
are present in Pound's second line as well ("Know out love's heart o'er
borne by overlove"), though the third line seems to emphasize a shift to
higher vowels ("my," "desire," "straight") and only "For" and "so" recalls
the openness of the second line.

In quite a different way, though still with an emphasis on sound,
Pound translates "The Seafarer," relying on the Anglo-Saxon alliterative

line to capture in English a more native sense of the residual echo that he desires. Only here the echo crosses time to involve the past of English in the possible sounds of the present:

> May I for my own self song's truth reckon,
> Journey's jargon, how I in harsh days
> Hardship endured oft.
> Bitter breast-cares have I abided,
> Known on my keel many a care's hold,
> And dire sea-surge . . .

Here, the kind of "organ-base" residual effect takes on a different shape than in the Daniel translation. The repeated long "i" sounds (in the "I" given three times in four lines, and again in the "abide" of the fourth line) play across the halting emphasis of the consonants ("Journey's jargon, how I in harsh days / Hardship endured oft"). Kenner points out that in Pound's attempt to match his version of the poem with the Anglo-Saxon, Pound turns his own poem into a "map" of the original's sound: "It maps the sound, not the meaning, tacitly judging that the local meanings are of secondary importance in that particular poem." Christine Froula too suggests that Pound "preserves . . . not merely the syntactic and prosodic *structures* of the original, but, as much as possible, its actual sounds." It is also important to note that even in these earlier works, before Pound has devised his notion of the "Great Bass," we see very clearly an attempt to make sounds cross or intersect each other, as though they are temporal frontiers capable of a kind of simultaneous presence. Such simultaneity or "spatiality" applies, as I have indicated above in regard to "The Seafarer," not only to the sonority of words, but to the different historical moments in which words occur.[18]

Pound's achievement is especially significant in terms of his own sense of the "melopoeiaic" aspects of poetry. In "How to Read" (1928), Pound defines melopoeia as a kind of poetry "wherein the words are charged, over and above their plain meaning, with some musical property, which directs the bearing or trend of that meaning." But he goes on to say that this property is "practically impossible to transfer or translate . . . from one language to another, save perhaps by divine accident, and for half a line at a time." Pound succeeds in translating not only the sense of these poems but some of the import of their sound as well. However, if the "divine accident" has occurred, it is still largely an achievement of a technical nature. I do not claim this is trivial; but I do maintain that this level of virtuosity, even as well as Pound performs it in these translations, secures little beyond itself. Pound's mastery of technique does not in itself lift the poetic act out of the need for a stronger bond between word and expression – of some kind or another.

Indeed, the tension between technical mastery and the "truth" of presentation is manifest in the very idea of precise presentation that Pound himself wants to formulate. In Pound's own sense of poetic melopoeia there is a latent threat to the exactitude and precision that elsewhere he claims is so necessary for technique. Again, in "How to Read," he points out that melopoeia may operate in direct opposition to "Phanopoeia," or "the casting of images upon the visual imagination." In the visuality of phanopoeia, Pound states that we find "the greatest drive toward utter precision of word," and that in melopoeia, we discover "a contrary current:"

a force tending often to lull, or distract the reader from the exact sense of the language. It is poetry on the borders of music and music is perhaps the bridge between consciousness and the unthinking sentient or even insentient universe.

Here, word and sound seem to be at odds with one another. But it is not as though Pound is willing to discard or suppress melopoeia in favour of the greater clarity of phanopoeia.[19] In fact, it is strikingly clear here that Pound's sense of the musical properties of poetry seem to have a connection to a universal sphere where, as he says, the conscious and the "insentient universe" are somehow brought together. Such a claim exposes the desire for poetic technique to be at once a place of totality, of absolute coordination between the word and what it is intended to express, while at the same time acknowledging that such a complete poetic project is somehow not possible. The melopoeiaic aspect of poetry, its "music," enters to fulfill the goal that the concreteness of phanopoeia cannot seem to do. So, for as much as Pound will emphasize clarity of technique and concreteness of presentation, both in the "Osiris" essays and in the imagist work to come, such claims will always be threatened by the need for the potentially supererogative return of "music."

The ongoing search for a necessary bond between word and expression may perhaps explain why the next section of the "Osiris" essays following the one on music turns toward "Pitch," and eventually returns to a discussion of the necessity of technique, and to the more vague implications of beauty: "'beauty of the thing,' certainly, but besides that 'beauty of the means'." And this "'beauty of the means'," insofar as it includes music as part of the indefinable quality of technique, participates in the logic of an exterior or material poetry which attempts to be certain of – in fact, to create – an interior of the poet which is somehow nearer to the "truth." As Pound puts it, " '[t]echnique' . . . means not only the suavity of exterior, but means the clinch of expression on the thing intended to be expressed."[20] At this moment of the intersection between inside and outside, it is difficult to tell whether the "beauty of the means" is expressing or making the very interiority it is meant to frame. Music, despite Pound's attempt to restrain it for the uses of a technique which welds together the language of the poem and that which this language is meant to express, announces the moment where technique must be *something else* in order to be itself; it must *be* the inside, not just the "gauge" of the poet's sincerity. Music is clearly the sign of the supplementarity of a precise and thorough technique – which is still not enough. Pound poses the question, introduces music, then backs off, with the result that the emphasis on technique is no longer sure of itself, but instead, has moved into a vague terrain where it may be all, rather than only the necessary shadow of the expressive ends of poetry. In Pound's attempt to revise the language of poetry and to justify such revision, he inadvertently throws into question the work that he claims it is necessary for the art to do.

ABSOLUTE RHYTHMAGISM; OR, WHEN THIS YOU SEE, WHAT DO YOU HEAR?

The connection between music and the search for a precise technique is an issue that Pound raises in several different places and at several different times. About the same time as the "Osiris" essays, Pound offers one of his clearest statements on the relationship between music and writing in the "Introduction" to his translation of Cavalcanti (1910). Here, as in "Osiris," he says that the strongest connection between the two arts lies in their shared affinity with rhythm. In a division of artistic labor reminiscent of Wagner, Pound states his belief in

an ultimate and absolute rhythm [just] as I believe in an absolute symbol or metaphor. The perception of the intellect is given in the word, that of the emotions in the cadence. It is only then, in perfect rhythm joined to the perfect word that the two-fold vision can be recorded.[21]

Though working with an ostensible focus on only the rhythmic connection between word and sound, the similarity between this statement and the theories of Wagner is clear, as is the implicit idea of the familiar split between the word (intellect) and sound (emotion). Like a composer, the poet must also pay attention to the melodic properties inherent in the language. The case is a little strained in Pound's version since, in poetry, the word must perform both functions of expressive sound and concrete sense. This is significant. In Pound, as in Joyce, there is always this tension between language as a kind of material entity and as a tool of expression. But Joyce, as we will see, will push the possibilities quite over the top, forcing this coordination of word (intellect) and sound (emotion) to absurd proportions. Joyce will, in other words, tacitly put the "absolute" nature of Pound's assumptions about the nature of language and its relation to music into serious doubt.

The interesting thing about Pound's concept of absolute rhythm is the way in which it conflates the surface and the depth of the text into one semi-mystical artifact. The perfect word joined to the perfect rhythmic element unites in a "two-fold vision." Somehow the language of musical inwardness plus the material perfect word results in yet another metaphorical state – that of the visual. The *visionary* is not, of course, the *visual*. But Pound's statements on the importance of the combination of the aural (rhythmic) and verbal elements suggests that *something* is being seen. Just who, poet or reader, sees what remains somewhat obscure at this point. The notion of a poetic seeing in terms of the visionary raises rather succinctly one of the primary issues in the development of Pound's poetics, starting even before imagism and lasting through the *Cantos*. The very idea of "the vision" combines interior and exterior properties. The inward vision is *seen*, a process usually performed by a subject on something exterior to itself, but this visionary seeing takes place out of sight, participated in by only one, or, at most, a select few. The idea of the vision articulates the very nature of the stress between surface and depth. It structures the inverse desire for the outside which does not merely reflect the world, while it maintains a revised exterior realm as an inward possibility. Moreover, the notion of poetic vision also suggests the implicitly hierarchical status of both the nature of the visionary *and* those with the ability to perceive it. The vision is both seen and unseeable. The idea of poetic vision is certainly nothing new by the time Pound gets hold of it. Still, in Pound's articulation of the "perfect word" joined to the "perfect rhythm" as necessary ingredients for the appearance of the vision, he resurrects the age-old necessity of poetic vision to supercede itself. But, significantly, for Pound it must do so within the work of the surface or technique of the poetry itself; in other words, in that which *can* be seen, though it is not the vision proper.

Martin A. Kayman characterizes Pound's struggle with the distance between the surface and the depth of the work in terms of the literary and cultural history of which Pound and other moderns are the inheritors. Kayman notes that from the eighteenth century on the poet is placed in growing opposition to a new "social reality/audience which appears to oppose itself to the higher 'spiritual' values." In part, the very hermeticism of symbolist poetry, in Kayman's view, stems from the poet's need to resist the growing naturalism of prose. But Pound, as a modern

inherits . . . not simply the subjectivity, mysticism and self-reference of late Symbolism, but also the imperatives exhibited in the realist novel. Modernism as a whole may indeed be characterised as that moment of crisis of subjective and objective realism which, inheriting "an apparently unresolvable cultural bifurcation between *symbolisme* and naturalism", sets about trying to resolve it.

In the conflict between inside and outside, especially as it is played out in the problematic realm of poetic practice, we find the basis for Pound's theory of imagism.[22]

Imagism, as the name suggests, emphasizes a poetry of the visual. This has at least been the predominant view of imagism, especially insofar as it is seen to be a break with symbolist poetic concepts. As Stanley K. Coffman puts it, the imagists, at least in theory, were attempting to avoid "earlier romantic posturing and [return] to exact consideration of the external world." The first two tenants of the imagist doctrine, as repeated in "A Retrospect," are clear enough on this point:

1. Direct treatment of the "thing" either subjective or objective.
2. To use absolutely no word that does not contribute to the presentation.

The third proposal, however, takes us back to the connection between sound and expression:

3. As regarding rhythm: to compose in the sequence of the musical phrase, not in sequence of a metronome.[23]

There are some interesting ambiguities here. The third proposition reintroduces music, or at least rhythm, as an element freed from mechanical or artificial supervision by prescriptive metrical forms. It is an echo of the idea of absolute rhythm that Pound mentions in his earlier Introduction to Calvalcanti. But in a sense, this appearance of music in the last of the imagist commandments restates the tension inherent in the first proposal: to render the "'thing'" accurately, whether "subjective or objective." If, for Pound, as we have seen elsewhere, music still signifies the subjective or inward, then we must recognize that the double possibilities for presenting the "'thing'" are more complicated than the call for "direct treatment" might at first indicate. Music, or at least some sign of music (here it is rhythm), seems to call on a different order of poetic necessity than the visual concreteness that Pound, both here in his imagist pronouncements and later in his statements about the vortex, conjures up.

The struggle here is between the musical inwardness of the symbolist past and the attempt to adopt (perhaps partly in the naturalist tradition of prose) what T. E. Hulme had described in his "Romanticism and Classicism" essay even before Pound as the necessity to achieve a new "dry hardness" in poetry: "The great aim is accurate, precise and definite description." As C. K. Stead puts it, the tension here seems to be between the tendency in symbolism to place "the sensuous emphasis . . . more upon the ear than the eye, [with] a music which casts the feeling inward," whereas for the imagists the emphasis is the other way around: "visual elements [predominate] over aural, and so the mind [is] turned outward towards the world."[24] But the case for a hard and fast split between the visual and the auditory in Pound's sense of imagism is difficult to make. To over-emphasize the visual dimension of imagism is to overlook Pound's struggle to reconcile the concrete and the expressive dimensions of poetry. This struggle is itself the attempt to invent a poetry which at one and the same time offers both an empirical and a "spiritual" security, and to do this, it must use "technique," especially as it applies to the sound of poetry, as its guarantee. The paradox is, however, that at the same time that this music of poetry must bear more of the weight of interiority, it also becomes more closely associated with the artifice or the exterior of the poem.

What is so interesting in Pound's sense of the imagist project is the relative weight he places upon the auditory as part of the necessary artifice of the poem, even though it is clear that the poem's rhythmic properties are meant to hold its emotional weight. In the section of "A Retrospect" dealing with *vers libre*, Pound sees the movement toward freer verse in poetry as a desire for "the sense of quantity reasserting itself after years of starvation." But despite the desire born of such deprivation, free verse should be used "only when the 'thing' builds up a rhythm more beautiful than that of set metres, or more real, more a part of the emotion of the 'thing', more germane, intimate, interpretive than the measure of regular accentual verse . . ." The interplay is between a verse that is not completely free (merely irregular in comparison with other verse forms), and – again – between a "'thing'" which is real, but either "subjective or objective": rhythm bears the trace of the true response to the "'thing'."

But the "'thing'" remains in quotation marks, because it stays at some remove, perhaps by virtue of the very craft which is necessary to produce, or to reproduce, it. The "'thing'" which Pound wishes *vers libre* to render accurately is, in a way, always inward: if it is ever outside the poet, the rhythmic necessity is to capture the response to the "'thing'"; if it is internal, then the poet must stage some kind of response to his or her response. The exteriority, and hence, all the talk about the concreteness and visual emphasis of imagism, remains at the level of the sign and of the arrangement of signs in their sonorous displacement of the "'thing'." It is implicit that the poet's response is foremost; the "'thing'" can suffer no liberation from the quotation marks of the poet's representation of the inside. Strangely, but perhaps against his own wishes, Pound transforms the musical mark of inwardness into a state of necessary difference. The level of metric, of the interposition of sound as purveyor of the inward leaves only the trace of the response, but not the "'thing'" itself.

When it comes to the visual aspects of the poem there is a similar complex interweaving between inside and outside. On the one hand, the poet must "[g]o in fear of abstractions," an appropriate corollary to the dictum of direct presentation that Pound lays down. For this reason, the "perfect symbol is [always] the natural object." The symbol must never obtrude on the sense of the poem so that for those "who do not understand the symbol as such," "a hawk is [still] a hawk."[25] But, if a hawk is a hawk (is a hawk), the question then becomes, when is it *not* a hawk, or, at least, not *only* a hawk. The answer to such questions about the potential symbolic or metaphorical meaning of the poem is clearly less important than its concrete continuity of presentation. But if concreteness is the poem's first order of business and, to a certain extent, is meant to be enough, then why call upon rhythm to render the "absolute" emotional correlative to the word as Pound requires the music of poetry to do? And, how are we to reconcile this internal necessity with the Pound who, in an essay on Wyndham Lewis dating from 1920, borrows from Lewis' character Tarr to state "that art 'has no inside'"? Admittedly, this is Pound now passed through the imagist stage proper and well into the later development of vorticism. But there is a continuity here between the imagist Pound and his attempt to make a precise coordination between image, sound, and "'thing'," and the later Pound of vorticism with its emphasis on the "primary pigment" or material of each art. The continuity may be found in what Marianne Korn calls Pound's "phenomenological"[26] approach to art.

What Korn means here is something we came upon earlier in our discussion of the "Osiris" essays, and that is Pound's overriding sense that knowledge is a matter of direct personal experience rather than the mere memorization of cultural or literary "fact." In other words, knowledge is always somebody's knowledge and pertains to a complex of thought, and felt, responses. If this seems to render the possibility of "objectivity" a dubious affair, it also, at the same time, supposedly allows for the greater possibility of an inter-subjective way of knowing, a way in which poetry (if it holds to the concrete) can participate. Korn places her comments in the context of a discussion of Pound's sense of history and literary tradition, but they have some relevance here in our discussion of the problems of the imagist poem. As Korn puts it,

[i]t is not in the end the objective fact or the physical construct which has primacy, but the grasp of the fact of the thing, the way in which the intellectual and emotional experience of the fact by the individual forms a new complex of significant meaning.

From here, Pound attempts to justify poetry through the concreteness of its presentation, since the poem, in its textual presence, is meant to be the site of recognition of the composite mixture of the experience of the poet, and of the "'thing'" experienced (either subjective or objective). If, then, the sense of tradition (Korn's concern) is to be discovered only "in the words of the text," and is to be grasped "in terms of the text itself," then the text must be able to achieve a certainty of knowledge which parallels that of experience. Behind imagism, as Pound sees it, is the sense that if fact is presented "without subjective comment or description,"[27] a truly objective poetry can be produced: hence, the natural object is always the perfect symbol.

   One immediate problem that we come upon here is Pound's ostensible conflation of textual and experiential domains. One of the usual ways of reconciling the need for art is to maintain its usefulness for "life." Pound says in "The Serious Artist," for instance, that "[t]he arts give us a great percentage of the lasting and unassailable data regarding the nature of man, of immaterial man, of man considered as a thinking and sentient creature." Similarly, in "How to Read," Pound states that the very nature of good government and social–political practice has something at stake in the work of the "damned and despised *litterati:*" "when their medium, the very essence of their work, the application of word to thing goes rotten, i.e. becomes slushy and inexact, or excessive or bloated, the whole machinery of social and of individual thought and order goes to pot."[28] Books are important to "life," but books must be superseded by "life." Thus, when it comes to good poetic practice, Pound says that "[n]o good poetry is ever written in a manner twenty years old, for to write in such a manner shows conclusively that the writer thinks from books, convention and *cliché*, and not from life . . ." "Life" is the target, art only the means (one could make here a variation on Hugh Kenner's phrase that "[t]he poem is not its language"[29] and say that the poetry is not the poem). But at the same moment, as Korn suggests, art – texts, and so on – is all there is, and, for the practicing poet, technique is the guarantee of the poet's sincerity. Pound's emphasis returns to the text as the only security of something outside it ("life," sincerity). Writing is never enough, it is not the outside; yet it is the only thing that saves this exterior realm.

Other issues are also at stake here. Notice the expansion of the arts' importance in the statements above. Pound's attempt to reinstall the importance of the arts within the scene of larger social and political realms is also part of his ongoing concern with the precision of language. Poetic precision of technique is necessary not only for the health of art and the damned literati, but for the whole of social *and* individual thought. If Pound's sense of the division between books and life remains fundamentally cloudy, his sense of the importance of the relations between the two is not – at least not for him. In fact, the connection these various realms share for Pound is precisley that of the propriety of order as such.

Technique very nearly comes to equal authority here, and authority is crucial if one is to invent a poetics of essentials, of the "luminous detail," of the " 'thing' " itself. The precision of language and the need for absolute orderliness, writ small in "How to Read," is given full moral, political, and aesthetic expression in the *Guide to Kulchur* (1938). There in the opening "digest" of the Confucian *Analects*, Pound, in the voice of Kung, gives what amounts to a kind of manifesto for the interconnectedness of moral, political, and aesthetic realms:

If the terminology be not exact, if it fit not the thing, the governmental instructions will not be explicit, if the instructions aren't clear and the names don't fit, you can not conduct business properly.

Pound's drive toward non-material truth leads to an ultimately dubious immanence which manifests itself in almost every aspect of his striving for precision – no less in his sense that money is (or should be) simply a "certificate for work done"[30] than in the imagist notion of the direct presentation of the " 'thing'." The security for such precision, for, as Korn puts it, the "grasp of the fact of the thing," as we shall see, leads ultimately to Pound and to his own problematic surety of relational knowledge; the "necessary" sense of hierarchy may be anything but necessary. Music is involved in all this, still as a sign of temporal art, but with temporality as such reinvented in the harmonic notions of "absolute

rhythm" and "Great Bass." With these concepts we see Pound attempting to reinvent temporality itself and to give to art ("good" art, that is)
an absolute and self-justifying basis, something which subsists in the very
ordering of the work's technique. This sense of absolute order within the
work of art matches the hierarchical order Pound thought was necessary
in the realms of politics and economics as well.

Pound's notions of "absolute rhythm" and "Great Bass" form the
foundation of what might be seen as his attempt to give the material of
poetry a kind of necessary immanence. (Such a desire is also part of
what links the imagist and vorticist phases of his thought.) In statements
Pound makes on both absolute rhythm and Great Bass, he transforms
the stuff of poetry and music into a kind of combined sensuous and spiritual material. Thus, to return again to the Introduction to the
Cavalcanti translations, Pound says that rhythm is common to both
poetry and music, and, is also "the most primal of all things known to
us." He then goes on to redefine the very nature of melody as not merely
the "variation of tone quality and pitch respectively," but as the coordination of pitch frequencies conceived of as rhythms:

> if we look more closely we will see that music is, by further analysis, pure rhythm;
> rhythm and nothing else, for the variation of pitch is the variation in rhythms of
> the individual notes, and harmony the blending of these varied rhythms. When
> we know more of overtones we will see that the tempo of every masterpiece is
> absolute, and is exactly set by some further law of rhythmic accord.

He continues by suggesting that any given "rhythm implies about it a
complete musical form . . . perfect, complete." Such is the case too with
poetry, wherein "the rhythm set in a line of poetry connotes its symphony, which, had we a little more skill, we could score for orchestra."[31]

In one way, the coordination of different pitch frequencies as a means
of composing a piece of music is not that far out. As R. Murray Schafer
reminds us, the frequency relationship between the tonic and the dominant (the crucial interval in Western tonal music) is based on a relationship of 2 to 3 in terms of frequency, and the octave upon a relationship
of 1 to 2.[32] So Pound is in a certain sense correct when he assumes that
frequencies of pitches, when thought of as *rhythms*, have a particular and
important relationship to the structure of a piece. But to relate such an
idea to the metrical conventions of music seems quite another matter.
Meter has to do with the duration of pitches, how long they (as basic
units) last in any given appearance within a bar, not with the frequency
of the pitches as such.

However, what is more significant here is the way Pound attempts to
think about the form of the work in terms of something intrinsic to its

material, be it a work of music or a work of poetry. The melding of form and material is of course fundamental to the notion of vorticism and its emphasis on the "primary pigment" of art. More importantly, and perhaps more clearly expressed here in his statements about music, is Pound's desire to join the synchronic and diachronic dimensions of art. When we know more about *overtones* – presumably through science – we will see the absolute and unalterable *form* of the masterpiece. As overtones (frequencies) become conflated with tempo (speed, or the rate at which notes are played in time) a kind of essential and very elaborate construct is supposed to emerge. Temporality itself, the diachronic, will become part of the fundamental synchronic formation of the work. That which seems to a certain extent arbitrary (or at least arbitrarily chosen) such as meter, will become *absolute*, determined by some "further law of rhythmic accord."[33] The audible surface of the piece of music, or the inwardly heard sound of the poem wander free of the imposition of mere convention, carrying instead their own necessary "inward" significance in the materiality of their presence within the work itself.

As in Pater, we seem to see again the figure of music as the paradigm of all art. Here, however, the temporal nature of music is not the ironic mark or reminder of the qualified epistemological situation of the subject. For Pound it is the case that *in time* we will discover an absolute space structured on temporality itself; its audible manifestations will rest not in liminality and the passing of tones but in the aural shape of the space such tones both create and point toward: an immanent space of necessary time. There is no sense of the provisional here as there is in Pater's use of music, and there is no need to burn with a flame gem-like or otherwise, since for Pound the business of grasping the fundamental structure in art is a very real possibility.

A similar emphasis upon the shaping of the manifest work by the unheard is present in Pound's later statements on Great Bass. In his *Guide to Kulchur* (1938), Pound states, with significant double emphasis, that

[d]own below the lowest note synthesized by the ear and "heard" there are slower vibrations. The ratio between these frequencies and those written to be executed by instruments is OBVIOUS in mathematics. The whole question of tempo, and of a main base in all musical structure resides in use of these frequencies.

The unheard frequencies are no longer just a possible means of organizing the piece as they were in the earlier statements on absolute rhythm. Science, in the form of mathematics, enters and, at least for Pound, solves the problem. No doubt the appearance of science/ mathematics occurs here to lend a kind of empirical status to the almost

mystical – yet for Pound, material – organizing principles of these
unheard frequencies, or, in Schafer's words, this "heterodyne of inscrutable to scrutable elements."

However, the appearance of science also acts as a veil for a certain
Mallarméan resonance. The reader may recall my earlier discussion of
Mallarmé's "Crisis in Poetry" in which he speaks of the interrelationships which constitute the spiritual artifact which is the Book.[34]
Mallarmé maintains, as Pound seems to be doing in another way here,
a certain crucial emphasis upon the material language of poetry, its
manifest aspect, at the same time as he seeks to draw from this very
material a kind of immaterial or "spiritual" significance from which the
language cannot be separated. Mallarmé speaks of the "rhythmic totality, which is the very silence of the poem," and of a silence which is
manipulated in the "hesitation" and "disposition" of the poem's language. This silent rhythm is what composes the poem. Similarly, in
Pound, the silence of the unheard sound, here supposedly demystified
and given a purportedly more concrete elaboration by references to
inaudible frequencies, vibrations, and mathematics, returns as the
ground of structuring the work of art. The science Pound calls upon is
meant to separate his notion of silence from that of Mallarmé's, though
his conception of the "main base" of these frequencies as they relate to
tempo may in the end be no more empirically demonstrable than
Mallarmé's conception of a silence which is "translated by each structural element in its own way."

"Science" is, also, however, part of a larger ideogrammic constellation
adumbrating the notion of Great Bass. As Pound seems to head down
into the depths of silent mathematics he also spreads out into the history
of vorticism, into philosophy and into the history of Catholic heresy –
with a Confucian turn. In the "Vortex" chapter which precedes "Great
Bass: Part One," Pound prints Gaudier-Brzeska's writing on the Vortex,
as well as his letter "Written from the Trenches," originally from *Blast*,
1915. "Great Bass: Part One" includes references to Spinoza, Leibniz's
"unsquashable monad," and to Scotus Erigena's heretical contention
that "Authority comes from right reason." Pound wants to be sure that
the reader takes these adjacent figures and themes as necessarily related:
*"These disjunct paragraphs belong together, Gaudier, Great Bass, Leibniz, Erigena,
are parts of one ideogram, they are not merely separate subjects."*[35] Unsquashable
truths can be known from "right reason," a contention more Confucian
than Catholic; right reason crosses time, abjures chronology and causality as well, but exists in the proper acknowledgment of the substance of
music, and perhaps of art in general, if the idea of Great Bass is to be

taken as illustrative. No doubt it is; for Pound's reach here is meant to extend beyond art for its own sake into the very depths of ethical and philosophical thought and belief. "Right reason" exceeds the boundaries of university "beaneries," and the traps of mere orthodox religious dogma: the interrelations between knowledge, moral and ethical concerns, and ultimately, aesthetic and political truths, exist for Pound at every juncture. These connections are not open for debate, nor are they demonstrable, or truly graspable, by means of reason. Pound's unreasonable relations between these disparate elements are meant to supersede rationality and the apparent narrowness of the usual categories of thought. At the same time, Pound's own anti-rationalism creates a set of "truths" which are every bit as absolute as those devised by reason.

Later in *Guide to Kulchur*, in chapter 42, "Great Bass: Part Two," Pound elaborates further on the notion of Great Bass, this time stating an even clearer link between pitch frequency and the idea of time. The greatest problem with deficient musicians, according to Pound, is their failure to understand the complex interplay of time as pitch frequency *and* time as tempo: "wobbly time is due to their NOT divining the real pace of the segment." He goes on to elaborate (figure 1):[36]

The 60, 72, or 84, or 120 per minute is a BASS, or basis. It is the bottom note of the harmony.

If the ear isn't true in its sense of this time-division the whole playing is bound to be molten, and doughy.

The sense of high order and clarity is not due to sense

pitch as between

and

alone

but to the sense of proportion between all time divisions from 10 to the minute or era up to top harmonic 8vo and 32mo above treble stave.

Figure 1 Ezra Pound, *Guide to Kulchur*.

The references to metronome settings are, we must assume, also meant to indicate, in some obscure fashion, pitch-frequency relationships as well. Here Pound explicitly links harmony, or that which in music is usually thought of as part of its simultaneity, with temporal (though not specifically durational) progression.

R. Murray Schafer suggests that we should not pay too close attention to Pound's discussion of harmonics and overtones, nor should we take too seriously Pound's "insistence on the efficacy of the metronome for divining absolute tempi . . ." In terms of the actual practice of music, Schafer is probably right. But in terms of Pound's continuing interest in the medium of art (present in his thought since the advent of vorticism) it is possible to see Pound as being in a certain sense quite consistent with the nature of musical "'primary pigment',," which must in part concern itself with the temporality of music, at least as music is traditionally conceived.[37] It will become clear, however, as we examine Pound's theories of the vortex and the ideogram, that temporality has little to do with organizing the poem in some continuous or causal sequence. Instead, continuity gives way to contiguity, to the interrelationship of elements, rather than to their "logical" development. It is this logic of contiguity, most explicitly outlined in Pound's statements on the vortex and the ideogram, which in fact lies behind the ideas of absolute rhythm and Great Bass.

In Pound's various statements on vorticism, there is an increasing connection between the materials of art and the specific emotional characteristics of the art itself. In *Gaudier-Brzeska: A Memoir* (1916), Pound quotes himself from the first issue of *Blast* (June 1914): "Every concept, every emotion, presents itself to the vivid consciousness in some primary form. It belongs to the art of the form." It is clear here, and elsewhere, that the work of vorticism is not necessarily mimetic.[38] Rather, the work of immediate impression from the world must translate itself into the appropriate artistic medium. Speaking of his attempt to render accurately his impressions in a Paris metro station, Pound says that his experience should have been translated, not into poetry, but into paint: "If instead of colour I had perceived sound or planes in relation, I should have expressed it in music or sculpture." Colour, in the present case, would have been more appropriate to the sense activated, since it was "the first adequate equation that came into consciousness," and would thus have constituted the "primary pigment" into which the impression should have been rendered. The process does indeed have less to do with placing the perceived world before the viewer/reader than with focusing attention upon the process, and the kind of perception taking place.

Speaking again of "In a Station of the Metro," Pound says that "[i]n a poem of this sort one is trying to record the precise instant when a thing outward and objective transforms itself, or darts into a thing inward and subjective." The "'thing'," either subjective or objective of imagism has shifted ground just slightly here. Though the vorticist concern is still with accuracy, it is now with the accurate rendering of the exchange between the inward and the outward. The time for thought or mediation in perception and in the re-representation of the work of art is meant to be reduced to the interplay of sensuous elements of "primary pigment":

There comes a time when one is more deeply moved by that form of intelligence which can present "masses in relation" than by that combination of patience and trickery which can make marble chains with free links and spin out bronze until it copies the feathers on a general's hat.

Hence, Pound can say, extending his definition of the image and of his own sense of imagism, that "[t]he image is not an idea. It is what I can and must perforce call a VORTEX, from which, and through which, and into which, ideas are constantly rushing."[39]

It is the primary pigment itself which constitutes the thread between the object outside, the inside of the artist, and the re-rendering of the experience in art. The image proper is that which goes beyond language: "[t]he image is itself the speech. The image is the word beyond formulated language."[40] In fact, the image comes in Pound's aesthetic to take up the same space as the "real." Herbert Schneidau points out that in Pound's imagist phase, "[t]he aim of 'presentation' or 'statement' . . . is the veridical registration of the form of an experience." The image is not adornment, or description, or even objective correlative. It is meant to be, in a sense, the experience itself. Schneidau later makes clear that this tendency to collapse difference is also helped along by Pound's research into Fenollosa's concept of Chinese language.

Fenollosa's influence on (or concurrence with) Pound has to do with what Schneidau calls "objective predication." In part, this concept depends upon Fenollosa's idea that the Chinese character is based, as he puts it, on "a vivid shorthand picture of the operations of nature," a shorthand which is, moreover, a "[picture] of actions and processes." All "truth" as witnessed in nature, according to Fenollosa, is "the *transference of power*. The type of sentence in nature is a flash of lightning. It passes between two terms, a cloud and the earth." By this (albeit erroneous) analysis, the Chinese language – and English too, insofar as it uses transitive verbs – is based upon an *identity with nature*:

The form of the Chinese transitive sentence, and of English (omitting particles) exactly corresponds to the universal form of action in nature. This brings language close to *things*, and in its strong reliance upon verbs it erects all speech into a kind of dramatic poetry.[41]

Fenollosa collapses speech and writing, as well as world and language, eliminating difference as a necessary, and problematic, factor in the operations of poetry. To a certain extent, this is the result of erasing the subject position as a necessity of language. In his own war against intransitive constructions, for instance, Fenollosa makes much of the imposition of the subject onto the "natural" process of language: "'uniting a subject and a predicate', the grammarian falls back on pure subjectivity. *We* do it all; it is a little private juggling between our right and left hands." At the same time, Fenollosa's whole idea of the need for a poetic language which is identified with nature must still require some subject somewhere, and at some point, to appreciate this language.

Nevertheless, he persists in outlining this poetics of interrelation, stating that it is not only the Chinese language itself which is continuous with nature, but that, when it comes to the workings of poetry, Chinese also has a great potential for metaphor, or, in Fenollosa's terms, "the use of material images to suggest immaterial relations." For Fenollosa, metaphor is not merely a process of analogy, but the perception of an "identity of structure." Hence, in these terms, "a nerve, a wire, a roadway, and a clearing house are only varying channels which communication forces for itself." One perceives not merely the likeness between things, but the essential structure that lurks beneath their relationship.

Two things are important for Pound here. One is certainly the sense that "metaphor . . . is at once the substance of nature and of language."[42] By reducing, if not completely denying, the issue of a split between subject and object, the language of poetry can become continuous with the "world." The difference within the signifier is gone and language loses its arbitrary and provisional possibilities. Language is then no longer a barrier to be overcome, but now, as part of nature, a sign of the certainty of unseen structures. This idea will be of some importance later in the discussion of the song in Canto 75. The second thing that fits for Pound, and is in fact part of the first, is Fenollosa's belief that

primitive metaphors do not spring from arbitrary subjective processes. They are possible only because they follow objective lines of relations in nature herself. *Relations are more real and more important than the things which they relate.*[43]

We can see how Fenollosa's emphasis upon the "reality" of relations between elements in the work becomes part of Pound's general thrust away from mimesis in vorticism, a move which stresses instead the idea of energy between elements. Implicit in all this is the parodoxical situation in which the search for technique seems now to have become a search for a way to have language, on the one hand, disappear, but at the same time, reappear as something else: the world, or reality, or truth. Whether poetry becomes continuous with the empirical world, or with this world's hidden truths, it remains instrumental to the truth. At the same time, however, poetry must make itself unavoidable in order to allow for the hidden pattern of energy to be revealed. The importance of poetry floats somewhere between its materiality and its instrumentality. The notion of the ideogram has a clear affinity with the later idea of Great Bass at least insofar as both concepts are concerned with a reconciliation between what is manifest and what is essential though unseen or unheard.

The attempt in vorticism and in the idea of the ideogram to achieve a concreteness of presentation *and* of mobility or movement in the relation of elements is meant to outline a poetics in which time and space are reconciled. Pound claims in the *ABC of Reading* (1934), that the "earlier imagist propaganda" had been diluted by those who "thought only of the STATIONARY image."[44] He goes on to say that "[i]f you can't think imagism or phanopoeia as including the moving image, you will have to make a really needless division of fixed image and praxis or action." Given that the image is not necessarily mimetic, we are cast back here to the "real presence in the symbolic medium," a realm which, if it is to accord with "reality," must include, as Pound puts it later in *ABC*, "a fixed element and a variable."[45] Such a concept lies behind the notion of absolute rhythm, where the temporal rhythm itself, as Stephen J. Adams puts it, "does not divide time into little units, but accumulates through time as a vital energy. Even where fluctuation is allowed, there must remain an underlying, almost mystical, binding force." Hence, "[t]he verse, the translation, the melody – each has ideally the same inflection, the same tempo. The rhythm itself, disembodied, is absolute." If the notion of absolute rhythm still remains obscure in terms of the actual workings of either music or poetry, it is, I think, partly because it is a somewhat polemical idea. In their manifestations as polemic, absolute rhythm and Great Bass recapitulate Pound's desire for a method of structuring the work of art by some means which reconciles the fixed and the mobile, or the synchronic and the diachronic. In a certain way, both ideas turn toward the concept of rhythm, especially in Adam's accumulative sense, as a way of attempting to make the successive part of the fixed, and the fixed itself much more fluid.

In *Antheil and the Treatise on Harmony* (1927), for instance, Pound moves directly against traditional thought on harmony and emphasizes not the movement of harmonic tones, nor their concurrence, but rather "the element of TIME."[46] As in the notion of the ideogram, so it is in the theory of harmony that the issue of relations between two sounds, here figured by time, becomes more important than the specific notes played:

A SOUND OF ANY PITCH, or ANY COMBINATION OF SUCH SOUNDS, MAY BE FOLLOWED BY A SOUND OF ANY OTHER PITCH, OR ANY COMBINA-TION OF SUCH SOUNDS, providing the time interval between them is properly gauged; and this is true for ANY SERIES OF SOUNDS, CHORDS OR ARPEG-GIOS.

The sense of time Pound implies here is not strictly linear, but it involves linearity itself as part of the residual *pattern* of the series of sounded notes:

The limits for the practical purposes of music depend solely on our capacity to produce a sound that will last long enough, i.e. remain audible long enough, for the succeeding sound or sounds to catch up, traverse, intersect it.

The "laws" of harmony and indeed of tonality in general are here dis-owned in favour of an "active, not static, harmony." One of the first effects of this dismissal of the laws of "static" harmony is the return to sound alone. Pound advises composers to "give up trying to compose by half-remembered rules, and really listen to sound." But the sounds are not simply freed from the logic of established rules, they are released (if that is the right term) into the realm of contiguous horizontal relations, wherein they must "catch up, traverse, intersect" each other. The guiding principle for this horizontal continuity is melody now conceived of as time, and it is time which also binds the larger construction of the overall piece, as is suggested in Pound's theory of Great Bass.[47] In *The Treatise on Harmony*, as opposed to his later statements in *Guide to Kulchur*, Pound uses a slightly more parodic version of mathematics to prop up his theory, again placing rhythmic and pitch relations in the same theo-retical space:

You can use your beat as a third or fourth or Nth note in the harmony.

To put it another way; the percussion of the rhythm can enter the harmony exactly as another note would. It enters usually as a Bassus, a still deeper bassus; giving the main form to the sound.

Even here in these statements which precede the more "complete" version of Great Bass, we find that the heard and the unheard constitute the foundation of structure. Though elsewhere in *The Treatise* Pound emphasizes sound alone, it is clear that this sound is always contained by some deeper structure, by something which exceeds the sound itself. The percussive element may enter the harmony within the realm of the heard, "exactly as another note would," but it does not constitute a mere figure of regularity; instead, it comprises a "still deeper bassus" which determines the "main form" of the piece. As Stephen J. Adams puts it, Great Bass becomes for Pound "the basis for a kind of Pythagorean music of the spheres:"[48] in other words, a place of putative stability and fundamental organization which subsumes within it – indeed, is based upon – the notion of temporality.

The theories of absolute rhythm and Great Bass develop alongside, or come out of, the theories of vorticism and the ideogram and are another version of Pound's attempt to reconcile both spatial and temporal dimensions of his work. Pound's musical theories not only move to take account of the temporal aspects of his poetry but also act to establish the unseen depth of structure within the poetry of concrete surfaces. Linking the diachronic and synchronic aspects of poetic practice is part of the whole project of creating a poetry of the "real" in which poetry and "nature," indeed, outside and inside, are made continuous by a contiguous procedure supposedly common to both.

Before I discuss the continuity of these musical theories with Pound's poetic practice, I want first to explore their possible implication in one of Pound's most important musical works, his opera, *Le Testament de François Villon*.

FIGURING TIME: *LE TESTAMENT*

My reservations about, and fascination with, Pound's theories of absolute rhythm and Great Bass are probably clear, and I will go on to elaborate on these in regard to the *Cantos* below. I mean too to implicate these musical aesthetic theories in Pound's larger poetics, and these with his political and economic ideas. However, no discussion of Pound and music would be complete (and I don't expect this one will be so either) without mention of one of his most remarkable achievements, *Le Testament de François Villon*. Pound is ever courageous in putting his practical energy where his theory lies, and *Le Testament* is as admirable a piece of "practice" of the theories of absolute rhythm and Great Bass as might be conceived. Whether or not the opera is the complete embodiment of these theories remains for me doubtful, since it is difficult to ascertain just how Pound's compositional practice can be considered "absolute" or "Great" in the way he uses this term in the theory of Great Bass. It is clear, though, that for whatever shadows may fall between Pound's ideas and their realities here, *Le Testament* remains arguably one of the most successful attempts by a poet to bring language and music into close, and for Pound, necessary, relationship.

Le Testament de François Villon (1923), is where we see Pound's most earnest attempt at connecting poetry and music in accordance with his theories of absolute rhythm and Great Bass. Significantly, though, the poetry is not his own; rather, he reaches back to the work of the fifteenth-century French poet François Villon for his reinvention of harmony and musical–poetic practice. It is not unusual for Pound to turn to the distant past in order to invent and justify his own musical present; in a way, *Le Testament* is simply part of his ongoing mission of inventing modernity itself. What is interesting is that Pound's choice of early French as the language of the opera and medieval pretonality as its compositional technique seem designed to assert special demands upon the listener as great as many that contemporary experiments in music might have required.

Pound began the opera in the early 'twenties.[49] There is no definitive *performance* version of the piece, no text which possesses full stage directions, instructions for costumes, set design, lighting, and so on. Murray Schafer does mention, however, Pound's stray plans for production, and there is an extant copy of Pound's 1931, BBC radio version of the opera. One of the most intriguing possibilities Pound mentions of the several Schafer records is the notion that the characters must be "zoned" into "The IMMOBILE" and "The fidgety." Villon, for instance, "is completely immobile from start to finish. *Beauté* moves only to close a shutter." It seems that consciously or otherwise, Pound may have been trying visually to convey the sense of the "fixed and the mobile" which is so much a part of his theory of music, and of art in general.

The score of the opera also exists in several versions, adjusted mostly for the various venues and instruments available. Schafer lists five significant different versions, which are: the early version, transcribed with Agnes Bedford, (early 1920s); the 1924 Antheil version, which Schafer suggests is the basis for the 1926 Paris premier concert; the 1931 BBC radio version; Schafer's own 1962 BBC version, and the Spoleto edition of 1965 which Schafer suggests "need not be taken seriously."[50] The unpublished Schafer manuscript does not mention the 1971, November 3 performance in Berkeley, by the Western Opera Theater, conducted by Robert Hughes. This led to the Fantasy Records recording of the same year (Fantasy 12001), which is clearly based on the Antheil/Pound manuscript. It should be noted that before the 1971 performance, Spoleto is really the first time that the opera received anything like a dramatic treatment, though it was offered there as a ballet. More significantly, for my purposes, is the remarkable fact that though different scripts remain quite consistent in regard to melodic shapes, they are very different in terms of the rhythmic writing. I will return to this point in a moment.

The opera exists as a series of arias with some brief instrumental interludes. The 1931 BBC version contains a scenario which includes Villon and his rather low-life friends being pursued by the police for "violence against particular [sic], for violence against the King's officers, for deception of the King's officers . . ." and most damningly it seems, "that he did speak foul language . . ."[51] The opera is in one act, the major portion of which deals with Villon's bequests to assorted friends and relations, faced as he is with imminent arrest and hanging for his crimes. The mortal tenor of the piece permeates many of the arias of the secondary characters as well: the lament of the aging prostitute, Hëaulmiere ("*Ha, vieillesse felonne et fiere* . . ."); the prayer for salvation of Villon's mother ("*Dame du ciel*"); and even the drinking song ("*Pere Noë*") that precedes the final *a capella* chorus of the hanged, which includes Villon himself: it seems that only song can outlast human life. Moreover, the contrast between the weighty themes of mortality and death, and the more trivial matters for which Villon and his coterie are being pursued, seems a fitting description of Pound's own circumstances as these existed in the twenties, and certainly in the years to come.

If time is a theme of the opera, it is also a concern of the composition of the music and the setting of the words. The relations between language and music as these are stated in Pound's prefatory note suggest a deliberate compositional practice wherein music will take the shape of linguistic rhythm. As Pound puts it

The "orchestration" in the first part of the opera is not in the usual sense "musical." It is simply an emphasis on the consonantal and vowel sounds *of the words*. I doubt if the instrumentalist will get much help from "counting measures." Let him learn the *words* and make his noises when the singer reaches the *syllable* the intrumentalist is to emphasize.[52]

Pound is evidently trying to break the conformity of language to musical structure and phrasing. If he does not quite reverse the order of precedence, then he at least means to disturb the status quo in regard to language's secondary role in opera and song. The emphasis is solidly upon rhythm, the rhythm of the language, and it is not concerned with obedience to bar lines and the regular divisions of phrasing or melodic shape.

As we have seen already, for Pound, rhythm is part of the whole issue of time and duration as these form the fundamentals of both musical sounds in themselves *and* harmony. Pound's sense of harmony as based on time takes on new meaning here; for his complaints about the solidification of harmony into the "mere" conventional deployment of "static" concurrence are really directed against the way time, duration and rhythm have come to be conceived in music. Though Pound does not explicitly acknowledge it here, he is in a sense turning music toward the rhythms of language, the durational properties of words themselves, since they too, like musical notes, take, and therefore, demarcate, time – to read, to speak, to hear. Words, as Pound has admitted, cannot be made to sound simultaneously; however, if words can be made to concur with a very different conception of harmony, one based upon time, upon frequencies of pitches and durations, then suddenly both words and music are now made of the same "primary pigment" and can be concieved of on a new-found equal footing.

George Antheil's presence as "editor" and scriptor of the opera is also reinforcement for Pound's conceptions of harmony and the writing of the opera. In the section on Antheil in the *Treatise on Harmony*, a book written around the same time as the opera (1927), Pound links Antheil to no less a figure than Stravinsky, again, not with terrible accuracy. Pound's claim is that both composers take especial care with the writing of rhythm: "Strawinsky's [sic] merit lies very largely in taking hard bits of rhythm, and noting them with great care. Antheil continues this; and these two composers mark a definite break with the 'atmospheric' school; they both write horizontal music . . ."[53] Through Antheil Pound hopes to make his own theories vault directly into the contemporary music scene. Still, there is an odd dualism at work here.

In Antheil's prefatory note to the opera which precedes Pound's, he makes much of the "entirely new musical technic" and of the accuracy of the written script. He does not go into detail about this new "technic," except to say that it "upholds its line through inevitable rhythmic locks and new grips" in a way "heretofore unknown, owing to the stupidity of the formal architects still busy with organizing square bricks in worn-out formal patterns . . ." His audacity seems linked to his further conviction that the opera is "written as it sounds!": "the editor would be obliged if the singer would not let the least bit of temperament affect in the least the correct singing of this opera . . ."[54] Antheil's claims for technique as embodied in the accuracy of scripting here seem to conflict with Pound's own prefatory suggestion that the "instrumentalist will [not] get much help from 'counting measures'." Antheil speaks of the precision of the notation, while Pound seems to point to that which escapes the mere technique of the writing; musicians must not merely read and count, but listen to the language as the true guide to instrumentation. The opera is both written "as it sounds," but at the same time, mere reading will not suffice to *make* it "sound" accurately. Again, the technique of writing is emphasized, but it is also technique which must be surpassed to realize the "thing" itself. Once again, the old tangle between the demand for precise technique and the overcoming of that technique plays itself out, this time in the unacknowledged divergence in the words of Antheil and Pound.

Perhaps the opera *as* written betrays this apparent tension throughout its writing. In the Antheil transcription, the writing of time signatures is so over-wrought as to make the "counting of measures" nearly impossible. The opening two lines of Villon's first aria, "*Et Meure Paris*," are set over seven bars, each of which possesses a different time signature: 11/16, 3/4, 5/8, 7/8, 2/4, 5/8, 11/16. Such complex figurations are the norm here. To illustrate the problem of precise rhythmic scripting, Murray Schafer reproduces five different versions of the opening two lines of "*Et meure Paris*" for each of the five different versions from the Bedford/Pound version to his own 1962 BBC version. The pitch selections and intervals are almost identical, but the rhythmic figurations vary considerably. I reproduce three of Schafer's transcriptions in figure 2.

As Schafer remarks, with some dismay, "What might have been fascinating evidence for the precise measurements of poetical diction from the lips of one of the twentieth century's great rhythmicists appears to be a nightmare of inconsistency." Schafer goes on to note, however, that "[t]his is partly explained by the interpretive variations of the reciter himself over the years."[55] Pound's own musical writing skills appear to have been limited, and his use of friends as amanuenses at different times over the years would clearly have lead to great variation in rhythmic shapes. What is rather more impressive is the relative *lack* of intervalic and pitch variation over the same period of time.

ET MOURUT PARIS

1) **Pound/Bedford Version**

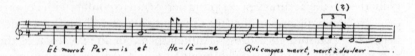

2) **Pound/Antheil Version**

3) **Version used for Paris Premiere (1926)**

Figure 2 Three variations of the same aria from Ezra Pound's *Le Testament de François Villon*. Transcribed by R. Murray Schafer.

The point here is not Pound's musicianship; rather, what is more significant is the strain under which rhythm is placed in the service of proving the case for the definitive or "absolute" rhythmic configurations of the piece. Pound's return to the pretonality of Villon's time is important insofar as it allows him both rhythmic and melodic freedoms which he clearly associates with older – and apparently, newer – musics.

One of the most famous Villon poems of *Le Testament* is set as the second aria of the opera, "*Dictes moy*" with its refrain, "*Mais ou sont les neiges d'antan.*" It is written as a typical *ballade*, with an ababbcbc rhyme scheme, and a four line *envoi* at the end. The octosyllabic line predominates here, as it does throughout *Le Testament*. The rhythmic figures are complex, in what seems to be an attempt on Pound's part to bend modern musical script into the flexibility of neumes, and thus to resist the conventions of time signatures, the durations of notes, and the rules of voice-leading. Pound is certainly suggesting a kind of medieval melodic phrasing here and throughout the opera, and the result is, if not always strictly "medieval" in practice, then at least enough to give the sonic impression of such a practice.

The rhythmic writing achieves this in part, but so do the melodic formations. If Pound is attempting to follow troubadour compositional techniques (a form of writing which appears in Canto 91), then there are many reasons to believe that he succeeds, at least in part. Hendrik van der Werf says that in the surviving manuscripts of the *chansons* of the troubadours and trouvères, it is "abundantly clear that the form of the poem must have been of far greater interest to everybody involved than the form of the melody." It is obvious that Pound is very much interested in the poetry, as he himself makes clear in the prefatory note, and in his disregard for the tonal conventions of voice-leading. We must remember, though, that Pound is putting aside such musical conventions in order to, in his view, reinvent a firmer grip between words and music, not to make one subservient to the other. Van der Werf also remarks upon the lack of melodic consistency from line to line in the compositions of the troubadours and trouvères. The rhyme scheme for the above *ballade* in fact would follow quite closely the "stereotyped form"[56] of the versification of the troubadours: that is, the rhyme scheme can be broken down into a *frons*, or two groups of two lines (each group known as a *pedes*, of two *pes*, or lines, each). The second section, here the last four lines of each stanza, was called the *cauda*. Correspondingly, the melodic setting of the *frons* would conventionally be set with "the formula A B A B X corresponding to the frons, pedes, and cauda of the poem." According to van der Werf, the A B represent "*antecedent* and *consequent* phrases" which are dependent on each other. But he also notes, that "[o]ne would expect the melody for the second pes to be a literal repeat of that for the first pes. Yet in reality the relation of the second melodic sentence to the first may be anything from a literal repeat to an elusive echo."[57] Add to this the variants of different manuscripts of the same *chanson*, as well as the possibility that some *chansons* are through-composed and therefore have no necessary repetitions, and we begin to see the possibility for melodic variation that could have appealed greatly to Pound. Even Pound's apparent lack of melodic emphasis for the ends of verse lines and rhymes is not inconsistent with the practice of the troubadours and trouvères:

Although there are chansons in which each melodic line appears to be a self-contained melodic entity, the prevailing situation is different. Especially in through-composed melodies and in the cauda of the melodies in the

Figure 3 Manuscript page from Ezra Pound's *Le Testament de François Villon*.

stereotyped stanza form the total melody is often shaped so that a performer could have stopped at the end of each line – or almost anywhere else – but he may also have sung as many lines to one breath as physically possible.

In the overwrought rhythmic scripting of the opera, Pound seems to have taken on himself the flexibility of line lengths as these may be sung.

Robert Hughes remarks that there is a "virtual absence of repetition" in the opera, which could suggest that Pound is intentionally following a troubadour technique of either melodic inconsistency or through-composition.[58] The setting of the first four lines of the *"Dictes moy"* aria show a great many repeated tones, usually moving step-wise above and below the F (the highest pitch being a G, and the lowest a D), but very little is present in terms of repeated phrase combinations. Each stanza ends with the refrain, and the last pitch a C, and though there is little here by way of exact repetition as we might expect with a refrain, in each of the four occurences of the refrain, the melodic phrase usually ascends from a D by step and then descends to the basis tone, C (figure 3).[59]

Perhaps more to the point is Pound's resistance to anything like tonal voice-leading. In *"Dame du ciel,"* Villon's bequest to his mother, the unusual harmony frustrates triadic listening, partly because of Pound's selection of accompanying instruments, and partly because of the great intervalic distances between the vocal line and the lower end of the accompaniment. The voice is set over a cello playing in the mid-range, and bells and piano playing single pitches vibrato two octaves below the cello. There is, as usual, great variety in the rhythmic configuration of the voice line, with signatures such as 27/16, 12/16, 36/32, etc. constantly directing the phrasing. The vibrato on the bells and the low-end of the piano, seems an attempt to put into practice Pound's contention that the similarity between pitch frequencies and rhythm is time, for the depth of the frequencies here send off very deep overtones, further enriching the already strange harmony. Thus, even a fairly mundane triad, such as the F major which opens the piece, is made strange by the configuration of the pitches: an A, written at the bottom of the bass clef, is marked "8va *bassa*," the cello sustains a middle C, and the voice sings an F above the C (figure 4).

The upper intervals move to a perfect fifth (C, G) which is disturbed by a G♯ in the lowest voice. This cluster turns again into an extended F major triad, but then changes in the next bar to an F in the bass beneath, again, a perfect fifth (C, G) in the cello and voice. Such unusual "progressions" create the harmony of the whole piece. In fact, it is remarkable how often Pound will use or imply a perfect or consonant interval either between the upper two voices, or between the lowest voice and one of the upper, only to disrupt it (at least from the point of view of tonality) with some much more dissonant interval. The major third, for instance, heard between the cello and the vocal line at the beginning of the third bar, is again off-set by the D♯ in the bass. In the sixth measure,

Figure 4 Manuscript page from Ezra Pound's *Le Testament de François Villon*.

a very unmedieval tritone is struck in the bass (D♯, A) beneath the fourth above (B, E). This, in the middle of a prayer for salvation, might in fact suggest a less than perfect heart in the supplicant, or, at the very least, a certain dubious sense of the possibility for the salvation requested. The pitch selection for the upper and lower voices is such that the voices are forced to remain outside of more predictable common-practice relationships. Pound uses only four pitches in the lowest voice, D♯, F, G♯, and A, while the vocal line is set, as Robert Hughes suggests, in a "studied hexatonic" fashion with the lowest pitch being a middle C, and the highest the A above it. But most of the melody is chanted in any given bar over F or G, and less often an E. The complex time signatures stress the pedaled tones which usually occupy the early parts of the bar in what seems a clear imitation of chant.[60] The selection and combination of musical pitches here is designed to avoid triadic consonance and dissonance, and to reinforce the sense of the lines as *separate* though simultaneously occurring horizontal lines. No doubt Pound is putting into harmonic practice here, and elsewhere in the opera, his contention that essentially any note can follow any other as long as the time interval between the notes is somehow correct – just how and why they are "correct" might be cause for discussion, at least insofar as the relationships of time and duration are supposed to be in some way "absolute."

Instead of relying on a triadic relationship between melodic and harmonic movement, Pound turns to duration and rhythmic figuration of the melody to structure the piece. Most of the arias are set syllabically (a pitch per word), but in the case of *"Dame du ciel"* Pound structures the melodic phrases in much tighter relationship with the poetic line lengths. At the end of almost every bar there is a change in the length of the notes in the melody. The end of the first bar above is typical: the sixteenth note figure changes to a dotted quarter note then to a quarter note. The lengthening of durations here is also usually accompanied by an intervallic shift as well, usually a major second or third up or down to the final note of the bar. This punctuates the line in a very emphatic and effective way.

The rich harmonic implications of *"Dame du ciel"* are a striking contrast to the accompaniment of earlier arias in the opera. What is notable in *"Dame"* is in fact the concurrence of pitches and the use of dissonances to maintain a sense of the independence of the various lines. Earlier in the opera especially, Pound uses a rather different technique to emphasize the separation of musical lines. In a practice which Schafer calls pointillisitic and Hughes suggests is *"Klangfarbenmelodie,"* Pound creates an accompaniment which moves across the instrumentation as the voice proceeds with the melody. *Klangfarbenmelodie* is a technique usually associated with Webern, though the term apparently originates with Schoenberg in the *Harmonielehre* (1911). The term literally means "tone-color melody," and is associated with the attempt to "establish

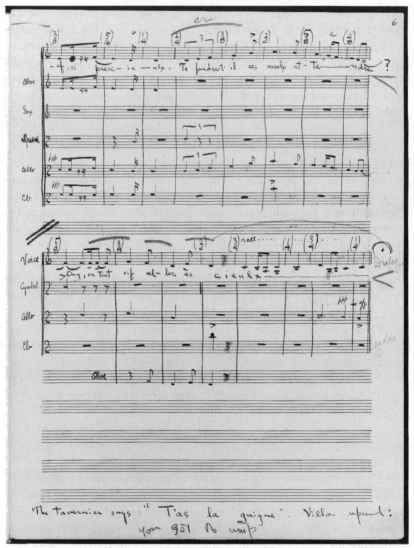

Figure 5   Manuscript page from Ezra Pound's *Le Testament de François Villon*.

timbre as a structural element comparable in importance to pitch, duration, etc."[61] Obviously, Webern or Schoenberg are not thinking of
"accompaniment" in the sense of instrumentation *supporting* a melody,
and though Pound's arias do have clear vocal melodies which are "supported," it is also true that the instrumentation Pound uses, and the way

he uses it, often partakes of a kind of independent coloration of the melody.

In the final measures of the opening aria, *"Et Meure Paris,"* for instance, we see in the upper system (figure 5) how the oboe matches the vocal line at the unison (E, E, F), the cello an octave below, and the bass a third above the cello (most of the instrumentation is simple – unisons, octaves, the occasional third or sixth – especially in the early part of the opera).

The cello takes over the accompaniment with occasional interjections from the drum, but in the next system we see that the oboe returns, and takes over from the cello in playing a unison with the vocal line. The procedure continues, and is perhaps most interesting when Pound works the percussion into the movement from voice to voice, as in the *rondeau*, *"Mort j'appelle"* sung by Ythier, Villon's friend. Pound does not really use the percussion to keep "time," but instead uses drums, cymbals, and even dried bones to insert yet another kind of "voicing," as can be seen in the drum figures of the first three measures of *"Mort j'appelle"* (figure 6), and in the sandpaper instrumentation in measures 14–15 of the same piece (figure 7).

The practice is consistent with Pound's contention that the percussion can be used as an "Nth" note in the harmony; but here the practice is notable because it takes the percussion *away* from mere time keeping and adds it to the coloration of the various lines, again, as part of the process of maintaining the lines as discrete temporal entities. Perhaps even more remarkable is the fact that the invention here seems to be Pound's own. As Schafer points out, such pointillisitic orchestration is not part of Antheil's style, nor is it clear that Pound knew of Webern's development of *Klangfarbenmelodie*.[62]

Even in the *a capella "Frères humains"* which ends the opera, with all the major characters swinging – and singing – from the gallows, the harmonies spread over the vocal ranges in such a way as to continue Pound's practice of separating the musical lines; this in fact adds to the remarkable vocal blends the final song acquires. Pound once again maintains a modal sensibility, especially in the upper lines, with versions of the stepwise ascent and descent, as in measures 3–4 of the opening (here, moving upwards from a C to an F, and falling to a D) being one of the principle melodic shapes of the aria (figure 8).

The first few words of the *ballade's* refrain, *"Mais priez Dieu . . ."* also have a recognizable four note step-wise pattern which is emphasized by repetition and variation, with the upper tenors often singing a descending

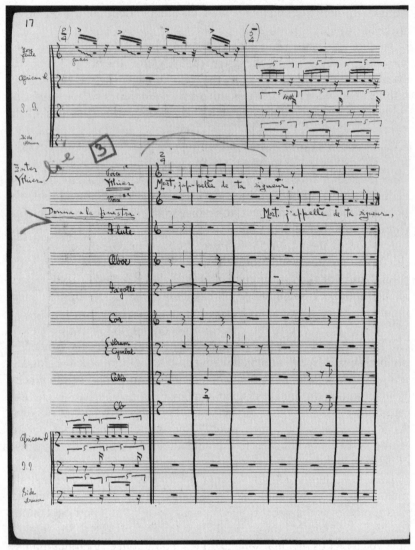

Figure 6 Manuscript page from Ezra Pound's *Le Testament de François Villon*.

variation which is answered in the lower voices, often by ascending, at the end of each stanza. Pound then is using recognizable motifs to demarcate and emphasize certain passages.

He is also using the technique of implying tonality and then avoiding it which we saw at work in *"Dame du ciel."* The very first pitches sung are

Figure 7 Manuscript page from Ezra Pound's *Le Testament de François Villon*.

essentially a D major triad in the upper voices, but they are hung (so to speak) over a B♭ in the bass. These are rather modern sounds for a medieval poem; even the very medieval cadence, which would be common at the end of medieval pieces, of the unison and the open fifth in the fourth measure (G, D) is disrupted by the A♭ in the bass creating a tritone

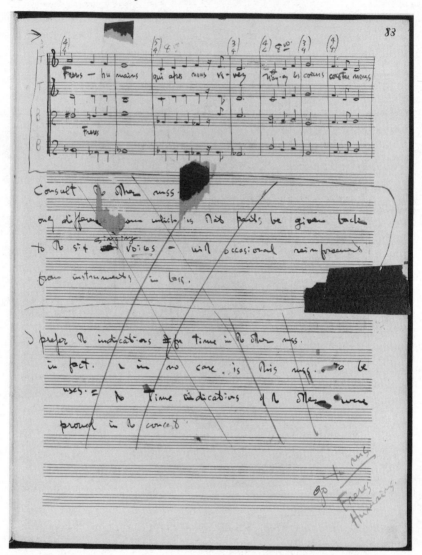

Figure 8 Manuscript page from Ezra Pound's *Le Testament de François Villon*.

(A♭, D) – which as we noted in "*Dame du ciel*" is hardly a common medieval interval. While the upper voices seem to move diatonically, the lower voices here move chromatically, and the very movement of the upper melody is often much more tensely articulated because of the lower voices.

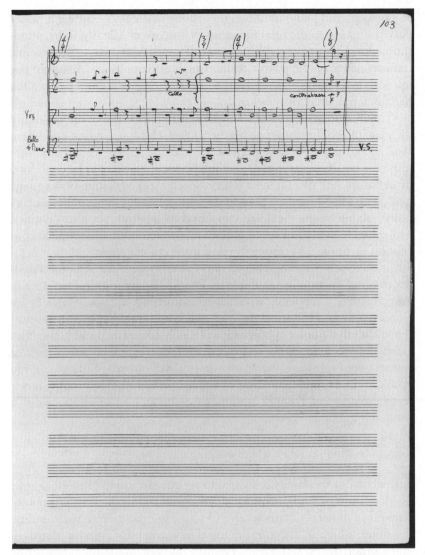

Figure 9 Manuscript page from Ezra Pound's *Le Testament de François Villon.*

Perhaps the clearest expression of the tension in the piece, and one which again stresses the independence of the lines, comes just near the end where the bells and the low end of the piano which first appeared in "*Dame du ciel*" return as the tenors sing an ascending version of the "*Mais priez Dieu*" motif (figure 9).

The bells and piano maintain the tritone in the bass, lending a rather dark resonance to the final moments of the opera. Clearly, in his admiration for Villon, the criminal poet, Pound flouts even the possible transcendence of the prayer, as the words apparently are meant to rise up, both in the invocation of God and in the melodic movement, but the harmony remains firmly below.

What Pound achieves in *Le Testament*, as remarkable as it often is, is not the absolute confirmation of his theories of absolute rhythm and Great Bass, since, as I have said already, it is hard to know precisely in what sense the rhythmic settings of the independent lines might be conceived of as "absolute." We do have a very closely worked setting of language here, with great attention paid to the independence, and to the concurrence, of pitches as these are conceived as separate temporal entities. Moreover, few poets of any age have attempted both a theoretical conception of musical harmony in relationship to language and then actually tried to put it into practice *as* music. In this sense, *Le Testament* stands out as a rather stunning example of Pound's desire to transform theory into practice, a tendency which is as disturbing when it comes to his larger poetic and historical theories as it is admirable here. For we must remember that music, insofar as it will finally concern Pound in the *Pisan Cantos*, follows in his larger scheme of the construction of poetry itself as transcendent signified, the place where time and space, those age-old problems in the understanding of nature, and of poetry, become facets of the "reality" of Pound's attempt to create an icon of temporality, "a fixed and a mobile" place.

SCORING POUND: THE MUSIC OF PISA

The second of the *Pisan Cantos*, Canto 75, gives us a map of musical time, an ideogram, perhaps, of musical temporality with the transcription of Janequin's motet, "Chansons des Oiseux" (see figure 10). Surrounding this figure which is "there in the mind indestructable" are the shards of many other voices, some from Pound's immediate surroundings (those of the other inmates, and the guards), some from the usual texts (Greek, Chinese, Frobenius, etc.) and some of personal reminiscence (of Joyce, Eliot, Lewis, among others). At the Disciplinary Training Centre just outside Pisa, Pound is without most of his books and all of his friends and therefore is forced to re-compose himself in a sense as yet a new "noman," an Odysseus figure at the blind end of time. For time itself has stopped, according to Pound, here "in the 23rd year of the effort" –

Mussolini's fascist effort, that is, with its new calendar and its concomitant attempt to make history coterminus with itself. In terms of the poem, too, time seems to have stopped and needs to be started again. Pound's identification of himself as "a man on whom the sun has gone down" takes us back to Canto I and Elpenor, whom Odysseus meets in Hades, and who wishes the inscription on his grave to be *"A man of no fortune, and with a name to come."* Pound in hell, as Odyssean visitor, yet, too, as his noman other, the forgotten Elpenor.

The *Pisan Cantos* seem to pour from this fractured self and make obvious the contradictoriness of the *Cantos* as a whole. Pound will renounce "neither the empire nor the temples / plural / nor the constitution nor yet the city of Dioce / each one in his god's name."[63] His curious combination of faiths are left intact: in fascism, in the Dionysion myths and his anti-Christianity, in the Confucian morality of right action and government, and, indeed, in the possibility of the manifestation of *"virtù,"* in the image of the "city of Dioce." This city is a crossover point between history and imagination, inside and outside. As Massimo Bacigalupo explains, in part, the city is Pound's own "dreamlike City of the *Cantos*," the "Ecbatan of c[anto] 4." It also echoes with Wagadu, city of a Sonnike myth related in Frobenius and Fox's *African Genesis*. The legendary city is built and falls four times, and is each time reconstructed alternatively as Dierra, Agada, Ganna, and Silla. As Leon Surette points out, this city is a perfect image for Pound, especially at this time, since, "[a]lthough the city . . . is repeatedly destroyed by vanity, falsehood, greed, and dissension, the dream cannot be destroyed." The perfect or ideal city figures a means of the interaction between internal and external realms, and so, "while history is internalized in the *Pisan Cantos*, Pound maintains a link between the city in the mind and the historical city, between the 'forméd trace' and 'the seen form'."

I use Surette here (and in a way probably much against his will) to state the very problem of the *authorizing* of precisely this kind of dialogue between internal and external realms. This is not to say there isn't such a dialogue; I believe that something very like Surette's conception did take place for Pound himself. But what authority can such a dialogue, and indeed, such a method of association, and non-linear interconnection have that is, as Pound would have seen it, *absolutely* necessary? Indeed, within the historical moment in which Pound is involved and in which he writes, it may seem inevitable that some such belief in the indestructibility of imaginary realms is necessary. At the same time, we come once again to one of the tensions within modernism itself (and perhaps within modernity as a whole, including the *post*modern, though expressed in different terms) which I mentioned in the Introduction, and that is, the struggle for "objective principals [in art] wholly distinct from human will," and the "freedom of the artist and the absolute priority of personal vision."[64] Such a polarity seems to describe Pound precisely. As we have already seen, Pound's efforts to account for a reconciliation between space and time in the theories of Great Bass and absolute rhythm suggest a coordination between any "true" work of art as manifest in the world, and the premises upon which such a work begins and to which it ultimately points. Moreover, as we will see shortly, such a premise is consistent with Pound's own conception of the ideogrammic technique and its requirement to be material, or at least perceivable, and its necessary connection to an immanent plane of truth. Pound eschews a transcendent aesthetics, it is true; at the same time however, he reintroduces a new plane of problematic authorization. It is as though he does away with one plane of authority to transplant himself as perceiver, and purveyor, of another. It is not simply the case, however, that such a move is somehow necessarily "fascist" or even more or less authoritative than any other poetic. But Pound, ever the one for attempting to put ideas into action, chose to act upon these beliefs as more than only – or merely – poetic and aesthetic concerns. He actively involved himself with fascism without, it seems, a perfect understanding of its practical workings. As such, his "totalitarian" cultural project dovetails with a related totalitarian political project, one which Pound perhaps too happily sought to make identical with his own.

Technique equals authority in Pound, and authority is crucial if one is to invent a poetics of essentials. Technique may not need to be conceived in this way; but for Pound it is the beginning and his ending; his strong point and his weakness. His resistance to mimesis quarrels with his need for accuracy.[65] His drive toward non-material truth leads to a dubious immanence, which manifests itself no less in his theories of social credit than in his musical speculations. The "truth" of either kind of thought, as we will see, leads only to Pound and to his own problematic surety of relational knowledge, and thus to the "necessary" sense of hierarchy which may be anything but necessary. Into this mixture comes music, still as a sign of temporal art, but with temporality itself reinvented in the harmonic notions of the Great Bass. Always there is the effort in Pound to reinvent with a sense of the propriety of order: historical, temporal, economic, and artistic order, all interconnected like one great ideogram with perhaps only Pound at the centre to verify, or enforce, the connections.

The concepts of absolute rhythm and Great Bass, unorthodox musical ideas as they may be, are part of Pound's larger purpose to create and justify his increasingly non-linear poetic practice, a practice which in its fullest form comes to be known as the "ideogrammic" technique of the *Cantos*. As should be clear from my argument so far, these ideas have less specifically to do with any strict analogy between the sound of poetry and that of music than with the method of putting the elements of the poetic or musical text together. Clearly, when Pound emphasizes the linear nature of harmony in *The Treatise on Harmony*, he does so in order to make it more amenable to the successive nature of language. Puns – aural or verbal – or homonyms are not, as they are in Joyce, Pound's style. It is not Pound's way to partake so much of the simultaneous possibilities of language, to obscure its referential capacities as such. Rather, he chooses to expand these capacities beyond the level where specific referents can contain the meaning. For Pound, the image, not the word, as noted earlier, is the poem's minimal unit of meaning. So, in his theory of an "active, not static" harmony, where the need is for a sound to "last long enough . . . for the succeeding sound or sounds to catch up, traverse, intersect it," the meaning, as John Tucker explains, "resides precisely in the catching up, traversing and intersecting." Tucker also points out that, in Pound's view, "[p]oetry [like music] also is built up of minimal units of this kind" and thus, he reminds us, "[t]his many-titled vortex, equation, image or gist is also known as the ideogram. The belief that such minimal units of juxtaposition can generate meaning is the basis of the ideogrammic method."[66]

TOWARD THE MUSIC OF THE *CANTOS*: FROM FUGUE TO THE IDEOGRAM OF CANTO 75; OR, WHERE THE BIRDS ARE

Canto 75 is the first written instance of music in the *Cantos*; but seeking musical analogues for the work as a whole has a long history.

Perhaps the most frequently mentioned musical form applied to the poem is that of the fugue, probably since the fugue seems to offer some rationale for the juxtapositioning of "minimal units" that Tucker mentions. Still, though the analogy with mucial counterpoint may be tempting, it is difficult to prove in any definitive way. In 1928, in "A Packet for Ezra Pound" (which precedes the introduction to *A Vision*), W. B. Yeats describes a meeting with Pound in which the latter is supposed to have said that when the "hundredth canto is finished [the work] will display a plot like a Bach fugue." Yeats, however, then goes on to say that there

LXXV

OUT of Phlegethon!
out of Phlegethon,
Gerhart
art thou come forth out of Phlegethon?
with Buxtehude and Klages in your satchel, with the
Ständebuch of Sachs in yr/ luggage
—not of one bird but of many

Figure 10 Canto 75, *The Cantos of Ezra Pound.*

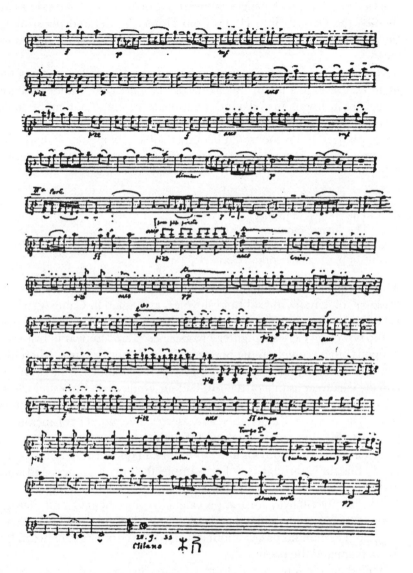

Figure 10 *(cont.)*

will be "no plot, no chronicle of events, no logic of discourse, but two themes, the Descent into Hades from Homer, a Metamorphosis from Ovid, and, mixed with these, mediaeval or modern historical characters."[67]

A year earlier, Pound had written to his father, himself suggesting the fugal nature of his poem. Speaking of the poem as "rather obscure, especially in fragments," Pound attempts to give an "outline of main scheme." The scheme, he contradictorily contends, is "[r]ather like, or unlike subject and response and counter subject in fugue." Pound goes on to outline the tentative possibilities of subject, response, and counter subject:

A. A. Live man goes down into world of Dead
C. B. The "repeat in history"
B. C. The "magic moment" or moment of
metamorphosis, bust thru from quotidien into
"divine or permanent world." Gods, etc.[68]

The descent is easy enough to discern in Canto 1 as Pound does the "nekuia" of Ulysses in Old English voice, and again in Canto 47 where yet another voice instructs: "First must thou go the road / to hell / And to the bower of Cere's daughter Proserpine." The "'repeat in history'" happens often enough in the poem: in Canto 4, for instance, where the cannibalistic story of Procne and Tereus is made to rhyme with the equally carnivorous tale of the troubadour Guillem de Cabestan whose heart was served up to his lover Seremonda by a jealous husband (history repeats itself first as dinner, then as dessert?). The moment of metamorphosis is also apparent enough all through the *Cantos*, especially in the *Pisan Cantos* where Dionysus and Aphrodite, in one form or another, are often "bust[in']" through (see, for example, the prayer to these gods that ends Canto 79).[69] The elements Pound outlines can be found in the *Cantos*, but they hardly form a prevalent "main scheme," and Pound's self-negating statement that the *Cantos* is both "like" and "unlike" a fugue suggests a certain hesitancy about any absolute correlation between the fugue form and the poem.

This does not stop others from carrying the musical – though not always fugal – analogy along. In 1931, for instance, Dudley Fitts and Louis Zukovsky both publish essays with sections devoted to the musical aspects of the *Cantos*. Only Fitts mentions any explicitly fugal properties of the poem, maintaining that it possesses both "counterpoint" and "harmony." What he means to indicate by this somewhat erroneous opposition is that the *Cantos* supply a kind of "'echo-counterpoint'," or sonorous recollection within the confines of the sequential nature of language by means of "repetition of pitch and rhythm." This is similar to Zukovsky's position that the "music of the words themselves" is important, but instead of repetition and echo, he speaks of "the music of juxtaposition (includ[ing] the pauses), of word and word, line and line, strophe and changing strophe, entire canto against cantos." While Fitts and Zukovsky do not quite agree about how the music of the poem works, they are both in agreement about Pound's sense of sound *and* space.[70]

Zukovsky, Fitts, and later writers who appeal to music in order to explain the *Cantos'* technique are trying to give reason to the discontinuity of Pound's form. Sidestepping the fact that tonal musical forms, especially contrapuntal ones, are anything but contiguous in the way they are describing, these authors are attempting to justify Pound's method of composition by an appeal to another art's means of structuring itself. It is true that both tonal music and language are similar insofar as each operates according to a differential procedure; notes and letters take on meaning (to a degree) depending upon their relationship to the other notes and letters with which they are combined. In fugue, and perhaps especially in Bach's contrapuntal work, the procedure of composition is very rational: it is the *interpretation* of the resulting music which – as should be clear from my first chapter and the idea of absolute music I discuss there – allows for the entry of the possibility of the non- or irrational. Pound's structure may be discontinuous, but it too has its logic, though this may well be a "logic" of the non-rational and the discontinuous. But this is a very different thing than the procedure of traditional counterpoint which could be more (or just as) easily adapted to sustain an argument for enlightenment rationality than one for modernist experimental poetry. For many critics then, music enters the discussion of the *Cantos* in order to rationalize the apparent irrationality of the design. "Meaning" is not, in this view, entirely held within the script, and certainly not in its sequential design. Fugue, or counterpoint, seems like a plausible analogy insofar as it places individual voices moving in time in *necessary* relationship with one another. But the rules regarding such placement must accord, at least in traditional counterpoint, with what amount to rules of harmony: the placement of pitches is not arbitrary and is governed by rules exterior to the composer. This is not the case with Pound's text, though the relationships between elements in collision are, in Pound's view, and in that of many of his critics, *absolutely* necessary. But they are in fact only part of Pound's arcanum.

However, Pound's disruption of a rational, or rationalizable, linear movement of language seems to inspire a need in most critics who are positive about the *Cantos* to see it as having an at least potentially unifiable design. Though the ostensible appeal may be to the rigor of the fugue and to its design of independent voices, this is really only to disguise – and perhaps not too well – an analogy between Pound's text and its anti-logical character. In other words, music enters for these critics as a means of signifying something beyond mere words, something supposedly essential to which language can only point but which it cannot encompass. Thus, Zukovsky maintains that there is a musical structure to the *Cantos* as a whole, though he admits that at the time of his writing there are only twenty-seven cantos in existence. He claims that there is in the *Cantos* "a music such as of horizontal melody, the further connection in the writing being not merely further but simultaneously conceived": that is, the "music" may be conceived as "an immediacy of the entire structure." Fitts is also willing to admit to a kind of breaking of the successivity of the language which forms instead "a harmony not only of sound, but of image."[71] He claims that through the accretion of sounds to a point of extreme density a kind of stasis of motion can be acquired in the sound of the poem. For images, too, a "true" harmony can be attained if the image "is broken, echoed back and forth, or adequated substantially or kinetically by another image . . ." While willing to grant the *Cantos* a very high degree of technical competence, however, Fitts concludes that the poem is only "very nearly the great music 'fit for the Odes'." In the end, though, neither Fitts, nor Zukovsky – despite the latter's claims – go very far in making the case for an overall musical structure of the work.

More recent claims about the fugal nature of the *Cantos*, however they might differ from these early attempts at explaining the poem, still make their fundamental appeal to the relationship between design and transcendence. Daniel D. Pearlman suggests a Hegelian scheme opposing "Spirit and Time . . . [as the] basic metaphysical pair" into which the *Cantos* polarize themselves. Based on this assumption, he proceeds to outline a possible fugal–Hegelian structure of "subject [thesis], response [antithesis], and counter-subject [synthesis]" which derive from the outline in Pound's letter to his father. Pearlman though does only one close reading of Canto 47 in which he reintroduces the fugue as a rather effective means of organizing the thematic material of the canto. This is what Kay Davis does on a larger scale in *Fugue and Frescoe*. Davis gives a much more detailed analysis of Canto 63 as fugue; indeed, more than any other critic who takes up the analogy, Davis spends much more time defining what a fugue is and how Pound's Adams Cantos are both like, and unlike, the fugue.

Though Davis is at pains to give a detailed explication of the canto according to the traditional elements of the fugue, she, like R. Murray Schafer, acknowledges that the fugue is a process and not a strict form, and that any similarity between the *Cantos* and fugue cannot be thought of as a "strict one to one analogy."[72] Schafer, discussing the "main" themes of descent, metamorphosis, and history, suggests that the *Cantos* are a fugue, "for despite the externalization of [these] themes, they themselves remain unchanged throughout." This consistency, in Schafer's view, is similar to the themes of a Bach fugue because, in musical terms, these themes are truly "ideas, not mere profusions of sound." Consistency of overall form lies, for Schafer, within these ideas. This can only be upheld as a notion of form, however, if we appreciate the fact that "[s]trictly speaking, the fugue is not a form at all, but rather a procedure." As such, the emphasis falls upon the "craftsmanship of [the work's] texture" rather than on its form. Perhaps beyond any specific analysis of the *Cantos*, or parts of the *Cantos* as fugue, the most important connection between Pound's poem and that of the fugue is precisely here in the idea of both as *kinds* of writing.

Two things are important to grasp here in the notion of the *Cantos* as a *kind* of writing, rather than as a fixed form: first is that, in coming to this conclusion, these critics begin to agree with Pound's sense of the importance of a method, not a simple representable symbolic truth. As Stephen J. Adams suggests (though he has no faith in the *Cantos* as fugue), what is useful for Pound in the fugal analogy is that the fugue is "abstract . . . melodic . . . intellectual," traits which work away from the expression or representaion of emotions and toward compositional virtuosity and the need for an intellectual grasp of this virtuosity on the listener's part. Adams also acknowledges, as do Davis and Schafer, that, for Pound, the fugue is both "'elastic'" and "open-ended"; it is not subject to the prescriptions of some more or less set form, but, instead, is "a musical procedure founded on certain principles," the development of which is an "on-going process." The downfall of the analogy, as Adams sees it, is that, though Pound is also interested in the juxtaposition of voices in fugue as having a certain affinity with his own ideogrammic method, Pound "does not seem to have arrived at any comparison between his techniques of juxtaposition and fugal counterpoint."[73] Pointing out that Pound himself admits that harmony (Adams adds in counterpoint as well) is possible in poetry only as at best a "residue of sound,"Adams concludes that there is no real analogy between fugal form and the *Cantos*.

I agree with Adams' point, but would suggest that there is yet another reason for the analogy. It is important to recall that the "ideogrammic" technique has its roots in Pound's interest in the concrete *visual* properties of the Chinese written character. What I think lies beneath the suggestion of fugality is in fact an attempt to portray, or indeed, *invest* Western writing with a spatial, less linear, even perhaps a more *visual* dimension, at least as this writing is used in Pound's poem. The impression we are meant to get is that Pound's *form of writing* (to recall Schafer's words), is, again, not quite itself. However, the difference within the technique must both precede it and exceed it; it must be *more* than linear Western script and enscripting. It must encompass both spatial and temporal discursive dimensions. In regard to the graphing of music itself – and "graphing" is Pound's word here – Pound states that

There is an enormous leeway even in the best graph, BUT it is a leeway of intensity, not of duration. It is a leeway in graduations of force and of quality, not of duration, or in the lapse of very small intervals between the beginnings of notes.

Graphing is the spatial designing of time, of absolute compositional time through the structuring of sonorous temporal planes in relation. Bad graphing can indicate bad composing; but more importantly, the theory that "there can be no absolute rendering of the composer's design, ultimately destroys all composition, it undermines all values, all hierarchy of values."[74] Writing or graphing, then has a great deal riding on it, and the fugal design of multiple and (to a degree) independent voices in time *and* space renders the "fugue" as a kind of aural model of absolute space–time relations. What I suspect both Pound and his commentators want from the fugue is an aural complement to the predominantly visual poetics of the ideogram. Moreover, they want really to keep the rigor of the fugal model about, as well as the non-lexical and potentially transcendent sense of the "musical." But this musical idea has in Pound's view already been saved from mere abstraction or amorphous emotionality by the "scientific" notions about time presented in the theory of the Great Bass. Add to this the sense that when scripted, the fugue may *appear* as a visual, though not linguistically discursive *graph* of these sonorous planes in relation, and we can begin to see the fugue as a kind of audio and visual icon for the precise coordination of synchronic and diachronic dimensions that Pound means to encompass in his own *Cantos*. Such a combination must, in Pound's view, be present in order for the absolute hierarchy of values, aesthetic or otherwise, to remain in place. For Pound, a great deal does indeed depend on writing.

Such is the "gist" of a text like the *Treatise on Harmony*. In *The Treatise*, Pound completely sidesteps the issue of tonal relationships. Harmony, like pitch, is now an issue of intersecting frequencies, some heard, some not, and these intersections are, for Pound, all conceived of as linear planes in relation. In writing, there is no question of one voice answering or countering another at some perfect interval, as there is in fugue. But there is the possibility of using several voices which not only supply their own temporal/historical contexts, but also their own discursive linearities which enter into relationship with other voices by means of contiguity. The force, indeed the weight, of contiguity, as these voices appear in Pound's text, disrupts the logic of textual progression in this new place of collision which is the *Cantos*. Paradoxically, then, the *progression* of voices can best be read in their non-linear interrelationships.

A slightly different, but clearly related, sense of multiplicity is involved in Pound's conception of the Chinese ideogram itself. If the subject-rhyme operates by the intersection or layering of different strands of discourse, the ideogram proper functions by the accretion of various smaller, "radical" ideograms. As Marianne Korn explains, "[e]ach ideogram presents the reader not just with an ultimate import, but with the factual data which, gathered, gave rise to that import." In other words, each ideogram carries with it "its own etymology." Pound demonstrates this in the by now famous example from *ABC of Reading*, where he outlines how the ideogram for "East" develops as a result of combining the various ideograms for "man," "tree," and "sun." Individual ideograms can in turn be combined into still larger units, as Kay Davis demonstrates is the case with the ideogram for "rays" in Canto 254. This ideogram, writ very large at the beginning of the Chinese/Adams section of the poem, is constituted of the ideograms for "bright," "feathers," and "flying."

But the "harmonically" accretive presence of the ideograms can also be further placed into a kind of syntagmatic relationship, as in Canto 53. Here, running vertically on the righthand side of the page, is a row of four ideograms beginning and ending with the ideogram *hsin*, meaning "to make new daily." In between is repeated the ideogram for "sun," *jih*. The import of the whole is given in the disrupted lines of verbal text going down the lefthand side of the page: "[Tching] wrote MAKE IT NEW / on his bath tub / Day by day make it new / cut underbrush, / pile the logs / keep it growing."[75]

Here, the text itself reflects the interplay between its own temporal and spatial procedures. The linear progression of the verbal text cuts back across its own successive plane. The script of the lefthand side, stacked, it seems, to parallel the line of ideograms on the right, follows an apparently linear syntactic progression which, moreover, forms a subject-rhyme with an earlier reference to Frobenius in Canto 38. Meeting with an unfriendly tribe in Biembe, Frobenius is saved by a chance thunderstorm attributed to him by the tribesmen. Their drums beat out the message, "The white man who made the tempest in Baluba [Pound's error for "Biembe"] / Der im Baluba das Gewitter gemacht hat . . . / they spell words with a drum beat, . . ." In Canto 53, two lines before the section I quote above, the German phrase is repeated, "der im Baluba das Gewitter gemacht hat," linking Tching's prayer for rain to end "7 years of sterility" with the Frobenius incident. Good fortune in both cases is amplified by good management in the second. But despite the thematic similarities and differences, the significant thing here is the way the text (as Schafer says of the fugue) "regenerates itself out of its own thematic material."[76] The poem is able to recall and transform itself at any given moment in its own temporal progression.

The linear progression of the text can be divided against itself, and the accretive mode of the ideogram can be placed in a kind of linear progression. The syntagmatic movement of the text does not so much "progress" as *continue*; it moves through the process of its own disjunctions, recalling and replacing and recontextualizing its own imagistic "minimal units" as it goes, thereby defining its own particular kind of accretive space. Conversely, the ideogram contains the simultaneous presence of the elements that constitute it. The ideogram and its elements can then be placed into their own syntactic chain. In other words, the linear aspect of the text may create its own mobile space, and the spatial/pictorial aspect of the ideogram may take up its own temporal position. And this is possible because of the logic behind Pound's sense of the harmonious contiguity of his writerly musical technique.

Contiguity is, then, not only the underpinning of Pound's "music" of writing, it is also the crucial element of the ideogrammic method which is Pound's technique for the presentation of the real and the true. The surface of radical discontinuity is for Pound in fact the means intended to include *and* overcome history and temporal division at the same time. Contiguity as a technical device is supposed to signify a continuity with reality. Here we begin to see the reason for the continuous emphasis in Pound on technique. The disjunctive procedure of the text is a corollary to Pound's conception of the process of knowing itself. His view of historical knowledge, presented in *Guide to Kulchur* is consistent with his view of knowledge as such:

We do NOT know the past in chronological sequence. It may be convenient to lay it out anesthetized on the table with dates pasted on here and there, but what we know we know by ripples and spirals eddying out from us and from our own time.[77]

Pound's method of fragmentation and display of textual manipulation is not designed to show us the artificiality or provisionality of his writing; on the contrary, the text's very disruptions are meant to be the very sign of continuity with our mode of perception. They are intended to be mimetic of our process of knowing the world. But here, of course, is the crux: if there is one ongoing struggle in Pound, it is his search for an "objective" art which is implicitly always at odds with his emphasis on the subjective status of knowledge. Technique, in one form or another, whether imagist, vorticist, or ideogrammic, is the place where the constant and "objective" truths which cross time and transcend it must be made manifest. Indeed, the whole "hierarchy of all values" depends on the accuracy of graphing music or writing poetry. At the same time, we seem to know things only from ripples and spirals "eddying out from us and from our own time." The question is, then, which comes first: the writing or the hierarchy of values? If we can only know things from the centrality of our selves and our own moment, then how can we be certain that we know them at all? Technique or good graphing, whatever these may be, might only be evidence of our solipsism, our enclosure within history, or worse, mere projections of our fantasies and desires. The real question is, what can give authority to technique? And it is Pound himself who has articulated this quandary within the parameters of an epistemology of poetry in which technique is meant to be "objective," a working out of non-syllogistic truth, and yet evidence of our "inner" connection to things. The problem with ideogrammic poetic knowledge, as Bob Perelman puts it, is that

The ideogram is true for Pound because it is made up of particulars, which in turn are true because they are not abstract. Such a circular method grants complete authority to the ideogram's fashioner, who is backed by the irrefutable singularity of the particulars . . . at the same time as he gets to assign them a more comprehensive ethical significance.[78]

This difficulty of authority can be seen in the inclusion of music as sign of the inward, in the otherwise visual poetics of imagism, or, in another way, in Pound's belief that the manifest sounds of music are, or can be, perceived and unified on some more silent, though no less "scientifically" objective, level of perception.

His move to make music a part of the objective process of poetry as "real," by attaching it to imagism as an element of composing "in the musical phrase," or, as part of the "scientific" unifying principle of art in general, is consistent with Pound's contradictory project of overcoming the problem of subject–object knowledge. It is also related to the process of discontinuity of presentation that makes writing continuous with the real. But music, as the *graphed* presence of the birds in Canto 75, at the same time is also part of the undermining of this writing of the real insofar as it inexorably marks the provisionality of Pound's text *as* writing, and, therefore, as part of the supplemental struggle behind Pound's epistemological and poetic design. This struggle appears perhaps nowhere as clearly as in the written music of Canto 75, since it is here that the complex conflict between graphing/writing and the authority of contiguity is most clearly inscribed. It is in Pisa that Pound struggles hardest to comprehend history and temporality, even as they are about to swallow him, and it is here that he calls upon his deepest faith in the immanent power of contiguity, even as his own dubious authority as the source of such hierarchical immanence becomes most dramatically clear.

Canto 75, the second of the *Pisan* series Pound completed in 1945 while he was detained at Pisa, contains a reproduction of Clement Janequin's "Chant des Oiseux" in the form of Gerhart Münch's transcription for violin. The complex textual heritage of this song is given by Hugh Kenner:

> . . . we hear the birds persisting in a violin part which Gerhart Münch made from Francesco da Milano's lute reduction of Clement Janequin's choral arrangement of perhaps some Provençal tune from some remote act of invention inspired by the form of bird-song.

Münch's transcription is only the most recent manifestation in an ancestry which Pound believes goes back "to Arnaut Daniel and to god knows what 'hidden antiquity'." Kenner says that the song's point of origin is in nature ("inspired by the form of bird-song"), whereas Pound suggests that the beginnings of the song have some "'hidden antiquity'," which implies an ancient human song, rather than some imitation of nature. But given Pound's conflation of the poetic and the real, there is a sense in which following the lineage of some ancient song may be very like following nature. As Pound also says in the *Guide to Kulchur*, pointing toward the imitative possibilities of music, "[i]n music there is representation of the sole matter wherein music can be 'literally' representative, namely sound. Thus the violinist reading Janequin's music transposed said: a lot of birds, not one bird alone."

Pound includes the violinist's (it was Olga Rudge) comment in Canto 75 itself: it is a quotation which precedes and is intended to lend credence to the quotation of Janequin's song. Quotation is nothing new at this point in the *Cantos*; as Marjorie Perloff points out, Pound, from "Near Perigord" on, is moving "toward an art of quotation that closely resembles the collagiste's appropriation of 'real' objects."[79] An art of citation, however, is not quite the same as the art of objectivity or fact that Pound seeks to establish. For what is the "real" object here? What is the nature of the "reality" of this musical citation? Pound quotes Olga Rudge in order to certify that the birds are there. If the transcription does somehow capture the essential form, as is supposed to be the case with the ideogram, then this kind of supplementary statement would seem to be unnecessary. If, however, such a statement *is* somehow necessary, then it betrays the verity of the textual citation as less a part of a procedure which presents "fact" than one in which *contingency*, as opposed to continuity, becomes the actual foundation.[80] Pound transcribes in Canto 75, not the sound of the birds, but the written presentation of the bird song. With this notation, the imitative possibilities of the song as sound – that dimension in which Pound himself claims music can be imitative – are lost. Moreover, Pound's statement that the song *is* "imitative" suggests a kind of difference between the medium and the imitated birds which the theory of the ideogram as "real" does not seem to allow. If the birds are "there" in the song, then they would not need to have been "imitated."

Still, it is his preoccupation with the presence of these birds which underscores Pound's long interest with the song. The "Chant des Oiseaux" was known to Pound at least as early as 1933. It was one of the pieces played in the very first of the Rapallo concerts that Pound helped to organize in the thirties. The first concert contained an arrangement of the "Chant" for piano and violin made by Gerhart Münch which was based on the sixteenth-century lute transcription by Francesco da Milano. Pound seems to have kept the song, or at least Münch's version of it, in his mind for most of the thirties. In the *ABC of Reading* (1933), Pound draws a clear connection between Janequin's song and the earlier troubadour tradition of Arnaut Daniel. What Daniel does "IN HIS

WORDS; [not] that he merely referred to birds singing," Janequin, some three hundred years later does in his song. The birds are not in Janequin's words, though his is a choral version, but in the music only:

... when Francesco da Milano reduced it for the lute, the birds were still in the music. And when Münch transcribed it for modern instruments the birds were still there. They ARE still in the violin part.[81]

The birds have transferred their position over time, shifting from the language of the troubadours to the intervals of Janequin. But this transference is not somehow complete until the Münch transcription, and even here, the birds are only really "there" in the violin part.

The copy of the violin part from Münch's transcription, which is reproduced in Olga Rudge's hand in Canto 75, has its first printed appearance in the *Townsman* article, "Janequin, Francesco da Milano," printed in January 1938. Pound's words accompany it in the *Townsman* article too. Pound states here that in the two pages of Münch's transcription, the Janequin is "there, indestructable." He goes on to say that "[t]he ideogram of real composition is in Münch's two pages, which belong to no man." On the one hand, Pound maintains that he does not "care a hoot about the authorship," since the "unbreakable fact" of the thing is maintained. On the other hand, it is clear that authorship, at least as some provisional site of origin, seems particularly important since the indestructable *fact* of the song is not really attained until Münch reduces the piece to its essentials. As Pound insists: "I doubt if choral performance underlines the thing that I mean. I doubt if Francesco da Milano's lute quite so concentrated the statement. The statement is in the violin part..."[82] Unlike his earlier suggestions in *ABC* in which Pound claims that in *all* versions the "birds are there," clearly they are not there until Münch has had his turn.

Pound wants to posit an accuracy of construction which is fundamental and unchanging in the work, a kind of timeless element common to any particular manifestation of these musical birds in history. The trouble is that he can only do so by inference from the last, and supposedly, most definitive appearance of the work in his own time. Thus, the timeless attainment of the intervals in Münch's violin part suggest, in a backhanded way, a historical progression: the moment of the perception of the timeless falls back into the necessities of time. The very attempt to eschew authorship is also part of an attempt to make the song, as artifact, part of the realm of "objective" fact; but at the same time, authorship slips back into the argument, introducing the security of the

"unbreakable fact" of the thing to the contingencies of further historical alteration.

Of course, the contingencies of history set the scene of the composition of the *Pisan Cantos* and are precisely that which Pound must most
resist. Pound's construction of himself as noman on the other side of
Lethe places him in the realm of the cultural preterite, of those who have
made the wrong bet with history but who, in at least Pound's case, are
the still-living dead, about to suffer the justice of mere winners (of the
war) not of the righteous. In a sense, then, Pound must now look *away*
from the material, at least as it pertains to the historical, and collect a
different, and for him, more pertinent set of particulars from which to
draw forth the eternal. So Pound sets about mounting a series of his own
"generalities" drawn from his own set of "sufficient . . . particulars."
Pound will position himself as a kind of natural force, one which will
draw these particulars together, just as the magnet invisibly draws
together the fragments of steel dust at the end of Canto 74.

And so Gerhart Münch himself appears "Out of Phlegethon!" at the
beginning of Canto 75, countering a Greek hell with an apparent escape
from a Dantean river of fire. Both Massimo Bacigalupo and Michael
Coyle comment on the striking rhythmic nature of the opening:
Bacigalupo noting how the "fine counterpoint of the *Gerhart-art-forth* and
of *thou-out*, and the ecstatic dactylic measure of the *Cantos* (art thou come
forth out of Phlegethon), come together in what is indeed a noble bit of
music," and Coyle, agreeing with Bacigalupo and extending the examination of Pound's formal practice to include assonance, alliteration,
internal rhyme, homeoteleuton, and other figurations, as well as the disposition of the words on the page:[83]

> Out of Phlegethon!
> Out of Phlegethon,
>   Gerhart
>   art thou come forth out of Phlegethon?
> With Buxtehude and Klages in your satchel, with the
> Ständebuch of Sachs in yr/ luggage
>   – not of one bird but of many

Coyle points out Pound's interest in the aural function of this kind of
spatial distribution of words as a kind of scoring and therefore a verbal
analogy to Münch's transcription of the Janequin. (The idea of spatial-
izing the text to suggest a musical analogy is a practice we have recognized at work in Mallarmé.) He suggests that the mention of Buxtehude,
Klages, Münch, and Sachs points to the Janequin's "accumulation of

other voices through time," a list that must include Pound now as well. Three of the names refer to figures who are composers and musicians (Buxtehude, Sachs, and Münch) whom Pound would have seen as aligned with the "linear" form of music which he thought the most important kind. Ludwig Klages, however, was a sociologist and friend of Münch's, and, as Coyle reminds us, a virulent anti-Semite. Coyle points out that Pound resisted Münch's attempts to interest him in Klages' work, and that even Pound found him offensive. Nevertheless, Klages is here. Of these seven lines, Coyle suggests that

. . . each line participates in a single associational unit or pattern. This is the informing principle of the post-bag or satchel. It is, moreover, the kind of technique to which Pound's combination of musical and metrical notation points. Although it is not "contrapuntal" in the usual sense of that term, "counterpoint" was Pound's way of conceiving of the simultaneous unfolding of several distinct themes or concerns.[84]

Coyle's reading is compelling, but also troubled in serious ways. He is correct I think in pointing out Pound's overt sense that music and language are discrete signifying practices which share some, but only some, properties. However, this sensibility seems to fall apart at the level of the *ideogram*, which, however much Coyle may not wish to see the Janequin *as* an ideogram, it is clear that it is still meant to function as one. The ideogram is a kind of writing which is meant not to be writing; it is meant to draw together the particulars of truth as manifested in nature, the political realm, the aesthetic, the moral, the ethical, and so forth. As clusters then these particulars are intended to become self-evident "truths" beyond rational argument, and, indeed, the authority of the author himself. But of course, the ostensible moment of the author's disappearance marks the moment of his greatest authority, and the disappearance of writing as rational, linear argumentation, is undermined by writing's reappearance as dispersion and insistence. Few who read Pound can do so without recourse to his copious other texts in order to discover his many and varied concerns. The self-evident nature of the ideogram, in any form, is anything but self-evident, and can only be authorized by referral to Pound's other written insistences and arguments. (This is not to mention the mass of critical texts concerning Pound and his work.) The plethora of allusions and associations to key ideas and figures within the *Cantos* themselves leads always to more writing; it does not really seem enough for Pound himself to "get it across e poi basta;"[85] insistence, repetition, reprise must take up the slack left by the loss of argumentation and supply the verity of the ideogrammic technique. But instead of absolute truth, we find Pound's assertions and the constant proliferation of text.

The "associational units" that Coyle points to do indeed recall a history of linear music, and such a connection also links back to the issue of the temporal–spatial interconnection which is part of Pound's theory of Great Bass, and of the efficacy of the non-linear work of art in general. As we have already seen, these ideas are essential to Pound's ideogrammic epistemology. Coyle is right when he points to the method of Canto 75 as anti-narrative – that is the procedure of most of the *Cantos*, just as it is with the ideogrammic method itself. The associations fit back together as a cluster signifying a linear musical practice which would have accorded with Pound's sense of the necessary temporality of harmony. If, as Coyle suggests, this is a representation of a "prelinguistic" grasp of the sound of many birds, then it is so not merely as an inclusion of music which would reproduce this multiplicity, but as a *graphing* of that multiplicity; in other words it is a *non-linguistic* writing of those birds, a spatio-temporal render-ing, or re-presentation of them, and the notion of a "prelinguistic" moment can be verified only through Pound and his insistence on these birds as present, yet still outside of language.[86] Moreover, the musical notation is still writing, not birds. The Janequin *is* an ideogram, clustering the temporality of associations, and also attempting to exceed time, even as it traces it in the conventions of musical notation.

The "Chants" is an ideogram which records not only Pound's sense of the prevalence of an essential kind of music through the enforced process of association which is the ideogrammic way, but it also links this hierarchical order of music and art with what appears to be a no less "necessary" ethos of anti-Semitism. Pound may not have liked Klages, but he seems willing to have him appear as one of Münch's familiars. We are once again forced to see Pound's inexorable connection between the aesthetic and the social here with the combined appearance of the necessity of "good" music and "proper" social attitude. The link, while implicit – a "gist," an intimation – is nevertheless clear enough. But oddly, Coyle's often insightful reading passes over the implications here of the connection between anti-Semitism and the requirements of "good" art: if the Canto is not read ideogrammically, and too much weight given to hermeneutic indeterminacy, then perhaps the "gist" of the hermeneutic elements that *are* present can be missed.

Interestingly, the Janequin is placed within the larger context of a the-matics of a forgotten musical and poetic tradition, one in which music and language were in closer relation. The violin transcription is the visual sign of a late-Renaissance tradition of "linear" music that Pound felt was all but lost. In a way it is Pound himself who plays further variations on the textual presence of the birds. Hence, the references to composers like Buxtehude, Sachs, and Münch, or to a scholar like Klages, interested in the music of these composers, link up with later references in the "libretto" of Canto 81 to other early composers (Dowland, Lawes, Jenkyns, Waller [not Fats]) and their more recent champions such as Arnold Dolmetsch:

> *Lawes and Jenkyns guard thy rest*
> *Dolmetsch ever be thy guest . . .*
>   . . . .
> Then resolve me, tell me aright
> If Waller sang or Dowland played.

All these allusions are sonorously linked by the reference to Ben Jonson's "Her Triumph" at the end of Canto 74: "Hast 'ou seen the rose in the steel dust / (or swansdown ever?)." Carroll F. Terrell notes that the "rose in the steel dust" is "[a] graphic image of the divine order operating in the material universe." The mystical moment, here alluded to in Pound's adaptation of Jonson, is reminiscent of the immanent quality inherent in the theory of Great Bass, where the sensorily perceptible has its foundation buried at some invisible level. At the end of the "libretto" section of Canto 81, Pound states abruptly that the union of music and words comes to a sudden end: "And for 180 years almost nothing."[87] The sense is that he himself is trying to reunite the two arts here in the *Pisan Cantos*.

But, if this is the case, then it is curious to see how separate the writing of words and the writing of music are kept. The visual presentation of music in Canto 75 contains no lyric; the "libretto" of Canto 81 has no score. Indeed, in Canto 75 Pound has seen fit to grasp this multiplicity of birds in only *one* of the parts, and he has followed Münch in the omission of Janequin's original words: the Janequin motet was of course written in counterpoint, and was originally for voices. Coyle suggests that Münch successfully recreates the sound of multiple birds (and imitates the Janequin verbal imitations too) through the use of pizzicato and double-stopping. If this is so, then it is another point of "imitation" which the ideogram as the composite of the "real" will not allow. Perhaps, the dominant musical/literary analogy in the *Pisan Cantos* resides in the transformation of the Janequin birds into (word) birds which Pound sees composing and recomposing themselves on the staff of barbed wire that surrounds the detention center.

The bird-notes appear in the dense early stages of Canto 79, the canto that begins with references to the reopening of the Salzburg Mozart festival and to the song "Amarilli mia bella" by Giulio Caccini, one of the early inventors of opera: "So Salzburg reopens / lit a flame in my thought that the years / Amari–li Am—ar–i–li!"[88] This is also the canto that ends with a kind of long chant or prayer to Dionysus, Aphrodite, and other gods associated with the Eleusian rituals of fertility and renewal, such as Demeter and Persephone. The canto begins with associations between music and rejuvenation, and origin within history (the return of the festival, the origins of opera), but it ends in an attempt to go beyond history, to link up with some sacred musical apotheosis with nature:

> O lynx, guard my vineyard
> As the grape swells under the vine leaf
> [Helios] is come to our mountain
> there is a red glow in the carpet of pine spikes
>
> O lynx, guard my vineyard
> As the grape swells under the vine leaf
>
> This Goddess was born of sea-foam
> She is lighter than air under Hesperus . . .

Between the beginnings of the canto "in" history, and the ritualistic and mystical conclusion come the birds. Pound's turn toward the natural world generally in the Pisan series seems to mark a retreat from the world of larger historical events, those which have overtaken him. Increasingly in these cantos, Pound focuses attention on the more minute, mystical, and decidedly ahistorical, realm of nature. The birds as part of this natural realm continue to enter into the dense allusive field of the text very often in close relation with some reference to music:

> with 8 birds on a wire
> or rather on 3 wires, Mr. Allingham
> The new Bechstein is electric
> and the lark squawk is out of season[89]
>
> . . . .
>
> in
>   discourse
>   what matters is
> to get it across e poi basta
>   5 of 'em now on 2;
>   on 3; 7 on 4

                        thus what's his name
                and the change in writing the song books
                5 on 3 . . .

    . . . .

                                                    2 on 2
        what's the name of that bastard? D'Arezzo, Gui d'Arezzo
            notation

                            3 on 3
                    chiacchierona   the yellow bird
            to rest   3 months in bottle
                                                    (auctor)

The adjacent musical allusions are related to change: the new electric
Bechstein, that "bastard" d'Arezzo who, in the eleventh century, developed a method of using vocables to render the tones of the medieval
hexachord more easily accessible to memory.[90] Arezzo is not really the
bastard Pound claims, since clearly Pound himself is attempting to make
a music of vocables: birds and pitches are being scored here, each is the
substitute of the other, and their unity is intended to mark the immanent
possibilities of nature, music, and poetic text. Word becomes bird
becomes musical note in the conflation of natural and aesthetic orders.
Moreover, Arezzo is also a crucial figure in the development of written
music, since he also invented a four line staff which allowed the organization of pitches to be much more clearly defined through more precise
written notation, thus freeing "music from its hitherto exclusive depen-
dence on oral transmission." With Arezzo in mind, then, Pound sets about
his own writing of music, though his is not a music strictly of sound, but
rather of writing, and, more importantly, not a writing which is imitative
or even descriptive of sound, but, instead, one which requires the "real"
birds of the camp to be transformed into the image of written music.

    The clearest manifestation of this occurs, in fact, in Canto 81, where
the bird-notes are drawn in as letter notes:

            f f

                d

                g
                write the birds in the treble scale

Finally, the birds fall to rest as
                three solemn half notes
                                their white downy chests black-rimmed
                on the middle wire[91]

The birds as written/graphed music seem now to stand outside of the changes that history brings, constantly reforming themselves, yet aloof from the particularities of time. With these bird-notes, nature is now music, and music is nature: the birds form the chant that changes in time, but does not change, just as the Eleusian mysteries of death and renewal go beyond particulars and create an image of reconciliation between the fixed and the mobile. And we cannot overlook the fact that it is not only nature and music which have become one, but that Pound's text is also meant to have united with these other two realities insofar as it attempts to identify itself with the processes of these, at the same time as it performs the unification of music/aesthetic and natural orders.

But, despite Pound's desire to have these birds act as the emblems of both flux and permanence, they remain ensconced among the layers of the text. Their direct presentation is muted by their contingent displacement among the double stops of the violin transcription, or as emblems which the poet transforms into an image of still another kind of writing. The point is that the positing of the birds as real, either as the presentation of "things," or of their mystical and immanent qualities, can only have reality by virtue of a text that insists upon this reality, but which cannot remove *itself* without removing the "real" along with it. The birds as double stops, or as "real" birds offering verification of the violin part's "unbreakable fact," are "there" as something which the text reinforces only by still more and more references, dispersions, and reappearances. The only thing that might stop such dispersion is the return of the poet as seer, a position that Pound must dispense with if he is to avoid the solipsism of what he himself would see as the romantic figure of the poet.[92]

It is Pound who has insisted that the text can be objective in its presentation, and that by the presentation of these facts the truth can be revealed. In the *Cantos*, Pound creates a kind of field of interrelationships which, in themselves, comprise a presence which is solid enough. But this textual field reaches no final conflation between world and text; instead, by its very design of contiguity and association it undermines any such identity. The text can provide constantly proliferating possibilities, connections, and exempla, but it cannot finally *be* reality. Music is part of the model for Pound's attempt at the reconciliation of surface and depth: in the theory of Great Bass, with its quasi-scientific reconciliation between the audible and the absolute underlying unity of silence; or, again, in the ideogrammic counterpoint of the *Cantos*, where spatial and linear aspects of writing attempt to overcome any rigid separation.

But, finally, Pound's use of music becomes part of the method of textual proliferation; it is one more factor or element in the struggle to make the text not only "objective," but the "truth." Such "truth" as is there, however, may depend much less on the reader's ability to perceive the meaning of the text as "objective" fact, than on the perception that this is Pound's attempt to project his own "truth," his own conceptions of what is important and how it is important into his text. There is a way in which his constant striving for objectivity and "direct presentation" leads back to the recognition of Pound's own subjective imprint. Try how one might, there is no way around Pound. It is Pound through whom we must see the elements of the text as significant, even though it is also Pound who asserts their "objective" importance. The proliferation of writing in Pound, both in the *Cantos* and in his multitudinous books and articles, sustain his conceptions as further writing, but do not cross into the domain of ultimate revelation. Pound's use of music as a provisional model for his textual procedures in the *Cantos*, or, further, as a way of conceiving, or explaining, or *asserting* an immanence in his text, and in the realm of politics, economics, etc., finally becomes part of the insistence of the text *as* writing – more of its surface. The text cannot finally exceed itself, but only produce more and more of itself in a procedure of continual assertion and association. The result is a process of constant supplementarity that "music," in any of its various appearances, cannot stop, but of which it can only become a part.

CHAPTER FOUR

"Sirens" and the problem of literary and musical meaning

Joyce and Pound had a small parting of the ways over the "Sirens" chapter of Joyce's *Ulysses*, purportedly the most "musical" writing in the book. In a letter to Frank Budgen dated June 19, 1919, Joyce relates that Pound "writes disapprovingly of the *Sirens* then modifying the disapproval and protesting against the close [i.e. of the chapter] and against 'obsession' and wanting to know whether Bloom (prolonged cheers from all parts of the house) could not be relegated to the background and Stephen Telemachus brought forward." Pound's dislike of the flatulent ending and the growing prominence of Bloom perhaps masks his more profound aversion to Joyce's supposedly "musical" experimentation with words. R. Murray Schafer points out that Joyce's literary musicianship runs "more to details, to [the] isolated sounds of words" than does Pound's.[1] Pound, for all his borrowings, citations, textual disruptions and renovations, at no point places the word as such under any particular stress. "Sirens" may not be the first place in Joyce's *oeuvre* where language comes to the fore, but it is certainly the first place where words themselves seem to take over. Interestingly, the eruption of language is performed under the auspices of music.

One important difference between the two writers is that Joyce's focus on "details" in "Sirens" is part of an exploration of the difficulty of how meaning gets made at all. The allusions to music, both within and outside the text, seem designed to call up that art's unmistakable tangibility, the clear force of its presence. But such a conjuring also brings with it the difficulty in ascertaining any singular kind of musical meaning. Joyce works explicitly with the very problem of "direct presentation"; Pound works, in various ways, from the assumption that such presentation is possible, however difficult it may be to attain.

Joyce's apparent attempt to "fuse" language and music in "Sirens" also constitutes part of an examination of the conflicting spaces of "reality," of the clash between the "inside" of the characters and their external, social worlds; it is both the provisionality and the necessity of making meaning which Joyce takes on in "Sirens." Such concerns are no less central to Pound's project, but for Pound, music is one way of both organizing and giving a deeper rationale to his poetic materials. For Joyce, the tension between the very idea of depth (especially as music constitutes the sign of such depth) and the material surface of the text forms the very critique he is staging. Joyce in fact seems to be suggesting in "Sirens" that there may be no unifying resolution to such a tension.

Joyce's own words on the chapter are contradictory, involving, as with Pound, the mention of fugue and counterpoint. Again, in Joyce, we find the musical model arriving as a justification of what amounts to a kind of literary spatialization. I mean here both that the continuum of the language is broken, and that the narrative space is divided among several simultaneous areas of action. His words may suggest more than just another analogy between writing and musical form. They may also signal the very contradictory nature of the search for meaning or significance as it involves both literary and musical works. The attempt to find a one-to-one analogy between fugue and "Sirens" is, as it was in Pound, probably not fruitful. But it is worth pursuing some of the complexities of the form as it has been outlined by various critics before I proceed with my own reading of the chapter.

In a letter to Harriet Shaw Weaver dated 1919, Joyce speaks of the chapter as having "the eight regular parts of a *fuga per canonem*." Elsewhere, Joyce calls the chapter a "fugue with all musical notations: *piano, forte, rallentando*, and so on."[2] The trouble is, however, that the fugue and the *fuga per canonem* are not the same form. *Fuga per canonem* refers to an early sixteenth-century form for a "fugue according to rule," or essentially what we would call today a canon. The reference to canon is still pertinent, since, as Imogene Horsley points out, "the Latin *canon* (rule) meant a short motto or sentence that indicated, in the manner of a riddle, the way in which a single part was to be performed or another part derived from it." Where it appears that Joyce is giving some solid clues to the nature of his writing, we find ambiguity, an intersection between two musical forms involving flight (fugue) and rule (canon). Significantly, the sense of "rule" that emerges from the notion of canon as Horsley describes it amounts to being a kind of puzzle or play. Moreover, Joyce's words about "regular notation" are a bit misleading too, since *piano, forte*, and *rallentando* refer to dynamic markings which could apply to any piece of music. Similarly, the mention of "eight regular parts" of the *fuga per canonem* is confusing since, as Lawrence

Levin points out, the form does not have eight regular parts unless Joyce is "referring to *voices* which are not necessarily confined to a specific number."[3]

Joyce's comments that his method of composition is fugal do not help matters since, as I have already made clear, fugue is a difficult form to define, though it is often the form preferred by critics who choose to analyze the chapter. For one thing, the fugue is subject to definition in terms of its historical context. The sixteenth-century *fuga per canonem* develops into two species of counterpoint, each referred to as *"fuga."* *Fuga legata* came more and more to refer to strict and continuous types of contrapuntal writing ("legata" meaning bound or strict). *Fuga sciolta* (or "free flight") became distinguished by "the use of short points of imitation followed by free melodic continuation [especially at] . . . the unison, fourth, fifth or octave." This latter develops into a still freer form able to "restate the theme in one part while the others move freely on."[4] The association of freedom and form, which might have appealed to Joyce, remains a part of the idea of the fugue even as it develops into the eighteenth and nineteenth centuries.

In order to illustrate some of the difficulties that lie behind Joyce's remarks about the fugue, I will give a brief account of the properties of this complex musical procedure. *Fuga sciolta*, or fugue, develops away from its canonic roots, but aside from the fugue's beginning, about all that can be considered conventional in terms of its formal properties are certain events that occur frequently enough to be considered part of its "form." Usually, the fugue contains a beginning or exposition in which all the voices, soprano, alto, tenor, bass (though a fugue in four voices is not an absolute) enter one after the other starting with a short melodic subject which is imitated or "answered" by another voice in another key, usually at a perfect interval. Often, another subject or "counter subject" is introduced. This follows the first subject and is played either above or below it. The subject and the counter subject are in double counterpoint to each other. Sometimes the exposition may be restated in a "counter exposition" where voices trade parts; the voices that stated the subject in the exposition now state the answer and so on. After the exposition or the counter exposition comes a freer "development" section where the subject or parts of it are played in various keys or voices. These re-introductions of the subject are known as "middle entries" which are joined by "episodes" that modulate from one key to the next by providing variations and new material derived from the subject and the counter subject. Toward the end of the fugue, a return to the tonic takes place.

The manner and length of this return usually vary, but the subject and counter subject are normally reintroduced in different voices than in the exposition. The ending may include a coda, and/or the use of "stretto," an overlapping of statements of the subject in different voices to give a tighter, more intense effect.[5]

Here, then, are some of the complexities that lurk beneath Joyce's contradictory statements, and which in turn muddy the critical waters for those who attempt to define the chapter in terms of either fugue or *fuga per canonem*. Critics can be divided in terms of which form they choose to see in the chapter. Early critics, such as Frank Budgen and Stuart Gilbert, having access to the voice of Joyce, often simply repeat Joyce's own contradictions. Budgen claims that "Sirens" is a "fugue in counterpart," while Gilbert asserts that the technique of the chapter is "*fuga per canonem*." One of the greatest difficulties, however, for those who wish to maintain a reading of the chapter as canon or fugue lies in trying to determine how the writing shapes itself into parts (subject, answer, etc.). Ann Hardy, for instance, believes in the fugal structure of the chapter and claims that the first subject is Man–Woman relationships; the first counter subject is music; the second subject is Bloom himself (note the shift from thematic concerns to those of character) and so on. Hardy's fugue varies from Gilbert's canon. He maintains that the subject is the Siren's song, the answer (an element missing from Hardy's analysis) is "Bloom's entry and monologue; Boylan is *Counter-Subject*." Other commentators, such as Lawrence Levin and David Cole come up with still different variations about subject, answer, counter subject and so on.

At least one critic, Heath Lees, suggests that the fragmented opening lines of the chapter in themselves constitute a kind of contrapuntal writing. Lees plausibly suggests that in the opening Joyce is following a fifteenth-century idea where the term "*canon* . . . referred not to the music but to the verbal directions placed before or sometimes within the music." From such directions an entire piece could be worked out. The message in the opening passage of "Sirens," as Lees sees it, is two-fold: first, there is the implication that the chapter is meant to be read "as much by the ear as by the eye" and second, Lees believes that the introduction "embodies the shape of a fugue and . . . alludes to specific works written in fugal style."[6] Lees proceeds to organize the introduction into three sections based on similarity of rhythmic patterns, patterns which he maintains correlate to subjects predominant in Bach's *Art of the Fugue*. While I can agree with Lees' point that the opening of the chapter does signal a certain shift in emphasis toward the aural, his second idea that the phrases of the opening have some affinity with Bach seems rather arbitrary. Moreover, Lees does not give any space to the problem of voices. If the introduction were truly fugal, then the distinctiveness of register for each voice would have to be made clear. Lees gives us no such clarity. Also, to take Lees' approach places an overwhelming emphasis on the sound of language, an emphasis which, if followed too far, leaves out other important considerations such as the problem of reference, spatiality, or the significant intertext of song. Perhaps, as is the case with Pound's *Cantos*, no definitive analogy with either fugue or canon can be maintained in "Sirens" since, as Harry Levin says, there is no clear way to know

whether it is the language or the situation that is being treated fugally. Should we accept each syllable as an interval in a melodic phrase? Or should we assume that the characters work out their own counterpoint, with Bloom as subject and Boylan as countersubject?

Still, Levin and others who deny the fugal analogy, such as Zack Bowen, do see the chapter as having a fundamental relationship with music. Bowen, like Gilbert points out Joyce's use of "leitmotif," or the "repeated metonymical phrases [such] as 'Bronze by Gold'" which stand in, so to speak, for characters especially in the opening moves of the chapter.[7] More significantly, Bowen notes the emphasis in "Sirens" on sound devices such as assonance, phrase repetition, alliteration, and onomatopoeia on the textual level, as well as Bloom's internal monologue on the origins, definition, effects, etc. of music on the thematic level. But for Bowen, of most importance are the "158 references to forty-seven different works of music" which constitute the "almost continuous music from which the chapter draws its existence . . ." Of these, there are five main songs – "Goodbye, Sweetheart, Goodbye," "All is Lost Now," "When First I Saw That Form Endearing," "Love and War," and "The Croppy Boy" – which are of most importance.

Bowen's impressive explication of song and narrative is something I will come back to later on, since the whole issue of song has so much to do with the allusive and intertextual strategies used to compose the chapter and, indeed, the whole of *Ulysses*. But remaining at the level of allusion may not tell us everything about the strange word to word method of the chapter. Moreover, such an approach fails to consider that the use of song may be in some ways reflective of the technique of "Sirens" itself, since the song is the most commonplace site for the meeting of language and music. Indeed, song signals here a certain kind of cultural presence which is deeply wound through the episode, and through *Ulysses* as a whole. It seems likely that the extensive use of song in this chapter, aside from its function as a particular kind of intertext, works as well to signify a complex identification between language and music that the narrative itself may be attempting to perform.

In an interesting and important conceptualization of the episode, David Herman links Joyce's technique (primarily in "Sirens," but with affinities to *Ulysses* as a whole) to a larger combinative method found in many of the arts and sciences of the modern period, and especially to Arnold Schoenberg's twelve-tone compositional technique. He maintains that "'Sirens' (self-reflexively) exploits the formal or constructional devices common to both musical and linguistic structures – devices or rules necessarily belonging to the syntactic dimension of those structures."[8] Herman goes so far as to see combinative procedures, rather than affective or mimetic ones, as being definitive of modernism across the arts and sciences.

Herman sketches the main features of the twelve-tone technique, emphasizing its combinatory principles as a means of destroying the organizing effects of tonality. Quoting often from Schoenberg's essay, "Composition with Twelve Tones" Herman refers to the composer's selection of the "basic set" – the initial ordering of the pitches of the chromatic scale – which Schoenberg himself meant as a "'. . . substitute for some of the unifying and formative advantages of scale and tonality'." Herman does not mention the variations on the basic set here – the basic set, inversion, reverse row, and its inversion, plus the fact that any of these may be transposed (i.e. they may begin on any pitch and follow the same intervallic progression). Instead, he presses Schoenberg's emphasis on the need to delay the repetition of pitches as long as possible, since to repeat a tone, such as a double octave, "'is to emphasize a pitch, and an emphasized tone could be interpreted as a root, or even as a tonic; the consequences of such an interpretation must be avoided'." The "principle of nonredundancy" "[i]n post-Saussurean terms, [suggests] that the twelve-tone row forces us to reconfigure the syntagmatic or combinatory dimension of musical composition vis-à-vis its paradigmatic or associative dimension. More precisely, we must now ascribe a combinatory or sequencing role to the very association of layering of tones along the axis of simultaneity itself."[9]

Herman is interested in the particular qualities of the twelve-tone system which resist the hierarchies and restrictions of tonality. Twelve-tone theory is an attempt to systematize, or at least to make rational or "objective," a means by which the constraints of tonality – the need to reassert a key or tonal center; the force of the "laws" of harmony for combining pitches, for creating and structuring chords, harmonies, and large-scale forms – can be overcome. Tonal "natural" laws of voice-leading, of relationships between pitches, of the dominance of keys, etc., are abandoned in the twelve-tone method by challenging tonality's most fundamental features and by asserting an equivalence among all pitches in chromatic space. Herman's analogy between "Sirens" and Schoenberg's method lies precisely here, with the challenge to the "naturalness" of compositional tonal, or "realistic" narrative patterns and techniques. This is one of Herman's most interesting points, and, too, as we will see, the major problem with the analogy.

Herman suggests that, in effect, the introduction to "Sirens" works as a kind of twelve-tone "basic set" from which elements are chosen and then ordered as the main section of the chapter proceeds. He notes that commentators who have considered the list have "failed to situate the structure of 'Sirens' in [the] early twentieth-century radicalization of fugal or polyphonic form" which is crucial to Schoenberg's compositional thought. Thus, as Herman sees it,

... even as the episode unfolds in time, we are forced to neutralize temporality itself: now by superimposing upon the extended sequence of motifs the initial repertoire that provides a taxonomy, legend, or key for the narrative as a whole; now by superimposing the episode proper back upon the initial repertoire, in order to check that system of coordinates against the (strings of) elements diachronically realized in the text.[10]

Ultimately, Herman considers "'Sirens' [as] reproduc[ing] the polyphonic technique of a specifically modern music. Joyce's narrating disrupts classical narrative form in a manner more or less strictly analogous to the way Schönberg's twelve-tone technique wreaks change on classical conceptions of music." Both Joyce and Schoenberg, then, set out the "unique compositional forms for specific compositions" with pieces that, in effect, work out specific formal paradigms for each individual compostion.[11]

Herman's reading is important in its locating of Joyce within a general twentieth-century context of a certain kind of combinatorial aesthetic practice, though, as Herman admits, this is more of a suggestion than something he proves in depth. Perhaps more significant is Herman's placing of "Sirens" within the context of Schoenberg's polyphonic practice itself. Now, I know of no evidence to suggest that Joyce was aware of the principles of the technique, and Herman offers none. In fact, Schoenberg's *Five Piano Pieces*, opus 23, 24, and 25, which give us the first compositional display of the twelve-tone technique, do not appear until 1923, four years *after* the writing of "Sirens" and one year after the publication of *Ulysses*. Herman is pointing to historical proximity, it seems, rather than connection in linking Joyce and Schoenberg. Such tangents, of course, have their risks, but so far as Herman goes, they also have some productive dimensions as well. For one thing, Herman's suggestion that the beginning of "Sirens" is a kind of basic set, removes the sometimes unusual fugue hunting that many engage in, and supplies instead a more flexible sense of form which still, in a way, maintains the idea of "flight" and "rule" which the somewhat confusing mention of fugue and *fuga per canonem* seem to bring forth. "Sirens" as twelve-tone polyphony may need more proving than Herman supplies here, and, indeed, more than I will attempt as well. It remains to be seen if a more exact connection between the episode and Schoenberg's technique can be carried out. But I have different reasons for my own reserve here.

It may in fact be more productive to take a reading of the chapter and its musical possibilities in a slightly different direction. One problem that seems to remain latent in Herman's essay is that, in fact, for Schoenberg, the difference between twelve-tone technique and tonality is not as great as it at first might appear. In "Problems of Harmony," (1934) also included in *Style and Idea*, Schoenberg attempts a systematic relating of all pitches, both diatonic and chromatic, through their relations to overtones: "In the major scale the relation of the tones to one another is firm and constant through their relation to the fundamental, but in the chromatic scale the relation of the tones is variable and dependent entirely on whether one of the tones is regarded as a fundamental." But differences in familiarity do not necessarily make for fundamental differences in *nature*, for as Schoenberg goes on to explain,

the chromatic scale flows from the same source as the major: from the elements which are the constituents of every tone [(i.e. from the overtone series)]. The difference is only that the one imitates the natural sound up to the sixth overtone, while the other reaches about twice as far, to the thirteenth overtone; in other words, the chromatic scale brings the more distant overtones within the possibility of relationship.[12]

Schoenberg makes his appeal to the "naturalness" of these tonal relationships by virtue of their shared basis in the overtone series, and it seems that it is in "nature" that the reconciliation of these apparently disparate tones and their relationships can be brought about. Indeed, the "interconnection" of these tones "is founded on the fact that in the sounding tone and its nearest relative, the union and the companionship of the tones is continuously demonstrated to our ear, so that we do nothing more than imitate nature when we make use of these relations." Schoenberg seems to be making a case for the relationship between any and all tones in a way that comes close to Pound's sense that any tone can be followed by any other tone. Schoenberg does not, like Pound, begin to conflate overtones with tempi and then move on to temporality itself. Still, there is an interesting similarity in their arguments here. The difference is that Schoenberg's ultimate appeal, at least at this point, is to nature, whereas Pound will call down "science" in order to coordinate nature and rationality.

But as Schoenberg goes on, there is a decided shift away from nature and toward the "artistic means" necessary for the establishment of the centrality of key. He notes, among other things, that every major triad "can of itself express a key," and that "every succeeding chord contests the feeling for [a given chord's] tonality and pleads for others." The classical solution to the ambiguity brought about by modulations and the suggestions of alternate tonalities was the repeated emphasis of the V-I cadence, with many additional reassertions of the I. In other words, by insistence, and a certain dependency upon the notion that "'the last prevails',"though as Schoenberg suggests, even this is debatable.[13] Schoenberg will go on to say that

since, in a word, tonality is neither a natural nor automatic consequence of tone combination and therefore cannot claim to be the automatic result of the nature of sound and so an indispensable attribute of every piece of music, we shall probably have to define tonality as the art of combining tones in such successions and such harmonies or successions of harmonies, that the relation of all events to a fundamental tone is made possible.

Suddenly, the basis for the continuity between *both* tonal and atonal music, nature, is now *not* the basis for tonal music – at least. But of course to sacrifice "nature" for one, according to Schoenberg's own argument, is logically to sacrifice it for the other. As he will later state, tonality is "no postulate of natural conditions, but . . . the utilization of natural *possibilities*." Really, in a kind of false opposition between nature and culture or artifice, Schoenberg is stressing an emphasis on the need for "coherence and articulation," or a rational and logical basis for the sustaining of musical structure, whether tonal or not: what one requires is a means of composing "which unifies all elements so that their succession and relation are logically comprehensible, and which is articulated as our mental capacity requires, . . . so that the parts unfold clearly and characteristically in related significance and function."[14]

This is not merely a search for a justification of his own twelve-tone system, though is it is clearly this too. Such a call for the rationality of structure is also designed to heal the potential rifts between the internal workings of music – in particular, of "new" music – and its apparently dissonant surface. More to the point, however, is the intention to offer a method – i.e. the logic of structure itself – as a model for explaining the affective dimensions of dissonance: the *internal* logic of the work is here suggested as a guide for, and maybe a guard against, the audible experience of dissonance. As Schoenberg puts it:

The criterion for the acceptance or rejection of dissonances is not that of their beauty, but rather only of their perceptibility. The recognition of coherence, logic, conclusiveness is one of the most important conditions for the apprehension of what occurs . . .[15]

The appeal to the rational here as a justification of an unconventional surface mirrors in a way Joyce's own claim to explain or give clues to the surface of the chapter, and, indeed, the claims of those who have followed Joyce's lead and examined the chapter on formal grounds alone. The difference here is that Joyce is clearly driving at something *irrational* in music: "fugue," "*fuga per canonem*," or even "twelve-tone polyphony" are not just signs of high cultural forms which offer a certain acceptability to this unconventional writing. This is partly the case, but not all. As the "flight" and "rule" combination suggests, they are also signs of a decidedly *intellectual* practice of composition. As Schoenberg himself seems to indicate, tonal or non-tonal music must always be rationally recuperable: indeed, such formal comprehensibility might be an essential property of *any* kind of musical compositional practice. But I think Joyce also wants to keep at play a certain *irrational* sensibility associated with music, a sense of its affective properties, however intellectually humble, clichéd, and even debilitating these may be.

Joyce fuses in "Sirens" a formally experimental writing practice with a clear sense of realism, even if this realism is at times of a kind we have learned from reading *Ulysses* itself: we know, for instance, the sound of Bloom's voice; we have a sense of where the characters are, whether they are across town or in the next room; and we have as well a sense of the irrational, yet powerful nature of rather more commonplace kinds of music than fugue or canon or serial polyphony in the portrayal of the songs. The linguistic practices of the episode do require attention in terms of formal literary analysis; perhaps they even require *rational* explanation. But there is also no doubt that they point to an irrationality at the heart of musical experience, especially – and this is crucial – as this applies to the social context of playing, hearing and interpreting: the social, the rational, the irrational, and the formal – musical or literary – cannot be separated here, nor one examined to the exclusion of the other.

As I will try to show later on, the songs in "Sirens" serve to emphasize the process, and the ironies, entailed in the production of "meaning" within a certain cultural context. The place of the voice raised in passionate lyric or patriotic narrative song becomes not a site of the absolute presence of the singer's innermost thoughts and feelings, but rather, the place where such feelings and thoughts are most invaded by cultural erotic and patriotic (and sometimes both at the same time) ideological codes and values. I try to include too a greater sense of the effect of the songs presented in the episode, and, therefore, I work with a clear sense of the importance of Zack Bowen's research on the songs, but with an eye less toward their unifying thematic virtues (as he might) than toward their clear cultural and epistemological critical possibilities.

Cultural criteria may influence in various ways most methods of attempting to understand music; and this seems true whether such methods involve the exploration, definition, or, indeed, the predication of codes of feeling, or more technical, musical examinations of "structural listening" which attempt to surpass the dangers of impressionism to which language is heir. As Subotnik points out, such detailed listening has its own historical and cultural limitations.[16] Graphs, charts, and mathematical computations do not themselves escape their own status as signs of objectivity, precision – or even hermeticism.

Joyce includes and extends the problems and powers of musical meaning into the equally complex sphere of narative, with due reference – and non-reference – to the cultural parameters of both realms. In "Sirens," problems of meaning in music are, to a certain degree, made to reflect upon problems of meaning in language, and vice versa. In the process, problems of "form" do not remain simply formal, and hence, neither do problems of meaning. To explore such issues in terms of music, Joyce questions the very means by which language – that other element of song and the stuff of his own chapter – is itself in a similar kind of supplemental place as is music: to what degree is meaning in either realm exposed to the contingencies and interpretive vicissitudes of the contexts each appears in, and which each is part of creating? At least part of the answer (though there is no complete answer) lies with the relations between music and language as sound, and it is to the problem of sound itself as it pertains to language that Joyce first turns.

"SIRENS" AND THE WRITING OF SOUND

Many critics, as I noted earlier, maintain that "Sirens" forces the reader into a greater recognition of the aural qualities of language. It is conceivable to see the idea of music in the chapter as a kind of horizon of possibility, a place for accentuating an analogy with writing in terms of the differential properties inherent to both writing and music. Joyce demonstrates the fact that phonemes and morphemes are, like the pitches of the diatonic, or indeed, chromatic scale, to a certain degree defined negatively or, to use Saussure's phrase, by "their relations with other terms of the system." What becomes in "Sirens" a more precise focus upon the word is partly an extension of a focus on language and textuality that is pervasive in the first ten chapters of the book. Much of *Ulysses'* force up until "Sirens" is directed toward a representation of the interior, a kind of radical subjective realism. But the two main voices of the interior, Stephen's and Bloom's, are far from monolithic; they are composed in large part of the threads of other texts. Stephen's walk along the strand in "Proteus" is a kind of compendium or re-interrogation of many of the primary texts of Western culture. Bloom too, though less erudite, mixes and matches many of the same texts as Stephen, as well as others (billboard advertisements, "popular" literature, etc.) which Stephen might not consider. But with the opening of "Sirens" there is a certain sense in which language seems to take over. Many commentators refer to this opening as a kind of "overture," an introduction of the major themes of the chapter. But the opening fragments present us less with themes in any conventional sense, than with themselves as phrases and apparent imitations of sounds that are adrift from any specific context. Marilyn French points out that the fragments are mostly in "recognizable English and recognizable syntactic units." But, while the fragments have a certain familiar quality, they remain, in Karen Laurence's words, "largely an encoded transcription of sound," an attempt on Joyce's part to reduce "sound, [both] verbal and nonverbal, to its written equivalent." With the opening of "Sirens" we are faced with the shards of the chapter to come, the pieces of the combinational narrative procedure gathered in one place; in a sense, the "langue" of the "parole" to follow.[17] The introduction to "Sirens" presents us with syntactically and rhythmically organized sounds, but sounds which are not, in a sense, authorized; they are lent neither narratorial presence, nor the suggestion that they are the utterances of characters. Lacking narrative context, the phrases are reduced to the organization of their phonemes alone. Instead of an assembly denoting linearity and the resulting impression of logical causality (the gesture of sequence, cause and effect, even rationality), the fragments are marked only by their rhythmic and apparent aural imitative properties.

Though I disagreed earlier with Heath Lees' assumption about the *kind* of rhythmic presence in the opening, it does seem true, as Lees and others suggest, that rhythm generally is emphasized in the opening. Even a simple long–short scanning of the lines reveals, if not a strict metrical patterning, at least a marked syllabic emphasis: "Bronze by gold heard the hoofirons, steelyringing. / . . . / A husky fifenote blew." This kind of scanning is subject to variation, but the point is that it would be hard to miss the rhythmic emphasis of these phrases. The result is a kind of phonic play of repetition and variation of sounds and words: "And a call, pure, long and throbbing. Longindying call."

The collapse of words back toward sound is also accomplished through the use of both lexical and non-lexical onomatopoeia. But even here, where language seems to be pointing us back toward a direct presentation of the world, we come to realize that it is still operating in accordance with linguistic conventions. Derek Attridge supplies compelling evidence of this in a discussion of the apparent tram sounds that appear toward the end of the "prelude." The "Kraa Kraandl," while non-lexical, maintains, in Attridge's view, clear "reference to the morphological system of the language and its semantic accompaniment."[18] In other words, readers must turn to the knowledge they have about reading, spelling, and writing English words in order to decipher the sound as it is presented. We "hear" other linguistic associations as much, if not more, than anything else. Attridge suggests that "Krandl" "evokes phonetically related verbs of movement and noise such as 'trundle', 'rumble', 'grumble', 'shamble', 'scramble'," as well as mechanistic associations with "'handle'" and "'krank'" which actually appears near the end of the chapter. Spelling also becomes significant in terms of what it avoids and includes. A "k" before "r" in initial position breaks with English spelling conventions which usually demand a "c" in such instances. The "k" also precludes unwanted associations with other words ("'cranium'," and "'cranberries'" Attridge suggests) while maintaining certain conventions about the "hardness" of the "k" sound as opposed to the potentially "softer" sound of "c" as /s/. The moment of direct presentation of sound becomes, in "Sirens," as much a matter of "*interpretation*" according to linguistic rules as anything else.

The knowledge of similar differential procedures also applies to lexical onomatopoeia, or words that refer to sounds rather than imitate them. A word such as "jingle" has clear associations with "jiggle" and "ring," words which, while descriptive enough of Boylan's jaunting car, have more ironic sexual implications in the chapter as well, as is the case with "jingle" itself in its association with the sound of Bloom's and Molly's bed. But as Attridge notes, in lexical onomatopoeia we cannot separate the sound of the word from its semantic content: "it is virtually impossible to hear a sound *as* a sound when it simultaneously informs us what sound it is supposed to represent." He suggests that in lexical onomatopoeia there is a reinforcing relationship between semantic and phonetic elements of the word which "intensifies *both* aspects of language." Most important for "Sirens" as a whole is Attridge's claim that there is a mutual interdependence between phonetic and semantic elements wherein the content "is relatable to some aspect of the physical characteristics of speech," this occurs even if there is no necessary connection between the phonetic elements and the content they describe. He points out, for instance, the "striking physical properties" of the description of Ben Dollard playing the piano: "His gouty paws plumped chords."[19] The words do not give a description or imitation of the way the chords sound, but rather a visual enhancement of the "gouty" way they are played; the physical properties that are emphasized by means of the repeated "p"s are ocular, not aural. Similar phonetic emphasis reinforces the visuality of Miss Kennedy's stroll of sadness: "Miss Kennedy sauntered sadly from bright light, twining a loose hair behind an ear. Sauntering sadly, gold no more, she twisted twined a hair. Sadly she twined in sauntering gold hair behind a curving ear." Here, an emphasis on phonemic repetition (mostly of "s" and "t" sounds) is joined with variations and repetitions of words (past participles become present, and vice versa) in different grammatical placement to create a kind of aural excess which goes beyond the simple requirements of visual description, and returns us to the movement and sounds of language as it seems to be produced.

The overall effect of this kind of interplay, however, is less to give priority to one aspect of language at the expense of the other, than to cast emphasis on language in the act of *producing* meaning and thereby momentarily fusing the abstractness of *langue* and the concreteness of *parole*, the ahistoricity of the system and the historicity of this moment in time, the shared social convention upon which language depends and the individuality of my vocal activities as I speak these words.[20]

Attridge's argument is especially significant since the kind of interaction between convention and individual which he is focusing on at the linguistic level, an activity in which we, as readers, are implicated, is played out in another way, as we will see later on, in Joyce's representation of song.

Joyce's first "musical" move, as we witness it in the introduction and throughout "Sirens" is both simple and very broad. It is comprised of a nudging of words away from their lexical properties toward a greater emphasis on their substantiality as sounds. Words do not only imitate or describe sounds; as often as not, any word seems available for Joyce's aurally inscribed variations. From the rhythm of syntax and the deceptive presentations of sound descriptions and apparent imitation, we note the sounds which constitute the words, and thus, words themselves, like the elements of narrative, as the "combination of constituent parts." The sense of Joyce's language is not lost, but instead, it is no longer primary. Though in the introduction the reader may not know as yet how "Bronze" or "Gold" can hear, or where a "peepofgold" is, these words still fit the fragments grammatically. Rhythmic, syntactic, and phonetic combination works away from sense, without total abandonment, back to sound.[21]

Implicit in the discussion so far is the understanding that language is not only sounded but also written. There is a great deal written in "Sirens" which does not meet the ear, but which does meet the eye. Joyce often plays the sound of words off against one another. To the ear, there is no difference between the sounds of "blew" and "blue." But there is a great deal of difference in written language, or in spoken too, if the context of the word does, or does not, supply enough information for the reader or listener to understand the difference. The point here is that we may be deceived by sounds; we may fall through their seams without hearing the lexical difference. Joyce is drawing us toward the surfaces of words while simultaneously reminding us of the difficult nature of the word as heard. Writing apprises us of the differences, the possibilities, and the deceptions of language *as* sound, possibilities which Joyce constantly uses in scripting linguistic sounds. Language, like music, has its seductions, and this kind of play occurs often as the chapter proceeds.

While Lenehan and Boylan urge Miss Douce to "*Sonnez la cloche,*" and Bloom is just entering the dining hall, Simon Dedalus is playing, though not singing, "Goodbye, Sweetheart, Goodbye." The text alone supplies the missing words: " – . . . *to Flora's lips did hie.* High, a high noted pealed in the treble clear." The "high" that follows "hie" makes a joke out of aural consistency, one which is played against lexical meaning. The note that goes with "hie" is, apparently, "high," but the "high" note plays a trick with a word that sounds like the note's description, but is not. Instead of note imitating word, or the other way around, the ear is deceived by a "high" and a "hie" which are not the same.

The aural punning and parodying is given its readerly counterpart: "A jumping rose on satiny breast of satin, rose of Castile." The repetition of "rose" tends to amplify the possibilities of the first "rose" as both noun (flower) and verb (to rise "on satiny breast"). This kind of linear pun, made through changing the grammatical function of words, becomes another of the prominent techniques of the chapter. In a description of Boylan we read: "Sparkling bronze azure eyed Blazure's skyblue bow and eyes." Here, "eye" is turned into both verb and noun, as well as twisted through a sound resemblance with "sky"; "azure," a kind of blue, is blown together with "bronze" in a suggestive dissolution of Boylan's first name. Sound and script both seem to threaten lexicality, implying a danger to assumptions about identity of reference.

In the recombination of elements of Boylan's name we also have an example of the kind play of phonemic spacing that Joyce often uses in his display of the dissonance between sound and script. Garrett Stewart notes this effect in the collapsing and reopening of recontextualized elements in such phrases as "A sail! A veil awave upon the waves" with its metonymic substitution of "sail" for ship, which is in turn likened to the wave that it is on. We can see similar principles at work in the fusion that occurs in something like "Longindying call,"[22] where the loss of conventional divisions in the scripted words supplies a more accurate writing of sound, both of the tuning fork, and indeed, of the way the words sound when read. Stewart suggests that the departures from written conventions alert us to an "accession to the phonic (if not the musical) within the linguistic, the metrical within the discursive, the note within the word."

The aural and verbal manipulations, which include puns, recombinant words and phonemes, work against the clarity of the language as well as narrative suppositions of linearity. Joyce's flexible phonemes, syllables, and words play upon the idea that "one can always lift a written syntagma from the interlocking chain in which it is caught or given without making it lose every possibility of functioning, if not every possibility of 'communicating' precisely."[23] Joyce exploits the recontextual possibilities of linguistic elements, their ability to recombine in discrete and at times deceptive shapes. If the method of the chapter is "musical" in some broad sense, it is so not because it fits itself into the shape of some musical form, or simply because it emphasizes descriptions or imitations of sounds, but rather because it points up the problem of finding complete meaning in sound, whether expressive, or referential, whether spoken, written, played, or sung. Joyce foregrounds the basic similarity between music and literature as combinational and substitutive procedures that constantly rely on context to establish meaning: the combination of sounds (notes, words) or "constituent elements" within particular written or performed context. The reassembling of parts of language connects the "prelude" to the chapter itself. Really, conceptions of the opening as a prelude, an overture, a Schoenberg-like basic set, or even a strange kind of establishment of key, all share (as different as these ideas are) the sense of a laying out of elements which will be recombined as the chapter unfolds. With varying degrees and kinds of complexity, and various kinds of emphases, each metaphor of technique acknowledges with more or less specificity Joyce's sense of the paradigmatic nature (to use now a structuralist metaphor) of the first section in its relation to the ensuing syntagmatic progression of the rest of the episode. In this sense the "prelude" is less an introduction to the themes of the following narrative than a recapitulation of that narrative's techniques as demonstrated on a more strictly linguistic level. When we come to the first lines of the second part of the chapter, we are able to give some identity to the "Bronze" and "gold" of the first section: "Bronze by gold, miss Douce's head by miss Kennedy's head . . .;" but only *some* identity. As we saw in the recomposition of Boylan's first name, the elements in the chain of syntax may be lifted out and reinserted with dismaying ease: Blazes + azure + (b)ronze + (b)lue = Blazure. Elements of the linear chain can become involved in an almost "harmonic" overlaying. In a less compressed fashion, Joyce is doing a very similar thing in the opening of the narrative proper. Placed in the sequence of a parallel construction, "Bronze" and "miss Douce's head" become linked or grafted on to each other, and, therefore, substitutes for one another. The same process holds for miss Kennedy. Both the head of miss Douce and "Bronze" are meant to be substitutes for a character named "miss Douce" (perhaps itself a double name). The partitioning is multiple; the parallel construction and the substitutional possibilities it gives rise to remind us of the part-making procedures of narrative as such (in the naming of characters; in the telling only of what is relevant, or "part" of the whole). The head of miss Douce is itself a synecdoche for an "entire" character whose "complete" presentation under the sign of her own name would still only be, as Roland Barthes suggests, the presentation of a "nominal unit [which stands for] a collection of characteristics . . . establishing an equivalent relationship between sign and sum." Furthermore, "Bronze" and "gold" are metonyms or single word substitutions not only for characters, but also for a set of silent or deleted metaphorical manipulations: her hair was the color of bronze = her hair was bronze = Bronze.[24] The metonymical "Bronze" or "gold" are contiguous substitutions for already performed metaphorical manipulations. Joyce is balancing part, or trait, and name, disassembling the proper noun into *its* constituent elements and thus giving trait and name equal possibilities for signification. The proper name is divided, recomposed, substituted for traits it is supposed to unite, or, in the case of Bloom, the name suffers direct linguistic interruption in the narration with such constructions as "Bloowho" or "Bloowhose." This kind of play on the name has the further effect of conflating the character's identity with its grammatical function as noun and possessive pronoun intrude upon each other's space.[25] In fact, space – grammatical, syntactic, and representational – will remain of primary importance as the chapter progresses.

"SIRENS" AND THE WORKINGS OF NARRATIVE MUSICAL SPACE

In the last chapter on Pound, I pointed out that reading the *Cantos* requires the juggling of various themes and references. Pound's contiguous method disrupts the linearity of the text, while at the same time supplying it with a more textured method of progression. I suggested that, in part, this method of intratextual recall and recurrence, as a process, has a certain affinity with the way a musical composition creates its own specific kind of "space" even as it moves through time. In a more intensified form, and with a greater emphasis on language, we have a somewhat similar process taking place in "Sirens." Cross-referencing and recalling are, of course, part of the process of reading any text; but few long poems or naturalistic novels require as much intra- and intertextual cross-referencing as do the work of Pound and Joyce. These texts resist traditional means of unification and recuperation through their play with linguistic, thematic, and representational levels of continuity.

But they also sustain themselves by virtue of the very plurality which constitutes them.

Plurality, the disruption of continuity, the attempt at simultaneity in writing do not, of themselves, make texts like *Cantos* or "Sirens" "musical." Indeed, in tonal terms, such disruptions would seem quite contrary to our usual modes of listening and understanding music in a very teleological or "goal" oriented way.[26] But, as we saw in Pound's, and in a slightly different way, Schoenberg's, definition of harmony as founded on the properties of linearity and contiguity, completion according to prescribed formal or harmonic laws is not the "point" of music, or, by inference for Pound at least, poetry. In a sense, as Pound works out his theories of music and attempts to identify and incorporate some of these into his poetry, his theoretical and poetic practice become a critique of traditional musical expectations and a display of the possibilities for a new kind of poetic and musical practice.

In Joyce's "Sirens," the writerly analogy with music is also part of an interrogation of teleological musical and readerly understanding. The linguistic performance I have been discussing so far is part of this interrogation. It is not as though the naturalistic elements of the text disappear with "Sirens"; we know where the characters are and where they go; we know what they say, the actions they perform; there is even a discernible beginning, middle, and (gaseous) end to the chapter, as there is to the book. But with "Sirens," naturalism or realism can only be seen as *one more* element at work in a text which will increasingly complicate the presentation of its story by an ever more complex and variable discourse. Joyce's foregrounding of the text as both sound and script returns us to its phenomenality, to its presence as something seen and (if inwardly) heard, not something seen through and immediately interpreted and understood. Joyce's particular way of clouding lexicality brings language into closer proximity with music, and, at the level of language, offers a kind of parodic continuity which the narrative itself picks up. Indeed, the phonemic play with recombinant words, the verbal and aural puns, as well as the metonymic and synecdochal substitutions of character traits give an even greater sense of language flowing through itself, repeating, varying, and moving through its own self-defined space in its own unique manner.

Moving our focus from the word or word sound to longer syntagmatic chains we begin to realize how Joyce is playing upon our expectations of continuity. The fragments of the opening section suggest unusual, though perhaps not totally improbable, connections:

> Bronze by gold heard the hoofirons, steelyringing.
> Imperthnthn thnthnthn.
> Chips, picking chips off rocky thumbnail, chips.
> Horrid! And gold flushed more.
> A husky fifenote blew.
> Blew. Blue bloom is on the.
> Goldpinnacled hair . . .

All the phrases in the first section end with periods, exclamation marks, or question marks, signs of completion or closure. But our desire to connect these units with those that follow them is present even though it is frustrated. The steelyringing hoofirons are curiously answered: "Imperthnthn . . ." If we read on into the text we discover that this is not the call of iron, but "bootssnout['s]" impertinent imitation of miss Douce:

> – I'll complain to Mrs. de Mansey on you if I hear any more of your
>   impertinent insolence.
> – Imperthnthn thnthnthn, bootssnout sniffed rudely . . .[27]

The unpronounceable syllables are themselves, we discover, a parody of another's speech (perhaps even a kind of parody of unpronounceabilty). Similarly, the "Horrid!" of the fourth line of the introduction seems to be a kind of response to "picking chips off rocky thumbnail." But just a little further ahead this "Horrid" is inscribed as miss Kennedy's response to miss Douce's apparently hilarious imitation of the old fogey in Boyd's:

> – O, miss Douce! miss Kennedy protested. You horrid thing!
>   And flushed yet more (you horrid), more goldenly.

Again, in the introduction, the continuation of the line, or the "response" to it, implies a strange relationship, one that *could* be plausible in the "right" context, though perhaps not in any that we find in the book. The same goes for "Blue bloom" actually being *on* the "Goldpinnacled hair." Or we may note as well the ". . . blew/ Blew. Blue bloom . . ." connection in which an aural pun creates the only continuity between syntactic units.

This parodic continuity of the opening of "Sirens" is one of the ways in which the chapter sustains itself. When Bloom receives change from the girl in Daly's, his mind plays over the ominous number four:

> – Twopence, sir, the shopgirl dared to say.
> – Aha . . . I was forgetting . . . Excuse . . .
> – And four.
> At four she.[28]

Bloom has in mind the coming tryst between Molly and Boylan, but the contingent connection between the amount of change he is receiving and the hour of infidelity enlightens us not only to the distraction of Bloom's mind, but also to the way in which expectation or intention acts to make connections which are, and are not, there.

As if to emphasize this problem of narrative continuity, the last line of the quotation above is soon repeated by a voice in yet a slightly different context. Boylan enters the bar and, in the process of buying a round, happens to ask about the results of the horse race: "– What's your cry? Glass of bitter? Glass of bitter, please, and a sloegin for me. Wire in yet?" A voice replies with a crude turn: "Not yet. At four she. Who said four?" Who indeed? And who is *this* still more distant voice who creates *and* points to the intrusion? Bloom, we must remember, has not yet entered the bar, so it seems unlikely that this is his voice, though these are, in part, his words. Though it is not unusual for the narrative voice to accommodate, without warning, the collision of description and interior monologue, this seems unlikely here given Bloom's location at the moment Boylan speaks.

This intervention by the narrative voice sustains a kind of aural ambiguity for which the introduction has prepared the way. At the same time, however, it also supplies another kind of continuity since it often gives the impression of a single voice "doing" other voices.[29] We are apprised here of a crucial subtlety: that to hear, or read, some*one* speaking is not really to know or understand the *location* of the voice; sound does not always make space precise, nor accomplish an identity. Vocality is subject to other stratagems since articulation itself always participates in the cultural shapes of a language or of sounds with precedence, of words and sounds already spoken and heard. Hence, identity, or the clarity of the site of expression is disintegrating here. Turning Lacan a bit askew, we could say that here vocal ambiguity is inherent to the moment of the entry into the symbolic. Phonemic and morphemic vocal play and inscription parallels the syntactic ambiguity of the "prelude." The entry into the second part of the narrative offers not only increasing ambiguities, but does so by displaying, and taking fresh advantage of, narrative conventions. The effect of entering into narrative here is that placement into the social nexus is by no means a guarantee of finding a location, nor of establishing an identity. On the contrary; entering into language, or in this case narrative, entails the risk of the loss of location, of identity within vocality.

And music? The risk of such loss is the other side of the musical sublime which the concept of "absolute music" of the early nineteenth century had established as a safeguard against mere subjectivism and self-indulgence (see chapter 1). The increasing chromaticism of Liszt, Wagner, Chopin (among others) through to the more or less complete dissatisfaction with tonality itself of Debussy, Scriabin, and Schoenberg (again, among others), suggests a reprise of the tension between the desire for inwardness and "expression" (even if justified by some form of "rationality"), and the explanatory power of a system or systems from which and by which the non-lexical power of music could derive and be justified.[30]

"Sirens" explores the very idea of signification in literarily formal and musically "popular" terms. In a way, though, the apparent high (literary)/low (musical) opposition here is false: it is too hard and fast a distinction to imply that the "high" art concerns of formal experimentation are portrayed in the discourse of the chapter and that the "low" or communal forms of musical and linguistic knowing are left to the songs. It is true that the chapter marks a significant stylistic shift in approach to narrative and narration that seems meant to parallel a kind of disintegrative anxiety which has surrounded, rightly or wrongly, "art" music for some time. But it seems clear too that, though the means for musical comprehensibility will be challenged through the portrayal of communally "popular" or well-known songs, implicitly, the stress under which language is placed throughout the episode does not merely mean that "high" art experimentation is somehow superior to the sentimentality of other forms of art. Ambiguity and dislocation of voice(s) will form instead the very means of the chapter, infiltrating every kind of expression, whether the transcripted language of popular song, or that of the narrative itself. Nothing resolves itself here into some monologically superior discourse; the songs and the narration of them face the same problems in regard to the Voice of the Father.

Throughout the episode small ambiguities point toward the presence–absence movement of the voice. The lack of conventional quotation marks, nothing new in Joyce, can cause slight confusions at times in determining whose voice is whose: "– Who? Where? gold asked eagerly. / – In the second carriage, miss Douce's wet lips said, laughing in the sun. He's looking. Mind till I see." The uncertainty is slight, but it does seem unclear whether it is miss Douce's "wet lips" that are "laughing in the sun" or the man in the "tall silk." The lack of clarity is dispelled a few lines later when we read that "Her wet lips tittered;" still, this small place of uncertainty warns us that the levels of discourse, the distances between narrator and speaker are never really secure.

Moreover, as if in imitation of the narrator, the characters themselves also participate in a kind of plurivocality. Bootssnout's "Imperthnthn" is a mocking imitation of miss Douce. Similarly, miss Douce herself does the voice of the old man in Boyd's: "– Here he was, miss Douce said, cocking her bronze three quarters, ruffling her nosewings. Hufa! Hufa!" The barmaids, again like the narrator, also perform synecdochic and metonymic part-making on those they discuss. While deriding the old fogey, they identify him by several "greasy" parts of his anatomy: "O greasy eyes! Imagine being married to a man like that! she cried. With his bit of beard! . . . Married to the greasy nose! she yelled." Later, other characters will do still other voices. There is Cowley's dubbing of Dollard as "the Warrior,"[31] and Tom Kernan's ginhot story of an irate husband who ruins the voice of Walter Bapty: "Well, sir, the husband took him by the throat. *Scoundrel*, said he, *you'll sing no more love songs.*" There is also Bloom's apparent imitation of Farrel ("Waaaaaaalk"), as well as his reading of Robert Emmet's last words, with flatulent variations, at the end of the chapter: "One, two. *Let my epitaph be . . . Written. I have.* Pprrpffrrppffff." Thus, even the voices of characters *do* voices here, and in a manner very reminiscent of the narrator's own methods.

In "Sirens," Joyce substitutes a disruptive and parodic narrative continuity for more traditional means. In part, this is accomplished through an emphasis on language as a sonic entity, an entity which, in the mouths of many in the chapter including the narrator, is capable of running across, and, in fact, creating multiple narrative spaces. Building from its emphasis on the contingent procedures of language, its recombinant and associative possibilities, the chapter begins a contingent representation of different coexisting "spaces." Earlier I discussed the linguistic performance that is part of miss Kennedy's sad sauntering contemplation of men. This passage ends with an abrupt change of focus: "Sadly she twined in sauntering gold hair behind a curving ear. / – It's them has the fine times, sadly then she said. / A man." Suddenly, there is a shift to a space of motion which runs parallel to the movement of those at the Ormond. Concomitant with this report of Bloom's movement is the description of his thoughts as they revolve around *The Sweets of Sin*, the prurient text he has purchased for Molly:

Bloowho went by by Moulang's pipes bearing in his breast the sweets of sin, by Wine's antiques, in memory bearing sweet sinful words, by Carroll's dusky battered plate, for Raoul.

In exquisite contrast, Bloom enters, first identified only as "A man"[32] not having, nor about to have any "fine times." Running counter to miss Kennedy's phonemic sauntering runs Bloom's: "by by Moulang's pipes bearing in his breast the sweets of sin, by Wine's antiques, in memory bearing sweet sinful words . . ." The motion here is manifold. Sound is in a way the most serious connection between the two passages, sound, and the ironic way in which Bloom, as "A man," is presented. The change of space might point to a man, but his identity remains obscured by the intersection of the space between his name and a pronoun which could also be that name's grammatical substitute: "Bloowho." Even as Bloom's movements are indicated through the use of repeated prepositional phrases ("by by . . . by"), his internal motion is marked by recollection of the "sweet sinful words" of *The Sweets of Sin*. The interweaving of Bloom's thoughts and his movements is also a kind of counterpoint between inside and outside, even though it is the narrative voice which describes, and indeed, constitutes the movement in both realms. After setting one represented space against another, the writing continues its multiplicity by describing and performing the internal and external spaces of the character in one elaborate interweaving of language.

Movement in "Sirens" always involves a simultaneity of various spaces, and within the various represented spaces (the singers in the room adjacent to Bloom and Goulding; the coming and going of Boylan; the approaching tap of the blind piano tuner; etc.) there is always movement. Though we cannot accord a relative "highness" or "lowness" to these quickly fluctuating shifts of place, as we might with the pitches or voices of a musical composition, this kind of quick-cutting between various narrative spaces is probably as close to a narrative counterpoint as Joyce can come.[33] We must attempt to keep in mind that, as the chapter moves, these are areas of concurrence. Though the chapter may make light of the idea of narrative and linguistic linearity in the name of music and its propensities toward teleological completion, it is also true that the use of this very linearity makes the illusion of the contemporaneous spaces possible. The text's display of the contingencies of language, both phonemic and narrative, makes the linear movement of language come to *seem* merely contingent, obedient to another logic (or, to other logics) of narrative emplacement. The puns and homonyms, the cramped and shared syntactic and grammatical spaces, the deceptive units of narration seem at times to overcome the linear tract of the script, and we can see the multiple areas of narrated space at least in part as regions of narrated sound. "Sirens" is neither

fugue nor canon in any strict sense; but perhaps, like the definition of
fugue which Ralph Vaughan Williams gives, it is a *kind* of writing, distinct in its own method of self-creation, in its own approach to the problems of space and movement even as it disassembles and reassembles
itself as it moves.

Language as sound permeates the contingent definition of various
kinds of represented space in "Sirens" including the very "interiority" of
its characters. The "typing" of characters, and especially of Bloom, in
this writing of the coalescence and dispersion of interiority is, like the
writing of any kind of space in "Sirens," comprised of a multiplicity of
substitutions. The priority of any given identity or sign of identity is generally hard to tell. The "Bloowho" which marks the ambiguous presence
of Bloom's first appearance carrying "sweet sinful words" signals the
indecisiveness of his identity. In Jackson Cope's words, Bloom appears
as one "seen hiding sexual luxury in the secret heart and [also] . . . as
castrate cuckold." Bloom's ambiguous identity is mixed further as the
narrative voice continues to make tangential connections. At a shrieking
moment in the discussion between the barmaids, the "goggle eye" of the
man in Boyd's comes up. Miss Douce rejoins to miss Kennedy "in deep
bronze laughter": "– And your other eye!" The other eye of the narrator then switches to "Blowhose dark eye read Aaron Figatners name,"
and to Bloom's thoughts on the indeterminacy of naming: "Why do I
always think Figather? . . . And Prosper Loré's huguenot name."[34] From
the seen, and only partially understood, Bloom turns to speculations
upon the unseen: "By Bassi's blessed virgins Bloom's dark eyes went by.
Bluerobed, white under come to me." The connections here are again
multidirectional. Later in the chapter, Bloom will contemplate the vir-
ginity of miss Douce: "Blank face. Virgin should say . . ." Bloom moves
from wondering about the "reality" of the anatomy of the icon, to the
transformation of the "real" woman into icon, a crisscrossing of substitutions: "See. Play on her. Lip blow. Body of white woman, a flute alive
. . ." If Bloom's dark other eye establishes a phallic seeing here, it also
presents this seeing as its own lack. The eye keeps up (so to speak) the
whole process of partitioning and substitution which allows for the
(male) seeing of woman as icon, and icon as woman.

A similar process of contiguity is performed on Bloom as he himself
is inscribed into a certain emblematic space with the old fogey in Boyd's.
The distance between the figures seems to collapse altogether when miss
Douce finally shouts the preposterousness of being "Married to the
greasy nose!" The peculiar shift of phallic substitutes from eye to nose

creates a kind of linguistic orgasm: "All flushed (O!), panting, sweating (O!), all breathless," in which the barmaids undergo a kind of linguistic fusion: "they urged each each to peal after peal, ringing in changes, bronzegold, goldbronze . . ." And then, another change occurs in which a voice speaks: "Married to Bloom, to greaseabloom." The changes rung in by bronze and gold seem to change Bloom as well: a rather greasy sea change which links him to the typology of the old fogey.

The mirroring syntax of Kennedy and Douce ("they urged each each to peal after peal . . . bronzegold, goldbronze") suggests an audio-visual reflexiveness (we "seehear" the words and the sentence pattern) which attacks the precise location of the utterance; it is the "narrative" voice we say, but it is not narration in any conventional sense.[35] It is the auditory–syntactic emblem of a mirroring echo which has its working out later in the chapter when Bloom *sees* miss Douce and Lidwell exchanging turns with the seashell she has brought back from her holiday:

Bloom through the bardoor saw a shell held at their ears. He heard more faintly that that they heard, each for herself alone, then each for other, hearing the plash of waves, loudly, a silent roar.

Bloom recognizes that "[h]er ear too is a shell," and also that "[t]he sea they think they hear. Singing. A roar. The blood it is. Souse in the ear sometimes. Well, it's a sea. Corpuscle islands." Jean-Michel Rabaté comments that, in this scene, the mirror–shell ". . . reflects only emptiness, the emptiness which nevertheless allows for the exchange of imaginary products." This auditory silence of the body in exchange with itself subverts, and reflects, the sexual–visual moment of offering, acceptance, and return of the shell between Douce and Lidwell. Exchange between is partially limited by its unconscious substitution for an exchange within. Such interference and self-reflexive exchange troubles the very possibility of expression, the exchange between inside and outside – never mind any kind of intersubjective moment. Noting the chiasmatic moment that crosses between eyes and ears, listening and seeing, Rabaté suggests that "the role of the echo is to redouble both song and look. The space of the shell is necessary for the reciprocal transformation of song into image (an imaginary song) and of vision into music (hallucination)."[36]

No doubt, there is a void at the core of hearing, and one which is central to the understanding of the sounds of well-known music. Such a paradox is not *only* a void, however, but the very sound of the other within (Douce and Lidwell it would seem "hear" the same vacant imaginary sound). If, from one angle, as Slavoj Žižek suggests (playing off Derrida), to hear oneself speaking is "that which undermines most radically the subject's self-presence and self-transparence . . .," nevertheless, the "stranger in myself acquires positive existence in different guises, . . . Voice is that which, in the signifier, resists meaning, it stands for the opaque inertia that cannot be recuperated by meaning." Exchange is possible and impossible at the same time. It is both incomplete and necessary. The status of the voice as "excess" is, for Žižek, "radically undecideable;" that is, it carries the danger of "sliding into a consuming self-enjoyment that 'effeminates' the reliable masculine Word," but at the same time, as that which gives articulation to the Word, it is subject to the Word's discipline which "regulates the voice as a means of asserting social discipline and authority . . ." This is no simple opposition of Word and voice, for Žižek sees the two opposing elements combine in something like the marching chants of the Marines, with their "debilitating rhythm and sadistically sexualized nonsensical content" as an exemplary case of "consuming self-enjoyment in the service of power . . ."[37] Žižek is in a way rearticulating the supplementary condition of music and notions of musical meaning in relation to literature that I have been pointing to throughout this book.

This supplementarity is recapitulated in "Sirens" by virtue of the visual transcription of *seeing listening occur* in the chiasmatic moment (as Rabaté has called it) where Bloom watches Douce and Lidwell exchange the shell. In "Sirens" we do not come upon the imaginary void at the center of hearing through the illusions of hearing itself, or not only through these, but rather when these are transposed, at least at this moment, into the realm of sight. Bloom *sees* the two hearing nothing: the visual check, insofar as seeing is not only believing, but in Western culture, knowing, produces no veracity at all. Still, Bloom *knows* what he sees: a hearing which is not hearing; he sees the illusory moment of exchange and the "substance" of that exchange, and knows very well there is nothing in the shell to be heard, yet too, he *knows* what this nothing sounds like. The very possibility of knowledge, and indeed, the very certainty of expressive audibility, later to be emblematized in the songs – those well-internalized pieces of occupied subjectivity – is here emblazoned by the visuality of substantial non-presence. Bloom sees them hearing the nothing that is not there, and hears the nothing that is.

At a perhaps more recognizable level, interiority, as it is inscribed in "Sirens" continues to operate in various possible exchanges of identities. Thus, if Bloom is castrate cuckold, then he is also borderline lascivious fogey, and perhaps, too, "that strong sailor rounding home toward Ithaca, toward Molly." Bloom will also inscribe himself later as the naughty Henry Flower, verbal lover of another potential Molly figure, Martha Clifford – if that is *her* "real" name. Amusingly, even as he writes under one name not his own (as Henry Flower) he murmurs, for Richie Goulding's view, the names of others while writing the possible pen-name of his verbal paramour: "Just copy out of paper. Murmured: Messrs Callan, Coleman and Co, limited. Henry wrote: / Miss Martha Clifford . . . ." In this scheme, Lydia Douce plays double for both virgin and Molly as icon of exotic Easternness, an association which miss Douce herself seems to sustain when she sings the line from the song of the East: "*O, Idolores, queen of the eastern seas!*"

The paradox of exchange, of identity as substitution, of language as sound, and sound as the ubiquitous and deceptive silent roar of textual space has its first small crescendo when Simon Dedalus enters the bar. Dedalus is part of the old fogey schema ("– Ah sure, my dancing days are done . . ."), though he still manages a "gentlemanly" flirtation with miss Douce ("– That was exceedingly naughty of you . . . tempting poor simple males"[38]), and when singing later on he becomes the lover-tenor "Lionel Simon." There is a suspension of singular identity in Simon's case, as there is in Bloom's, which manifests itself linguistically in Dedalus' reflections on the Mourne Mountains wherein he mixes the languages of affirmation and morbid self pity: "Must be a great tonic in the air down there. But a long threatening comes at last, they say. Yes. Yes." Then all falls silent in an oxymoronic moment where words of self pity and affirmation float upon the narrator's voice: "None nought said nothing. Yes." But out of this linguistic suspension movement again seems to appear. Miss Douce will trill, Dedalus revives ("– Was Mr Lidwell in today?"), into the bar comes Lenehan, and across the bridge of "Yessex" comes Bloom, himself a new context for the word of affirmation, for Molly's word: "Mr Bloom reached Essex bridge. Yes, Mr Bloom crossed bridge of Yessex." The change of space, of context, also changes the word. The end of the book resounds in the middle, as the place of crossing is crowded phonemically by the place of affirmation.

But the affirmation is ambiguous, the space is in doubt. Is this the sign of Bloom's acceptance of Boylan as surrogate for himself as Molly's lover? Boylan will cross the same bridge in a moment as "a grey hat riding on a jaunting car." Or is this the sign of Bloom's imminent sexual rejuvenation ("Too late now. Or if not? If not? If still?"[39]), or is this a shared linguistic figure for Bloom's and Molly's potential congruence?

We cannot choose, for here again, the sign of Joycean narration resists enclosure or complete exchange. "Yessex" offers a peculiar concreteness (we can trace its constituent elements) and ambiguity (can we finally say what it means?) which may mark this writing strongly in an analogy with music. Simultaneity and motion, flux, change, and concurrence will continue to preside in this writing of voices, identities, and spaces, even as the Ormond bar itself will fill with song.

WORDS? MUSIC? . . .: THE INTERTEXT OF SONG

Song is usually treated as part of the universalizing process at work in Joyce's general allusive scheme; it is considered but one more kind of text which fits into the web of intra- and intertextual references which are commonly seen as lending a kind of universal significance and overall unity to the text. Zack Bowen, who has done perhaps the most work on "Sirens" and song, notes, for instance, the matrix of connections that circulate around Stephen, the blind piano tuner, and the figure of the croppy boy. Both Stephen and the tuner, for different reasons, tap their way through part of the text: Stephen in "Proteus" ("I am getting along nicely in the dark. My ash sword hangs at my side. Tap with it: they do"), and the tuner, most audibly, during Ben Dollard's singing of "The Croppy Boy" in "Sirens." Stephen's relation to the croppy boy occurs obliquely: the "false-father motif" of the song relates to Stephen's opinion of his own father, and the croppy boy's failure to pray for his mother's rest links to Stephen's refusal to pray for his mother on her death bed. The "bitches bastard" phrase of the tuner echoes during Dollard's singing of the song, and the tuner's entering the "'lonely Ormond hall' at the end of 'Sirens' puts him directly in the croppy boy's place." Moreover, Bowen points out that Bloom gives aid to Stephen, at the end of "Circe," and to the tuner in "Lystregonians." Bloom thus becomes symbolically the true "father-figure." The theme of betrayal in the song and in *Ulysses* ultimately includes Bloom, and, according to Bowen, "[e]ventually everyone can be linked with the croppy boy . . . as the song, like other major musical works in the chapter, takes on overtones of being both the means and the end of the universalizing process."[40]

The "universalizing process" is for Bowen the means by which characters and their situations are identified with the figures or situations in the songs and, in turn, the stories that are alluded to create a kind of absolute stratum of verification for the figures and figurations in the chapter. Though this kind of procedure has been used for many years to recuperate the many and disparate allusions and texts of which *Ulysses* is composed, it does seem possible that the multiple allusions and figurations, both literary and more broadly cultural, which surround and connect the characters may in fact be undercut by the very narration which includes so many possibilities. Bloom, as we have been tracing him so far, may be old fogey or cuckold, a true-father figure, or even, as the narrative voice suggests at one point, the "unconquered hero." But I would suggest that any one type, or allusion, or figuration will never constitute a securely universal place of reference. I will attend to the intertext of song in "Sirens" not as a set of universal repetitions or figurations of a truth which pervades, transcends, and yet links any and all of its manifestations, but rather as the site of the problem of citation, as a critique of the expectation of the universal in the repetition of songs. They are threads to and from other texts, both written and unwritten, whose value, as Stephen Heath puts it,

is to be found in the heterogeneity, in the very distance between . . . diverse elements that the writing will cross in a ceaseless play of relations and correspondences in which every element becomes the fiction of another. The unity of these elements is not, then, . . . one of content, of meaning, but one grasped at the level of their reality as forms, as fictions.

Thus, the intertext of song in "Sirens" can be seen as part of a "discontinuity in progress,"[41] rather than part of a "universalizing process."

Song is a complex kind of presence in "Sirens," partly because of its own composition as the meeting place of music and language. As Roland Barthes puts it, in song, the voice is in a "double posture, a double production – of language and of music." "Doubling" of various supplementary kinds is, as we have already seen, very much in evidence in the chapter. The narrative of "Sirens," with all its recombinant and substitutive linguistic play and its strange manipulations of time and space, identities, and crossed modes of knowing, is itself always in some kind of "double posture." But there is also another kind of doubling in the musical and vocal intertext of "Sirens" which has implications for the narrative technique. Marc E. Blanchard, in a discussion of Elias Canetti's *The Voices of Marakesh*, makes a point which may prove germane to "Sirens":

Words belong to everyone, the voice, one voice only to someone. It is this ambiguity of a body like no other and of this sound like all others with which Canetti confronts us.

Joyce's use of song works very much with this paradoxical sense of the particularity of the voice like no other, and the lack of uniqueness of words, or sounds like all others. But in "Sirens," the song in its efficiency as a cultural utterance is used to expose the loss of distinction between private expression and the means of "public tonality,"[42] an assumption shared by the majority of singers and listeners in the chapter. This is done by the predominance of a narrative voice which maintains difference through phonemic and syntactic play, as well as through its selection and citation from the "common" cultural fictions of tonal interpretation.

One of the more striking moments of this kind of exposure occurs when Simon Dedalus plays "Goodbye, Sweetheart, Goodbye." The movement into this song is preceded by an interesting loss of a clear referent for the pronoun "he," something which the narrative voice, in apparent imitation of some readerly voice, draws attention to:

Upholding the lid he (who?) gazed in the coffin (coffin?) at the oblique triple (piano!) wires. He pressed (the same who pressed indulgently her hand), soft pedalling, a triple of keys. . . .

The interpolated questions happily resolve as the voices seem to join in their recognition of the "(piano!)." The unnamed Dedalus is signified only by his earlier gentlemanly posing with miss Douce: "(the same who pressed indulgently her hand)." Pronominal confusion persists as Dedalus strikes the tuning fork left by the blind piano tuner:

From the saloon a call came, long in dying. That was the tuning fork the tuner had that he forgot that he now struck. A call again. That he now poised that it now throbbed. You hear? It throbbed, pure, purer, softly and softlier, its buzzing prongs. Longer in dying call.[43]

At the sound of the fork, Dedalus seems to disappear, lost in the pronouns that unite him to the tuner, and yet obliterate both.

Significantly, this moment of the decomposition of identity occurs amidst the sounding of an "absolute" pitch. Hugh Kenner suggests that in this passage, Joyce is "abrogating syntactic canons in adhering to imitative ones." But what exactly is being imitated here? The interpolated "You hear?" seems to ask the same question. In a sense, the description is not of the fork's sound but of its absoluteness – a description which is performed in less than absolute terms. If we consider Jackson Cope's suggestion that this early section of the chapter is "dominated by tumescence – a sort of group [and mainly male] masturbation . . .[in which] Simon flirts with Douce; Lenehan, put down by Kennedy . . . is brought up by Douce again

. . ." and so on then we can view the language here in quite a different way. Note how Dedalus' hand moves from an initial overture with miss Douce ("He held her hand. Enjoyed her holidays?")[44] to the pressing of the piano keys. From the substitution of the piano keys for miss Douce, it is but a little way to the replacement of the tuning fork for the piano. The fork is apparently struck and, hence, swells, "poised" and "throbbing," then detumesces, growing "softlier." Words such as "throbbed," "poised," or "prong" have less to do with sound than with a kind of figuration of the onanism surrounding the absolute. The sound of the pure pitch resides within a web of humorously over-played sexual double entendre; it is rendered "impurely," mediated and displaced by the language that describes it, and which suggests the *way* in which it may be heard. The implication seems to be that hearing can become a collaboration of sense data and already internalized sublimations. Hearing is not innocent though the forms of interpretation may not be totally conscious. The over-the-top phallic language here, and elsewhere in the chapter, suggests not only a somewhat more crude sense of "inwardness" than the language of a love song or a patriotic ditty might at first seem to warrant; it also indicates that the "inward" may already be informed or shaped by an ideological design – in this case, a very masculinist design – which functions at one and the same time to control the heard, even as it designates it as *beyond* control, as expressive of eternal design. This will become even more apparent when, later on, Dedalus will actually sing "Come Thou Lost One."

These first hints of the parodic sublime occur here even before Simon has begun to play the song which is itself the context for another set of displacements. In a significant performance of narrative and musical doubling, we hear the unsung language of the song: "– *The bright stars fade* . . . A voiceless song sang from within, singing." The voice is missing, though the words are there, if only literally for the reader. The words enter as signs of their non-presence, and give notice of the partiality of song. Joyce is inscribing the division within song and upon which it is based. This division exposes the song's supplementary nature: note adds to word what it cannot "express." It supplies another level of expression to the completeness of the discourse, and, in a sense, displaces it, and vice versa. Joyce's presentation of song lyric as the substitute for music plays across this division, offering us the deceptive presence of language which is not "there" for music which supposedly is.

The music of the song, like the sound of the tuning fork, is also less imitated than figured or rendered in the imagery of cultural conceptions of listening:

A duodene of birdnotes chirruped bright treble answer under sensitive hands. Brightly the keys, all twinkling linked, all harpsichording, called to a voice to sing the strain of dewy morn, of youth, of love's leavetaking, life's, love's morn.[45]

Once more, the language has less to do with imitating sound than with how sound is heard. This is, of course, the sentimental imagery of affects ("birdnotes chirruped bright treble . . . all twinkling . . . all harpsichording"), of the expectation of "subjective expression" through the public determinations of song. The music calls "to a voice," but nobody in particular need answer. The "voice like no other" is here deferred and becomes instead, it seems, the voice of *any* other. For "them in the bar,"[46] what is heard is immediately interpreted, held under control by the "laws" or unspoken conventions of expression, thus producing a condition of *in*different participation in the public and private paradox of tonal song. But indifference is not the condition of the narrative, for the very figurations that stand in for sound, borrowed as they are from certain ideological fictions of expressivity, are self-conscious disfigurations of hearing, designations of a language which has already interpreted and displaced what it would describe.

Syntax too plays a part in the double gesture of illucidating this amorphous public–private space. Phrases such as "all twinkling," or "all harpsichording" are peculiar kinds of verbal adjectives which could be rendered more commonly as predications: "the keys were all twinkling," or, "the keys were all harpsichording." Such predicative locutions have, in Barthes' phrase, a certain "economic function":

the predicate is the rampart by which the subject's image-repertoire protects itself against the loss that threatens it . . . music has an image-repertoire whose function is to reassure, to constitute the subject, who hears it.

The moment of hearing, and in "Sirens," of singing, in a way obliterates the subject, but also allows a space for it to creep back in, however transformed. A voice may enter into the place of public expressivity, may become the "voice like no other" only to take its place in the image-repertoire of expression as *some* other voice or speaker of the song. In this process, the subject is constituted, and also deferred. The intertextual moment of song is a writing of displacement and replacement in which identity is dispersed and reconstituted; it is also a process of which those in the Ormond, except perhaps Bloom, are unaware.

Appropriately then, dispersion marks the actions of those who are present in the bar, or who arrive, as Simon is playing the wordless song.

Boylan shows up, and his arrival is sounded by a synecdochic entrance: "Jingle jaunted by the curb and stopped . . . Blazes Boylan's smart tan shoes creaked on the barfloor where he strode." The barmaids are given a synecdochic response ("Yes, gold from anear by bronze from afar"). And amidst all this fragmentary coming and going prepare themselves to assume their "like lady, ladylike" roles: ". . . fair miss Kennedy . . . smiled on him. But sister bronze outsmiled her, preening for him her richer hair, a bosom and a rose." Miss Douce, by her trilling of "The Shade of the Palm" ("– *O, Idolores* . . ."), is already associated with the sexual, exotic East, and the sexual in this case, and probably for most of the chapter, may be considered as male sexual fantasy. The speaker in "The Shade of the Palm" is male, as is indicated in the correct version of the line which miss Douce has trilled in error: "*O, my Dolores, Queen of the Eastern Sea!*"[47] Douce, in constituting herself through song, takes part in a double displacement. Her mistake of "*I*dolores" for "*my* Dolores" situates her as the speaker of the song, but at the same time, the "I" for "my" transposition relocates her as the object of the other speaker's desire: she is still the "Queen of the Eastern Sea." With the words of the song still playing about her lips, she becomes the manifestation of the song's deferred object of desire:

Lenehan still drank and grinned . . . at miss Douce's lips that all but hummed, not shut, the oceansong her lips had trilled. Idolores. The eastern seas.

There is also a sense of bartering here ("– Fine goods in small parcels. / That is to say she") that emphasizes the double displacement of miss Douce in the economy of the song and the bar. As she returns Boylan's change, the narrator interpolates lines from the song: "Fair one of Egypt teased and sorted in the till and handed coins in change. Look to the west. A clack. For me." The culmination of all this splitting and division comes when miss Douce, at the begging of Lenehan, makes yet another transformation when she rings the bell of her body which echoes all the masturbatory displacement of the songs:

– Go on! Do! *Sonnez!*
Bending, she nipped a peak of skirt above her knee. Delayed. Taunted them still, bending, suspending, with wilful eyes.
– *Sonnez!*
Smack. She set free sudden in rebound her nipped elastic garter smackwarm against her smackable a woman's warmhosed thigh.
– *La cloche!* cried gleeful Lenehan.[48]

All of this takes place while the voiceless rendition of "Goodbye, Sweetheart, Goodbye" continues in the background. This song is part of

a reflexive narrative organization which subtly emphasizes the displacements going on in the bar. While the scene with miss Douce is building
toward its climax, the voiceless song is making the deceptive correspondence between the apparently high note and the "hie" word: "– . . . *to
Flora's lips did hie.* / High, a high note pealed in the treble clear." But, to
go along with this deceptive moment, there is also the fact that the silent
singer is singing wrong words. According to Bowen, the line from the
song is actually, "And morn to floral lips doth hie." The error cannot be
Bloom's, since he is not there; nor can it be Dedalus', since he is not
singing. Is this Joyce nodding, or in fact a portal of discovery in which
the musical intertext again enacts the presence–absence gesture of song?
Recalling Barthes' discussion of the predication of the subject through
song, I think it is possible to see this "error" as a kind of linguistic demonstration of music's constitutive effect. An adjective, "floral," is turned
into a proper noun, "Flora"; a part, "floral lips," is turned into a "whole"
figure. The potentially erroneous repetition of the song constitutes the
textual cipher of an identity which is neither in the song, nor, past this
mention, in *Ulysses*. The moment of "error" exposes the process of substitution and displacement that comprises the musical context of the bar.
"Flora" is forever deferred in the quotation of words that are not
present, and this simultaneous creation and absenting parallels the
absenting of miss Douce and her own deferred situation in the Ormond.

   Into this complex system of narrative and musical relations comes
Bloom who is both participant and recalcitrant, insider and outsider of
the general tonal tendencies of his peers. Technically, Bloom seems to
have very good ears. He knows, for instance, that the piano "[s]ounds
better than last I heard. Tuned probably,"[49] and can even distinguish the
peculiarities of Cowley's touch at the piano: "Piano again. Cowley it is."
To a certain degree, he also shares in the interpretive leanings of those
around him. When Richie Goulding whistles "All is lost now," Bloom
recalls the story of the opera, *La Sonnambula*, from which it comes, and
then brings it into his own context: "Yes, I remember. Lovely air. In sleep
she went to him. Innocence in the moon." Soon, the public text takes on
a generalized significance in Bloom's reverie: "Still hold her back. Call
name. Touch water. Jingle jaunty. Too late. She longed to go. That's why.
Woman. As easy stop the sea. Yes: all is lost."

   From the particulars of the story, Bloom moves to generalizations
about "Woman." Differences seem to collapse as he identifies with the
tragic voice of Elvino: "– A beautiful air, said Bloom lost Leopold. I
know it well." We observe here an instance in which what is recalled by

the music, the story of *La Sonnambula*, and in particular, Elvino's misguided grief, becomes the signifier for a whole mythology of relentless "Woman," and "Man's" concomitant chagrin. As is usually the case with such mythologies, to quote Barthes again, "[t]he meaning is *already* complete, it postulates a kind of knowledge, a past, a memory, a comparative order of facts, ideas, decisions."[50] Bloom identifies with Elvino, and in doing so, he supplies himself with a certain "knowledge" of identity. Part of a song (a bit of melody, no words) fills in the blank, and the reconstructed subject becomes just another participant in the "eternal" struggle between "Man" and "Woman." This moment is an inversion of the audio-visuality of the shell, insofar as here Bloom seems to be *hearing* that which he cannot see; the "jingle jaunty" certainly suggests more than the sound of Boylan's carriage. The mythology of the eternal war between the sexes (a war in fact to which Bloom will never completely subscribe) affords Bloom at least a possible, and momentary, self-figuration.

Such stories of listening may be part of a more sublimated dimension of the heard. Joyce's intertext of song has been establishing all along a kind of semiconscious erotics of listening, or of the fetishism that is part of a certain kind of tonal expression. Joyce offers an examination of the heard and unheard, of the more or less conscious assumptions of interpretation, such as Bloom's, and, of the displaced hearing and interpreting which shadows the codes of the communal ear.

A moment where the communal unconscious is dramatically exposed occurs during Simon Dedalus' version of "When first I saw that form endearing." True to the ongoing process of displacement in the chapter, Simon sings the English version of an Italian translation from the German opera, *Martha*. The sensation of the music seems to bridge the differences in language as the song permeates the nervous systems of its ready listeners: "Braintipped, cheek touched with flame, they listened feeling that flow endearing flow over skin limbs heart soul spine." Body and soul, inside and outside become neatly identified in this language of sensation. Sound continues its inward translation as it quickly transforms into image: "Through the hush of air a voice sang to them . . . touching their still ears with words, still hearts of their each his remembered lives." Public and private distinctions break down as the "lovesoft oftloved word" offers its "mercy of beauty": "sorrow from them each seemed to from both depart when first they heard." Finally, it is not simply a voice, but, as Bloom identifies it, "Love that is singing" or the "Language of Love."

Beneath the euphemisms of the language of love, the voice becomes increasingly, and parodically, phallic ("Tenderness it welled: slow, swelling, full it throbbed . . . a pulsing proud erect),"[51] and its entrance into Bloom's ear is related in phrases suggestive of a kind of voyeuristic orgasmic pleasure:

> Bloom. Full of warm jamjam lickitup secretness flowed to flow in music out, in desire . . . Tipping her tepping her tapping her topping her. Tup . . . . Flood, gush, flow, joygush, tupthrob. Now! Language of love.[52]

Here again the description of the inwardness, as tawdry as it is, is presented less as imitation of the song, than as a visual description of affects amplified by the sounds of language which portray the somewhat less lovely dimensions of this "language of love." The lexical onomatopoeia forms its own linguistic rhythm ("Tipping her tepping her tapping her topping her. Tup . . ."; "Flood, gush, flow, joygush, tupthrob") which is extraneous to the music itself. It is as though at this communal moment of auditory collectivity, a linguistic rhythm sets up the visual properties of the affects, and in the transfer between the two sensory emphases, the void of a certain ideology behind the "language of love" makes an appearance as the song is heard. Just as Bloom knows what the silence of the shell exchanged between Douce and Lidwell *sounds* like, so too does the narrative voice here turn outward by means of visuality the interpretive moment of hearing. Whether or not we know what the song sounds like, we do "know" its meaning by virtue of the sonorous yet visual rendering of its affects.

We must also note, however, that the song, for all the humorously sexualized imagery here, is nevertheless effective; it "moves" the listeners, and in a very powerful manner. At the crescendo of the song comes an orgasmic fusion of the identities of Bloom, Dedalus, and Lionel, the forlorn speaker in the song:

> – *Come . . .*!
> It soared, a bird, it held its flight . . . soaring high, high resplendent, aflame, crowned, high in the effulgence symbolistic . . . everywhere
> all soaring all around about the all, the endlessnessnessness . . . . . .
> – *To me*!
> Siopold!
> Consumed.

Usually, this moment is seen as the place where Bloom takes over from Simon as the true father of Stephen. The idea is plausible if we hold to the symbolic and mythic ordering of the text, and to the idea of thematic recuperation and wholeness as they might surround the theme of paternity. But given the practice of synecdochic and metonymic part-making and substitution that is such a constant feature of "Sirens," it seems just as likely that there is "perhaps no meta-language – such as myth" which offers some totalizing way of recuperating the text. Rather, there may be only an "ironic, relativistic sense" of the possible ways narrative events may come to have meaning.[53] The narrative goes to great lengths to exploit the substitutional possibilities of language and narrative in order to make an analogy with the problematic nature of musical meaning. This process suggests that the nature of "meaning," be it musical, narrative, mythic (in the usual sense), or even paternal, may not be possible as a unity. Thus, the moment of ostensible union between listener, singer, and the figure in the song, may also be viewed as a moment of dispersion. The fusion of names must be seen within the context of the narrative tactic of phonemic recombination and intrusion that prevails in "Sirens," and of the dispersion of identities that goes along with such manipulations. The two-way movement of the word "Siopold" makes it a signifier of desire. At one moment it is part of a whole homo-erotic iconographic union which seems to disparage conventional sexual mythologies. At the same time, as a recombination of phonemic elements, it seems to block out the very sounds of the song that it represents. The moment of the "loss" of the song, may well be the sign of the song *as* loss, a place where even the conventional codes of hearing may founder under the weight of unknown desire. As Arthur Nestrovski suggests, "[t]he threat of song is the threat of forgetfulness," and further, "[t]he moment of thrust is the moment of delusion – not vision, not satori, but rather alienation." The place of textual melodic coming may be one of dissolution, not – or not only – of the symbolic passing on of paternity. The unsteady "Siopold" coming at the crescendo of the song, again serves to remind us of the potential ambiguity and concreteness that may be shared by both music and Joyce's narrative form: we may not doubt the presence of a signifier, but there is perhaps no single or secure way to understand what it means.

From this point on, Bloom seems to shift away from his position as an indifferent listener, and begins to reassert the arc of his peculiarly discerning mind. In the wake of Dedalus' song, Bloom marvels at the "human voice, two tiny silky chords, wonderful, more than all others." The silent aural pun on "chords" nicely suggests a kind of space in the production of vocal music: vocal pitch is created in the space between vibrating vocal cords; chords are created by the intervals between simultaneously sounded pitches. Bloom notes the presence and absence aspect of vocal music in terms of the song he has just heard: "That voice was a lamentation. Calmer now. It's in the silence after you feel you hear. Vibrations. Now silent air."[54] Bloom is here working backward from conventional figurations of the heard voice (here as "lamentation") toward the problems of the doubleness of hearing ("in the silence after you feel you hear") and of the voice as the figure of both silence and sound ("Vibrations. Now silent air").

Bloom seeks his own metalanguage in order to explain the way music works:

Numbers it is. All music when you come to think. Two multiplied by two divided by half is twice one. Vibrations: chords, those are . . . Do anything you like with figures juggling. Always find out this equal to that. Symmetry under a cemetery wall . . . And you think you're listening to the ethereal. But suppose you said it like: Martha, seven times nine minus x is thirtyfive thousand. Fall quite flat.

The numerical metalanguage fails because the precision of its schema correlates numbers and sounds without difference. What the body hears is not numbers; the difference is "on account of the sound." But even the sound offers no particular security: "Instance, he's playing now. Improvising. Might be what you like . . ." Bloom knows too that once "you hear the words," a certain supplementary situation occurs, that from the moment of this addition, music does not "mean what you like," but instead, becomes part of the codes of hearing and expressing: of love, of war, of "flow," or of "Thou lost one. All songs on that theme."[55]

But, of course, music, even with words, can offer no guarantee of its meaning, since words also have their sonorous and deceptive shapes. Much of Bloom's meditation on music takes place while he writes to Martha Clifford. Here, the expression of his "naughty" desires is given vent under the concealing and revealing pseudonym of Henry Flower. The narrative, continuing its method of writing the inside and the outside of Bloom, offers an appropriate sense of the doubleness of his writing. Bloom is, of course, very interested in concealment ("Remember write Greek ees") at the same time as he is trying to express a camouflaged prurience: "Why do you call me naught? You naughty too?" The narrative locates the reader on the borderline between Bloom's concealing and revealing inscription and his thoughts which are themselves working on multiple levels: "my poor little press: p.o. two and six. Write me a long. Do you despise? Jingle, have you the? So excited." The synecdochic sound of Boylan's intrusion, aside from functioning as a sign of Bloom's repression of events elsewhere, again links the issue of writing and music, at least as it is presented in "Sirens," as arts of substitution and dispersion.

Bloom's thoughts about music blend into the context of his writing. As he adds the postscript to his letter ("P.S. The rum tum tum. How will you pun? You punish me?"), he notices that Cowley's improvisation "[t]rails off sad there in minor" and wonders "[w]hy minor sad?" Fittingly, he decides that "[t]hey like sad tail at end," and adds, "P.P.S. La la la ree. I feel so sad today. La ree. So lonely. Dee." Under the influence of the sad–minor convention, Bloom shapes the "tail" of his letter, with a pun also shaping the literal and figurative aspects of his conclusion. But Bloom moves outside of conventional codes as he completes his self-inscription, and, in characteristically oblique fashion, implicitly indicts the mythologies of meaning that surround both music and writing:

Too poetical that about the sad. Music did that. Music hath charms. Shakespeare said. Quotations every day of the year. To be or not to be. Wisdom while you wait.

Bloom, as insider and outsider, is himself in a kind of double posture of blindness and insight.[56] At one moment he sees through the conventional wisdoms of hearing and seeing, the next he is drawn in by them. At one moment he sees the desire beneath the heard, as when he watches Lidwell and Douce exchange the auditory inwardness of the seashell. But during Dollard's "heroticized" version of "The Croppy Boy," as sexual excitement ("On the smooth jutting beerpull laid Lydia hand. . . . Fro, to: to, fro") colors nostalgic martyr-worship ("Thrill now . . . To wipe away a tear for martyrs that want to, dying to, die"), Bloom seems unable to recognize his own desire. He gazes at miss Douce with the hope of contact through a "Song without words": "Say something. Make her hear. With look to look." But, like one with an ear to the shell, Bloom finally realizes that it is only a reflection of his own desire that he feels he sees: "Ha. Lidwell. For him then not for. Infatuated. I like that?"

Bloom decides to "[g]et out before the end," surviving, though not unscathed. He seems to pass safely "[b]y rose, by satiny bosom, by the fondling hand, by slops, by empties, by popped corks . . .," away from the particular conventions of musical meaning used by those in the bar where "[t]hinking [is] strictly prohibited." But he leaves with the shards of his identities, amidst the parts that have adumbrated him and dispersed him; in short, he leaves as a figure of self-division:

Up the quay went Lionelleopold, naughty Henry with letter for Mady, with sweets of sin with frillies for Raoul with met him pike hoses went Poldy on.

Those he has left behind receive similar fragmentary recapitulation in a parodic cadence: "before bronze Lydia's tempting last rose of summer, rose of Castile. First Lid, De, Cow, Ker, Doll, a fifth,"[57] and as well, the blind stripling enters who, with his perfect ears and blind eyes, perhaps stands as an emblem of the presence and absence procedure of the chapter: "He saw not bronze. He saw not gold. . . . Hee hee hee hee. He did not see," and too, of Bloom's own partial perfections of hearing, as well as seeing what goes on in the bar, and *not* seeing what is happening elsewhere.

But it is Bloom, or Bloom's body, that makes the final combination of "air and words." Even here, as the last words of Robert Emmet blend with Bloom's other voice, the procedure of linguistic and sonic interruption is maintained. The words speak of a time and place of written fulfillment: "*When my country takes her place among . . . Nations of the earth . . . Let my epitaph be . . . Written.*" Bloom's music, however, speaks of more immediate needs: "Prrprr. / Must be the bur. / Fff! Oo. Rrpr. / . . . Pprrpffrrppffff." Air passes, the odour of nostalgic martyr-worship, perhaps not. And in this last parodic moment of phonemic recombination, where cultural codes and need, if not desire, clash, nothing is finished, nothing is "*Done.*"[58] The performance and critique simply stop under a guise of finality. The end is in a different place.

CHAPTER FIVE

Gertrude Stein and her saints

Gertrude Stein, perhaps more than any other early twentieth-century writer, is most often associated with the visual arts, not those of music. If one knows little else about Stein, one is sure to have heard of her connection with Picasso especially, if not with Matisse, Gris, Braque and others. The analogy between her work and cubism is one fostered by Stein herself (in *Picasso*, for example) and extensively elaborated by critics. There is also Stein's own peculiar kind of literary portraiture which comprises a significant facet of her ongoing exploration of writing. But this exploration also includes – though with little regard for traditional definitions – experiments in the various genres of poetry, prose, drama, lecture, and opera. This last category seems to be conceived with little specific attention to its musical component. As Jane Bowers points out, Stein made few distinctions between her operas and her plays when discussing them. Indeed, in Stein's own estimation, "music was made for adolescents and not for adults," and her early experience in listening to opera seems merely to have been a phase through which she passed on her way to a fuller knowledge of drama.[1] Unlike Pound, then, for whom the idea of music held a significant place within his thinking on art and knowledge, Stein's regard for music, and its position within the parameters of her artistic concerns, seems to be of little import. Nevertheless, throughout her working life Stein would come back to opera, and her operas remain among her best known works. Stein's apparent indifference toward music did not deter musicians from being drawn to her writing.

Recent feminist interpretations of Stein's writing might supply a partial explanation for the attractions that Stein's difficult language holds for music. Critics such as Lisa Ruddick, Harriet Scott Chessman, and especially Marianne DeKoven, among others, have reread Stein within the context of poststructuralism and French feminism.[2] In various ways they see Stein's writing as participating in (and anticipating) the rhythms and "musicality" of a semiotic, or preoedipal resistance to patriarchal/symbolic language. Keeping in mind the notion of Stein's writing as a kind of *écriture féminine* is useful. I take for granted in what follows that Stein's work is indeed anti-patriarchal especially in the sense that it refuses culturally established procedures of meaning, and it does so in ways that most of her contemporaries would not have conceived (I refer here to Stein's almost complete dismissal not only of readily available methods of symbolization and allusion, but also of the modernist practices of acquiring eccentric aesthetic precursors, intertexts, and concomitant allusive procedures). Having said this, however, I maintain that the notion of the semiotic or preoedipal will not be entirely sufficient to describe what happens when Stein's language meets music *in fact*. The tonal tradition of Western music has its own history of meaning, its own rules of coherence and expression, however mutable and much debated these may be, which defines it in terms rather different from the notion of "music" in Kristeva's sense. The music that Virgil Thomson wrote for *Four Saints* is very tonal, and as such participates in the traditions of Western harmonic coherence. If anything, Thomson's music in *Four Saints* resists the experimentalism and dissolution of tonality with which so many composers of the early part of the century were involved. Stein's language may resist patriarchal hierarchy, but Thomson's music may not, at least not in any obvious formal way. We would be wrong to assume, however, that Thomson merely capitulates to the traditional discourses of musical composition; his deep admiration for Stein's language and her practice of writing, indeed, his deep *understanding* of her practice – so clear in the composition of *Four Saints* – marks Thomson as perhaps a truly unique practitioner of tonality especially when writing for Stein's language. Part of my interest is precisely in the ironic dissonance in the relations between the music and the language of *Four Saints*.

Such a doubleness in the opera finds a literary critical homology in some recent criticism on Stein. Many – and I count myself among them – feel the need to negotiate some critical path between the playfulness and mobility of Stein's language, and the potential for meaning which often seems present in her work, if at the same time not quite within reach. Searching out the possible autobiographical and/or homoerotic details of the writing, or maintaining the polysemousness of Stein's texts are two fruitful, at times diverging and at others overlapping, means of reading Stein. My own contention is similar to Jayne L. Walker's idea that Stein's work is mimetic finally of the "unbreachable gulf that separates the chaotic plenitude of the sensory world from the arbitrary order of language." I would contend, though, that however distant and uncertain the gulf between the sensory and the linguistic may be for Stein, there is also, as I will show in a moment, a crucial and unavoidable connection between language and the world, an interpenetration of fundamental importance. In Stein's remarkable *Tender Buttons* (1910–12) we are given the directive to "[a]ct so that there is no use in a centre" which seems to suggest the possibility that, to a certain extent, language is the creator of its own time and space. Stein's attempt to reconcile the "chaotic plenitude of the sensory world" with the "arbitrary order of language" might remind us of Pater's difficulties in the Conclusion to *The Renaissance*, where the problem of bridging the sensory and the subjective remains a dominant concern. Stein's resolution to epistemological difficulties is at least in part, aesthetic, as it was for Pater. But her most difficult work, including *Four Saints*, is not only a demonstration of the difference between language and a chaotic sensory plenitude, it is also a delineation of a possible – and impossible – interface between the two. As one critic puts it, with reference to *Tender Buttons*, "[e]verything stands apart as well as in relation."[3] But such a static undecidability can only be established by temporality; only time can create the space for such separation and connection. For Stein, as I will try to show in the discussion of "Composition as Explanation" below, the creation of the work – here an opera – is part of the creation of the world, of the space of time, and the time of space.

The interesting question, then, in terms of approaching *Four Saints in Three Acts*, has less to do with the issue of "why opera?" than the question of "*how* opera?" It is important to remember that the majority of Stein's operas exist as texts to be read, without obvious or easy translation into the space of performance. Some, however, such as *Four Saints* and *The Mother of Us All* (1945–46), were intended to be performed. The text-operas and the libretti are not radically different in character; the major difference between works has more to do with Stein's own writerly preoccupations at the time of composition than any specific generic distinctions. The problems of knowledge and writing are of course central to Stein's notion of the continuous present, and to her conception of drama as "landscape." What I want to do here is refocus these ideas onto the specific territory of *Four Saints in Three Acts*.

Stein's particular designation of "opera" to certain of her writings is a request to consider them as a particular form of "writing after otherness." By borrowing Pater's phrase I mean to indicate that though the claim of "operaness" is not enough to make a certain writing an opera

– or even operatic – it does serve a kind of ludic notice about the generic status of the text. While I do not want to enter into the whole debate about the issues of genre and textuality, I do however wish to signal that I take Stein's own specific generic designations as both playful and earnestly interrogative.[4] The sign "opera" seems tacitly to ask *why not* opera? Why not an implicit allusion to that which writing cannot contain (music) and which was never part of the text in the first place? One can respond by saying that Stein could have been referring to the "music" of language, to its own specific sonority of internal or even objective performance. This is possible, but it does not explain the similarities in uses of language and syntax between works variously designated as poems, plays, prose works, or portraits. The full title of the opera I am considering here is *Four Saints in Three Acts: an Opera to Be Sung*; only the directive of the title marks the writing that follows in any distinctive way as a particular *kind* of writing.

Stein's language, both in her text-operas and in *Four Saints*, defeats easy generic categorization partly because it always seems to contain and inscribe a striving after otherness, though not in any obvious Paterian sense. Her work attempts neither a kind of imagistic representation of the "thing" (though a definite sense of the concreteness of language pervades her writing), nor the melopoaeic sonority in which subject matter and sound are reconciled. The language of *Four Saints in Three Acts* constitutes an interrogation into the possibility of "making" with language – in this case the possibility of making an opera libretto. A good many of Stein's own theoretical concerns about writing come to bear here. *Four Saints* recapitulates the problems of time, space, and knowledge which concerned her throughout her career. For Stein, the exploration of these issues is one of the characteristic features of modernity, or "the inevitable problem of anybody living in the composition of the present time."[5] Before entering into a discussion of the opera itself, then, I want first to focus upon some of Stein's own ideas concerning composition, presence, and time.

OPERA AND THE COMPOSITION OF LOST CAUSES

"Composition as Explanation" (1926) was written a year before the libretto of *Four Saints in Three Acts* (1927) and can be useful for giving the opera some context. The lecture appears about midway in Stein's career and is one of her earliest and most interesting attempts to explain her work within the context of *its* own time: that is, in terms of its relation

to temporality, if not explicitly to its historical context. The emphasis of
the piece is not upon an abstract concern with the notion of a literary
tradition or past to which the contemporary writer must respond or try
to transform (as, say, in Eliot's view); rather, Stein's emphasis is doubly
focused upon the issue of literary change, or the appearance of what will
become the "new," and also upon the complex issues of writing's relationship to time. The two themes are locked in a paradoxical connection
which the opening moves of the piece outline:

> There is singularly nothing that makes a difference a difference in beginning
> and in the middle and in ending except that each generation has something
> different at which they are looking. By this I mean simply . . . that composition
> is the difference which makes each and all of them then different from other
> generations and this is what makes everything different otherwise they are all
> alike . . .

Stein's statements in the passage above are complicated, first of all, by a
certain pronominal ambiguity.[6] The singular "generation" becomes
divided into "they," and "all of them." The phrase, "each and all of
them" could refer to the "they" of the now multiplied "generation," or
it could be consistent with the later reference to the many "other generations." Implicitly, Stein seems to be indicating that the "past" is no
single or easily identifiable place, and possesses none of the possibilities
for a straightforward narrative of "beginning," "middle," or "ending."

The play with pronouns is small but consistent with, and constructive
of, Stein's ambiguous method throughout the lecture of making an
assertion and then qualifying it to the point of doubt. Such moments
create a kind of two-way rhetorical procedure in which claim and
counterclaim seem to occupy the same instant. The first clause in the
passage subtly links the idea of linear *textual* progression ("beginning . . .
in the middle and in ending") with that of the *historical* progression of
generations. But the very idea of "progression," textual or historical,
remains somehow in question. The opening sentence asserts that there
is "singularly nothing that makes a difference" in this historical and
textual movement except "composition." But as Stein will point out a
few sentences later, composition itself depends on "what is seen and
what is seen depends upon how everybody is doing everything." Seeing
and composing are simultaneous acts, neither of which is able to claim
an anterior time. Part of what "everybody" is doing is, of course, making
compositions, and "[t]his makes the thing we are looking at very different and this makes what those describe make of it, it makes a composition, it confuses, it shows, it is, it looks, it likes it as it is, and this makes

what is seen as it is seen." It is not simply that "things" are looked at differently from generation to generation, but that they are made differently within the act of looking itself. From an ostensibly transhistorical assumption that "[n]othing changes from generation to generation," we arrive at a place where it seems that everything is open to change across time, a place where "everything" is subject to the "composition" of "the thing seen."[7] The "seen" both is and is not the source of difference; what is composed relies upon and creates what is seen. The link between perceptual knowledge and temporality outlined here becomes further entwined with the problems of art and historical change later when Stein begins to describe her own notion of the "continuous present."

The paradox in Stein's theoretical work, as Marianne DeKoven points out, is that "literature must be absolutely pure, . . . but at the same time it must express and create its time . . . It must both renounce the world and embody the deepest nature, the essence of its cultural moment." Elsewhere, however, Stein complicates the issue even further. In *Picasso* (1938), for instance, Stein makes it clear that the word "composition" refers not only to painting or writing (art works), but to anything done within a certain historical moment which effectively *composes* that moment. Stein in fact explicitly links the issue of composition to history:

Really the composition of this war, 1914–1918, was not the composition of all previous wars, the composition was not a composition in which there was one man in the centre surrounded by a lot of other men but a composition that had neither a beginning nor an end, a composition of which one corner was as important as another corner, in fact the composition of cubism.

Less dramatically than Great Wars and Cubism, however, Stein maintains that

people remain the same, the way the frequented roads are frequented is what changes from one century to another and it is that that makes the composition that is before the eyes of everyone of that generation and it is that that makes the composition that a creator creates.[8]

Wars and local roads, cubism and "generations"; clearly this is not just (or only) the birth of yet another formalist or *art pour l'art* scheme. Instead of the call for a radical break with the past we are quietly turned toward the making of the present in its small- and large-scale particularity and concreteness. If art must remain "pure" then its purity is based upon a separation from the common conceptions of causal relations, the narrativity that presumes a timely explanation. At the same time, however, the composition of art is of a piece with the composition of the daily, the ordinary, especially as these relate to, and come to constitute time itself. This is perhaps an artist's view of history, where art and "the world" become so conflated as to be indistinguishable. Still, to so dislodge both art and history from the discourses of causality and progression is to move the discussion implicitly onto epistemological grounds. For Stein seems to be inquiring as to how any "one" can *know* when and by what means change or progression occurs. It is not that history or change more generally do not exist; Stein is by no means entering upon some elitist program of the removal of art from time and history. On the contrary. She is in fact launching a penetrating critique of knowledge which she believes can never be coeval with the "thing" that is known. "Knowledge," as causality, always comes after the fact, and the discourses which perpetuate it may not, as Stein knew, be innocent, and are for her, rarely helpful.[9] The idea of "composition" is in fact Stein's attempt to substitute temporality for history and the discourses of continuity. As such, Stein's notion of composition, then, sounds very much like a kind of phenomenological reduction but without a final transcendental recuperation. "Knowing" remains at the perceptual level without the imposition or assumption of an ultimate essence – unless "essence" can be thought as necessarily including temporality, which, for Stein apparently, it must.

What is at stake in *Picasso*, in "Composition," and in Stein's concepts of the continuous present and landscape, as these notions concern *Four Saints* is nothing less than an inquiry into knowledge as a perceptual problematic in which temporality itself always remains crucial. If Stein seems to skew her focus away from history it may be because she is trying to slip the forms of history, the "essential" stories of causality and knowledge which, for her, may preclude the immediacy of knowing itself. One critic has suggested, with particular reference to *Four Saints* that "[t]his is art without history. Immediacy lacks the vertical dimension. Elements occur 'one at a time' as the mind focuses on them." If the opera, and perhaps much of Stein's writing, lacks "history" (you do not have to know anything about these saints to hear the opera, nor in listening will you learn much about them), it is nevertheless *making* time, and happening in space. What *Four Saints* does – and what "Composition as Explanation" explains and performs – is to mark the composition as the *making* of both space and time, *and* to represent this very process.

In "Composition as Explanation," "composition" does seem to be primarily focused on the literary, though the expanded sense of the term that I have been outlining can be inferred in many places. Stein is inquiring into the means by which writing can lead us into an exploration of the sensory and perceptual. Stein's examination is immensely complex since it requires the maintenance of the possibility of meaning, the sustaining of coherence. But this possibility must remain secondary to the fitful dispensations of a writing which always interferes with itself. Stein writes against the line, against the inherent "meaning" of progression and continuity as these are either depicted in the narrative unfolding of a causal chain of events or in a language whose syntagmatic operations play against their own rules.[10] In other words, Stein's language maintains a double sense of instrumentality (as something functioning in the possiblity of a meaning beyond itself) and as a phenomenon in itself, as its own field of perceptual confrontation.

From the complex beginnings of "Composition as Explanation" the piece proceeds to a general discussion of the idea of change in art then moves to a discussion of Stein's own compositions. The quality that joins these two parts of her discussion is the lost sense of causality that constitutes both historical and artistic change. Progression and development are secondary to contiguity, to a succession of appearances that comprise the endless isolated compositions of the "new." Indeed, progression and development seem to be ideas that only a present looking backward imposes upon the past: "[t]hose who are creating the modern composition authentically are naturally only of importance when they are dead because by that time the modern composition having become past is classified and the description of it is classical." Classification and classicalization seem to be functions of history; but the change involved in the acceptance of the new work also occurs without apparent reason: "[f]or a very long time everybody refuses and then almost without a pause almost everybody accepts." The acceptance of the work as "classic" involves a recognition of its beauty, but beauty here is never defined, perhaps because it is not some timeless quality "now" discovered to be intrinsic to the work, but instead, a *timely* quality which in a sense composes the time of its recognition: "[a]utomatically with the acceptance of the time sense comes the recognition of the beauty and once the beauty is accepted the beauty never fails anyone." Beauty is the mark of acceptance, of an imposed timelessness which the work will now carry into its future, and which the composition is also in part responsible for creating. A sense of cause and effect, or of progression in the history of art, gives way to a series of appearances or eruptions which compose the time of recognition itself: "Beginning again and again is natural even when there is a series."[11]

Stein does begin again by further linking and complicating the issues of composition and temporality. She points out that "[e]verything is the same except composition and as composition is different and always going to be different everything is not the same. Everything is not the same as the time when of the composition and the time in the composition is different." But, "[t]he time when and the time of and the time in that composition is the natural phenomena of that composition . . ." Everything is the same, except nothing is the same – and this is "natural." The quality of this naturalness seems somehow to reside in the composition as the site of conflicting temporal qualities. Stein is attempting to reconcile the temporal differentiation that occurs within any text in terms of represented time and the time of the actual composition, as well as the problem of a future present which will be forced to deal with the past presentness of the text. These issues will return again at the end of the piece, but at this moment Stein is still primarily concerned with how the composition constructs its own time. She says that "any one creating the composition in the arts does not know it . . . they are conducting life and that makes their composition what it is . . ." At the same time, though, the "[c]omposition is not there, it is going to be there and we are here. This is some time ago for us naturally." In this description of the composition, and implicitly, of living as a kind of future pastness of the present which is yet to be, Stein marks the composition as a kind of temporal intersection. "Nobody knows" that they are making the composition which makes the present, or the "composition of the time in which they are living."[12] The present is elusive, yet structured in the process of composition even while the composition of the present bears the mark of a temporal disjunction since it is only recognized in the future, when it is already passed. Thus, the composition is not "there" since we are "here," in it, but this can only be recognized later, when "there" and "here" are already "some time ago."

The effect of this temporal instability is to dislocate the composition, and the present, from any sense of strict continuity, and at the same time, to join the artistic composition implicitly *with* the present, the "time in which [one is] living." As Stein notes elsewhere, the purpose of most of her work is to disentangle herself from the "inevitable narrative" of cause and effect. The causal necessities of story-telling give way to a coincidence between the temporality (or temporalities) of composition and the "living" which is going on and being created by the composition at the same time. The relationship between the *when, of,* or *in* of the composition of the present does not allow for the making of a narrative beginning, middle, and ending. The emphasis now comes to be on the composition as a matrix of temporal intersections.

What is crucial here, especially for a consideration of *Four Saints*, is precisely the idea that the composition creates its own time and space. As I will demonstrate a little later, the method of the libretto enacts the procedure of creating *now* the opera which will occupy some future present. Such a futurity is put off, however, by the continuous present which defines the operatic space by challenging the very idea of future continuity in the present of its making. This present also founds the performance space in its own temporal dislocation, in a liminality which, as we will see, constitutes the space of the opera itself.

Stein remarks at the end of "Composition as Explanation" that, in fact, one of the great dangers of composition is the very presentness of the present which it creates: "Now there is still something else the time-sense in the composition . . . The quality in the expression the quality in a composition that makes it go dead just after it has been made is very troublesome." The problem lies not so much in the time described in the composition, though this may also be an issue; but even "if there is no time at all in the composition there must be time in the composition which is in its quality of distribution and equilibration." "Distribution" and "equilibration" seem to refer to the method of the writing, apart from any referential qualities it may have. A composition always "comes now"[13] no matter when or how it may have been made. But such a nowness is, we must assume, part of the composition's own making, and it is this very presentness which seems to endanger the longevity of the work. Stein speaks to this problem with the ideas of distribution and equilibration, but these ideas remain rather obscure; she claims that the idea of distribution refers to "expression and time," and that "composition is time." Though time is the essence of composition it seems necessary to translate equilibration and distribution in a particularly spatial way. Clearly, Stein recognizes that temporality is both a problem, *and* a solution: it simultaneously poses the largest difficulties (those of memory and causal succession – cultural, personal, aesthetic conventions of continuity, the bane of composition) and the clearest opportunities for her own work, since opposing common conceptions of temporality will constitute in various forms the "composition" of her own techniques. This difficult struggle with temporality lies beneath Stein's attempt to develop the "continuous present."

Stein addresses the complexities of time and composition with reference to her own methods:

In my beginning it was a continuous present a beginning again and again and again and again, it was a series it was a list it was similarity and everything different it was a distribution and an equilibration. That is all of the time some of the time of the composition.[14]

What lies behind this list, especially as it is articulated in Stein's famous notion of the "continuous present," is a kind of spatial–temporal reconciliation which is meant to overcome the issues of narrative continuity. In describing her own early work, *Melanctha*, Stein states that she "created . . . a prolonged present naturally I knew nothing of a continuous present but it came naturally to me to make one." It came "naturally" because the composition forming around her was a prolonged present.

   The distinctive quality of the continuous present resides chiefly in its sense of the relationship between time and knowledge, a quality which Stein articulates when she speaks elsewhere about the difference between repetition and insistence:

. . . repetition that is if you like the repeating that is the same thing, but once started expressing this thing, expressing any thing there can be no repetition because the essence of that expression is insistence, and if you insist you must each time use emphasis and if you use emphasis it is not possible while anybody is alive that they should use exactly the same emphasis.

"Insistence," as Stein uses the term here, is meant to define a new focus on a coincidence of time as it is both represented *in* the composition and experienced by the reader *of* the composition.

   The attention on the now-ness of writing, upon the coordination of temporal discrepancies, is part of Stein's conception of art as "entity," an idea most thoroughly elaborated in *The Geographical History of America, or The Relation of Human Nature to the Human Mind* (1935). Here, Stein works out a crucial distinction between human nature and the human mind. In Stein's terms, human nature is related to linear time, to a sense of audience, to memory and identity. It is human nature which constructs the self as social: "Now identity remembers and so it has an audience and as it has an audience it is history and as it is history it has nothing to do with the human mind."[15] The human mind, by contrast, "cannot does not look forward and remember . . .," for the human mind "has to say what anything is now." Writing, in Stein's sense of the composition, is the particular provenance of the human mind: ". . . the writing that is the human mind does not consist in messages or in events it consists only in writing down what is written . . ." Writing which has to do with "events" is "connected with human nature," and therefore "has to be written over."

The human nature/human mind division is not reducible to a simple opposition between the timelessness of art and the mundanity of history. It is, again, a refocusing of the issue of composition as part of the very production of time and space. As Stein says in *Geographical History*, using a geographical–temporal metaphor, ". . . land connected with the human mind [is] only flat land a great deal of flat land is connected with the human mind, I can say so but what I do is to write it so." America is a kind of quintessential modern space for Stein, a land without (to mix metaphors appropriately) the depths of a past, a space–time matrix in which progression gives way to the immediacy of perception, to a means of apprehension in which Stein "trie[s] not to capture the world and its relations (what it means, how it progresses) but the world in itself . . . moment by moment."[16] The "world in itself," however, as Stein knew, may not be enirely knowable, at least in any final or essential fashion. This is especially so since clearly for Stein the notion of "essence," or of "the world in itself" must include temporality, and thus, the very idea of "knowing" cannot be achieved in some synchronic way. The idea of the continuous present, like the related issues of composition and entity, implies that there is a tension between the "now" and the way in which several "nows" might be brought into relation.

WHAT'S OPERA GOT TO DO WITH IT; OR, OF DRAMA, LANDSCAPE, AND SAINTS.

Such a tension is crucial to Stein's conception of writing, and especially to her dramatic writing, as "landscape." The idea is one which Stein applies specifically to drama with a special emphasis on *Four Saints*. Stein claims that her plays are a natural extension of her portraits. Anything that "was not a story could be a play," and just as is the case in Stein's portraits, the essence of the play is "to express this thing each one being that one and there being a number of them knowing each other . . ." The idea is to "express this without telling what happened in short to make a play the essence of what happened." Such a telling without telling stems from a desire to "say what you nor I nor nobody knows but what is really what you and I and everybody knows . . . everybody hears stories but the things that make each one what he is is not that." Early plays, such as *What Happened: A Play in Five Acts*, (1913) or "Ladies Voices," (1916) have much in common with the selective and combinative procedures of

Tender Buttons. The grammar and syntax are generally regular, but the selection of elements that fill grammatical places is incongruous:

Length, what is length when silence is so windowful. What is the use of a sore if there is no joint and no toady and no tag and not even an eraser. What is the commonest exchange between laughing and most.[17]

There is also a new element of dialogue that appears in many of the plays which seems to accord with Stein's sense of interaction between portrait figures as "ones"; but such dialogues remain in an undefined space and time:

Act II
Honest to God Mrs. Williams I don't mean to say that I was older.
But you were.
Yes I was I do not excuse myself. I feel that there is no reason for passing an
    archduke.
You like the word.
You know very well that they all call it their house.

The vaguely situated and unassigned speeches, and the establishing of concrete references without context are methods which appear later on in *Four Saints in Three Acts.*

What is remarkable in these plays, and in *Tender Buttons* as well, is the impression that knowledge is not entirely representable. In drama, as in other dimensions of her work, Stein is concerned with eliminating the different temporalities between the audience and the play they are potentially to witness. Ordinarily, there is a "syncopation" between the "emotional time of the play" and that of the audience. The result is "nervousness"; the two temporal dimensions "do not progress together." Note that the imperative of crisis here is set in terms of interiority; but it is a *perceptual* interiority only, not that of a referential or symbolic or otherwise "meaningful" inside, a point which is emphasized in the essay when Stein inquires if "the hearing replace[s] the seeing or does the seeing replace the hearing. Or do they go together." The sensory or perceptual is, in a way, far more important than any definition or necessity of meaning that interiority could supply. In "Plays," Stein suggests that knowledge is itself a kind of enigma which seems beyond explanation or representation. Knowledge is "what you do know." But what you do know rarely seems out of sensory range, even if the poem or play is not presenting the "'thing'" with attention to any language of description. In Stein's view, plays, since they are at least ideally present before an audience, preclude the possibility of getting acquainted with the characters over time as one gets to know people in ordinary life or the "double time" of the novel.[18] In novels that tell stories there is always the discrepancy between the present of the telling and the time, usually the past, of the story's action. It is precisely the double time of story which Stein means to lose in her notion of theatre. For it is the immediate without extension which comprises the play in Stein's terms; the immediacy of the perceptual is emotion. This conflation is implicit in Stein's turn toward the cinema for an analogy with her own solution to the problem of "sight and sound and its relation to emotion and time, rather than in relation to story and action." The cinema offers a particularly contemporary example of such a solution in its own changes "from sight to sound": "and how much before there was real sound how much of the sight was sound or how much of it was not."

Questions about the relations between seeing and hearing in theatre or, analogously, sight and sound in film, demonstrate Stein's focus upon the perceptual immediacy of aesthetic experience. However, unlike Pound, Stein does not confound the "thing-in-itself" with the poem in some kind of absolute continuity between writing and world. Rather, for her, the emphasis on art's materiality serves to focus attention on the immediacy of the composition as a *potential interface* with the world, upon the stature of its ordinariness, and also upon its capacity to compose the world in its very immediacy. As Stein puts it, with specific reference to "Composition as Explanation," "The business of Art . . . is to live in the actual present that is the complete actual present, and to completely express that complete actual present."[19] Inside and outside, in a sense, become equivalent, not in the loss of the self *within* truth, but in the limitation to the writing of the perceptual *as* "truth." The being of the "thing" is its specificity as it is produced – and deflected – in the text itself.

It is precisely such a material conception of the theatre's language, and of language in general, that underlies Stein's notion of "landscape." Stein's statement of the idea in "Plays" recalls the sense of "equilibration" and "distribution" which she raises in "Composition as Explanation" and is clearly a way of adjusting the temporal disparities of theatre in terms of the immediacy of writing. Stein claims that a "landscape . . . [is] a thing, [and] a play . . . [is] a thing," and, further, that

if a play was exactly like a landscape then there would be no difficulty about the emotion of the person looking on at the play being behind or ahead of the play because the landscape does not have to make acquaintance. You may have to make acquaintance with it, but it does not with you, it is there and so the play being written the relation between you at any time is so exactly that that it is of no importance unless you look at it.[20]

The art-object is given the same status as the supposedly natural object. But at the same time, by referring to the natural world in terms of the painterly language of "landscape," Stein complicates the priorities of the "real." The act of calling both landscape and play "things" implicitly emphasizes the phenomenal nature of both and blurs the ontological priority of one over the other. The equivalence between the "thing" of writing and playing and the "thing" of nature relies most emphatically upon perceptual apprehension. The time of perceiving rests upon no causal foundation other than that which the viewing subject allows for the witnessing of the thing. Unlike Pound then, who sought for an image or vortex in poetry that could be both concrete *and* ripe with immanent meaning, Stein's interrelating of writing and perception asks no more than the recognition of immediacy. The Steinian image does not lead us to greater realms of significance or deeper levels of connection than are offered at any moment in the temporal experience of the viewer.

Stein, in her lecture, "Plays," quotes extensively from *Operas and Plays* in order to demonstrate just how little "acquaintance" is necessary for the viewer of the landscape play. One citation is from *A List* (1923) which displays the use of the line worked rhythmically through several variations and combinations:

Maryas. Accidentally in the morning and after
      that every evening and accidentally every
      evening and after that every morning and after
      that accidentally every morning and after that
      accidentally and after that every morning.

The cycle of day and night seems reduced to chance, having no longer any symbolic or even "natural" reason for its movement. In a similar way descriptions which appear to approach a more conventional narrative function occur but are given no justification within a story, or dramatic moment. In many cases the moment of description seems designed to invite the expectation of continuity only to abandon it:

Maryas. If five are seated at a table and there is
      bread on it and there are pomegranates on it and
      one of the five is leaning on the table it does
      not make any difference.[21]

Such descriptions have a kind of meta-dramatic quality to them; it is as though they describe dramatic possibilities which are almost brought into being but which never appear. The language suggests them, but simultaneously makes them disappear. This technique, as we will see, is fundamental to the workings of *Four Saints*. The same process of writing the possible scene can also be observed in *Say It With Flowers* (1931) where we read under the heading "Scenery," apparently before the play begins:

The home where they were waiting for William Long
to ask them to come along and ask them not to be
waiting for them.
Will they be asleep while they are waiting.
They will be pleased with everything.
What is everything.
A hyacinth is everything.
Will they be sleeping while they are
waiting for everything.[22]

Here, and in many of Stein's plays, the lines of dialogue seem to be written in response to one another; there is a sense of possible interaction between statements, but it rarely leads to a sustained or ordinary development. Often, words or ideas are picked up and played upon, sometimes with interesting inexplicit thematic possibilities, such as we see above with the idea of "everything," or, again, with the notion of "twins" in *Photograph* (1920):

Twins.
There is a prejudice about twins.
Twins are one. Does this mean as they separate as they
are separate or together.
Let me hear the story of the twin. So we begin.
                    Photograph.
The sub title. Twin.
Two a twin. – Step in.
Margot. – Not a twin.
Lilacs. – For a twin.

There is the tantalizing possibility of a thematics of twinning somehow related to the photograph, but it is sidetracked into an almost childlike play with language. The possibility of "Margot" or "Lilacs" being photographs with the respective "sub title[s]," "Not a twin" and "For a twin" are potential connections which cannot be solidly ascertained. In a slightly different way we have, as I mentioned earlier in regard to *Tender Buttons*, another instance of semantic inequivalence.

The problem of identity, implicit here in the adjacency of photographs and twins, is also apparent in Stein's play with names. Often names are doubled, or even doubly gendered, as in *Paisieu* (1928), in which names show up in several formations: "Poplar chestnut and oak trees and not maiden fern, not planted Arbuthnot Geronimo Caesar a plainly fairly watered plain"; "Gregory Alice photographed in earrings"; "A cake in water in care of Gertrude Geronimo." In some plays, such as the later *Doctor Faustus Lights the Lights* (1938) there is a character who is doubly named as "Marguerite Ida and Helena Annabel."[23] And there are in *Four Saints*, (added by Virgil Thomson) both a St. Theresa 1 and a St. Theresa 2: a means of identification without, it seems, identity, which works against the idea that any particular historical person is being portrayed.

Unassigned or confusingly assigned speeches, word games, long and varied word combinations, possible moments of dialogue, and, of course, variations on proper names and identities, are all elements at work in the "landscape" of *Four Saints in Three Acts*. The idea of landscape is clearly linked to Stein's notion of entity, and to the idea of creating an art in which "the intensity of movement [is] so great that it has not to be seen against something else to be known . . ." Speaking of *Four Saints in Three Acts*, Stein claims that "all these saints together . . . were the landscape and the play really is a landscape." The movement contained within such a dramatic configuration is meant simply to be "there," and its immediacy is founded only upon the choice to look or not to look:

> . . . the movement in it was like a movement in and out with which anybody looking on can keep in time. I also wanted it to have the movement of nuns very busy and in continuous movement but placid as a landscape has to be because after all the life in a convent is the life of a landscape, it may look excited a landscape does sometimes look excited but its quality is that a landscape if it ever did go away would have to go away to stay.

Stein translates the dramatic into the painterly, with a concomitant intermingling of the temporal and spatial, in an attempt to make a theatre which "moves but . . . also stays."

"Landscape," like the conceptions of composition and the continuous present, is another version of Stein's struggle with the idea of causality. Situated as it is within the context of dramatic writing, landscape seems designed as a kind of reconciliation between the temporality of language and the immediacy of dramatic presentation.[24] Stein's notion of "landscape" crystalizes what might be called a pleasurable anxiety of continuity. For Stein seems to anticipate (even perhaps invent?) Lyotard's notion of the postmodern sublime as the "threat of nothing further happening." Lyotard's concept sounds very much like the temporal dislocations that we saw at work in Stein's concept of the composition. For him, the "event," or simply the "occurrence," like Stein's composition, "happens as a question mark before it happens as a question." The question of Lyotard's sublime is the same as that which dominates *Four Saints*: "*Is it happening?*"; and this question, always belated, yet also productive of the present about which it asks, involves the pleasurable suspense constructed in this present:

Not elsewhere, not up there or over there, not earlier or later, not once upon a time . . . Here and now there is this painting [this landscape?, this opera?] rather than nothing, and that is what is sublime. [It lets go] of all grasping intelligence and of its power, disarming it, recognizing that this occurrence of painting [landscape-opera] was not necessary and is scarcely foreseeable, a privation in the face of *Is it happening?* guarding the occurrence 'before' any defence, any illustration, and any commentary, guarding before being on one's guard . . .[25]

Lyotard recognizes Stein's *How to Write* as one of the literary avant garde's "most rigorous realizations" of this sublime question. I will not quibble about which of Stein's works should be handed the avant-garde palm; but I will continue with the recognition that this question is at work within the opera as *it* is happening.

FOUR SAINTS IN THREE ACTS: "TO KNOW, TO KNOW . . ."

There is this opera then, not nothing. And even while it *is* apparently happening it continues to inquire into the possibilities of its own status. This ongoing self-inquiry seems always to refer, implicitly, to the infinitives which open the opera – "To know, to know . . ." – and these verbal/epistemological assertions seem to have no other response than the coming into being of the opera itself. From a certain point of view, given the contingent temporality inscribed here, one could say that perhaps *Four Saints*, like much of Stein's work, is an attempt (not entirely modernist, certainly not existentialist in the traditional philosophical sense) to come to terms with chance.[26] Stein's sense of landscape is a version of the finite world of things struck through with the indefiniteness of linguistic permutations, and it is precisely the sense of indeterminacy which makes for a connection between language and perceptual experience outside of literary or epistemological convention.

The task now for one turning to this language is to see it in its doubled

relationship with Virgil Thomson's music. The issue is further complicated by the fact – a fact which anyone trying to deal with drama or
opera must come to terms with – that there is no single object, or performance at which I am looking. The queries posed by the language (not
only "*Is it Happening?*" but also "It is happening?" – always the question,
and the questionability) are literally *performed*, or at least performable. I
will focus primarily on the musical–linguistic relationship here, though I
am fully aware of the absent and most necessary dimension of the visual
staging of the opera. I will however return to the rather interesting issue
of Thomson's selection of only black performers for the original cast of
the 1934 production. The reproduceability, but necessary non-identity,
of stage performance seems in itself to embody Stein's distinction
between repetition and insistence: there can be no repetition since there
can be no absolute identity between events, no matter how formally
similar they may be. Maurice Grosser, the original designer of the opera,
seemed in fact not even to wish to outline a definitive staging for *Four
Saints*. In the Scenario which prefaces the piano–vocal score of the opera
– the text to which from here on I will be referring – takes very seriously
the necessary playfulness required to stage such a work as Stein's:

> One should not try to interpret too literally the words of this opera, nor should
> one fall into the opposite error of thinking that they mean nothing at all. On
> the contrary, they mean many things at once. The scenarist believes that any
> practicable interpretation of the text is legitimate and has allowed himself, in
> consequence, considerable liberty. He counsels equal freedom to stage directors
> and choreographers, in the hope that they will find in this deeply fanciful work
> stimulous to their own imaginations.[27]

And fanciful it was, and is. In the original production, designed by
Florine Stettheimer, the setting, as Grosser tells us, was "composed out
of lace, feathers, gold paper, glass beads, cellophane, tarlatan, and tulle"
and was meant not to represent the "naive altar decorations characteristic of Latin countries," but rather the "tinsel and glitter, the exhuber-
ance [sic] and informality" of such decorations. The Compère and
Commère – two beings added by Thomson as his "'end men'" – are not
saints and were not characters at all in Stein's text; similarly, Thomson
made two Saint Teresas as identical twins, again, an addition not in
Stein's text. The words sung and spoken by these added characters are
however all Stein's. Thomson claims to have set all of Stein's text, including the directions, and many of these are spoken and/or sung by cho-
ruses or by the Compère and Commère. The opera is, however, about a
third shorter than the Stein text, since Thomson was forced to cut it for

the original production. Choreography was done by Frederick Ashton, who included the then popular and relatively new tango; the original director was John Houseman. Grosser points out that the "Pigeons on the Grass" aria was intended by Stein to be a vision of the Holy Ghost, and that the "Letting Pin In Letting Let" section at the end of Act III was also intended by her to suggest a religious procession. The ballets were also her suggestion, but largely the scenario is Grosser's.[28] The freedom of the collaborators seems evident and telling: the opera was to be "practicable" and imaginative despite the apparent obscurity of its text.

The issue of "understanding" in any conventional sense is itself undergoing renovation here. It may be incautious of me to trust so to the comments of a writer on her own work; but I think in Stein's case it is possible and important to keep the texts of apparent intention at play when focusing on a single piece. *Four Saints* is a text very much at the interstices of music, writing, and theatre, and as such it may also call for a shift in critical practice as well. The opera achieves a kind of plurality which escapes ordinary interpretive analysis. For the text unthinks us, returns language to spectacle, to the sacral and social, though not to the religious, not to the Father. It poses and escapes the functions of orderly representation and sonorous embellishment and expression. At the moment of its juncture with music, theatre, and the "practicable" nature of production and design, it still excedes them, allows them to go on, permits collaboration (perhaps necessitates it), but still functions somehow outside all of these. What I think truly does mark *Four Saints* as *écriture féminine* – to speak only of this one text – is the fact that it can call upon, or call forth, all these other symbolic systems, yet clearly (keeping in mind Grosser's sense of the endless possibilities for "interpreting" the language) it is contained by none of them – musical, hagiographic, dramatic.

I will no doubt speak of the text with a literary emphasis, given my own training; for me, though, "reading" the opera will mean reading the language and music together. Most readings of *Four Saints* say little about Virgil Thomson's score, but in a sense, the score is a kind of inscription of the first and perhaps the text's ideal reader, a reader responding (if not "talking") at the same time as he is reading Stein's language land-scape. The score is one of the most extensive responses to Stein's writing, a response which must try to take on the complexity of the landscape whole: that is, over the whole potential space of its duration.

For Thomson, it is precisely Stein's language which was so amenable to music: "Putting music to poetry so musically conceived as Gertrude Stein's has long been a pleasure to me. The spontaneity of it, its easy flow, and its deep sincerity have always seemed to me just right for music."[29] Thomson's description of Stein's language seems simple enough. Such epithets as "spontaneity," "easy flow," and "deep sincerity" could be used to describe (or as Barthes might say, "predicate") texts as unlike Stein's as possible. Thomson, however, also appreciated the fact that Stein's language seemed to possess none of the ready-made meanings and responses which would require an all too constricted musical response:

With meanings already abstracted, or absent, or so multiplied that choice among them was impossible, there was no temptation toward tonal illustration, say, of birdie babbling by the brook, or heavy heavy hangs my heart.

Spontaneity, flow, and sincerity may be hard adjectives to apply to a work where the choice among meanings remains so "multiplied." If Stein's is a language of flow it is not an easy or familiar poetic brook, and such sincerity as may reside in Stein's libretto may have little to do with the depths that musical poetry is usually assumed to possess.

Thomson's attraction to Stein resides in his "theory . . . that if a text is set correctly for the sound of it, the meaning will take care of itself." Thomson's own sense of English musical declamation resides not with expressivity first of all – and in this he seems to accord with Stein's own distrust of the usual forms of literary expression. In a passage from *The Musical Scene*, Thomson's words seem to recall Wagner's theorizing about the constitution of the *Gesamstkunstwerk*, but without the rhetoric of inwardness:

. . . way back in the mind, where music gets born, it has a closer concordance with language and with gesture than it can ever possibly have with obscure movements of the viscera or with states of the soul.

This is not to say that Thomson does not believe in musical expressiveness;[30] but, especially in terms of *Four Saints*, it is not (and really could not be) his first order of business. Thomson recognizes Stein's paradoxical approach to language, the "cadences and contradictions," of her "subtle syntaxes and maybe stammerings" which amount to a "quite expressive obscurity." But at the same time, this obliqueness comes "out of real English words, each of them having a weight, a history, a meaning, and a place in the dictionary." From his own perspective, *Four Saints* required focusing on "the rhythm of the language, and its specific

Anglo-American sound, adding shape, where that seemed to be needed, and it usually was, from music's own devices."

Thomson claims that he was drawn to Stein's texts, even before *Four Saints*, in order to "break, crack open, and solve for all time anything still wanting to be solved, which was almost everything, about English musical declamation." He set "Susie Asado" before meeting Stein, and went on to set many other pieces, including *Capital Capitals* before the opera came into being. It is striking that it is Stein's language he chooses for his personal quest to solve the setting of English; we must assume it was precisely the lexical liberty her works offer which drew him and gave him the space he needed. By applying the musical rhythmic patterns of "lengths and . . . of stresses," Thomson felt he was responding to the music that was latent in Stein's texts. For him, Stein's language *"likes"* music, it does not lack it; it simply needs his own music to "[explode] into the singing and give [these words] shape." He is perhaps more defensive when justifying his tonality, his potentially "backward-looking musical idiom [placed] in connection with a forward-looking literary one." His attention to "verbal speeds" however, as he himself points out, seems to justify his tonal practice – and besides, he saw, as he states, no need to "protect[ ] such composers as had invested in the dissonant manner . . ."[31] It is for others to decide upon the propriety of this choice in strictly musical terms; for me the tonality is clearly one of the opera's most important features. It becomes the perfect foil for Stein's language in a way which more "difficult" music might not have succeeded in becoming.

Partly, this is so because of Thomson's deep appreciation of language, and Stein's language in particular, as sound. In his *Music with Words: A Composer's View* Thomson explains his method, a method he would first have begun to learn by setting Stein, by making it clear that he does not work first of all from a sense of the "meaning" or interpretation of the text – lexical, symbolic, or otherwise. He works instead from the rhythmic sense of word groups: "Words, translated into sounds, do have meanings, often several quite different meanings; but the transmission of thoughts or of feelings requires that the words be pronounced (or read) as word-groups." For Thomson, these groups are where communication begins: "All word-groups behave like words . . ., " that is, the constituent words must be spoken or sung as though they are one entity, with accents falling on the appropriate words. To demonstrate, Thomson cites poems from Blake, Milton, Shakespeare, and Stein (this in itself is an interesting grouping and might have pleased Stein as well). He groups the opening lines of her "Susie Asado" thus:

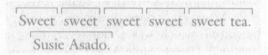

Compare the groupings to the setting Thomson includes at the back of the text (figure 11):[32]

Figure 11 Virgil Thomson, *Music With Words: A Composer's View.*

Thomson allows the language to take up its rhythmic space here; nothing of the language is shortened or truncated to make the setting of the music easier. The groupings of five units in the first line, and one in the second, are set with respect to the syllabic organization as well. The two opening bars of 5/4 time allow for both the word-groups and their syllables to occur freely, as though two rhythmic senses were being maintained at once: the one musical, which then accommodates the linguistic, with the five groups of the opening line and its six syllables. The five syllables of "Susie Asado" are treated as one word group, but set with two triplet figures in a bar of 3/4. The units of word-groups are given particular attention as musical phrases, as we can see especially in the time signatures that change with the phrases here, and these with the rhythmic structure of the linguistic line with its firm emphasis on each word. This is more like Renaissance setting where the music seems to follow the language which makes the rhythmic concerns of the music follow suit.[33]

   Thomson does know and employ tonal music's own devices of expressiveness, and he does so with a deliberateness verging on parody. Stein's libretto will over and over again throw itself into question, reminding us that there is no reason for it to be, while at the same time confronting us with its presence. Thomson's music in part conceals and in part reveals the obscurity of the libretto. It gives a tonal impression of causality, the sense of a "goal" or direction which counterbalances Stein's writing of the "*Is it happening?*" Setting Stein's "expressive obscurity" through tonal means creates an illusion of continuity; it supplies a progression which the language does not have. But at the same time, Thomson's tonality plays a kind of parodic dance with the language, as if one were the discontinuous image of the other.

This is well illustrated in the opening moves of the Prologue of *Four Saints* (see figure 12). Here we see a more complex version of the combination of linguistic and musical timings that we witnessed with "Susie Asado." The Prologue begins in F major with accordion and orchestra setting a pulse in 3/4 time, as Thomson might say, with an "oom pah pah" rhythmic alternation between an F major and a C dominant. However, when the full chorus enters singing in unison the melody is set in 4/4 time, changes to 3/2 at bar 7, 4/4 at bar 8, 5/4 at 11 and back to 4/4 at 12. Still, the strong 3/4 pulse remains beneath, giving emphasis and a kind of alternate organization to the melodic and linguistic lines. Thomson's setting adjusts itself to the language. The words he has chosen to emphasize fall generally on the first beat of the bar and are underlined below:

> To *know* to know to *love* her so.
> Four *saints* prepare for *saints*.
> It makes it well *fish*.
> Four *saints* it makes it well *fish*.
> Four *saints* prepare for *saints* it makes it well well *fish* it
> makes it well *fish* prepare for *saints*.[34]

Words falling on the first beat of a bar are emphasized, but against this emphasis the 3/4 pulse, even though it is distributed over bars of varying length, remains a strong influence here. Thomson generally places these words on the stronger beat of the bar and gives them a clear prominence in the tonality: "know" is sung on an F, "love" is sung on C as part of an arpeggiated descending F major chord sung in the melody, two of the first three "saints" are sung on a C, the second occurrence falling on a G which finishes the melodic phrase that began on the fourth beat of bar 5. In bars 10, 11, and 14 the word falls on the first beat of the bar and is sung on F, C, and F respectively.

Of particular interest here is the way Thomson both conceals and reveals the word "fish." Three of the four times it occurs at the end of the phrase "It makes it well fish" it is given an eighth note's duration, and comes at the end of a melodic phrase even though it falls on the first beat of the bar (at bars 9, 12, and 13). In its first appearance at bar 7, it falls

Figure 12   Gertrude Stein and Virgil Thomson. *Four Saints in Three Acts.*
Piano-Vocal Score.

on a weak beat of a bar of 3/2. At bars 7, 9, and 13 it is sung on an A, and even though this is a relatively strong pitch in F major, it is sung over the C dominant chord which weakens its relationship to F major. At bar twelve it is sung as B♭ over a G minor chord where it is part of a transition signaling the coming of a true cadence as the G minor resolves quickly into an F major where "fish" is again sung on an A. Though three of its appearances occur on downbeats the incongruity of the word is also downplayed by its relatively weaker relationship in the tonic-dominant of the section, and by its weak placement relative to the 3/4 time pulse which lies beneath the melody.

The "obscure prominence" of "fish" is part of what could be called a doubled acoustical image: "fish" is a striking disjunction on the grammatical continuity of the sentence, in fact, it throws us back upon what comes before ("to know" what or whom?; what "it" makes "it" "well fish"?) and impedes the logical, if not the syntactic, flow of the language. However, since the word is also partially veiled musically, worked in, but also worked against, the linguistic–musical progression overcomes the grammatical obscurity, though it does not erase it.

In a different fashion, the two early recitative passages of the Commère and Compère perform a similar doubled procedure (figure 13). After the initial moves I have just been describing, four saints, some invented, some not, talk of "A narrative of prepare for saints in narrative prepare for saints" (*2, plus 2 bars*). This is about to occur, or, it may be occurring already: it seems in fact to be doing both at once. Variations of this verbal theme are played upon by St. Stephen, St. Settlement, St. Plan, and St. Sarah. The closest we get to a plainly sung (and partially spoken) narrative, however, occurs with the first entries of the Commère and the Compère. At *3* plus 4 bars, the Commère sings the following, predominantly over an F:

We had intended if it were a pleasant day to go to the country it was a very beautiful day and we carried out our intention. We went to places that we had been when we were equally pleased and we found very nearly very nearly what we could find and returning saw and heard that after all we were rewarded and likewise. This makes it necessary to go again.

The Compère seems to respond to this near-story with one of his own at *3* plus 6:

He came and said he was hurrying hurrying and hurrying to remain he said he said finally to be and claim it he said he said feeling very nearly everything as it had been as if he could be precious to like like it as it had been that if he was used it would always do it good and now this time that it was as if it had been just the same as longer when as before it made it be left to be sure and . . .

The Compère sing-speaks his long non-story on an A with the orchestra sustaining a C diminished chord underneath. The tension created by this dissonant chord in the second instance, and by the rapidity of the articulation in both, gives the impression that momentous information is being revealed. But the Commère's story reveals only the jumbled

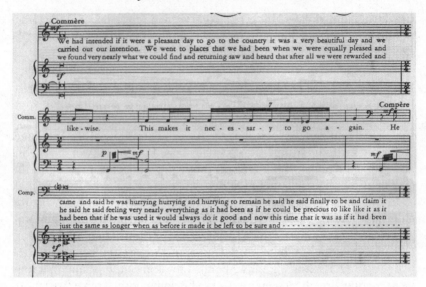

Figure 13　Gertrude Stein and Virgil Thomson, *Four Saints in Three Acts.*
Piano-Vocal Score.

events of a country outing, while the Compère's rushing discourse is "hurrying to remain," rushing to a harmonic, rather than a discursive conclusion. The tension breaks on the next word as the phrase continues:

. . . soft softly then can be changed to theirs and speck a speck of it makes blue be often sooner which is shared when theirs is in polite and reply that in their be the same with diminish always in respect to not at all and farther farther might be known as counted with it gain to be in retain which is not to be because of most.

At "soft" the chord changes to an F diminished then to a D minor 6, and finally the melody moves over series of chords which takes the language through a series of changes. We safely end up after the last portion of the sentence, from "as counted with it gain," working from an F without accompaniment upward in the bass to a D, the second degree of the C-major scale. The diminished chords resolve, or dwindle away; the "hurrying" almost-narratives leave off their haste and still seem to move on.

In this early section Thomson allows the language to take aural precedence, placing it out in front of the accompaniment. It is not, of course, "coherence" which emerges. The tension of the diminished chords and the haste of articulation give an impression of portentousness which

Figure 13 *(cont.)*

does not arrive in the language itself; rather the language takes on the aural *image* of a heavy burden which it syntactically and grammatically possesses not. Language is allowed to emerge as sound. This is not done, as in Joyce's "Sirens," through the play of the sound of language, though Stein does use puns and other aurally playful devices in *Four Saints* and elsewhere. Predominantly, Stein's return of language to sound depends upon its transformation into a chain of sounds; it *sounds like* the language of a narrative, though it possesses no story, it is musically *displayed* is if fraught with meaning, though it does not disclose anything. The length of the passages and their reduced punctuation allow the limitations of the performer only to determine the length and emphasis of the articulated unit. The structures of the performance as determined by designers, directors, and conductors become practical determinations which will shape meaning in any given performance of the piece; but the "sense" as it might usually be understood will not intrude. For "sense" at this point has become a matter of syntax as an allusion to its own coherence. In a truly Steinian paradox, it is precisely with regard to this sense of the shell of form as the model, and the problem, of meaning to which the language will in fact refer when it chooses to do so at all.

At the interface between language and music something particularly striking is happening. Lawrence Kramer suggests that in song (and here I think we can safely apply this to opera) there is "a partial dissociation of speech: a loosening of phonetic and syntactic articulation and a dissolving of language into its physical origin, vocalization." In song, "the vocal line becomes an image of speech in much the same way a mimed movement is the image of an action." I would say that this is true of *Four Saints* as it might be with any sung language, despite Thomson's continuing emphasis on clarity of articulation. However, in *Four Saints* the notion of song as the *image* of speech is further complicated by the fact that Stein's language is already transformed into an image of speech before it comes to music. Thus, the very dissociations of speech which sung language might normally undergo are, in this particular instance, ironically changed into images of potential *expressivity*, overcoming the language's already partially distorted condition.

Stein's wordplay, her unusual paradigmatic selections, and the general discontinuity between units of speech should not be mistaken for incoherence. There are "themes" or at least repetitions of phrases and words which suggest a certain thematicality to the work, even if these may often go no further than the recognition that *this* language is part of an opera, and this opera is "about" saints. This "aboutness" is not exterior to the confines of this language, this music, this (potential) spectacle and, indeed, the very discontinuity which seems to be the foundation of the language. Critical responses to the opera vary, but usually try to reconcile the thematic possibilities of saints and saintliness with the notion of landscape and/or the notions of the human nature-human mind dyad.[35] Most also emphasize the sense of immediacy given by the self-referential language as it attempts to bring the opera into being:

> Saint Teresa something like that
> Saint Teresa
> Saint Teresa half in doors and half out out of doors
> (Prologue, *20* plus 2)
>
> Ask Saint Teresa how much of it is
> finished. (Act 2, *113* plus 7–8)

Jane Bowers suggests that action here is a quality without reference to time (time, that is, as a measure or a sign of progression) which helps sustain the "improvisational illusion" that composition, rehearsal, and performance all occur at once. Like other critics, Bowers sees this temporal conflation or discontinuity as part of Stein's landscape technique. Critics such as Marianne DeKoven and Norman Weinstein suggest that the tension between movement and stasis within the language of the opera is emblematic of the saints' condition of existing between the earthly and the transcendent.

The territory of linguistic devices which sustains the tension between movement and stasis within the piece is also pretty well covered by critics. I have already pointed out one of the major devices which is the technique of combining more or less conventional syntactic movement with odd paradigmatic selections ("It makes it well fish"). Also apparent in the recitative passages quoted above is the use of repetition ("He came and said he was hurrying hurrying and hurrying to remain he said he said . . ."). Word-play, including phonemic variations, confusing grammatical placement, and puns are prominent features of the libretto: "With be there all their all their time time there be there vine there be vine time there be there time there all their time there" (Act 3, *195* plus 5–12). Bowers notes how the elimination of verbs and their replacement by noun phrases or transformation into adjectives works to resist the progression of the language while still maintaining a sense of movement: "There are very sweetly very sweetly Henry very sweetly René very sweetly many very sweetly" (*167* plus 6–10). Conditionals work to achieve a similar suspension of progression:[36] "Might be with them at that time all of them might be with them at that time" (*58* plus 5–8). I would add to this list the emphasis in many parts of the libretto on infinitive verb forms especially of the verb "to be": "To know to know to love her so . . ." (Bars 3–5); "Four saints later to be if to be one to be to be one to be" (*18* plus 3–4); "Begin to trace begin to race begin to place begin and in . . ." (*213* plus 1–5). And one of the most significant features of Stein's language is the pervasive sense of contradiction or uncertainty: "Saint Teresa seated and not surrounded (*27* plus 1–2) . . . Saint Teresa

not seated" (*27* plus 8); "Four saints are never three. / Three saints are never four" (*8* plus 3–4); "Saint Teresa very nearly half inside and half outside outside the house and not surrounded" (*30* plus 5–8).

Movement and stasis can be seen as not only the method of structuring the landscape of the opera, but as part of the more crucial articulation of the relationship between knowledge and temporality which is central to Stein's work as a whole. *Four Saints*, in its combination of language and music, enacts the playful anxiety of the question "Is it happening?" but always with the half-knowledge of the *next* moment, the sense of futurity which cannot arrive since it is always displaced by the present. At the same time, such a displacement forms the very possibility of the future and in turn this futurity may in fact constitute knowledge of the present. In this sense, I would have to disagree with Bower's idea that the language takes place without reference to time, since it seems more the case that Stein is concerned with the formation of time itself in its constant perceptual appearance. Thomson's tonality, rich in its teleological tendency, its constant emphasis upon reaching, if not some ultimate symbolic goal, at least a series of provisional points of reorientation, establishes not only an ironic interaction with Stein's language which is always in some sense "about to be," but more crucially, it enacts the temporality of movement and stasis which constitutes the Steinian landscape.

The Prologue, as we have seen so far, begins to establish the complex temporalities of this landscape. This is clear in the way Thomson has combined rhythmic and melodic structures. Legatto moments are few here, and the tendency for the most part is to set a single pitch almost for every word, or at least a single attack. Thus, after the ostensibly dark non-narratives of the Compère and the Commère, these two "end men" and the chorus of sopranos continue with the indirect allusions to both temporality and to space (see figure 14). The indirection of references to time, here achieved mostly by grammatical locutions without definite reference ("Why while while in that way was it after this that to be seen made left it" [*4* plus 9–10]) of the Compère is countered by the Commère's obscure reference to the fact that "It is very easy to be land" (*5* plus 2–3). Then the speculation seems, again portenteously, to turn to the being and non-being of the setting (figure 14, *5* plus 3–8).

The haste of the sixteenth-note figures here, combined with the repeated pitches, move quickly to the resolution over a D minor 9 chord; but then this "darkness" fades immediately as the chorus enters and the key changes abruptly from C major to D major at *5* plus 9.

Figure 14 Gertrude Stein and Virgil Thomson, *Four Saints in Three Acts*. Piano-Vocal Score.

This kind of quick change in musical direction is typical of the opera. The tempo increases slightly (quarter note equals 144), and the rhythm changes highlighting figures which will occur in various configurations throughout the whole piece: the dotted eighth notes tied to a sixteenth, and the reverse; and especially the triplet figures seen in the Commère and Compère's passage (5 plus 7–8). The sudden change in the music accommodates a shift not so much in focus, but in the direction of the

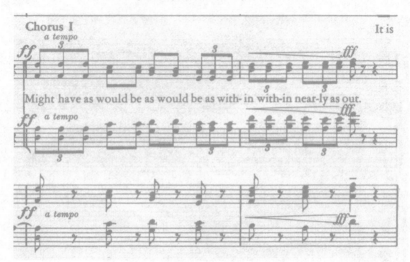

Figure 15   Gertrude Stein and Virgil Thomson, *Four Saints in Three Acts*. Piano-Vocal Score.

language. The swerve from benches (though benches return in tight choral harmony at *6* plus 2) seems merely a "progression" to the reinsertion of the temporal dimension of the "being" of character, setting, theatrical space – indeed, of the opera itself. The choral entry of "That makes it be not be makes it not be at the time" (scored here predominantly with descending and then ascending scale-steps) proposes the presence and absence of the opera and all it may be said, or expected, to possess. This is a process which will continue, and really only be held off (so to speak) by the assertion of the appearance of characters. The questioning, however, will never cease.

Thomson very clearly keeps the movement and stasis of the landscape in process here: the lilting changes in melodic/rhythmic figures, repeated often, are contrasted with the return of the Compère, and a modulation back to F major from D major by his singing an A natural below middle C (figure 15).

This is not quite a return to chant, but the pedaled single pitch – a frequent occurrence in the opera for soloists and ensembles – in this instance again seems to address us directly, to require us to attend to the voice's words. The Compère's line keeps reasserting the new key (D minor, the relative minor of F) which breaks finally into a double forte at *7* plus 2, moves to just the quartet at *7* plus 4, to just the altos at *7* plus

Figure 15 *(cont.)*

6, then to straight declamation at 7 plus 8 by the Compère: "Believe two three."

The libretto here jumbles the transformation of water ("snow, show, water to water") and portrays the possible transformations merely as a series of discrete moments almost unrelated, or in relation only syntactically. At the moment where water might be transformed somehow into snow, the language breaks up and scatters: "This is where to be at at water at snow . . ." The text moves from the present tense "is" to the infinitive "to be," to "at water," "at snow" – to non-grammatical preoppositional phrases, indirectly implying two distinct states of water (though which is *more* water than the other?) joined but not related as such. As with water, so with saints. St. Teresa and St. Ignatius could not possibly have had any connection historically, but here, they are brought together. Most of the saints declaimed at the end of the Prologue by the Commère and Compère at *22* plus 1 and 2 have no historical reality at all. This is typical of the libretto and the presentation of the entire opera. Its "assertions" are tangential, contiguous; the scenario presents, but not always in relation to the language. The characters inhabit an imaginary space which is not just fictional, but also "real" in the sense of being *there*, not elsewhere in time or in space. And having no story to tell, the explorations of linguistic and musical permutation are free to continue and *be* the opera.

Thomson uses conventional musical means – as we have just seen, the shift from D major to D minor, as well as frequent and often abrupt modulations, the dynamics of orchestra and voices, changes in tempo, in rhythmic–melodic figures – to move the text along. Moreover, the constant shuffling of voices, from pedaled tones, to unisons, to choral moments with counter movement, to continual shifts in the centres of sound – from one voice to quartet, to chorus, or various combinations of these – leads to constant variation in the overall sound of the opera. Perhaps most significant is his tendency to stop or redirect the musical flow of the opera and establish a constantly shifting sense of continuity. This is, in a way, I think the primary musical technique of the opera: Thomson basically, though not simply, begins again and again, as Stein might say, and in doing so really adopts for tonal music a Steinian technique not of the continuous present, but of what might be called continuous presentation.

In the Prologue, then, we have at *8* plus 10 a sudden change from E♭ major to G major, and the imperative in the libretto to "Begin four saints . . ." At *10* plus 5, after the Commère, the Compère, and the chorus pun through several variations of "Four Saints have to have to have at a time," all stops, and the Compère speaks grandly of "The difference between saints forget-me-nots and mountains have to have to have to at a time." There is then a complete change in key – from G major to B♭ major – tempo ($\quarternote = 108$), and there are repeated variations of the line "It is very easy in winter to remember winter spring and summer" beginning on the tonic and descending successively from soprano to tenor (down a third), alto (down a third), and bass (down an octave). Again, while the descent has a kind of musical continuity, the libretto and its

Figure 16 Gertrude Stein and Virgil Thomson, *Four Saints in Three Acts.*
Piano-Vocal Score.

variations defer any sense of progression between seasons, and the issue of remembering has no center-point from which to base itself: *when* is it easy to remember these seasons, and *who* is doing the remembering? Is there any "memory" here?[37]

Other notable interruptions and apparent new directions occur at *13* plus 2, with the shift from Bb major to A major for a bar of 2/4 and one of 3/4. The passage is sung by the chorus *lento*, and seems to refer to the opera itself: "There is no parti parti color in a house / there is no parti parti parti color in a house."[38] The opera as house will be picked up subsequently even as late as the Prologue to Act 4, where the Compère, apparently counting saints, sings: "One two three four and there is no door. Or more. Or more. Or door. Or floor or door" (*207* plus 9, to *208* plus 3). There is a complete return to the beginning of the opera at *15* plus 10, followed appropriately by a chant section, this time by St. Stephen, who sing-speaks a B natural over a D half diminished chord. This leads to the amusing and slightly dissonant crescendo which points ahead to the "Pigeons on the grass, alas" aria of St. Ignatius in Act 3 (figure 16, *16* + 10, to *17* + 1).

Panic may come, but then is overcome with the lively hymn-like intrusion in tight harmony at *17* plus 7; but this dwindles to an almost Gilbert and Sullivan sounding quartet at *17* plus 9.[39] Later, after a citation of "My Country 'Tis of Thee," St. Settlement (soprano) abruptly ends the 3/4 time of the quote with the humorous, and perhaps exasperated, "St.

Teresa something like that" at *19* plus 9. The entry of St. Teresa I (Thomson used two St. Teresas meant to be identical twins) occurs at *20* plus 2, and though she does not sing, the chorus responds with a double forte at octaves of F over a G♯ diminished seventh. The words they sing over this undecided chord are fittingly doubled: "Saint Teresa half in doors and half half out of doors." (Saint Ignatius gets no such response verbally or musically at his entry at *21* plus 2.) Just before the Prologue ends, the Commère and Compère chant the names of twenty-one saints (*21* plus 1 and 2), and the Prologue finally concludes with the playful "Anyone to tease a saint seriously" (*22* plus 3), perhaps a warning about, and instructions for the viewing of, what is to follow.

My reading so far of the music and language of the opera has tried to point out the detail of their interconnection; mainly, the discussion has pointed up Thomson's perspicacious use of tonality in relation to Stein's words. But to "analyze" in this way is almost to rework, and this is perhaps a testimony to the way the opera will not allow us to make standard identifications with settings, characters, speeches, or sung language. I have discussed the Prologue at some length in order to show how it designs for the reader/listener/audience the opera's fundamental interrelations of music and language. This is to say that Thomson's ironic tonality in relation to Stein's words is part of the serious and complex working out of the "rules" of the piece, even as the piece constantly questions its own presence, and therefore, the possibility of having rules at all. Get the saints on stage. Are the saints on stage? Where are we? What is happening? How many acts are there in it? All these questions in one way or another arise, but are included and disqualified somehow by the very impetus of the opera which forces us to ask them. Thomson's often abruptly tangential, yet tonal and very intelligible settings, relate to Stein's language in precisely this way: they are the temporal articulation of the space of the play as *it is happening*, but *not* as it can ever be repeated. There is no necessity for this opera, for this combination of music and language; yet, it goes on, it moves, it "likes it as it is," and makes itself as it is at the same time.

In my reading of the rest of the opera I would like to go a bit further. I mentioned above the way in which the opera disallows any easy sense of identification on the part of the audience. This is, I believe, an extension of its enactment, indeed, its *anxious* enactment, of the problematic status of the "Is it happening?" This problem is one not only of an aesthetic and epistemological nature, but also one which participates fully in a rather more social problematic than we might first expect. This

complexity manifests itself in two related ways. In the first case, the issue
of non-identity, or non-identification, is part of a strange process which
is enacted by the opera, and which may be best discerned through
Lacan. I want to suggest that the opera proposes a kind of negative invocation of the imaginary in so far as the *language* offers a series of visual
possibilities regarding the predication of itself as opera, and, indeed,
especially of its two main characters, St. Teresa and St. Ignatius. But it
also *negates* these possibilities at the same time. I realize that for Lacan,
the imaginary has to do with the realm of making and breaking identifications which are largely *visual* in kind.[40] But I want to suggest here that
the very nature of Stein's libretto resists the symbolic and invokes instead
a kind of continual re-imagining of the visual properties of this language
as opera. Thus, there are verbal cues which seem to contradict the visual
presence of the characters, and indeed, of the opera itself, at the same
time as the opera remains a visual spectacle – at least ideally. In contrast
also to the conventional conception of the symbolic, which is usually
related to language and partly, too, to the means of creating the social
(the Law of the Father), I would propose that Thomson's tonality suggests an order of meaning which, in its musical predictability takes the
place of language. It implies, though cannot confirm – as I have tried to
show above – the *course* of meaning which could be present if the language would play along. Of course, it won't, and as a result Thomson's
tonal exercises in keeping the opera moving, in suggesting a direction
and then diverging from it, are largely to give the *impression* of meaning
and direction, to give a scaffolding to a language which will not itself
move to any ordinary symbolic ordering. But it is also clear that the
libretto is disavowing its own "possession" of language, rejecting its usual
symbolic and social, communicative functions. In a sense then, it is
rejecting the formation of the subject as, according to Lacan, it is "normally" consituted. At the same time, moreover, I would maintain that it
is partly because of Thomson's conventionality here that the opera is
made *socially acceptable*. Perhaps a more significant objection might come
from those such as Lawrence Kramer who maintain that "[l]ike the
process of imaginary identification, music offers a seamless band of
pleasure and presence, but nonetheless one 'open to disruption by recur-
rent intimations that the supposedly self-present ego is always already
alienated, that its desire is the desire of (desire for, desire determined by)
the Other'." In this regard, Kramer stages a most compelling argument
that music in the West is regarded as "sinister and enchanting alike
because it has the putatively *feminine* power to combine promiscuously

with any other expressive modality and to exceed whatever it combines with." I do not dispute this insightful reading of music as being associated with the imaginary and with the woman/other; indeed, in both Wagner and Pound, for instance, it is clear that music is "feminine" and language-rationality is "masculine." However, I am instead pointing to one of the possible functions of Thomson's music in this specific opera. In so far as its tonality is so pronounced, so to speak, it becomes a parody of itself, an almost over-orderly ordering of these recalcitrant words.

What fascinates me here is not so much that this language, like so much of the language of avant-garde texts, does not address us as subjects in any conventional sense, but rather that *it sings to us*, that it *is* addressed, or rather, *is* an address. But the subject who hears cannot be predicated by hearing it, the subject does not, in Barthes' terms, return, but rather, swept along with the abrupt redirections of Thomson's tonality, the subject keeps almost appearing, almost being heard. The saints, the places they inhabit in the "action" of the piece, the relations between them, and indeed, their relations with themselves, all "exist" (again potentially) on stage, but never precisely in accordance with the language they speak, and which speaks them.

Act 1, then, begins with the Commère who pedals a G in the key of C major. St. Teresa 11 sits, as Grosser's tableau description says, "under the tree painting flowers on very large eggs."[41] The Commère sings, as almost everyone else does in the opera, of St. Teresa only, not of a St. Teresa 1 and/or 11. Visually then, another woman is actually on stage at this point, other than the woman we saw in the Prologue as St. Teresa 1. The language of the Commère makes no such distinctions. Instead, she sings "St. Teresa in a storm at Avila there can rain and warm snow and warm that is the water is warm the river is not warm the sun is not warm and if to stay to cry" (*22* plus 5–10). Only the description of the tableau tells us it is St. Teresa 11. The language is trying to find a setting, to make distinctions (there "can" be "rain and warm snow . . . the river is not warm the sun is not warm . . .") but seems unable to decide anything firmly, though Grosser's provisional scenario has.

The dissonance between the language and the description of the scenario seems to go unnoticed by the music which pumps nicely along with a tonic-dominant pulse on one and three. Indeed, this one and three pulse dominates much of the first act.[42] The second chorus picks up blithely upon the Commère's indecisive "and if to stay to cry," the altos and sopranos repeating and varying the phrase, the tenors and basses "ah"-ing angelic fifths (figure 17, *25* plus 5).

Figure 17 Gertrude Stein and Virgil Thomson, *Four Saints in Three Acts.*
Piano-Vocal Score.

The music does not seem to listen to the words, or if it does, it does not really care what they are saying. It keeps on moving as if there were no possible discord between language and scene, between the presence of *this* St. Teresa and that *other* one we saw in the Prologue (but which is the other?). The music then continues to shape the language, to force it ahead and give it the image of its teleology, its sense of direction. This propensity in the music makes me want to suggest that *it*, and certainly not the language here, takes on a kind of "symbolic" function in the opera. This is to say that Thomson's very structured tonality and rhythms *suggest* the image of a syntactical and ordered progression and acceptable *social* structure. The *language* on the other hand, keeps making verbal appeals and creations, assertions it does not care to prove or make clear. Grosser's scenario very cannily takes this language and shapes his tableaux of the first act as a series of events which the language might suggest, and might not. The provisionality of the tableaux is, as he states, very intentional; moreover, such provisionality is also consistent with the character of the language which keeps drawing up possible images and scenes, and then dissolving them. In this sense then, the non-predication of the language offers possible visual articulations and identities – of saints, of water, of scenes for saints – but keeps frustrating them, or changing them before they can verbally "appear." The language thus makes a kind of appeal to the imaginary (as the scene of visual identification) through the negative or multiple possibilities it provides. The scenario, meanwhile, keeps making the saints and situations appear, whether or not the language concurs. And, all along, Thomson's music keeps directing us, like a Good Daddy (not a big Law of the Father) to hear this scene and that, as though music, "in place of situations" (37 plus 1), will be enough to give us the illusion of coherence and perhaps even meaning.

The opera signals its own means of operation, its propensity to move by sequence or contiguity rather than by progession. It has built into it Stein's own "explanation" (truly, more like another composition) for her choice of the characters St. Teresa and St. Ignatius. Grosser's second tableau suggests that St. Teresa II should be seen "with dove, being photographed by St. Settlement" (37 plus 3). Though the key signature is E♭, the melody seems really to be in C major: briefly, while the words seem to take over and describe a potential scene, the music is momentarily indefinite. The alto chorus sings, predominantly over a G♮, "Saint Teresa could be photographed having been dressed like a lady and then they taking out her head changed it to a nun and a nun a saint and a saint so." The words echo Stein's reported viewing of such a series of photographs on the Boulevard Raspail:

They take a photograph of a young girl dressed in the costume of her ordinary life and little by little in successive photographs they change it to a nun . . . [T]he thing takes four or five changes but at the end it is a nun . . . [W]hen I was writing Saint Therese in looking at these photographs I saw how Saint Therese existed from the life of an ordinary young lady to that of a nun.[43]

Figure 18 Gertrude Stein and Virgil Thomson, *Four Saints in Three Acts.* Piano-Vocal Score.

This passage *seems* to explain the transformation process from one state of being to another; but of course it does nothing of the kind. The succession of photographs forms an apparent narrative. However, as the language in this passage suggests, the series is composed of static moments. It is not so much a "history" or the display of a progression which Stein recounts, as it is an acknowledgment of various states, of discreet configurations placed in sequence. The young girl in Stein's language is changed both into an "it" rhetorically, and a nun physically; but the girl moves less in a progression than through a series of states in which she "existed." Change resides on the surface of passing and discreet moments. Thus, the photographs function for Stein as suitably as any recorded history of St. Therese might. St. Ignatius is "not as actual" as St. Therese, but "still actual" enough. Stein claims to have seen a porcelain group in yet another window, and there, the figure is of a "young soldier [who] gives alms to a beggar and leaves his armour with another." This is apparently reminder enough for the play to be written, and enough so that we may see that the static nature of these representations supplies Stein with models for the opera which "moves but . . . also stays."[44] The description of St. Ignatius is cited in the opera during tableau v, as Ignatius shows St. Teresa ii a model of the Heavenly Mansion. As St. Stephen sings of St. Ignatius, he is interrupted with an undecided assertion by St. Plan (figure 18);

apparently St. Ignatius will not be allowed to become quite as "actual" as St. Teresa.

The opera's allusions to Stein's viewing of representations which *remind* her of saints, and of change, are part of the whole process of presenting visual configurations and of frustrating them as well. The actual visual formation of any production of the opera may *allude* to or borrow from the language, but, as is the case with Grosser's scenario, there is no *necessary* connection between the visual proposals of the language and the visuality of the opera as a staged event. Thus is the opera stitched together; linguistic verbal–visual proposals are made which rarely solidify, and the music then links these in a syntax of series (not quite of serialization) without progression. Though there is much variety in the musical *means* of accomplishing this, the principle is established early and is used in a variety of effective ways.

In St. Teresa's first aria, she sings predominantly in scale steps in E♭ major, "Not April Fool's day a pleasure" (*26* plus 2–3). The first chorus chants back on the tonic, "Saint Teresa seated" (*26* plus 3); eventually, the tenors and basses will proclaim at octaves of B♭, "Saint Teresa not seated" (*27* plus 8). Whatever might be happening on stage, the language keeps deciding and undeciding: it is not April Fool's day, and this is a pleasure; Saint Teresa is both seated and not seated, imaginable aside from any visual properties on stage, as both there and not there, both temporally and spatially. St. Teresa will vary the language too, as if to restate Stein's own version of the play as landscape: "There are a great many persons and places near together" (*27* plus 8–10, *28* plus 1–2).

Melodic continuity at times seems a mere excercise structured so as to foreground the articulation of the language, to make its curious articulations clearly heard. Such is the case from *47* plus 8 to *51* plus 4, where St. Teresa I (soprano) and St. Teresa II (contralto) trade triadic arpeggios moving upward by half-steps from E♭ to B (figure 19).

The modulations seem limited only by vocal and instrumental range, and they give the impression of being both unmotivated – since it is unclear precisely what dramatic purpose they might serve – and yet highly structured – what is more basic to Western music than the triad? They suggest an ordering on into perpetuity without any kind of necessary resolution. The arpeggios extend over a two octave range, though the pitches are always restricted to those of the triad, ascending or descending. The movement is only stopped by an equally arbitrary intrusion from the Compère at *50* plus 5, with "Saint Teresa come again to be absent" peddled over a C, and descending an octave on the last syllable. This rather definite (manly?) assertion of the octave does not, of course, answer or conclude the musical debate between the St. Teresas; it simply stops it.

The language seems to be indifferent to such constraints as are placed upon it in this rigid, if playful, setting. It is shaped by odd predications, conditionals, indefinite pronouns, and, except for very brief transitional passages, is unaccompanied. It inquires into the possibility of various states, or, just as likely, various possible *appearances* of things: I say "states" *or* "appearances," since the ontological status of both seem equivalent in the opera. In the first bar of figure 19, St. Teresa I suggests that "She is to meet her," and St. Teresa II answers with an inquiry: "Can two saints be one" (*47* plus 9 to *48* plus 1). "Oneness" seems to lack any anxiety of identity; visually at least, if not musically, two saints are indeed one, and not one, here. The question ostensibly needs no answer and none is given. Neither is the inquiry about Negroes and beards at *48* plus 7,[45] nor those regarding saints: "Who separated saints at one time" (*50* plus 3–4).

This procedure of combining what we might call the "directedness" of the music with the non-identificatory nature of the language pervades the whole opera in a multitude of small- and large-scale ways: there is a counting game at *82* plus 4–7 ("One two three four five six seven all good children go to heaven . . .") over a descending D major scale, variations of which will return in the second act (e.g. *97* plus 1–3, 5); somehow too, "All saints make Sunday Monday Sunday Monday Sunday Monday set. One two three saints" at *71* plus 2–6, a predication obscurely referring to another ordering system – the days of the week – and sung in counterpoint by the first chorus, with the tonic forcefully reasserted on the last four words. The second act continues a line of inquiry into the constitution, apparently, of the opera itself at *84* plus 8 (figure 20), and at *97* plus 10 all through *99*, there is a questioning of the number of saints (figure 21). As well, there are references to saints somehow changing "from the evening to the morning" and from "the morning to the morning" (*89* plus 1–5). Just what the change entails is never mentioned, though the suggestion of the overnight nature of the change seems to signal neither progress, nor recurrence.

Perhaps the most well-known and even amusing section of the opera in which the musical symbolic is resisted by the language comes in the third act, with the "Pigeons on the grass" aria sung by St. Ignatius. This begins at *146* in G major, and is set in 3/2 time. The aria is conceived in Grosser's scenario, apparently at Stein's request, as a "Vision of the Holy Ghost." The visuality of this vision, which is stated so clearly in the first

Figure 19 Gertrude Stein and Virgil Thomson, *Four Saints in Three Acts*.
Piano-Vocal Score.

Figure 19 (*cont.*)

bars of the aria ("Pigeons on the grass alas"), dissipates almost immediately: "Short longer grass short longer longer shorter grass" (*146* plus 3–4). The bird too undergoes variation from pigeon on the grass to magpie in the sky (*147* plus 2). It is almost as if the language is driving the melody here, since phrases rarely begin or end on the tonic, but rather pass through it on there way to uncertain periods. At the same time, however, the harmony, even in counterpoint, is working to underpin the melody with a recurring G-C major pattern (figure 22).

The concern with distinctions and identities is taken up again later in the act by the men's chorus and an unspecified tenor at *154* plus 8 and is in part a variation of the "pigeons" aria. Here, the tenor and chorus go through a series of modulations, musically, from G major through various keys back to G again, and verbally, with various combinations of "He asked for a distant magpie as if that made a difference" (figure 23).

Figure 20 Gertrude Stein and Virgil Thomson, *Four Saints in Three Acts.*
Piano-Vocal Score.

The assertion of the request does not overcome the imprecision concerning exactly what difference the reqest might make. It is as though the language, especially in this third act, is making an apparent call for distinctions – especially by the male saints – *and* its lack of necessity. Earlier in the act, St. Chavez declares: "Never to return to distinctions" (*150* plus 8–10), and at *169* plus 2–6, the magpie–pigeon theme returns, "Allegro militare," again in G major, as the men's chorus asserts, "There is a difference between Barcelona and Avila, there is a difference between Barcelona" up and down by step from the fifth to the tonic. This is a rather stiff assertion, both musically and verbally, which does not seem to hold, since the last phrase, "there is a difference beween Barcelona," seems to send the notion of distinction inward, beyond any sense of immediacy or possible identification. St. Ignatius may indeed state, with unequivocal equivocality, "Foundationally marvellously aboundingly illimitably with it as a circumstance" (*172* plus 2–6) as if to ground in some absolute way the status of saints ("fundamentally and saints" [8–9]). However, at *176* plus 10 to *177* plus 1, the women's chorus declares simply: "Ordinary pigeons and trees." And later, the *whole* chorus seems to agree, since they repeat the statement. Any sense of

Figure 21 Gertrude Stein and Virgil Thomson, *Four Saints in Three Acts.*
Piano-Vocal Score.

some kind of hierarchy of saints, especially male saints, will not solidify.[46]

Indeed, the solidity of verbal predication and any concomitant imaginary identifications are always suspended, if also at the same time, alluded to or proposed. At *185* plus 10, the full chorus sings "One two three as one one and one" in unison (figure 24), and as the Commère and Compère begin the slow, and musically "somber" "Letting pin in" procession, a kind of semi-unity is suggested, with the slow play of phonemes (e.g. "wet" and "wed") and dead rhymes ("led wed dead").

Figure 22 Gertrude Stein and Virgil Thomson, *Four Saints in Three Acts*.
Piano-Vocal Score.

This motif floats through the final moments of the act, and leads ultimately to what may be considered the crescendo of the opera, though
of course there is still another brief act tagged on. It consists of a series
of only three pitches, E, F♯, and G, alternating between the Commère
in the alto, and the Compère in the bass. It is simply harmonized and
clearly in E minor. Grammatically, there is no clear subject here, but
rather a collection of prepositions, possible predications (some "one"
may be led, wed, and dead, some "thing" may have been said), verbs or
verbals, all stated or discretely "said" as "One one and one" (*186* plus 3).
Unity, we can infer, seems to lie in singularity, in the setting off of each
moment in its separateness – and this separateness is precisely what joins
it to any other moment. Each moment of led, wed, dead, or said, is a

Figure 23 Gertrude Stein and Virgil Thomson, *Four Saints in Three Acts.*
Piano-Vocal Score.

kind of "Now differing from annointed now," as St. Ignatius seems to
admit (*181* plus 1).

The "pin" theme returns at *190* plus 7 to *191* plus 5, with only the
Compère stating, "Across across *a* cross coupled across crept across . . ."
If there is a certain flavor of the religious here in the play between
"across" and "a cross," it is, as are most of the possible religious suggestions of the opera, less irreverent than intrigued. The opera at times suggests the earthly and transcendent interconnection, but, as in the kind of
aural pun between "across" and "a cross," the absolute character of the
spiritual is put aside, or at least deferred in the presence and non-
presence of the *possible* visual suggestions made by the language. Indeed,
somberness, spirituality, gayness, and so forth, are really, if present at all,
made so by the conventional image repertoire created by the music. The
language itself will never completely concretize anything, as we have
seen.

So, as the first attempt at a final crescendo begins at *193* plus 8, we
hear again the full chorus in 3/2 time, and the phrase climbing by step

Figure 24 Gertrude Stein and Virgil Thomson, *Four Saints in Three Acts*.
Piano-Vocal Score.

at each half note and pause, then downward again in predominantly the
same way (figure 25).

Again, puns, prepositions, infinitives, rule the language, and the sense
of build-up and release is sustained only by the music. The "pin" theme
enters again as the key switches from G major to E minor, and then, the
finale completes itself (figure 26).

Clearly, and with simplicity, Thomson attempts to bring together in
these final stages, both major and minor concerns in major and minor

Figure 25 Gertrude Stein and Virgil Thomson, *Four Saints in Three Acts.*
Piano-Vocal Score.

keys: the possibility of death at any beginning (at being wed, for instance) is concomitant with, and contrasted by, the "Maestoso" dynamics of the full choral passages in the major key, and their uncertain, but grandly framed, assertions of uncertainty: "With be there all their all their time there be there vine there be vine time there be there time there all their time there."

The act soon ends with an intermezzo which returns us to the opening of the opera, though this time with passages of some dissonance, especially at *204* plus 5 to 6. Then begins the prologue to the extra act, the one not accounted for in the title, but which nevertheless appears. The Commère asks several times "How many acts are there in it" (*205* plus 9) and the Compère demurs time after time ("Ring around a rosy" [*206* plus 8]), though he finally admits with his usual descending octave that there is an "Act four" (*210* plus 1).

The final act is brief, but it contains one of the opera's most direct moments of address which points up the crucial division and association between language and music that I have been elaborating here: this is the moment when the full chorus in a reprise of the opening of the opera

Figure 26 Gertrude Stein and Virgil Thomson, *Four Saints in Three Acts*.
Piano-Vocal Score.

– except here, the melody is in 4/4 time – requests that "When this you see remember me" (*214* plus 5–7). This occurs just after St. Teresa 1 has engaged in her own solo reprise of the finale of the third act. The moment is sometimes taken as *Stein's* direct address, with the implication that this language is somehow a representation of Stein's "human mind."[47] But where could she possibly be? There are in fact so few places in which any kind of *clear* imaginary identification could be made. Even at this moment of apparent directness in the opera, the request is stated in terms of singularity, but it is of course a *group* of saints making it. Even the structure of the opera itself slips easy identification: there are four acts, not three "in it," and it is never clear who the four saints of the title might be: no matter which names one puts forward, there will always be a fifth, since there are two St. Teresas. Some scenario or other might be able to explain or contain these possibilities, even going so far as to make it clear that this *is* somehow Stein's address. But any such containment would only be provisional; nothing in either the libretto or the music can make such certainties appear, though it is clear that the music has guided the opera to its ending, given the language a kind of simulacrum of teleology, and stopped it – if not exactly conclusively. And perhaps it is only the ending, the very "Last act" (*217* plus 9–10), as the Compère puts it, with an almost predictable descending octave on C, "Which" as the full chorus shouts, "is a fact" (*217* plus 10 – *218* plus 1). It is a fact at least in the sense that this last Act, *contains* the last act, this shout, unpitched and unset to music, music which enters only after the declaration, and proves it true with a final drum roll, and a full orchestral F.

There is, however, in *Four Saints in Three Acts*, yet another potential "visuality" which is not necessarily inscribed in the score, but which is part of the history of the opera nonetheless: indeed, we could say that it defines, in a sense, the *historicity* of the opera itself – this in a piece which is so decidedly resistant to history in any conventional sense. I refer here to the fact that Thomson used only black singers and dancers in the original 1934 production – and in the 1947 recording, and in the 1952 New York/Paris revival. Indeed, the recording with which I am most familiar is the 1984 Electra/Nonsuch version which again uses all black singers. According to Thomson, the choice of singers had nothing to do with race, but only with these singers' carriage, bearing, and unselfconsciousness.[48] Of course, from one point of view, such assessments have *everything* to do with "race," or at least the *racializing* of the "other," even though, as is clear in Thomson's autobiography, he contrasts the performers, he believes favorably, with white performers. The properties which Thomson cites are both visual and aural; these are of course important features for an opera, but at the same time, obviously, they have their usually more insidious prominence in relationship to racial matters as well. Even though the idea of using black performers occurred to Thomson *after* the opera was composed, the issue of "race" is nevertheless related to the issue I have already taken up, which is that of the peculiar dual interplay between the imaginary and the symbolic. Indeed, the use of "Negroes," as Thomson himself says, is one of the only dimensions of the opera, unlike the text and the music, which never received "both praise and blame"; the use of black performers was generally praised by the mostly white reviewers.[49] As I suggested above, Thomson's music in fact makes the operatic text socially acceptable, and in perhaps another reversal of expectations, so too did the black cast of performers and dancers. This is, I would maintain, because they visually solidify the "otherness" of the text – that is, at least, for the *white* viewer/listener, and indeed, for the *composer* as well. The performers take the edge off any disturbance that could be caused by the language, and in another way, by the music; they manifest it in the image of its otherness. This might have been a more difficult thing to do if the opera viewers had been able to bring any expectations to the piece; that is if they had come to view a black *Barber of Seville*, or *Tristan*.

However, the "classical" opera/theatre is not at "risk" here; but clearly, in a very "anxious" way, something else is. It was Thomson's idea to use black performers, and his stated reasons were, as I've said, as visual as they were aural. The visual–aurality has its origins in Thomson's and Grosser's apparent exposure, according to Richard Bridgman, to the work of Marc Connelly (*The Green Pastures*, 1929) and Hall Johnson, whose "*Run Little Chillun*, seems to have made its effect, since Carl Van Vechten reported that at its intermission, Virgil Thomson exclaimed that he would have *Four Saints* sung by Negroes." The prospect of the transposition of black voices and bodies onto Stein's avant-garde language seems to have delighted Thomson; but in correspondence with Stein, in order to sooth *her* anxieties, Thomson's own lack of ease appears. Stein seemed principally concerned about black bodies:

"Your Negroes may sing and enunciate ever so much better than white artists, but I still do not like the idea of showing the Negro bodies," she wrote, envisaging no doubt the women as sketchily garbed and the men in loinclothes. "It is too much what modernistic writers refer to as 'futuristic.' I cannot see its relevance to my treatment of my theme . . .

Hoover's interpolation suggests, perhaps accurately, that perhaps Stein's exposure to, or at least knowledge of, contemporary African-American popular culture was limited to the cabarets, or at least the reputation, of such figures as Josephine Baker, and the usual stereotypes regarding black sexuality. Thomson's response, however, is equally telling in another way. He assures Stein that "'[t]he Negro bodies, if seen at all, would only [be] divined vaguely through long dresses. The movements would be sedate and prim, and the transparence is aimed primarily not at titillating the audience with the sight of a leg but at keeping the texture of the stage as light as possible'." Thomson claims that the Negro bodies would be better than white ones in giving the "'same magnificence'" to the opera as "'they give to classic religious painting and sculpture'."[50] The Negroes are, after all, "'a purely musical desideratum, because of their rhythm, their style and especially their diction'." The idea, put forth by the set designer, Florine Stettheimer, of painting the faces of the performers white, did not come to pass (so to speak); however, it is interesting to note that just after mentioning this possibility, Thomson adds, in a phrase *not* included in the autobiographical version of this letter, that " '[n]obody wants to put on just a nigger show."

The ambivalence of this last statement rings loud and not so clear. One would expect black performers themselves in a certain way to have agreed with Thomson. They had been attempting since the nineteenth century to work out from under the stereotypes of the minstrel show, and indeed, many had used these conventions and stereotypes to begin working into the world of entertainment, eventually with the hope of subverting these constraining images. So, certainly, the performers themselves might not have wanted such a show. At the same time, there is in Thomson's phrasing a certain anxiety, even perhaps horror at the prospect of a "nigger" show.

What he meant by such a phrase is not clear. For one thing, the often reprinted pictures of the original production make it clear that black bodies, male and female, were certainly used, though the bodies of the principal saints seem to be well covered. Moreover, as David Harris points out in regard to the choreography, Frederick Ashton used steps for the untrained dancers which "made allusion to the Charleston and Snake Hips (invented in the 1920s by Earl Tucker), if not to the Savoy's own Lindy Hop." Like the allusions in Thomson's music, and in Stein's libretto (especially to nursery rhymes), "[i]n the dancing, the allusions were almost as explicit. In addition, they were the only acknowledgement in '*Four Saints*' [sic] – with the possible exception of the Gospel music quality (itself a sort of quotation of style) – of the traditions of the black performers."[51]

Harris is right for the most part here; however, there is little in the score that one can clearly discern as being "Gospel" in quality, though there is a certain sense of quotation (aside from the actual quotations) in the music which goes along with the wholesale changes in direction that I describe above. I do not know either what he means by Gospel being a kind of "quotation style," though certainly one can hear *it* quoted often enough in popular American music. But nothing in the opera is swung; there are no "blue" notes or passages; there is little or no syncopation at least of the kind that might recall African-American music up to the thirties. Indeed, the music by both Western avant-garde *and* African-American standards of the time is extremely "straight." The attraction to "blackness" superimposed on the language and music after both had been completed, speaks precisely to what the music *lacks*; and here, perhaps, is the anxiety. Both Stein and Thomson are worried that the presence of these "others" especially *visually*, will overshadow their own work. Put another way, the concern is that the visual or the imaginary will overcome the purported "substance" of the show. At the same time, however, we can infer especially from Thomson's attention to Negro bearing and pronunciation even *more* anxiety that without them, the "substance" of the work might *not* be seen at all.[52] It is no doubt possible that Thomson may have been capitalizing on the current fashion of the twenties and thirties of things Negro. At the same time, he must have come to feel the work of black performers as integral to the piece, since they worked in the 1952 Paris revival, and in the earlier recording of 1947 which included many of the original cast: the notion of blackness as chic had certainly waned by the fifties, fraught as they were to become with the struggle for civil rights.

Even though there is, as I have said, no specific performance or production at which I am looking, I have recalled the original production in order to bring forth a certain dimension of the opera – one could say a certain *repressed* element – which is inscribed nowhere in the music or words, but which nevertheless could be said to trace along in silence just outside, and just out of sight, of any possible reading of the piece. Indeed, this repressed "blackness" actually forms the historical shadow, a silent shadow in the midst of all the music and words, which even now, many years after the first performance, insinuates itself into the opera as the known historical horizon of its possibility. It cannot be performed now, or even be read, without a further addition to the question, *Is it Happening?* since now the question must always be added: *And is the cast entirely black?* For the question, staged as it must be against the historical backdrop of the black voices and bodies, with the sense of both their pastness and futurity in mind, in effect reasserts the terrible paradox of Ellison's *Invisible Man*, which is, of course, that blackness renders one both highly visible in a white world, and also highly invisible at the same time. The Stein/Thomson anxiety about the presence of "blackness" within the opera (be it vocal or visual) finds at the same time in the possible presence of the uninscribed (perhaps because for them it was uninscribable?) "blackness" a perfect sounding "look" for the attractions and repulsions which pervade the opera, a tonal-visuality which, in the parlance of the opera itself, "makes it be not be."

With this uninscribed, this invisible – yet of course, in the original performance, very visible – "blackness" in mind we see then how the opera enters, despite Stein's best intentions, into history, or more accurately, how history crosses or marks inalterably, the opera. She did not of course at the time of her writing see the opera's actual performance with black bodies and voices as a possibility. We can recall too her anxiety in the "Composition" essay about the "time sense" of the work, and the particular way in which a work's historicity subjects it to decay in the face of the very temporality which it helps create; and we can also see that her worry about the use of black performers as too "futuristic" is a kind of concern about the mere popularization of the opera. However, even though history may have lacked acceptable narratives for her, resisting history and narrative did not mean that even her landscapes could finally out-maneuver them. The attempt to put the opera on *in fact* brings it into a collision with a multiplicity of discourses and practices with which it must involve itself. To fall into history is to fall into a place where one's work and one's self know and control less and less. Thomson's attempted "integration" of black popular performance, or at least, the *spectacle* of such performance for the white viewer – a motivation which he does not acknowledge himself – involves not only his unconscious attraction to and repulsion from this culture, but also his capitulation to it in so far as he chose only blacks to play in the opera. What Eric Lott says of the original white players of blackface minstrelsy might also, with revisions, be said of Thomson here: "[t]he very form of blackface – an investiture in black bodies – seems a manifestation of the particular desire to try on the accents of 'blackness' and demonstrates the permeability of the color line."[53] Clearly, for Thomson, if not for Stein, the *investment* in black bodies and voices betrays an attraction, *and* a repulsion, to these bodies and voices at one and the same time. Time enters, history enters, whether it is acknowledged or not, and plays across his tonality even as it plays across Stein's language. I mean here not that this historical dimension of the first performance so much *rules* the meaning of the opera, but rather that meaning must take on this nearly invisible addition. We cannot hear the opera (*I* cannot hear the opera) without hearing the trace of the historical incursion which the piece itself refuses to sound out, but which it also cannot help but make "heard." Whether or not the black performers *need*, or needed, to be there – i.e. were part of the "original" idea – or not, clearly, in some sense they *are* there, even when repressed.

Such an incursion of historicity might, as Lyotard says of the sublime, be "scarcely foreseeable." But it is here, *un*written into this text, rather than elsewhere. This amounts to more than the appropriation of "blackness:" that is there, but it is not all. Rather, with this conjunction between a certain modernist, anti-historical writing, and the historically sanctioned and therefore, "coherent" teleology of tonality – what I have described as the ironic interplay between the potential imaginary identifications of the language, and the quasi-symbolic continuity of the music – we arrive unexpectedly at an instance of the relations between words and music which seems to belong neither to the Mallarméan Book, nor to the Wagnerian, *Gesamstkunstwerk* – or, in another way, perhaps to both, but in no expected way. There is, of course, no absolute coordination between language and musical expression in the opera. There is instead a kind of surface interaction between the two, the hint at a symbolic limit which is really the interaction of two "images," one linguistic the other tonal, which slide past and across each other. Moreover, the entry of history is not mythic and defining, at least in some essentializing sense. Rather, history manifests itself as a defining *accident*: the "appearance" and invisibility of African Americans doubtless marks the "Americanness" of the opera, but offers no grand or mythic necessity which it must express. History here is instead the historicity of the absent presence of the repressed, the return of the other by chance, by the contingent nature of the work as it travels back into the culture, already carrying part of the cultural constellation with it.[54] By "chance," I simply mean "not by choice." Thomson certainly chose the black performers for "his" opera, but it seems that he in no way saw his choice as defining the opera as such. (Indeed, he will often speak of the performers as *his* Negroes.) This choice, then, is circumscribed by both the immediate context of black cultural renewal which we call, now, the "Harlem Renaissance," but at the same time it is defined by the historical parameters of the presence of Blacks in larger American history. It is not that he couldn't have chosen differently, that something else might not also have marked the choice of performers for the opera in some other equally "American" way. But, clearly, to have chosen the performers he did, during the period he did, *and* considering the anxiety which surrounded the choice – all this suggests that the choice is in itself constrained, already marked, and though unforeseen, nevertheless takes part in a very culturally unconscious "return."

On the other hand, if the opera is read as a kind of parodic manifestation of the "Book," we find that the original "openness" of Mallarmé's concept is moved here to a realm far less esoteric than he might have wished. The chance incursion of temporality as an "accident" of historicity sets a limit on the open semiosis of the word, even as it opens a set of other possibilities quite unexpected, quite unprepared for. This "accident" is, however, hardly accidental, though it was not at all foreseeable. It was the very condition of the "*Is it happening?*" the query established by the opera itself, and asked over and over again in various ways throughout its course. Now, however, we ask not only how many acts, or doors or windows might be in "it," but we also *ask after* movements and vocalities of the black performers shaping and and re-shaping silently the opera's tonal and lingusitic complexities.

It may be, then, that the actual collision, or even collusion, of words and music, sets in operation a new or different kind of "book" (without a capital b), offering a kind of hint of "totality" or a sense that there is *more* here, but "here" is always somehow dislocated, constantly disrupted by its own presence. Even as the question "*Is it happening?*" is being answered by the occurrence of this opera, and not something else, "something else" is already at play with the particularity of this event. And this is perhaps the "*It is happening,*" of some cultural temporality already not thought of, always at bay, but nevertheless, cutting across the event in ways beyond its control.

Endings

We have returned to our beginnings with the Stein/Thomson opera, but what we might know of these origins has changed. I began with an heuristic opposition between Mallarmé's Book, and the total art work of Wagner, and teased out some of the possible implications that this relationship between music and language might possess for writers who followed. This was not simply or only an attempt to see the formation of a single, all-encompassing line of aesthetic thought; I have made no case for "development" or for the predictable arguments of inheritance and "progress." The final collaboration of Stein and Thomson returns us to both "Book" and music but without either Wagner's sense of their potential totality or Mallarmé's notion of the mysterious fulfillment of meaning in deferment. What the Stein/Thomson collaboration confirms is mystery replaced with the problems of perception and knowledge and without the desire for prospective fulfillment. The surfaces of language and music here seem to acknowledge the perplexity of the problems and possibilities of their union. However, music is no longer the answer to the problem of expressivity, but rather part of the articulation of the complexities of meaning and expression. It is as though this collaboration joins both Book and music together as the reformation of an aesthetic ideal, but one now defined in what I take to be more modernist terms. For what has taken place is the implicit performance of the inside turned out, but with no guarantee of, and it seems little concern for, the sense that meaning in any ultimate sense can be confirmed. Language and music here cooperate in their own propinquity, and in effect, demonstrate the problem of the supplementarity of modernist formal experimentation by refusing any final totalizing synthesis – mythological, symbolic, psychological. The issue is not just one of "expression," the guarantee (or lack of it) that the inside can be turned out and made to "mean." This last text instead elaborates and also exposes the anxiety of the surfaces of language and music as these structure the modernist attempt to guarantee the authenticity of the interiority they construct. The very problems of knowledge and aesthetic practice are articulated in the ambivalent conception of music as an aesthetic ideal in Pater. The point is plain enough too in Joyce's amplification of the codes of hearing as these construct the multiple spaces of Dublin. The desire for a revitalized security of surfaces is clear in Pound's efforts to theorize music and to make it into part of his practice of an aesthetics of absolute immanence. His own operatic performance, shaped as it is within his conceptions of absolute rhythm and Great Bass, does not so much prove his theories true – those of harmony or those concerned with the overall basis for poetry – as offer him a method for structuring a particular, interestingly executed, work.

The Stein/Thomson collaboration points to still another dimension of modernist–musical relations. The critical history of modernism often speaks of its concern with form, and its desire to affirm an order of meaning separate from the culture of modernity itself. But in Pound's musical and poetic theorizing, and in his practice, we have seen quite clearly that, however dubious the results, he is greatly concerned about the reformation of form precisely *because* of its relation to his own time and culture. In a rather different, but no less complex, way, *Four Saints* presents us with a more unexpected cleavage between the aesthetic and the social. This is, of course, the collision with the contemporary history of American culture itself. In regard to music's own relations with the social, Theodor Adorno remarks

The demands made upon the subject by the material [of music] are conditioned much more by the fact that the "material" is itself a crystallization of the creative impulse, an element socially predetermined through the consciousness of man. As a previous subjectivity – now forgetful of itself – such an objectified impulse of the material has its own kinetic laws. That which seems to be the mere self-locomotion of the material is of the same origin as is the social process, by whose traces it is continually permeated. This energy pursues its course in the same sense as does actual society, even when energy and society have become totally unaware of each other and have come into conflict with each other.[1]

I don't mean here in the final moments to introduce a completely new set of ideas courtesy of the Frankfurt School; but I am fascinated with Adorno's defense of the difficulties of the New Music. This passage comes from *The Philosophy of New Music*, a book in which Adorno is in part defending Schoenberg's music from the charges of bourgeois hermeticism; it is a text which goes to great lengths to explain the historical necessity of this "ugly," and potentially elitist, music. Adorno clearly links here the social and the aesthetic in an unavoidable interplay between inside and outside. If the social "returns" so to speak in the operatic collaboration of Stein and Thomson, it does so despite the efforts, especially by Stein, to resist history. However, such resistance might in fact be her very necessary response to the shape of history that she knew, the composition of her present time. For her very resistance becomes the site of history's return in Thomson's tonal practice and the presence and absence of the Negro performers. Perhaps what music signals in the work of modernists who attempt to take on its non-lexical power is not an "excess" of meaning beyond the grasp of mere words, but the excess of time and history as these collide with and shape the composition (as Stein might say) in ways unforeseen and uncontrollable by any aesthetic design. My sense is that whether consciously or not, this is what "music" comes to mean within certain areas of literary modernism. It is not merely that the Paterian "wall of personality" cannot be broken through, but that such a wall is never in itself complete or totally impermeable to the contingencies of history, culture, time, or the various combinations of these. Rather, such a "wall" is always in part constructed by these. Even when one attempts a kind of thorough-going incorporation of time and form through music, as Pound does, the attempt can backfire and reinforce the isolation of the "wall of personality," not simply because personality itself is some matter which involves the problem of making a correspondence between inside and outside, but because there is *always* a constant interplay between the two, and the meaning of surfaces, immanent or otherwise, can never be fully controlled. "Music" in its non-lexical but very powerful immediacy marks out for these moderns both an attempt to overcome this contingency, but in another way, it also tends to reinforce or even reinvent it at the same time. Music, as practice, as linguistic ideal, or even as accompaniment tends to reinforce and amplify the anxiety of modernist formal experimentation, to maintain its supplementarity, its desire to point to some place of potential transcendence, even as it invents that place.

What I have tried to trace here, or, in a way, that which I have "discovered" is not simply that music, however conceived, is the ultimate model for the formal separation of writing from history or the social realm. Rather, music becomes the means for writing's return to such a realm, but it returns with its surety shaken, with its anxiety of form now exposed, and is at last set upon the search for less ghostly demarcations, keener sounds.

Notes

INTRODUCTION

1 Alex Aaronson rightly points out that the notion of such transcendental harmony goes back to Pythagoras; numerical order on earth participates in the same kind of harmoniousness which structures the universe. See Alex Aronson, *Music and the Novel: A Study in Twentieth-Century Fiction* (Totowa, NJ: Rowman and Littlefield, 1980), especially chapter 1.

2 Ibid., p. 32.

3 Often, as is the case with Franz Liszt, the expressivist view is stated in quasi-religious terms: "Music . . . presents at one and the same time the intensity and the expression of *feeling*; capable of being apprehended by our senses, it permeates them like a dart, like a ray, like a dew, like a spirit, and fills our soul. If music calls itself the supreme art, if Christian spiritualism has transported it, as alone worthy of Heaven, into the celestial world, this supremacy lies in the pure flames of emotion that beat one against another from heart to heart without the aid of reflection . . .", Franz Liszt, "Berlioz and His 'Harold' Symphony," 4 vols., *Source Readings in Music History: The Romantic Era*, ed. Oliver Strunk, vol. 4 (New York: W. W. Norton, 1965), p. 109.

4 Michael H. Levenson, *A Genealogy of Modernism: A Study of English Literary Doctrine 1908–1922* (Cambridge: Cambridge University Press, 1984), p. 134.

5 Ibid., p. 135.

6 Ibid.

7 Some perhaps obvious figures may be overlooked here, such as T. S. Eliot, and W. H. Auden, two poets (among many other writers) with very different, but very definite relationships with music. I have taken up Eliot elsewhere: "Eliot's Impossible Music," *T. S. Eliot's Orchestra: Critical Essays on Poetry and Music*, ed. John Xiros Cooper (New York: Garland, 2000).

8 This cooks down in Wilde into the aphoristic "All art is at once surface and symbol," Oscar Wilde, "The Preface," *The Picture of Dorian Gray*, ed. Peter Ackroyd (Harmondsworth: Penguin, 1985), p. 6.

9 *The Mother of Us All* (1946), Stein and Thomson's second and final collaboration, is more conventionally "historical" in its use of figures and music from American history to tell the story of Susan B. Anthony, the mother of the title. The earlier *Four Saints*, I believe, "returns" to history despite itself,

and for my purposes here, this fact reinforces my argument about the supplementarity of modernist form and the idea of music.

I PRELIMINARIES: OF MUSIC AND MODERNISM

1 Paul Valéry, "A Foreword," *The Art of Poetry*, trans. Denise Folliot, ed. Jackson Matthews, Bollingen Series XLV, *The Collected Works of Paul Valéry*, vol. VII (Princeton, NJ: Princeton University Press, 1958), p. 41.
2 Ibid., pp. 42, 43.
3 Sanford Schwartz, *The Matrix of Modernism: Pound, Eliot, and Early Twentieth-Century Thought* (Princeton, NJ: Princeton University Press, 1985), p. 38.
4 Oscar Wilde, "The Preface," *The Picture of Dorian Gray*, ed. Peter Ackroyd (Harmondsworth: Penguin, 1985), p. 6. Frederick Nietzsche, *The Birth of Tragedy and the Case of Wagner*, trans. Walter Kaufmann (New York: Vintage, 1967), p. 45.
5 Nietzsche, *Birth*, pp. 43, 36. Nietzsche's opposition between Apollo and Dionysus is part of a larger late nineteenth-century concern with the two-fold figure of Marsyas, or Pan. Marsyas, master of the flute, challenged Apollo, god of the lyre, to a music contest – a bit of audacity which literally cost Marsyas his skin. Marsyas is another figuration of Pan, the goat-god connected with Dionysus. J. E. Chamberlin points out that Marsyas is both a figure of "melancholy rebellion", J. E. Chamberlin, *Ripe was the Drowsy Hour: the Age of Oscar Wilde* (New York: The Seabury Press, 1977), p. 155, and, as Pan, is associated with "the energies and intensities of primitive forces" (p. 156). Late nineteenth-century authors such as Wilde and Pater related Dionysus and Pan with an affirmation of life as "defined by sorrow and suffering" (p. 158), and with the "artist's need to find expression" (p. 159). The implication is that the suffering of loss becomes its own affirmation (see Nietzsche, *Birth*, p. 40, in regard to a similar idea). This idea will show up again, with some variation, below.
6 Jorge Luis Borges, "Tlön, Uqbar, Orbis Tertius," *Labyrinths: Selected Stories and Other Writings*, trans. James E. Irby, eds. Donald A. Yates and James E. Irby (New York: New Directions 1964), p. 3.
7 Modris Eksteins, *Rites of Spring: the Great War and the Birth of the Modern Age* (Toronto: Lester and Orpen Dennys, 1989), p. 16.
8 Ibid., pp. 13, 14, 14–15.
9 Charles Baudelaire,"The Painter of Modern Life," *Baudelaire: Selected Writings on Art and Artists*, trans. P. E. Charvet (Cambridge: Cambridge University Press 1971), p. 420. This does not begin to illuminate the complexities of the dandy as a nineteenth-century figure of resistance to conventional culture. For more, see Wylie Sypher, *The Loss of the Self in Modern Literature and Art*. (New York: Vintage, 1962), p. 38.
10 Harold Bloom, "The Internalization of Quest Romance," *Romanticism and Consciousness: Essays in Criticism*, ed. Harold Bloom (New York: W. W. Norton and Co. 1970), pp. 4, 6.

11 Frank Kermode, "The Modern," *Modern Essays* (London: Collins, Fontana Books, 1971), p. 61. In *Romantic Image* (New York: Vintage Books, 1957) Kermode points to the ongoing belief in the necessary isolation of the artist, and of the artist's mission to encapsulate some kind of extra-social truth: ". . . how is the artist different, and what is the nature of his special access to truth . . . [?]" (p. 19). Kermode sees these issues as central to both nineteenth- and twentieth-century poetics.

12 Edmund Wilson, *Axel's Castle: a Study in the Imaginative Literature of 1870–1930* (New York: Charles Scribner's Sons, 1931), pp. 1–2.

13 Ibid., pp. 16–17, 17.

14 Edgar Allan Poe, "The Poetic Principle," *The Works of Edgar Allan Poe*, biographical introduction by Hervey Allen (New York: P. F. Collier and Son Co., 1927), pp. 769, 770.

15 Poe, "The Philosophy of Composition," *The Works of Edgar Allen Poe*, pp. 819, 813.

16 In *The Decadent Imagination, 1880–1900*, trans. Derek Coltman (Chicago: University of Chicago Press, 1981), Pierrot gives a clear summary of Poe's influence on the French. Pierrot establishes a provisional distinction between symbolism and decadence in terms of the different reactions to Poe: ". . . one might say that the [symbolists], guided by Mallarmé, were most receptive to Poe's ideas on creativity, the poetic consciousness, and the theory of effect . . . whereas the 'decadents' proper were primarily imitators of Poe's taste for the morbid, his macabre effects, his interest in dreams, and his descriptions of abnormal nervous phenomenon" (p. 33). Daniel Hoffman, in his insistently titled, *Poe Poe Poe Poe Poe Poe Poe Poe* (Garden City, NY: Doubleday and Co., Inc., 1972), discusses Poe's "Philosophy of Composition," and says that Poe's portrayal of himself as "a master-creator working out the details of his preconceived plan" (p. 96) points the way to the symbolists and to "their self-consciousness as artists" (p. 96).

17 Wilson, *Castle*, p. 20. As Wilson also points out, "[t]he symbolists, full of the idea of producing with poetry effects like those of music, tended to think of images as possessing an abstract value like musical notes and chords" (Wilson, *Castle*, p. 21). It is true that the romantics, especially those in England, were concerned with issues of poetic language. Much of the "Preface" to the *Lyrical Ballads*, for instance, is concerned with the nature of poetic language, and, of course, there is Coleridge's reaction to Wordsworth in the *Biographia Literaria*, as well as his own views on poetic language both in the *Biographia*, and elsewhere. Arthur Symons had noted before Wilson the same tendency especially in Mallarmé. See his discussion of Mallarmé in *The Symbolist Movement in Literature*, 2nd revised edn. 1919, introduction by Richard Ellmann (New York: E. P. Dutton and Co., Inc., 1958), especially, p. 72.

18 Kathleen Henderson Staudt, "The Poetics of 'Black on White': Stéphane Mallarmé's 'Un Coup de dés'," *Ineffability: Naming the Unnameable from Dante to Beckett*, eds. Peter S. Hawkins and Anne Howland Schotter (New York: AMS Press, Inc., 1984), pp. 151, 148, 153, 158–159.

19 Think of the prefaces or notes that precede many of their works, and, too, the way in which so much romantic poetry desires to keep the reader informed as to the movements of the poet's mind as it responds to perception.

20 There is little doubt of Mallarmé's hierarchical tendencies. But for a more complex and rich view of his position toward mass culture, see Paula Gilbert Lewis, *The Aesthetics of Stéphane Mallarmé in Relation to his Public* (Cranbury, NJ: Associated University Presses, Inc.,1976) especially chapter one.

21 Eduard Hanslick, *On the Musically Beautiful*, 8th edn., trans. Geoffrey Payzant (Indianapolis, IN: Hackett Publishing Co., 1986), pp. 70–71, 42.

22 The interstice between language as sound and language as written is that which constitutes the "phenomenality" or materiality of language as I speak of it here. At various times, authors speak of writing as though they mean only sound, as if writing itself is not an issue. For instance, some of Pound's early statements on the use of sound in poetry seem to separate the two dimensions of language (see chapter three). But clearly, in Mallarmé's sense of poetry as the redemption of language, or in Joyce's play with aural and scripted puns in "Sirens" (chapter four), there is the sense that writing and sound are both at work, though perhaps often at odds, as elements of the text. There is no fixed sense of one aspect taking priority over the other.

In recent years, discussions have appeared which counter the older notions of music and writing as strictly temporal arts. W. J. T. Mitchell has recently revised Joseph Frank's argument on spatiality in literature, originally put forth in 1948 and extended in Frank's *The Widening Gyre: Crisis and Mastery in Modern Literature* (New Brunswick, NJ: Rutgers University Press, 1963). Mitchell says that it is erroneous to regard space and time as "antithetical modalities," (W. J. T. Mitchell, "Spatial Form in Literature," *The Language of Images*, ed. W. J. T. Mitchell (Chicago, IL: Chicago University Press, 1980), p. 274, as many literary critics do, and to speak of spatial form as "'static,' or 'frozen,' or as involving some simultaneous, instantaneous, and wholistic impression of that which is 'really' temporal" (p. 274). Mitchell points out that the "linear track of the script . . . is literally a spatial form, and only metaphorically a temporal one" (p. 276). Noting the distinction between represented time and the text as a temporal object, Mitchell goes on to point out that no matter what sense of time we get from a text, we must realize that we are "decoding a spatial form . . ." (p. 276). In these terms, then, Mitchell concludes that any literary text is spatial and that "[w]e cannot experience a spatial form except in time, [and] we cannot talk about out temporal experience without invoking spatial measures" (p. 276).

Similarly, in response to Stravinsky's reiteration of the very old claim that music is a "chronologic art," and that it "presupposes before all else a certain organization of time, a chronomony . . ." (Igor Stravinsky, *Poetics of Music in the Form of Six Lessons*, trans. Arthur Knodel and Ingolf Dahl (Cambridge, MA: Harvard University Press, 1942), p. 28), Robert Morgan has argued that space is an essential element not only of musical experience, but also of the basic elements of Western tonality and its methods of composition. Speaking of the space between octaves which is separated into segments by means of different pitches, he points out that "one can speak of a total space subdivided into a number of equal segments, each of which contains the same twelve pitches, these pitches recurring regularly throughout the entire range" (Robert P. Morgan, "Musical Space/Musical Time," *The Language of Images*, ed. Mitchell, p. 262). Thus, "[t]here is absolutely nothing temporal about this space; it is an abstract system of mutual relationships, existing prior to and logically independent of a particular compositional ordering" (p. 262). Morgan goes on to point out how the conventions of tonality, as they focus on the centrality of one pitch, and the hierarchical relationship between this pitch and the others in the scale "defines a highly structured and largely conventional 'musical space'. . ." (p. 262). The particular design of a given composition distinguishes itself only as it "moves temporally through this prescribed space" (p. 262). In other words, a composition "not only defines its own space, but does so by moving through this space in its own unique manner" (p. 261). Hence, he argues the inseparability of musical time and space (p. 261). Morgan extends his argument to include the twelve-tone system as well. See pp. 266–268 especially.

23 Stéphane Mallarmé, "Crisis in Poetry," *Selected Prose Poems, Essays, and Letters*, trans. Bradford Cook. (Baltimore, MD: Johns Hopkins University Press, 1956), pp. 40, 41.

24 Mallarmé, "Crisis," p. 42. In *The Mirror and the Lamp: Romantic Theory and the Critical Tradition*, (London: Oxford University Press, 1953), M. H. Abrams reminds us of the neoplatonic tradition which held that the realm of Plato's ideas "in addition to the region of their transcendental subsistence, . . . were given a secondary location within the human mind itself" (p. 43). As versions of this notion come down to the nineteenth century, this secondary location is, for the romantics, of primary importance in establishing poetic credibility. Unlike Bloom and others who, as we saw above, claim that romanticism marks a movement away from nature to the imagination, Abrams maintains that, in whatever form this philosophy reaches these later poets, the location of the ideas "maintain[s] their theoretical grounding in the nature of the external universe" (p. 45). In either Bloom's view or Abrams', the poet is still featured as the basis of poetic truth.

25 Stravinsky, *Poetics*, p. 28.

26 Peter Dayan, *Mallarmé's "Divine Transportation": Real and Apparent Sources of Literary Value* (Oxford: Clarendon, 1986), p. 193.

27 Immanuel Kant, *Critique of Judgement*, trans. J. H. Bernard (New York: Hafner Publishing Co., 1951), sec. 53, pp. 172, 173, 174.

28 G. W. F. Hegel, *Aesthetics: Lectures on Fine Art*, 2 vols., vol. II, trans. T. M. Knox (Oxford: Oxford University Press, 1975), pp. 903, 904, 955.

29 Arthur Schopenhauer, *Die Welt als Wille und Vorstellung. Music and Aesthetics in the Eighteenth and Early-Nineteenth Centuries*, eds. Peter le Huray and James Day (Cambridge: Cambridge University Press, 1981), pp. 312, 325, 328.

30 Ibid., pp. 325.
31 Ibid., pp. 328, 329, 329–330.
32 Carl Dahlhaus, *Esthetics of Music*, trans. William W. Austin (Cambridge: Cambridge University Press, 1982), p. 43.
33 Carl Dahlhaus, *The Idea of Absolute Music*, trans. Roger Lustig (Chicago, IL: University of Chicago Press, 1989), pp. 17, 54.
34 Walter Pater, *The Renaissance: Studies in Art and Poetry*, 4th edn., edited with an introduction by Adam Phillips (Oxford: Oxford University Press, 1986), p. 86. Hanslick will in fact try to reconcile a kind of veiled Hegelianism with the non-lexical dimensions of intrumental music. His idea of musical meaning as "tonally moving forms" (Hanslick, *On the Musically Beautiful*, p. 29) is an attempt to move the Hegelian concept of the *content* ("spirit, [or] essential form, form created from the inside out" [Dahlhaus, *Absolute Music*, p. 111]) of art to the level of form itself, so that "The ideal content of the composition is in these concrete tonal structures, not in the vague general impression of an abstract feeling. The form (as tonal structure), as opposed to the feeling (as would-be content), is precisely the real content of music, is the music itself . . ." (Hanslick, *Musically Beautiful*, p. 60).
      Dahlhaus disparages any necessarily causal connection between the history of absolute music and symbolists such as Mallarmé and Baudelaire. Still, he admits that his own "sketch of structural connections between music aesthetics and poetic theory is intended as support for the claim that the concept of absolute music . . . was a secular idea that represented the artistic feelings of an entire age" (Dahlhaus, *Absolute Music*, p. 143).
35 Jacques Derrida, *Of Grammatology*, trans. Gayatri Chakravorty Spivak (Baltimore, MD: Johns Hopkins University Press, 1982), pp. 144, 145. Music may in fact possess a certain doubled identity for modernity rather like that described in Baudelaire's famous definition of the modern in "The Painter of Modern Life": "Modernity is the transient, the fleeting, the contingent; it is one half of art, the other being the eternal and the immovable," Charles Baudelaire, "The Painter of Modern Life," *Baudelaire: Selected Writings on Art and Artists*, trans. P. E. Charvet (Cambridge: Cambridge University Press 1971), p. 403. What is veiled in Baudelaire's definition is, of course, the past, the sense of history and tradition. It is subsumed in the sense of contingency of the present, and thus points up the fact that, as Paul de Man says in a discussion of Nietzsche, modernity itself is "a generative power that not only engenders history, but is part of a generative scheme that extends far back into the past," Paul de Man, "Literary History and Literary Modernity," *Blindness and Insight: Essays in the Rhetoric of Contemporary Criticism*, Theory and History of Literature VII (Minneapolis, MN: University of Minnesota Press, 1983), p. 150.
36 Mallarmé, "Crisis," p. 42.
37 Mallarmé, "The Book: a Spiritual Instrument," *Selected Prose Poems, Essays, and Letters*, trans. Bradford Cook (Baltimore, MD: Johns Hopkins University Press, 1956), pp. 25, 26, 25, 24, 27, my emphasis.

38 Elwood Hartman, *French Literary Wagnerism* (New York & London: Garland Publishing Inc., 1988), p. 10. See M. H. Abrams' discussion in *The Mirror and the Lamp*, pp. 89–94, especially pp. 93–94. See also, for example, Friedrich von Hausegger, *Music as a Form of Expression, Music and Aesthetics in the Eighteenth and Early Nineteenth Centuries*, eds. Peter le Huray and James Day (Cambridge: Cambridge University Press, 1981), p. 110; Johann Gottfried Herder, *Kalligone, Music and Aesthetics in the Eighteenth and Early Nineteenth Centuries*, eds. Peter le Huray and James Day, p. 257; and Wilhelm Heinrich Wackenroder, *Phantasien über die Kunst für Freunde der Kunst, Music and Aesthetics in the Eighteenth and Early Nineteenth Centuries*, p. 250. A more recent proposal of the transcendent nature of music appears in George Steiner's *Real Presences*. Steiner claims that "[t]he messianic intimation in music is always present," George Steiner, *Real Presences* (Chicago, IL: University of Chicago Press, 1989), p. 19, and that such musical intimations remain beyond the scope of language (p. 20).

   More recent critics suggest that music's apparent lack of semantic precision is what gives it its emotional power. Suzanne K. Langer, for instance, believes that music does have semantic import, Suzanne K. Langer, *Philosophy in a New Key: a Study in the Symbolism of Reason, Rite, and Art*, 3rd. edn. (Cambridge, MA: Harvard University Press, 1980), p. 218, but that its scope of potential meaning goes beyond language (p. 243). She says that though music may lack "'dictionary meaning'" (p. 229), it nevertheless traces "*the morphology of feeling*" (her emphasis, p. 229). For Langer, music is an "*unconsummated symbol*. Articulation is its life, but not assertion; expressiveness, not expression" (p. 240).

   Langer, and other writers on the expressive nature of music, such as Carroll C. Pratt, *The Meaning of Music*, (New York: McGraw-Hill, 1932), Leonard Meyer, *Emotion and Meaning in Music*, (Chicago, IL: Chicago University Press, 1956), and Peter Kivy, *Sound Sentiment: an Essay on the Musical Emotions, including the complete text of 'The Corded Shell'* (Philadelphia, PA: Temple University Press, 1989) are, in their various ways, concerned with reconciling formalist and expressivist thought on music.

39 E. T. A. Hoffmann, "Beethoven's Instrumental Music," *Source Readings in Music History: the Romantic Era*, ed. Oliver Strunk, 4 vols. (New York: W. W. Norton, 1965), vol. IV, pp. 35, 35–36.

40 Franz Liszt, "Berlioz and His 'Harold' Symphony," *Source Readings in Music History*, ed. Strunk, vol. IV, p. 109.

41 Richard Wagner, "Beethoven," *Music in European Thought: 1851–1912*, ed. Bojan Bujic (Cambridge: Cambridge University Press, 1988), p. 65. I should note that later on in this work, Wagner attempts to give expressive precedence to "drama." He compares Beethoven's music to Shakespeare's movement of plot and characterization (p. 72). "Drama," in this later essay is conceived in terms more "expressive" than narrative in any conventional sense (pp. 74–75). The "Beethoven" essay is heavily influenced by Schopenhauer.

42   Wagner, *Wagner on Music and Drama*, trans. H. Ashton Ellis, selected and arranged by Albert Goldman and Evert Sprinchorn (New York: Da Capo Press, Inc., 1988), p. 152.

43   Ibid., pp. 197, 199, 199–200, 203, 204. Wagner joins the process of musical modulation to the construction of verse in *Stabreim*. A key associated with *"Liebe giebt Lust zum Leben"* ("Love gives delight to living") (p. 210) can be changed (indeed, in terms of Wagner's theory of linking words and music, it *must* be changed) when we come to the darker import of the first few words of another phrase, *"doch in ihr Weh auch webt sie Wonnen* ("But with her woe she weaves things winsome") (p. 211). But, as Wagner points out, at *"webt . . .* [there appears] a tone leading into the first key, as from *here* the second emotion returns to the first, but now enriched, emotion" (p. 211). The idea is to link emotions through the kinship of consonant and vowel sounds, as well as through the harmonic progress of the music.

44   Wagner, *Wagner on Music and Drama*, p. 208. There is an interesting parallel to Wagner's drive toward an expressive and representational musical art in Wassily Kandinsky's later concern with the spiritual in his abstract art. Kandinsky, like Wagner, maintained that "the soul is affected through the medium of the senses – the felt," Wassily Kandinsky, *Concerning the Spiritual in Art and Painting in Particular*, trans. Michael Sadleir, Francis Golffing, *et al. The Documents of Art* v (New York: George Wittenborn, Inc., 1947), p. 23, note 1, though the means of art, the "'how'" is ultimately less important than the "'what' which forms the spiritual necessity of the nascent awakening" (p. 29). Kandinsky, however, sought such an awakening through a decidedly non-representational and antimaterialist means. See Sixten Ringbom, *The Sounding Cosmos: a Study in the Spiritualism of Kandinsky and the Genesis of Abstract Painting*, Acta Academuae Aboensis, ser. A, vol. xxxviii nr. 2 (Abo: Abo Akademi, 1970), pp. 39–48; and chapter 3.

45   Ibid., p. 210.

46   Ibid., pp. 217, 215, 218, 219.

47   Ibid., pp. 217, 218.

48   Ibid., pp. 229, 222. Wagner at no point in his theoretical work uses the term "leitmotif." Wagner illustrates the motivic property of remembrance with reference to the end of Act ii of *Lohengrin* where Ortrud appears at the last moment, much to the dismay of Elsa. With the entry into the ostensibly happy scene of a character who threatens the main character, the audience is filled with "foreboding" (p. 227). This foreboding is underscored with a "remembrance" elaborated by the orchestra with "the emphatic repetition of a melodic phrase which we have already heard as the musical expression of words referring to the threat . . ." (p. 227). The reappearance of the threat in the form of the motive thus becomes, as well, a prophecy of future trouble for the character.

49   Suzanne Bernard, *Mallarmé et la musique* (Paris: Librairie Nizet, 1959), p. 32. See also David Hertz, *The Tuning of the Word: the Musico-Literary Poetics of the Symbolist Movement* (Carbondale, il and Edwardsville, il: Southern Illinois

University Press, 1987), pp. 62–63, and Wagner, *Wagner on Music and Drama*, p. 191.

50 Stéphane Mallarmé, *Oeuvres Complètes* (Paris: Gallimard, 1945), p. 364; Mallarmé, "Crisis in Poetry," p. 38. On the salvation of language by verse: ". . . philosophiquement rémunère le défaut des langues, complément supérieur"(*Oeuvres Complètes*, p. 364); on the diversity of languages: ". . . la diversité, sur terre, des idiomes empêche personne de proférer les mots, qui, sinon se trouveraient, par une frappe unique, elle-même materiellement la vérité"(*Oeuvres Complètes*, p. 364).

51 Mallarmé, "Mystery in Literature," *Selected Prose Poems, Essays, and Letters*, pp. 32, 33. Here Mallarmé repeats an age-old belief, and an essential of musical romanticism: i.e. the idea of music's immediacy, its power to go beyond mediation. For a more recent statement of the idea, see George Steiner, "Silence and the Poet,"" *Language and Silence: Essays on Language, Literature, and the Inhuman* (New York: Atheneum, 1982), pp. 42–43, or his *Real Presences*, pp. 18–21. Interestingly, Mallarmé may in fact be trying to win back a space for poetry that had been lost to the romantic metaphysics of music. Dahlhaus notes that "the pathos used to praise instrumental music was inspired by literature: were it not for the poetic conceit of unspeakability, there would have been no words available for reinterpreting the musically confusing or empty into the sublime or wonderful" (Dahlhaus, *Absolute Music*, p. 63). See all of chapter four of *The Idea of Absolute Music*.

52 Mallarmé, "Music and Literature," *Selected Prose Poems, Essays, and Letters*, p. 47. For more on Mallarmé and the silence of poetic language, see Maurice Blanchot, "Mallarmé and Literary Space," *The Sirens' Song: Selected Essays*, trans. Sacha Rabinovitch, ed. Gabriel Josipovici (Bloomington, IN: Indiana University Press, 1982), especially p. 113: "The language of poetry is not one person's idiom: nobody speaks it and nobody is what speaks it but it is as if speech talked to itself" (p. 113).

53 Bernard, *Mallarmé et la musique*, p. 41; Mallarmé, "Crisis," p. 40; "Music," pp. 48, 50; Mallarmé, *Oeuvres*, p. 649.

54 Mallarmé, Letter to Henri Cazalis July 1866, *Selected Prose Poems, Essays, and Letters*, pp. 89–90.

55 Mallarmé, "Mystery," p. 34. For examples of such "blanks," see *Un Coup de dés*, and "Le vierge, le vivace, et le belle aujourd'hui." For more on the problems of the thematics of "blankness" in Mallarmé, see Jacques Derrida, "The Double Session," *Stéphane Mallarmé: Modern Critical Views*, trans. Barbara Johnson, ed. Harold Bloom (New York: Chelsea House Publishers, 1987), pp. 80–86. However, Paul de Man has shown that the referential dimension of Mallarmé's poetry cannot be dismissed. See "Lyric and Modernity," *Blindness and Insight*, pp. 166–186; especially, pp. 175–180.

56 Derrida, "Double Session," p. 85.

57 Bernard, *Mallarmé et la musique*, pp. 43, 43–44. This need not preclude the possibility of either art "representing" or imitating other objects or sounds: such local imitation is common in music (i.e. the imitation of cuckoo clocks,

knocks on doors, etc.), and architectural forms can be made to resemble, for better or worse, other non-architectural objects.

58 Hanslick, *Musically Beautiful*, pp. 29, 78. The self-consistency Hanslick has in mind is of course that of the creation of music within the boundaries of tonality. Geoffrey Payzant explains that Hanslick is referring to "[t]he system of [connections] between . . . auditory relationships [which are] objective though purely mental. [Such a system] is a formal artifact of human culture and not a material manifestation of nature. It is what musicians call 'tonality' . . . It is the system of varying tensions surrounding a home-note, the *Tonika* to 'tonic'; it is the system of major and minor scales and everything that follows from them such as rules of harmonic progression, voice-leading and melodic interval . . . [including] [r]hythmic motion . . . [and] the waxing and waning in loudness and, presumably, in tempo," Geoffrey Payzant, "Hanslick, Sams, Gay, and 'Tonend Bewegte Formen'," *Journal of Aesthetics and Art Criticism* 40.1 (Fall 1981), 45.

59 Bernard, *Mallarmé et la musique*, pp. 46, 49. "The literary advantage . . . of this copied distance which mentally separates groups of words or words from one another seems to be from time to time the acceleration and the slowing up of the movement, stressing it, conveying it even according to a simultaneous vision of the Page . . . The difference of type-faces between the predominant motif, a secondary one, and those adjoining dictates its importance to the oral utterance, and its range, average, up and down the page, will mark whether the intonation rises or falls. Certain very bold directions alone, infringements, etc., forming the counter-point of this prosody . . .," Mallarmé, Preface, *Un Coup de dés jamais n'abolira le hasard. The Poems*, trans. Keith Bosely (Harmondsworth: Penguin, 1977), pp. 210–211.

60 Mallarmé, *Oeuvres*, p. 71.

61 Mallarmé, "Richard Wagner, Reverie of a French Poet," *Selected Prose Poems, Essays, and Letters*, pp. 73, 75, my emphasis. See Mallarmé, *Oeuvres*, p. 543.

62 Mallarmé, "Reverie," pp. 76, 77. This is a Baudelairean notion of the City which resists, and is entangled with, the idea of beauty within the realm of the fallen world. See, for example, such Baudelaire poems as "Paysage," Charles Baudelaire, *Selected Poems*, trans. Joanna Richardson (Harmondsworth: Penguin, 1975), p. 161, or "Les Petites Vieilles," where the god that appears is "implacable" (p. 169).

63 Mallarmé, "Reverie," p. 77, 78. It is interesting to note that the *Festspielhaus* in Bayreuth is built half-way up the "Green Hill." See Robert L. Jacobs, *Wagner. The Master Musicians Series* (London: J. M. Dent & Sons, Ltd., 1980), p. 107. The "édifice" of the French text seems more suggestive. See Mallarmé, *Oeuvres*, p. 546.

64 Jean-Pol Madou says that in "la mimesis mallarméenne se veut abolition de l'être," Jean-Pol Madou, "Langue, mythe, musique: Rousseau, Nietzsche, Mallarmé, Levi-Strauss," *Littérature et musique*, ed. Raphaël Célis (Bruxelles: Publications des Facultés Universitaires Saint-Louis, 1982), p. 85. But "[d]égagé de toute insertion dans le réel, libéré de toute finitude qui le cap-

turait en une forme figée, l'être ainsi aboli se retrouverait, dans son anéan-
tissement même, riche de toutes . . . virtualités" (p. 85).

2 WALTER PATER: MUSIC AND THE AESTHETIC RESISTANCE TO
HISTORY

1 Walter Pater, *The Renaissance: Studies in Art and Poetry*, 4th edn., edited with an
introduction by Adam Phillips (Oxford: Oxford University Press, 1986),
Pater's emphasis, p. 86. Many critics feel that the political implications of
modernism's detemporalizing aesthetics are plain enough: they point to its
elitism, Andreas Huyssen, *After the Great Divide: Modernism, Mass Culture,
Postmodernism* (Bloomington, IN and Indianapolis, IN: Indiana University
Press, 1986), p. x, or consider it as "aloof [and] hieratic," Ihab Hassan, "The
Question of Postmodernism," *Bucknell Review* 25.2 (Fall 1977), p. 90 in its pre-
disposition toward "transcendence" (p. 92). In part I agree with such assessments; but it will become clear, if it has not already, that I believe there is
quite another anxiety lying beneath modernism's (or, more properly, *modernisms'*) concerns with art.
2 Clive Scott, "Symbolism, Decadence and Impressionism," *Modernism:
1890–1930*, eds. Malcolm Bradbury and James McFarlane
(Harmondsworth: Penguin, 1981), p. 209.
3 Pater, *The Renaissance*, p. xxix. Matthew Arnold, "The Function of Criticism
at the Present Time," *The Complete Prose Works of Matthew Arnold*, vol. III, ed.
R. H. Super, with Sister Thomas Marion Hoctor (Ann Arbor, MI:
University of Michigan Press, 1962), p. 258. Pater's provisional location of
the critic in relation to the work of art can be seen as part of a growing sense
of the historical relativity of theories of art. Wilhelm Worringer, in his
volume, *Abstraction and Empathy: a Contribution to the Psychology of Style*, trans.
Michael Bullock (New York: International Universities Press, 1953), for
instance, suggests that an analysis of the changing "need for style" (p. 13)
could reveal the reasons behind the historical changes in styles of art. Such
a study would seek to expose "the psychic state in which, at any given time,
mankind found itself in relation to the cosmos . . ." (p. 13). Shifts in feelings
about the world could be "gauged from the stylistic evolution of art, as well
as from the theogony of the people" (p. 13). This concern with changing
styles is part of Worringer's own project in outlining the opposition between
abstraction and empathy.
4 Graham Hough, *The Last Romantics* (London: Methuen; New York: Barnes
and Noble, 1961), p. 137. Percy Bysshe Shelley, "A Defense of Poetry," *English
Romantic Writers*, ed. David Perkins (New York: Harcourt Brace Jovanovich,
Inc., 1967), p. 1073. William Wordsworth, "Preface to the Second Edition of
the Lyrical Ballads," *English Romantic Writers*, ed. David Perkins, p. 326.
5 Walter Pater, *Appreciations, with an Essay on Style* (Evanston, IL: Northwestern
University Press, 1987), p. 66. Roland Barthes, *Writing Degree Zero*, trans.
Annette Lavers and Colin Smith (New York: Hill and Wang, 1977), p. 61.

6 Walter Pater, *The Renaissance*, pp. 16, xxix.

7 Ibid. p. xxx. Patricia Clements, *Baudelaire and the English Tradition* (Princeton, NJ: Princeton University Press, 1985), p. 114; see Pater's Preface, *The Renaissance*, p. xxx.

8 Pater, *The Renaissance*, p. 151. Many critics have noted such an isolation in Pater. Ian Fletcher in his essay, "Walter Pater," *Modern Critical Views: Walter Pater*, edited with an introduction by Harold Bloom (New York: Chelsea House, 1985), notes that Pater's method in *The Renaissance* of exploring "not so much a period as a movement of history through related individuals" (p. 49) is appropriate "for a writer who believed passionately in the fruitfulness of the tentative approach, and in the isolation of individuals within the 'flux'" (p. 50). Harold Bloom also says that Pater's "aesthetic man, surrounded by . . . decaying absolutes[,]" "accepts the truths of solipsism and isolation . . . and glories in the singularity of his own peculiar kind of contemplative temperament," Introduction, *Selected Writings of Walter Pater*, edited with an introduction and notes by Harold Bloom (New York: Columbia University Press, 1974), p. xvi. Billie Andrew Inman states the dilemma of the first half of the Conclusion: ". . . Pater shows that modern science can only integrate the human being into the chemical universe and that philosphy, when it presumes to convey truth . . . can only consign the human mind to a solipsistic isolation," Billie Andrew Inman, "The Intellectual Context of Pater's 'Conclusion'," *Modern Critical Views: Walter Pater*, ed. Bloom, pp. 139–140. The Conclusion is absent from the second edition of 1877 but reinserted for the third, 1893. The changes that Pater made for this last version are slight and mostly designed to veil his lack of orthodox religious sentiments. Bloom catalogues the differences in his notes to the Conclusion in *Selected Writings of Walter Pater*, pp. 62–63.

9 Pater, *The Renaissance*, p. 150, 151, 152. Fletcher, "Walter Pater," p. 53. Bloom points out Pater's awareness of Darwin here. See Bloom, *Selected Writings of Walter Pater*, p. 62, note 2.

10 Pater, *The Renaissance*, p. 150.

11 Ibid., pp. 151, 151–152, 152.

12 Carolyn Williams, *Transfigured World: Walter Pater's Aesthetic Historicism* (Ithaca, NY: Cornell University Press, 1989), pp. 24, 24–25, 25. Frank Kermode, in his *Romantic Image*, states Pater's position thus: ". . . art, for all its refusal to worship the *idola* of vulgar morality, is the only true morality; indeed it is nothing less than life itself," Frank Kermode, *Romantic Image* (New York: Vintage Books, 1957), p. 20. In Pater's own time, the question of knowledge even in scientific circles was a contested issue. Karl Pearson, in *The Grammar of Science* (1892), places the whole issue of the objectivity of scientific knowledge in doubt by posing a theory which claimed that the "thing-in-itself" could never be known. All one has is the intersection between immediate sense-impressions and remembered "sense-impresses," Karl Pearson, *The Grammar of Science*, (London: J. M. Dent and Sons, Ltd., 1937), p. 58, which combine to form "*constructs*" (p. 58). There is, then, no distinction between

the inside of the self and the outside, since such a distinction relies solely on the arbitrary division "between one type of sense-impression and another" (p. 60). There is thus no way of escaping the self and possessing a knowledge of the "thing-in-itself." As Pearson puts it, in a very Paterian image, "[w]e *know* ourselves, and we *know* around us an impenetrable wall of sense-impressions" (p. 62), and that is all we can know.

13 Wolfgang Iser, *Walter Pater: the Aesthetic Moment*, trans. David Henry Wilson (Cambridge: Cambridge University Press, 1987), pp. 30, 31, 77. Pater, *The Renaissance*, p. 32.

14 Stephen Spender, *The Struggle of the Modern* (London: Hamish Hamilton, 1963), pp. 79, 80, 71.

15 Lionel Trilling, "On the Teaching of Modern Literature," *Beyond Culture: Essays in Literature and Learning* (New York: Viking Press, 1955), p. 3. Similarly, (though by no means identically) Linda Hutcheon, in her various studies of the postmodern, clearly outlines the interconnections in historiographic metafiction between "literature, history, [and/] or theory," Linda Hutcheon, *A Poetics of Postmodernism: History, Theory, Fiction* (New York: Routledge, 1988), p. 5. Such contemporary writing maintains a "theoretical self-awareness of history and fiction as human constructs (historio*graphic meta*fiction) [which] is made the grounds for its rethinking and reworking of the forms and contents of the past" (Hutcheon's emphasis; p. 5). See also Ihab Hassan's "The Question of the Postmodernism": "Thus postmodernism . . . demands a double view. Sameness and difference, unity and rupture, filiation and revolt. All must be honoured if we are to *attend* to history, apprehend, (perceive, understand) change," Ihab Hassan, "The Question of the Postmodernism, *Bucknell Review* 25.2 (Fall 1977), Hassan's emphasis, p. 121.

16 Virginia Woolf, "Mr. Bennett and Mrs. Brown," *The Captain's Death Bed, and Other Essays* (London: Hogarth Press, 1950), pp. 90, 103, 99. Speaking in yet another "modern" moment in the development of the novel, Alain Robbe-Grillet points out that "[a]ll writers believe they are realists. None ever calls himself abstract, illusionistic, chimerical, fantastic, falsitical . . . It is the real world which interests them; each one attempts as best as can to create 'the real'," Alain Robbe-Grillet, "From Realism to Reality, *For a New Novel: Essay on Fiction*, trans. Richard Howard (New York: Grove, 1965), p. 157.

What is remarkable here is the emphasis on the issue of form as the means of gaining access to "reality," even though such a place has little shared meaning for the three moderns I mention above: one fascist, one high-Anglican conservative, one anti-imperialist. We could, no doubt, also tease out various senses of elitism in these writers. However, the variety of ideological and aesthetic positions covered even among these few writers underlines the importance, *and* the diversity of approaches to formal concerns and their ability to grasp some kind of "realistic" moment.

17 Hayden White, *Tropics of Discourse: Essays in Cultural Criticism* (Baltimore, MD: Johns Hopkins University Press, 1978), p 58. In *Appreciations*, Pater discusses the "imaginative sense of fact," Pater, *Appreciations*, p. 8, possessed by all

writers of fine art. Including the historian in his discussion, he points out that "[y]our historian, for instance, with absolutely truthful intention, amid the multitude of facts presented to him must needs select, and in selecting assert something of his own humour, something that comes not of the world without but of a vision within" (p. 9).

18 Pater, *The Renaissance*, p. xxx. Wolfgang Iser, *Pater*, pp. 36, 37.

19 Pater, *The Renaissance*, p. 153. Harold Bloom, *Selected Writings of Walter Pater*, p. xv. It is debatable, though, whether Pater's passing on of the epiphany to the twentieth century (from Wordsworth's "spots of time") made it into a moment "when the mind will know neither itself nor the object but only the dumbfoundering abyss that comes between" (p. xv). A discussion of the differences and similarities between, say, Joyce's sense of the epiphany and Woolf's "moment of being" would be much more complex than the word "dumbfoundering" can properly describe. For a more complex discussion of epiphany see Morris Beja, *Epiphany in the Modern Novel* (Seattle, WA: University of Washington Press, 1971).

20 For a concise sense of the division, see, for instance, the second paragraph of chapter sixteen of Gotthold Ephraim Lessing, *Laocoön: an Essay on the Limits of Painting and Poetry*, trans. with an introduction and notes by Edward Allen McCormick (Baltimore, MD: Johns Hopkins University Press, 1984), p. 78.

21 Hanslick in his *On the Musically Beautiful* resists similar unifying tendencies in the aesthetics of music. See Eduard Hanslick, *On the Musically Beautiful*, 8th edn., trans. Geoffrey Payzant (Indianapolis, IN: Hackett Publishing Co., 1986), p. 2, and note 2. I think Pater sets the tone for the later moderns who require the need for artifice and a need to legitimize this artifice both aesthetically and historically.

22 Pater, *The Renaissance*, pp. 83, 84. This emphasis on the sensuous is, of course, fundamental to the very idea of the aesthetic. As Terry Eagleton puts it, the study of aesthetics as it appears in the eighteenth century entails a turn toward a "territory [which] is nothing less than the whole of our sensate life together – the business of affections and aversions, of how the world strikes the body in its sensory surfaces . . ." Terry Eagleton, *The Ideology of the Aesthetic* (Oxford: Basil Blackwell Inc., 1990), p. 13. Given Pater's apparent uncertainty about the senses, however, his return to them marks a significant moment in his own aesthetic project.

23 Pater, *The Renaissance*, p. 85. In her discussion of Pater's "Conclusion," Carolyn Williams reminds us that "ecstacy" literally means "'standing apart from (oneself),'" Williams, *Transfigured World*, p. 30. Thus, Pater's phrase, "To burn always with this hard, gem-like flame, to maintain this ecstacy, is success in life," Pater, *The Renaissance*, p. 152, implies the establishment of a "provisional objectivity," Williams, *Transfigured World*, p. 31, a figurative shift away from the "essential self as 'prisoner'" (p. 31). This active sense of self figuratively stands outside the self as prisoner and allows for a much more active response to the world: "In his description of the aesthetically mobile, experimental state of mind, Pater describes a rhythm of identification and

detachment that is, in effect, the mobilization of this internal distance" (p. 31). It is my sense that this method of moving up close, and then backing off is at work in Pater's discussion of aesthetic premises throughout "The School of Giorgione."

24 Pater, *The Renaissance*, p. 85. See Bloom, *Selected Writings of Walter Pater*, p. 58, note 3.

25 Pater, *The Renaissance*, pp. 89, 86 Pater's emphasis, 87. F. C. McGrath says that for Hegel, "the absolute Idea provides the content and its sensible embodiment the form," F. C. McGrath, *The Sensible Spirit: Walter Pater and the Modernist Paradigm* (Tampa, FL: University of South Florida Press, 1986), p. 198, while Pater identifies "form with the underlying intellectual vision [of the artist] and content with the subject matter (the scene or incident) . . ." (p. 198). McGrath also points out, however, that Pater is consistent with Hegel in that Pater "conforms exactly to Hegel's emphasis on the indwelling spirit of art, and the subordinate sensuous elements are important only insofar as they express the spirit" (p. 198). I would say, however, that this idea of Pater's belief in the "expressivity" of the artist's inner vision is somewhat less Hegelian than McGrath claims, since the whole issue of the subject position is made so problematic in Pater. "Vision," in Pater, seems always to mean in some sense re-vision.

26 Pater, *The Renaissance*, pp. 86, 87, 89, 91, 90. In his *Esthetics of Music*, Carl Dahlhaus quotes Herder in response to Lessing: "Music and all energetic arts work in time, not merely in but through temporal sequence by means of an artificial temporal exchange of tones," Carl Dahlhaus, *Esthetics of Music*, trans. William W. Austin (Cambridge: Cambridge University Press, 1982), p. 9. The notion is historically pervasive in Pater's time. Perry Meisel has said of Pater's notion of music (with a somewhat different emphasis): "The 'first' note in the sound of music . . . emerge[s] only as a function of what follows it, thereby situating it even harmonically as a product of the unavoidable retrospect of temporality," Perry Meisel, *The Myth of the Modern: a Study in British Literature and Criticism after 1850* (New Haven, CT: Yale University Press, 1987), p. 58.

27 Pater, *The Renaissance*, p. 95, 94. Earlier in the paragraph which contains the famous "[s]he is older than the rocks among which she sits" passage, Pater, with an obvious allusion to the evolutionary theory of gradual development, describes the face as having the beauty "wrought out from within upon the flesh, the deposit, little cell by cell, of strange thoughts . . ." Pater, *The Renaissance*, p. 80. The sense here, as in the later, more famous passage is the fusion of all historical experience into one moment. Interestingly, Yeats, in *The Oxford Book of Modern Verse*, (1936) published the Mona Lisa passage in what he called "*vers libre*," "Introduction," *The Oxford Book of Modern Verse: 1892–1935*, chosen by W. B. Yeats (Oxford: Oxford University Press, 1936), p. viii, breaking up Pater's sentences, and putting them in stanza form. Yeats justified this being the best way to show Pater's method of developing his image rhythmically ("cell by cell"). See Yeats, "Introduction," pp. viii–ix.

3 THE MUSICAL POETICS OF EZRA POUND

1 See William Cookson, ed., *Ezra Pound: Selected Prose: 1909–1965*, introduction by William Cookson (London: Faber and Faber, 1973), p. 200. The disease metaphor occurs with alarming frequency and avidity when Pound speaks of supposed Jewish influence on language and economics. For instance, in Pound's assessment of T. S. Eliot's most *explicitly* anti-Semitic book, *After Strange Gods*, Eliot "has not come through uncontaminated by the Jewish poison. / Until a man purges himself of this poison he will never achieve understanding. It is a poison that lost no time in seeping into European thought . . . Not a jot or tittle of the hebraic alphabet can pass into the text without danger of contaminating it," "A Visiting Card," p. 290.

2 Ezra Pound, *Guide to Kulchur* (1934. New York: New Directions, 1970), pp. 270–271; "A Visiting Card," p. 284; "An Introduction to the Economic Nature of the United States," p. 144.

3 Robert Casillo, *The Genealogy of Demons: Anti-Semitism, Fascism, and the Myths of Ezra Pound* (Evanston, IL: Northwestern University Press, 1988), p. 18. As Casillo suggests, it is probably the case that the Pound industry has spent the majority of time separating the "intrinsic" value of Pound's poetics, and the "extrinsic" nature of his less tolerant (and tolerable) political positions. See pp. 16–20. Donald Davie, "Critics Who Made Us: Ezra Pound," *Sewanee Review* 92 (July–September 1984), p. 427. Evidence of the necessary connection between politics and art is everywhere in Pound's work. Michael Coyle, *Ezra Pound, Popular Genres, and the Discourse of Culture* (University Park, PA: The Pennsylvania State University Press, 1995) has devoted much space to the relations between Pound's ideas of culture and art. In part, Coyle, without apologizing for Pound's political ideas, points out that "Pound's concern to infect 'purely aesthetic experience' with the germ of history and economics identifies his perpetuation of a tradition in English writing sustained over two centuries, and which in the nineteenth century included among others Coleridge, Carlyle, Ruskin, Arnold, Morris, and Bosanquet" (p. 41). Pound, *Kulchur*, p. 27.

4 Pound, *Kulchur*, p. 47.

5 Marianne Korn, *Ezra Pound: Purpose/Form/Meaning* (London: Middlesex Polytechnic Press; Pembridge Press, 1983), p. 13.

6 Pound, "I gather the limbs of Osiris," *Selected Prose: 1909–1965*, ed. Cookson, p. 23. It is at times perhaps too easy to point out the gaps and contradictions in Pound's arguments. What I am concerned with here is not so much his logic, or the lack of it, as with Pound's attempt to reconstruct the meaning and usefulness of art especially as this project concerns the idea of music.

7 Pound, "Osiris," p. 23.

8 Peter Nicholls, *Modernisms: a Literary Guide* (Berkeley, CA: University of California Press, 1995), p. 9; emphasis added, p. 10.

9 Pound, "Osiris," pp. 23, 25. This does sound a lot like the sentiments

expressed in Eliot's "Tradition and the Individual Talent" (1919), and those of Borges in "Kafka and His Precursors" (1954).

10 Korn, *Purpose/Form/Meaning*, pp. 30, 26. The translations Pound speaks of in "I Gather the Limbs" were included in the original and are now accessible in *The Translations of Ezra Pound*, Introduction by Hugh Kenner (New York: New Directions, 1970).

11 Pound, "Osiris," pp. 26, 27.

12 Ibid., pp. 41, 30, 28.

13 Ibid., pp. 33, 34.

14 Ibid., pp. 38, 39.

15 Korn, *Purpose/Form/Meaning*, pp. 68–69, 69. Ezra Pound, "A Retrospect," *Literary Essays of Ezra Pound*, edited with an introduction by T. S. Eliot (London: Faber and Faber, 1954.), pp., 6–7.

16 Pound, "Osiris," p. 27; Hugh Kenner, *The Pound Era*, (Berkeley, CA: University of California Press, 1971), p. 370.

17 Pound, *Translations*, pp. 179, 178. The reader should note that the translation given in *The Translations of Ezra Pound* is not the same as the one used in the "Osiris" essays, though they are in the same order. Stuart Y. McDougal discusses the variants in his *Ezra Pound and the Troubadour Tradition* (Princeton, NJ: Princeton University Press, 1972), pp. 111–114. The translation of *"Sols sui"* given in *Translations*, and which I cite above, is from 1917. See Arnaut Daniel, *"Sols sui." The Translations of Ezra Pound*. Pound seems to adhere to the elaborate extended rhyme scheme, however, and the later translation still works to make my point.

18 Pound, *Translations*, p. 207; Kenner, *Era*, p. 351; Christine Froula, *A Guide to Ezra Pound's Selected Poems* (New York: New Directions, 1982), p. 35. In the *Selected Poems of Ezra Pound* (New York: New Directions, 1956) two commas have been inserted in the first line after "I" and "self." To me they seem like a grammatical redundancy; the consonants keep interrupting, and yet facilitating, the movement of the line. The commas are probably added to improve the clarity of the line, but not its sound. For a detailed, and different, account of Pound's attempt to include history through the technique of the sound of the line as borrowed from Browning's *Sordello*, see Nicholls, *Modernisms*, pp. 37–41.

19 Pound, "How to Read," *The Literary Essays of Ezra Pound*, ed. T. S. Eliot, pp. 25, 26. Though it is probably true that, as Pound goes on into vorticism, his emphasis does become increasingly visual, music, in some form or another, never leaves his aesthetic theory, as we will see later on in the discussion of absolute rhythm and Great Bass.

20 Pound, "How to Read," pp. 41, 42.

21 Pound, *Translations*, p. 23.

22 Martin A. Kayman, *The Modernism of Ezra Pound: the Science of Poetry* (London: Macmillan Press Ltd., 1986), p. 10. Kayman's quotation comes from Michael Bell's "Introduction: Modern Movements in Literature," *The Context of English Literature: 1900–1930*, ed. Michael Bell (London: Methuen and Co.,

Ltd. 1980), p. 18. "Imagism" was of course no single thing. I am concerned
here mainly with Pound's version of the movement. The story of the formation of this none too coherent group, with particular emphasis on
Pound's involvement, is readily available. See Stanley K. Coffman Jr.,
Imagism: a Chapter for the History of Modern Poetry (Norman, OK: University of
Oklahoma Press, 1951), ch. 1; Noel Stock, *The Life of Ezra Pound*, expanded
edition (San Francisco, CA: North Point Press, 1982) especially ch. 11, pp.
132–134; Kenner, *Era*, pp. 173–191; and Glenn Hughes, *Imagism and the
Imagists: a Study in Modern Poetry* (New York: The Humanities Press, 1960),
ch. 1.

23 Coffman, *Imagism,* p. 91. See too C. K. Stead, *Pound, Yeats, Eliot and the
Modernist Movement* (New Brunswick, NJ: Rutgers University Press, 1986), p.
38, where he states that the imagists "tied the poem to things, images,
colours, sounds, scents, escaping equally from abstraction." Pound, "A
Retrospect," *Literary Essays of Ezra Pound*, ed. T. S. Eliot, p. 3.

24 T. E. Hulme, "Romanticism and Classicism," *Speculations: Essays on
Humanism and the Philosophy of Art*, ed. Herbert Read (London: Routledge and
Kegan Paul, 1987), pp. 126, 132. I suggest the connection to naturalism
because of the point I raised earlier about the potential relationship
between symbolism and naturalism as part of Pound's modernist inheritance. Hulme makes no such connection and in fact is quite derogatory
when it comes to prose. He considers prose a kind of "counter language"
(p. 134) in which "concrete things are embodied in signs or counters which
are moved about according to rules, without being visualized at all in the
process" (p. 134). Poetry, on the other hand, is a "visual concrete" (p. 134)
language which uses images not as "mere decoration, but [as] the very
essence of an intuitive language" (p. 135). Stead, *Pound, Yeats, Eliot*, p. 38.

25 Pound, "A Retrospect," pp. 12, 5, 9.

26 Pound, "Wyndham Lewis," *Literary Essays of Ezra Pound*, ed. T. S. Eliot,
p. 430. Korn, *Purpose/Form/Meaning*, p. 31.

27 Korn, *Purpose/Form/Meaning*, pp. 31, 64.

28 Pound, "The Serious Artist," *Literary Essays of Ezra Pound*, ed. T. S. Eliot,
p. 42. "How To Read," p. 21.

29 Pound, "A Retrospect," p. 11. Kenner, *Era*, p. 149.

30 Pound, *Guide to Kulchur*, Pound's emphasis, p. 16. Pound, *ABC of Economics*,
in *Selected Prose*, ed. Cookson, p. 206.

31 Pound, *Translations*, pp. 23, 23–24, 24.

32 See R. Murray Schafer, ed., *Ezra Pound and Music: the Complete Criticism*, commentary by R. Murray Schafer (New York: New Directions, 1977), p. 479.

33 Pound, *Translations*, p. 24.

34 Pound, *Guide to Kulchur*, p. 73. R. Murray Schafer, *Ezra Pound and Music*, vol.
II, unpublished, p. 276. See chapter one of this volume.

35 Mallarmé, "Crisis in Poetry," *Selected Prose Poems, Essays, and Letters*, p. 41.
Pound, *Guide to Kulchur*, pp. 63–68, 68–70, 74, Pound's emphasis, 75. For
more on the similarities and differences between Pound's imagism and sym-

bolism in general, see Herbert N. Schneidau, *Ezra Pound: the Image and the Real* (Baton Rouge LA: Louisiana State University Press, 1969), especially pp. 28–30. Schneidau notes the imagist rejection of "non- discursive ineffability" (p. 29), and also, the imagist turn away from the symbolist tendency to "present the emotion without the object" (p. 29).

36 Pound, *Guide to Kulchur*, p. 233.

37 Schafer, *Ezra Pound and Music*, p. 479. Pound, *Gaudier-Brzeska: a Memoir* (New York: New Directions, 1960), p. 81. The double quotes are given here since Pound is quoting himself from the *Fortnightly Review* September 1914. It should be noted that Pound has shifted his focus in this second entry on Great Bass from meter to tempo or the actual *pace* at which a piece is played. He seems, in fact, to be conflating speed, duration, and frequency of pitch here.

38 Pound, *Gaudier-Brzeska*, p. 88. For more on Pound's resistance to mimesis see Sanford Schwartz, *The Matrix of Modernism: Pound, Eliot, and Early Twentieth-Century Thought* (Princeton, NJ: Princeton University Press, 1985), pp. 105–108.

39 Pound, *Gaudier-Brzeska*, pp. 88, 89, 93, 92.

40 Pound, *Gaudier-Brzeska*, p. 88.

41 H. Schneidau, *The Image and the Real*, pp. 27, 65. Ernest Fenollosa, "The Chinese Written Character as a Medium for Poetry," in *Prose Keys to Modern Poetry*, ed. Karl Shapiro (New York: Harper and Row, 1962), pp. 140, 141, Fenollosa's emphasis 142, 143.

42 Fenollosa, "Character," pp. 142, 148, 149.

43 Ibid., my emphasis, p. 148.

44 Pound, *ABC of Reading* (New York: New Directions, 1960), p. 52. Speaking of the influences, and confluences, of languages that go into the making of Canto 1, Hugh Kenner remarks that the Canto "recapitulates the story of a pattern persisting undeformable while many languages have flowed through it and many more pronunciations in the thousands of years it has been a property of the Western mind" (Kenner, *Era*, p. 149). In other words, the particulars may change, but they always refer to the basic pattern.

45 Pound, *ABC*, pp. 52, 201. Schneidau, *The Image and the Real*, p. 73.

46 Stephen J. Adams, "Are the 'Cantos' a Fugue?", *University of Toronto Quarterly* 45.1 (Fall 1975), 60, 58–59. Pound, *Antheil and the Treatise on Harmony* (New York: Da Capo Press, 1968), 9.

47 Pound, *Treatise*, pp. 10, 21, 29. See Stephen J. Adams, "Musical Neofism: Pound's Theory of Harmony in context," *Mosaic* 13.2 (Winter 1980), 59.

48 Pound, *Treatise*, p. 27. Adams, "Theory," 63. Pound obviously believes in his own quasi-mathematical statements concerning frequencies and rhythms, but he has little patience for those who might wish to justify conventional harmony through scientific mathematical means: "170 pages of mathematics are of less value than a little curiosity and a willingness to listen to the sound that actually proceeds from an instrument," Pound, *Treatise*, p. 33. Clearly, Pound is ambivalent about "science" and what it can offer aesthetic explanation. At

times he seems to seek out scientific explanation; at other times, such as here in the *Treatise*, he will put it into question, even while using it.

49 It is true that the opera is finished more than a decade (1923) before the full-blown version of Great Bass which appears in the *Guide to Kulchur*. Nevertheless, the concept is clearly related to the earlier notion of absolute rhythm, which I think does motivate the scripting of the opera. If the idea of Great Bass is not yet written, it seems clearly in evidence in Pound's thinking here.

One of two other Pound operas is known to have been completed. Pound's *Cavalcanti*, which had been believed lost, was finally pieced together from known material and from manuscripts supplied by Pound's long-time musical associate and lover, Olga Rudge. Conductor Robert Hughes was the one responsible for finally piecing the opera together, and on Monday March 28 1983, at the Herbst Theatre, Civic Center, in San Francisco, the completed version of *Cavalcanti* was premiered. As is the case with *Le Testament*, however, the world still awaits publication of the score. Pound's third opera, *Collis O Heliconii*, never seems to have been completed. Information on *Le Testament* can be gathered from many sources, but one of the most complete and well-informed readings is R. Murray Schafer's unpublished second volume of *Ezra Pound and Music*. See *Ezra Pound and Music*, vol. 2, unpublished. National Library of Canada. File No.: 246–3–2–S1. Figure 2 actually comes from Schafer's manuscript. The manuscript, virtually complete, languishes in the National Archive in Ottawa, Canada. I am grateful to the National Archive for access to the manuscript. I thank Murray Schafer too for the opportunity to use the work here. This second volume reproduces the opera as transcribed in George Antheil's hand; this is, according to Schafer, the most definitive version of the music. It is in any case clearly the version used in the 1971 recording of *Le Testament* conducted by Robert Hughes (Fantasy 12001). This recording is my primary listening source. All references to the opera, unless otherwise noted, will be to Schafer's unpublished reproduction of it.

50 Schafer, unpublished manuscript, Pound's emphasis, pp. 19–23, 25.

51 Cited in Schafer, unpublished manuscript, ellipsis in original, p. 141. For a useful listing of these versions of the opera, see Larry Lyall, "Pound/Villon: *Le Testament de Francois* [sic] *Villon*," *Paideuma* (1973) 2, 17–22. The 1971 recording has the character Villon reading in English sections of the poetry which act to link the arias together.

52 Ibid., Pound's emphases, p. 38.

53 Pound, *Treatise*, p. 46. Murray Schafer notes that here and elsewhere Pound makes a false distinction between Stravinsky and Schoenberg. Pound continually extols the virtues of Stravinsky's "horizontal," rhythmic music in comparison with Schoenberg's supposedly "vertical" theories. The opposite is of course the case (see Schafer, *Ezra Pound and Music*, p. 258, n. 21). Pound may be confusing Stravinsky's dedication to the accurate scripting of rhythm with his own theories of linear harmony, Schafer, unpublished manuscript, ellipses in original, p. 38.

54 Ibid., p. 47.

55 Schafer, unpublished manuscript, pp. 29–30.

56 Hendrik van der Werf, *The Chansons of the Troubadours and Trouvères: a Study of the Melodies and their Relation to the Poems* (Utrecht: A. Oosthoek's Uitgeversmaatschappij NV, 1972), pp. 63, 60. Certainly the music is worth the examination of someone with more knowledge of ancient music than I possess. The opera has mostly been of interest to composers and musicians: Murray Schafer, Robert Hughes, Ned Rorem are the most notable. None of the above, however, would probably claim great expertise in medieval notation or troubadour composition and performance techniques. The problem with this opera is in knowing whether or not Pound saw himself as using specifically troubadour techniques in setting the poetry of Villon, who was not a troubadour or trouvère, and who wrote more than a hundred years after the high point of the troubadours and trouvères.

57 Van der Werf, *The Chansons*, p. 63, emphasis in original 64. The first verse of the "*Dictes moy*" is as follows:

> Dictes moy ou, n'en quel pays,
> Est Flora la belle Romainne,
> Archipiades ne Thaïs,
> Qui fut sa cousine germaine,
> Echo parlant quant bruyt on maine
> Dessus riviere ou sus estan,
> Qui beaulté ot trop plus qu'humaine?
> Mais ou sont les neiges d'antan?

(François Villon, *The Testament. The Complete Works of François Villon*, translated with a biography and notes by Anthony Bonner. Introduction by William Carlos Williams (NewYork: David McKay Co., Inc. 1960), p. 38.

58 Van der Werf, *The Chansons*, p. 65. Murray Schafer remarks on Pound's sense of musical phrasing in relation to the poetry: "Interesting also is Pound's use of a form of enjambment, where the thought-endings and punctuation of the verse are carried across the music without pause or breath-point," Schafer, unpublished manuscript, p. 25. In other words, Pound will not always use the melody or the rhythm to emphasize the end of a line or its sense of pause. This is not always the case, however, as we will see in my discussion of "*Dame du ciel*." Robert Hughes, dir., *Le Testament de François Villon* by Ezra Pound. Fantasy Records, 12001, 1973. Long-play record. Liner notes.

59 I use the term "basis tone" following van der Werf in order to signal the fact that we are not in a tonal compositional mode here with Pound's opera in the same way that the troubadours would not have been either. The term suggests a lack of harmony, as we know it, which the word "tonic" might conjure up (Van Den Werf, *The Chansons*, p. 52). The word, by chance, has fortunate overtones with Pound's own conception of the Great Bass as a "basis."

60 Hughes, *Le Testament*, liner notes. The tritone was known as the *Diabolus in musica* (the Devil in music) in the Middle Ages. I am grateful to my colleague,

composer Michael Matthews, of the Department of Music at the University of Manitoba for a particularly enjoyable and enlightening discussion of the Pound's hexatonic practice here.

61 Schafer, unpublished manuscript, p. 26. Hughes, *Le Testament*, liner notes. Don Michael Randel, *Harvard Concise Dictionary of Music* (Cambridge, Mass.: Belknap, Harvard University Press, 1978), "*Klangfarbenmelodie*," p. 254.

62 Schafer, unpublished manuscript, p. 26. Robert Hughes lists the instrumentation of the 1971 performance as consisting of ". . . nose-flute, flute and piccolo (one player), oboe, saxaphone, bassoon, trumpet (for two bars only!), horn, two trombones, mandolin, violin, cello, three contrabassi, a variety of drums (including tympani), bells, 'bass bells' [sic] – performed here on prepared piano – gongs, sandpaper, dried bones and a percussionist whistling," Hughes, liner notes.

63 Ezra Pound, *The Cantos of Ezra Pound* (New York: New Directions, 1970), p. 456. All references to this edition will henceforth be given by Canto number, followed by the page number: e.g., C 74, p. 456. C 74, pp. 440, 444, 448–449; CI, Pound's emphasis p. 4.

64 Massimo Bacigalupo, *The Forméd Trace: the Later Poetry of Ezra Pound* (New York: Columbia University Press, 1980), p. 101. Carroll F. Terrell, *A Companion to the 'Cantos' of Ezra Pound*, 2 vols. (Berkeley, CA: University of California Press, 1980–1984) notes that Ecbatana was made by Median Deïoces, and constructed in such a way as to correspond with the plan of the universe: "Ecbatana is archetypal as a concept of perfect human order, a reconciliation of nature and civilization as paralleled in other cantos by Ithaca, Troy, Mt. Segur, Thebes, Rome, Wagadu, and later Trinovant (= London)" (p. 14). Leon Surette, *A Light from Eleusis: a Study of Ezra Pound's Cantos* (Oxford: Clarendon Press, 1979), pp. 180–181, 186. Michael H. Levenson, *A Genealogy of Modernism: a Study of English Literary Doctrine 1908–1922* (Cambridge: Cambridge University Press, 1984), p. 135.

65 "Totalitarian" for Pound, has a slightly different meaning than it might in the usual political context. In the *Guide to Kulcher*, Pound devotes an entire chapter to the idea, but refuses an outright definition. The concept seems to include the totality of cultural thought and production: so, from the metaphysics of Plato, he proceeds to the economics of Aristotle, then (among other topics) he includes mention of his own struggles for accurate definition on the artistic front (p. 49) and the need for a similar struggle to begin in economic matters (p. 50). The "totalitarian" concept seems thus to include all cultural matters, not only political ones. The totalitarian idea of culture, in Pound's view, must take into consideration all "the enduring constants in human composition" (p. 47). See Sanford Schwartz, *The Matrix of Modernism: Pound, Eliot, and Early Twentieth-Century Thought* (Princeton, NJ: Princeton University Press, 1985), pp. 105–108 for more on Pound's ideas regarding mimesis.

66 John J. Tucker, "Pound, Vorticism and the New Esthetic," *Mosaic* 16.4 (Fall 1983), 94.

67 W. B. Yeats, "A Packet for Ezra Pound," *A Vision* (London: Macmillan; Papermac, 1989), p. 4. Yeats also describes how Pound scribbled sets of letters on the back of an envelope, which, Yeats thought, represented "emotions or archetypes" (p. 5), and which repeated and reversed themselves with a purpose that escaped Yeats. In the 1936 Introduction to *The Oxford Book of Modern Verse*, Yeats wondered if the poem's "impressions that are in part visual, in part metrical [could] be related like the notes of a symphony," W. B. Yeats, "Introduction," *The Oxford Book of Modern Verse: 1892–1935*, chosen by W. B. Yeats (Oxford: Oxford University Press, 1936), p. xxiv, a statement which Pound, in a letter to Herbert Creekmore dated February 1939, felt was particularly inaccurate: "God damn Yeats' bloody paragraph. Done more to prevent people from reading Cantos for what is *on the page* than any other one smoke screen," Ezra Pound, *The Letters of Ezra Pound: 1907–1941*, ed. D. D. Paige (London: Faber and Faber, 1951), p. 417.

68 Pound, *Letters*, pp. 284, 285.

69 Pound, C 47, p. 236; C 4, pp. 13–14; C 79, pp. 503–506.

70 Dudley Fitts, "Music Fit for the Odes," *The Hound and Horn* 4.2 (January–March 1931), 279, 280. Louis Zukovsky, "The Cantos of Ezra Pound," *The Criterion* 10.40 (April 1931), 433. I say that Fitts' opposition between counterpoint and harmony is erroneous because it is simply too hard and fast. Following Pound's lead about the static nature of traditional harmony (Fitts mentions Pound's *Antheil and the Treatise on Harmony* on 278), Fitts claims that counterpoint "slumped" (278) into harmony after Bach: in other words, into stasis and stagnation (by harmony, both Pound and Fitts seem to mean nineteenth-century romantic harmony). The separate lines of melody in Bach's work are not "unharmonic", they are, by matter of degree, only a more mobile kind of harmonic music. Clearly, both Fitts and Zukovsky are very much under Pound's spell in their sense of the *Cantos*' music. Interestingly, though both writers cite from the Cabestan section of Canto 4 to prove their points, what one calls repetition and echo, the other seems to feel is juxtaposition, though Zukovsky also includes "words *echoing* words, line and line" (my emphasis, 433) as part of the juxtapositioning music of the poem. Juxtapositioning suggests the bringing together of disparate elements, a kind of paratactic procedure, whereas "echoing" seems to indicate a recalling of similar verbal events. I do not see why you could not have juxtaposed elements which echo other elements, but this seems to be something different than the conflation of the two poetic procedures would indicate.

The 1969 New Directions *Cantos* accords with Fitts' version. Zukovsky's citation replaces "Swung" (C4, p. 13) with "Swing", and after ". . . the swallows crying" has "Ityn, Ityn!" instead of "'Tis. 'Tis. Ytis!" Perhaps he quotes from an earlier version.

71 Zukovsky, "The Cantos of Ezra Pound," 433, note 1, 433. Fitts, "Music Fit for the Odes," 280. I will have more to say about the technical practice of counterpoint in the next chapter where I take up Joyce's "Sirens." The

reader will see there that the traditional procedures for counterpoint are rigorous indeed.

72 Fitts, "Music Fit for the Odes," 281, 289. Daniel D. Pearlman, *The Barb of
Time: on the Unity of Ezra Pound's 'Cantos'* (New York: Oxford University Press,
1969), pp. 17, 18, 173–175. Kay Davis, *Fugue and Frescoe: Structures in Pound's
'Cantos'.* (Orono, Maine: The National Poetry Foundation, University of
Maine, 1984), pp. 72–75, 75–76. Fitts, and, indeed, Pound, may suffer from
too narrow a view of harmony as "static" and stagnant. Fitts seems to feel
that Pound's "harmony" is not static, but rather full of the ideogrammic
energy of collision of elements.

   These are Pearlman's interpolations. Thus, the descent is "the thesis, or
Spirit" (p. 18); the "'repeat in history'" is "the varied embodiment in time
of timeless myths" (pp. 18–19). In other words, Time is the "antithesis or
complement of myth and the medium in which Spirit must operate" (p. 19).
Antithesis and complementarity do not seem to be quite the same thing to
me, however. Finally, the "'magic moment'" of metamorphosis "is the synthesis resulting from the interaction of the human spirit with time" (p. 19).
Pearlman maintains that this Hegelian fugue operates both in Pound's
"imagistic structure" (p. 19) and in the overall organic shape of the poem,
in the correspondence between "microscopic and macroscopic crystal
structure"(p. 19). Beyond this, however, Pearlman has little specific to say
about the fugal structure of the *Cantos*; obviously, the idea of the fugue is
really here to do service for the Hegelian scheme.

   Davis' reading gives a voice by voice exposition of Canto 63: first subject
– "conflict caused by lack of morality in government" (p. 83), stated in the
voice of Charles Francis Adams. This is answered, in the voice of John
Adams "in a different key [with] a prayer that the morality necessary for
good government will be found at the nation's capital" (p. 83), and so on. I
mention the "traditional elements of the fugue" here but, as I will explain
in the next chapter on Joyce, the fugue is a kind of musical writing which
changes over time. It does not always have the three-part design which most
literary critics attribute to it. Thus, to speak of subject, answer, countersubject and so on, is really to identify the fugue with the high point of its practice with the work of Bach. These are discernable elements in his work, but
not absolutes of musical theory.

73 Schafer, *Ezra Pound and Music: The Complete Criticism*, pp. 18, 22. Stephen J.
Adams,"Are the 'Cantos' a Fugue?", 68–70, 73. Schafer's notions regarding
musical "ideas" recalls Hanslick's notion of theme as "[t]he independent,
aesthetically not further reducible unit of musical thought . . ." Hanslick,
On the Musically Beautiful, p. 80. Davis and Schafer seem to echo Ralph
Vaughan Williams' suggestion that "we should speak of a composition
being written in 'fugue', just as we speak of a poem being written in hexam-
eters," Ralph Vaughan Williams, "Fugue," *Grove's Dictionary of Music and
Musicians*, ed. Eric Blom, 5th edn., vol. III (London: Macmillan; New York:
St. Martin's Press, 1954), p. 513. Fugue is more a way of organizing inde-

pendent voices than a prescriptive form (p. 513). Pearlman (*The Barb of Time*, pp. 11–12, quotes from the Williams essay too, though he does not cite Williams as the author. Pearlman seems to want to avoid the potential open-endedness of Williams' definition. As I have already shown, Pearlman attempts to recuperate the analogy between the fugue and the poem with his version of Hegelian organicism.

74 Pound, "Retrospect," pp. 6–7. Pound, *Guide to Kulcher*, p. 198.

75 Korn, *Purpose/Form/Meaning*, p. 121; see too Fenollosa, "Chinese Written Character," p. 150. Pound, *ABC of Reading*, p. 21. Davis, *Fugue and Frescoe*, p. 52. Pound, C 53, p. 265. See John Hamilton Edwards and William W. Vasse, *Annotated Index to the 'Cantos' of Ezra Pound. I-XXXIV* (Berkeley, CA: University of California Press, 1957), p. 269.

76 Pound, C 38, p.189. See Froula, *A Guide to Ezra Pound's Selected Poems*, p. 170. Pound, C 53, p. 264. Schafer, *Ezra Pound and Music*, p. 22.

77 Pound, *Guide to Kulchur*, p. 60.

78 Bob Perelman, *The Trouble With Genius: Reading Pound, Joyce, Stein, and Zukofsky* (Berkeley, CA: University of California Press, 1994), p. 44. Perelman goes on to suggest that, for Pound, "there were finally only two opposing yet inter-locked ideograms, the pure and the impure: light, health, hierarchy, the phallus, nature, the classics, . . .; and darkness, sickness, swamps, sodomy, Jews, usury . . ." (p. 46).

79 Kenner, *Pound Era*, p. 250. Pound, *Guide to Kulchur*, pp. 152, 152–153. Marjorie Perloff, *The Dance of the Intellect: Studies in the Poetry of the Pound Tradition* (Cambridge: Cambridge University Press, 1985), p. 48.

80 Michael Coyle, in his *Popular Genres*, might disagree. He follows Richard Sieburth's suggestion in *Instigations: Ezra Pound and Remy de Gourmont* (Cambridge, MA: Harvard University Press, 1978) that Pound is not merely copying the world but including it in his "art of quotation" (p. 121). Coyle rightly cautions against the notion of too literal a sense of inclusion; but the inclusion of music does not, in Coyle's view, equal a collapse between poetry and music, and he notes Pound's resistance to Paterian synaesthesia. I agree that Pound attempts to be inclusive in the *Cantos*, and that Pound may at some level indeed see words and music as having "different integrities" (Coyle, *Popular Genres*, p. 165). However, at the level of the ideogram, and, insofar as the ideogram is the basic structural unit of the poem, Pound is clearly trying to close the distance between the *graphed* ideogram (be it musical notation, or quotations from Malatesta's letters, etc.) and the "real" (in a non-Lacanian sense). Once transformed into the ideogram the integr-rities of textual and non-textual worlds seem to lose their discrete boundar-ies. Coyle too sees the introduction of the musical script as a means of opposing a "linear and strictly rational conception of 'sense'" (p. 168). Thus, the transcription from Münch can't be read, as others have done (and I am about to do), simply as an ideogram, nor can the music be naturalized in any other fashion, since it is "beyond sense . . . [Thus,] accepting the integrity of Pound's generic combination means accepting hermeneutical

limits" (p. 170). For Coyle, then, the inclusion of (not merely allusion to) music makes Pound both a popularizer of ancient music, since the micro-photography of the score "associates [it] with informal and oral history – with the popularization of scholarship" (p. 171), and a poet able to discern in Münch's score his ability "to recover the original, firsthand perception of the birdsong: the recovery of a prelinguistic experience" (p. 173). Pound may indeed have wished to become a popularizer, but on his own terms. It seems to me that Coyle falls for Pound's claims that he can somehow present reality directly in his text. We might have to accept hermeneutic limits, but it will be Pound directing us as to where those limits are, or *should* be. It is, of course, precisely this idea of the authority of poetic immanence which I am questioning here.

81 See Schafer, *Ezra Pound and Music*, p. 340. It seems that Pound received a copy of the Janequin proper also in 1933. In a letter dated tentatively March 1934, Pound thanks the Princess Edmond de Polignac for sending him "the Janequin," Pound, *Letters*, p. 339, which, as he says elsewhere, is the volume edited by Henry Expert, Schafer, *Ezra Pound and Music*, p. 357. Schafer doubts the date of the letter and suggests it was more likely written in December 1933. See Schafer, *Ezra Pound and Music*, footnote 58, p. 357. Pound, *ABC of Reading*, pp. 53, 54.

82 Cited in Schafer, *Ezra Pound and Music*, p. 435.

83 Pound, C 74, pp. 463, 455. Bacigalupo, *The Forméd Trace*, p. 115. Coyle, *Popular Genres*, pp. 178–179.

84 Pound, C 74, p. 465. Coyle, *Popular Genres*, pp. 178, 179. See too Eva Hesse, "Klages in Canto LXXV/450: a Positive Identification," *Paideuma* 10.2 (Fall 1981), 295–296.

85 Pound, C 79, p. 500.

86 Coyle, *Popular Genres*, p. 174.

87 Pound, C 75, p. 464; C 81, pp. 533, 534; C 74, p. 463. See Margaret M. Dunn, "Eine Kleine Wortmusik: the Marriage of Poetry and Music in 'The Pisan Cantos'," *Perspective on Contemporary Literature* 13 (1987), 104–105; See Terrell, *A Companion to the 'Cantos'*, p. 388. Terrell also points out the influence of Allen Upward (*The New World*) here and elsewhere in like moments of mystical immanence.

88 See Dunn, "Marriage of Poetry and Music," 105, and 108. Coyle, *Popular Genres*, pp. 173–174. Pound, C 79, p. 498. Unless otherwise noted, most of the background on allusions in the *Cantos* comes from Terrell, *A Companion to the 'Cantos'*.

89 Pound, C 79, pp. 506, 499. Peter Nicholls comments on the pathos of Pound's turn toward nature and the increasing demands such a turn makes upon writing:

> Since the ideology of agrarian mysticism can no longer be systematically main-tained, Pound finds himself confronting the perilously fragile base upon which his dream of social order has been constructed. It becomes clear that the only form of materiality which can now be entertained is the minutely local detail of nature . . .

[T]he writing . . . opens up none the less an unbridgeable gap between social and natural worlds. At certain pivotal moments in "The Pisan Cantos," the very lightness and bouyancy of the landscapes threaten to dissolve those intuitions of social order which Pound hopes to induce from the specificity and control of his writing . . . (Nicholls, *Modernisms*, p. 179)

Nicholls' remarks apply to Canto 83 specifically, but also to the larger shape of the Pisan series.

90 Pound, C 79, pp. 500, 501. See Randel, *Harvard Concise Dictionary of Music*, 1978), p. 221.

91 Donald Jay Grout, with Claude V. Palisca, *A History of Western Music*, 3rd edn. (New York: W. W. Norton and Company, 1980), p. 63. Grout suggests that the development of the staff was as important to Western music as the invention of writing was to language (p. 63). Pound, C 81, pp. 539, 541.

92 For a more extended working out of Pound's Eleusian sense of death and regeneration see Helen M. Dennis, "The Eleusian Mysteries as an Organizing Principle in *The Pisan Cantos*," *Paideuma* 10.2 (Fall 1982), 273–282, especially, 277–278; see also Leon Surette, *A Light from Eleusis*, ch. 7. Marianne Korn, in her discussion of the ideogrammic method as it is both described and performed in Pound's *Guide to Kulchur*, points out the contradiction between Pound's statements that knowledge can be achieved through direct presentation and his continual assurances that this is the case. She says that "[t]he problem lies in a solipsistic confusion between himself and the reader or other, the subject in whose mind the ideogram must spring to conclusion," Korn, *Purpose / Form / Meaning*, p.125. She goes on to say, in a passage that seems to have great relevance for the *Cantos*, that "[t]he ideogrammic method might be giving us a rain of data; but in fact that turns out to be an account of achieved meaning" (p. 125). Facts might be facts, but first and foremost they are *Pound's* facts, not unmediated presentations of the "truth."

4 "SIRENS" AND THE PROBLEM OF LITERARY AND MUSICAL
MEANING

1 James Joyce, *Letters of James Joyce*, ed. Stuart Gilbert (New York: Viking, 1957), p. 126. R. Murray Schafer, ed., *Ezra Pound and Music: the Complete Criticism*, commentary by R. Murray Schafer, (New York: New Directions, 1977), p. 18. Schafer also claims that, considering Pound's attention to more serious music, and his grander thought on music in the theories of absolute rhythm and Great Bass, Pound was the more serious musician of the two. This, to me, is debatable.

2 Joyce, *Letters*, p. 129. Richard Ellmann, *James Joyce*, rev. edn. (New York: Oxford University Press, 1982), p. 459.

3 Imogene Horsley, *Fugue: History and Practice* (New York: The Free Press, 1966), p. 7. Lawrence Levin, "The Sirens Episode as Music: Joyce's Experiment in Prose Polyphony," *James Joyce Quarterly* 3.1 (Fall 1965), 12.

4 Horsley, *Fugue*, pp. 187, 53; 11, 52, 53. Ralph Vaughan Williams, "Fugue," *Grove's Dictionary of Music and Musicians*, ed. Eric Blom, 5th edn., vol. III (London: Macmillan; New York: St. Martin's Press, 1954), p. 514. See also Kent Kennan, *Counterpoint: Based on Eighteenth-Century Practice*, 2nd edn. (New Jersey: Prentice-Hall, Inc., 1972), p. 200, and R. O. Morris, *The Structure of Music: an Outline for Students* (London: Oxford University Press, 1935). Kennan says that there "are various possibilities in fugal architecture, so that it is impossible to single out any one of them as 'fugue form'" (p. 200).

5 Morris, *The Structure of Music*, p. 91. Kennan, *Counterpoint*, pp. 217, 291, 131, 225, 224, 93. Horsley, *Fugue*, pp. 174, 142.

6 Frank Budgen, *James Joyce and the Making of 'Ulysses'* (Bloomington, IN: Indiana University Press, 1960), p. 130. Stuart Gilbert, *James Joyce's 'Ulysses': a Critical Study* (New York: Viking, 1955), pp. 252, 253. Ann Hardy, "A Fugal Analysis of the Sirens Episode in Joyce's 'Ulysses'," *Massachusetts Studies in English 2* (Spring 1970), 61. L. Levin, "Episode," 16–17; David W. Cole, "Fugal Structure in the Sirens Episode of 'Ulysses'," *Modern Fiction Studies* 19 (Summer 1973), 223–224. Heath Lees, "The Introduction to 'Sirens' and the *Fuga Per Canonem*," *James Joyce Quarterly* 22.1 (Fall 1984), 40, 42. See also Horsley, *Fugue*, p. 7. Gilbert seems unclear about which form he is using. He also assumes that the "Siren's song" is the speech of the barmaids, Douce and Kennedy. This seems difficult to uphold since they are only part of what endangers Bloom–Ulysses. They themselves are as vulnerable to the seductions of music as anyone in the bar. Lawrence Levin tries to establish "the eight regular parts" as voices of characters. But, since there are at least twelve characters who are mentioned or do in fact speak, he must make somewhat arbitrary decisions about who will be included as major voices (Levin, "Episode," 14). Cole, like Hardy, introduces the sexual theme as part of his analysis, saying that the subject and answer of the chapter are "complementary masculine and feminine aspects" (Cole, "Fugal Structure," 223), while the countersubject is hunger. Those who analyze musical fugues or canons would probably not have such difficulty in agreeing upon the major sections of a piece.

7 Lees, "The Introduction," 47. Harry Levin, *James Joyce: a Critical Introduction*, rev. and augmented edn. (New York: New Directions, 1960), p. 99. Gilbert, *A Critical Study*, p. 243. Zack Bowen, "The Bronzegold Sirensong: a Musical Analysis of the Sirens Episode in Joyce's 'Ulysses'," *Literary Monographs*, vol. I, eds. Eric Rothstein and Thomas K. Dunseath. (Milwaukee, WI: University of Wisconsin Press, 1967), 248.

8 Bowen, "Bronzegold," 251. Cultural examinations of *Ulysses* continue to pour forth, but one of the most important remains Cheryl Herr's, *Joyce's Anatomy of Culture*, (Urbana, IL and Chicago, IL: University of Illinois Press), 1986. There is some affinity between her sense that Joyce "foregrounds the repetitive nature of institutional messages" which direct us to the "the strictly conventional packaging of experience by institutions" (p. 4), and my own notion of the paradoxical public–private nature of song as Joyce pre-

sents it in this episode. See David Herman, "'Sirens' after Schönberg," *James Joyce Quarterly* 31.4 (Summer 1994), 476, 475–476. I have come upon Herman's piece late in the revisions of my own text, and there are certain resemblances between them, mostly residing around the issues of music and language as combinative procedures. My own emphasis is more on a kind of (post)structuralist linguistic view of musical–linguistic relations; Herman's is, as I try to show above, clearly placed upon a similar concern with linguistics, but he also makes a very astute connection with the experimental musical tenor of modern times, especially with Schoenberg. The reader will note that in my own reading, I will take a slightly more Jakobsonian approach and include *substitutive* procedures as well, since these seem to help us understand Joyce's synecdochic methods somewhat better than combinative ones alone can. Herman uses the German spelling of Shoenberg's name: Schönberg. Unless quoting Herman directly, I will remain with the Anglicized spelling: Schoenberg.

9 Arnold Schoenberg, "Composition with Twelve Tones," *Style and Idea: Selected Writings of Arnold Schoenberg*, ed. Leonard Stein, trans. Leo Black (London: Faber, 1975), p. 219, quoted in Herman, 480. Herman, "'Sirens'," 481. Herman's premises here in designating the twelve-tone method "combinational" are problematic. James Anderson Winn suggests that in fact it is the tonal system, where the "notes of the chosen key are the norm," *Unsuspected Eloquence, a History of the Relations between Poetry and Music* (New Haven, CT: Yale University Press, 1981), p. 311, which is combinational, and the twelve-tone system which is "permutational": that is, "no matter what the chosen row, all twelve [pitches] are equal: the universe of any twelve-tone piece is total chromatic space; the ordering of that space which the composer enforces by devising a row is one of factorial twelve . . ." (p. 311). Herman might see this as a difference of degree, not necessarily one of kind. This last point will become significant for me, however, later on when I take up the issue of whether or not the apparent opposition between tonal and chromatic thinking is as pronounced, even in Schoenberg's own thinking, as it appears to be in Herman's essay. Charles Rosen, in his *Arnold Schoenberg* (Princeton, NJ: Princeton University Press, 1975) points out that "the first note of one form of a series may be repeated as often as a composer likes, provided it always sounds like the first note (in other words, as though the note was sustained with intermittences); it must not sound as if it had a second position in the series" (p. 83). Rosen also notes that the sanctions against octave doubling mentioned above, really only apply in Schoenberg's earlier serial work, and for much the same reason as repetition of a note must also be delayed – to avoid the sense of centring or grounding the work around a pitch (p. 82). The irony here, as Rosen sees it, is that "[t]he series, in fact, is not an order of pitches but of what is called pitch-classes [meaning that once a series is chosen, the register of the pitches, high or low, is immaterial, so long as they follow in the particular sequence]. . . . Tonal music had gone only part of the way to asserting the

equivalence of all octaves, but Schoenberg's serialism went much further, and made it the structural foundation of his music" (p. 82). See too p. 83.

10 Herman, "'Sirens'," 482, 483, 483–484. See too Theodor W. Adorno, *Philosophy of Modern Music*, trans. Anne G. Mitchell and Wesley V. Blomster (London: Sheed and Ward, 1973), pp. 64–67.

11 Herman, "'Sirens'," 484, 481. This comes very close to a kind of Lyotardian suggestion that each work establishes it own rules after the fact. I will speak about this concept in regard to Gertrude Stein in the next chapter. Herman admits that his analogy does not go far enough to make conclusions about the prominence of combinatory procedures in modernity in general, nor does he feel that he has completely proven in detail the analogy between Joyce and Schoenberg (486).

12 Schoenberg, "Problems of Harmony," in *Style and Idea*, p. 272.

13 Ibid., pp. 272, 274, 275, 273. Schoenberg mentions the B-flat Allegretto of Beethoven's *Eighth Symphony*, which ends on a B flat, but functions as the V of E flat major.

14 Ibid., pp. 275–276, my emphasis 284, 279.

15 Ibid., p. 283, emphasis in original. Rose Rosengard Subotnik suggests Schoenberg is less concerned with the actual *sound* of a piece than with its coherence at a level other than the concrete level of sound. See Rose Rosengard Subotnik, *Deconstructive Variations: Music and Reason in Western Society*, (Minneapolis, MN: University of Minnesota Press, 1996), pp. 161–163. This is due, in her perspective, to the emphasis, especially in Schoenberg and Adorno, upon what she calls "structural listening," or the "attention primarily on the formal relationships established over the course of a single composition" (p. 148). In a fascinating discussion of Schoenberg, Adorno, and Stravinsky, Subotnik points out how even Schoenberg and Adorno, though more aware of the social position of art as a cultural practice than Stravinsky, tend, in their justification of the twelve-tone technique and their concomitant emphasis on the formal justifications of structural hearing, to be unselfconscious of their own cultural moment. Noting, for instance, the "widespread unresponsiveness to Schoenberg's music," she points out that neither Adorno nor Schoenberg could view such responses as anything other than "an immature unwillingness or intellectual incapacity on the part of the public to master the technical demands of structural listening . . ." (p. 166). Of Adorno, in this regard, she goes on to say that "[h]e could not bring himself to characterize either Schoenberg's unpopularity or nonstructural modes of listening as functions of legitimate differences, among listeners, in cultural or stylistic orientation" (p. 166). The basis of her argument might fit into critiques of literary formalism as well.

16 For "structural listening" and its limitations, see the previous note.

17 Ferdinand de Saussure, *Course in General Linguistics*, trans. Wade Baskin (London: Collins, Fontana, 1974), p. 117. Brook Thomas suggests that consciousness, as represented in *Ulysses*, is "conditioned by books, works of art, [and] language." See, Brook Thomas, *James Joyce's 'Ulysses': a Book of Many*

Happy Returns (Baton Rouge, LA: Louisiana State University Press, 1982), p. 17. The idea of the opening section of "Sirens" as "overture" is common-place. Marilyn French, *The Book as World: James Joyce's "Ulysses"* (Cambridge, MA: Harvard University Press, 1976), p. 127; Karen Laurence, *The Odyssey of Style in "Ulysses"* (Baton Rouge, LA: Louisiana State University Press, 1982), pp. 90 91; Stanley Sultan, "Sirens at the Ormond Bar: 'Ulysses'," *The University of Kansas City Review* 26.1 (October 1959), 85. The idea of narrative as a combinational form of writing is by now very common. Combination is associated with realist prose in Jakobson's idea of metonymic writing. In such prose, Jakobson points out that the writer follows the path of "contig-uous relationships, [wherein] the realist author metonymically digresses from the plot to the atmosphere and from the characters to the setting in space and time," Roman Jakobson, "Two Aspects of Language: Metaphor and Metonymy," *European Literary Theory and Practice: From Existential Phenomenology to Structuralism*, ed. Vernon W. Gras (New York: Dell, 1973), p. 214. See also Roland Barthes, "Introduction to the Structural Analysis of Narratives," *"Image-Music-Text*, trans. Stephen Heath (New York: Hill and Wang, 1977), pp. 122–124; and Seymour Chatman, *Story and Discourse: Narrative Structure in Fiction and Film* (Ithaca, NY: Cornell University Press, 1978), pp. 27– 29.

18   References are to Hans Walter Gabler, *et al.*, eds., *Ulysses: a Critical and Synoptic Edition*, 3 vols., vol. 1 (New York and London: Garland Publishing, Inc. 1984), ch. 11, 1, 12, 60. Citations will be given by chapter and line number. Line numbers will refer only to the first line of the quoted passage. Derek Attridge, *Peculiar Language: Literature as Difference from the Renaissance to James Joyce* (Ithaca, NY: Cornell University Press, 1988), p. 139.

19   Joyce, *Ulysses*, ch. 11, 1290, 15, 19, 452; ch. 4 303. Attridge, *Peculiar Language*, pp. 139, 141, 140, 148, 149, 151.

20   Joyce, *Ulysses*, ch. 11, 81. Attridge, *Peculiar Language*, p. 152. I will return to this aural–visual interconnection later on in the chapter.

21   Joyce, *Ulysses*, ch. 11, 1, 10. I borrow a phrase from Jakobson here. It appears in his discussion of the processes of combination (of sounds, words, sen-tences) and selection (from the "repository of all possible constituent parts," or the "code") which are required for the making of a recognizable message (Jakobson, "Two Aspects of Language," pp. 121–122). A. Walton Litz, in his *The Art of James Joyce: Method and Design in "Ulysses" and "Finnegans Wake"* (London: Oxford University Press, 1964), complains that Joyce's "overture" (and much of "Sirens" as a whole") does not succeed precisely because of his emphasis on what Litz considers the "secondary qualities" of language: i.e. its sound. Litz believes that this kind of focus ruins the possibility of "full communication" and thus demonstrates the "weaknesses of a compromise between the two arts" (p. 70) of music and prose. But Joyce is counting on the similarity between the two arts as methods of culturally determined, ambiguous kinds of expression to throw into question the whole issue of "full communication."

22 Joyce, *Ulysses*, ch. 11, 404, 396, 8, 394, 21,12. Garrett Stewart, *Reading Voices: Literature and the Phonotext*, (Berkeley, CA: University of California Press, 1990), p. 243.

23 Stewart, *Reading Voices*, pp. 243–244. Jacques Derrida, "Signature Event Context," *Margins of Philosophy*, trans. Alan Bass (Chicago, IL: University of Chicago Press, 1982), p. 317. Jean-Michel Rabaté, in "The Silence of the Sirens," *James Joyce: the Centennial Symposium*, eds. Morris Beja, *et al.* (Urbana, IL and Chicago, IL: University of Chicago Press, 1986), also notes how such conflations and expansions of intervals between linguistic elements create a kind of "system of echoes" (p. 85) out of which the entire chapter is composed. He also claims that the musical analogy does not work in the chapter, and that most of what goes on in terms of language can be explained by reference to classical rhetorical devices.

24 Joyce, *Ulysses*, ch. 11, 1, 65. Roland Barthes, *S/Z*, trans. Richard Howard (New York: Hill and Wang, 1975), p. 95. Seymour Chatman, in *Story and Discourse*, notes that, in a sense, "a narrative, as the product of a fixed number of statements [a specific "discourse"], can never be totally 'complete', in the way that a photographic reproduction is, since the number of plausible intermediate actions or properties is virtually infinite" (p. 29). David Lodge, in *The Modes of Modern Writing: Metaphor, Metonymy, and the Typology of Modern Literature* (London: Edward Arnold, 1977), p. 76, mentions deletion as a part of the metonymical process, but it is interesting to see here how Joyce overcomes any strict opposition between metaphor and metonymy by performing his metonymic troping on already metaphorical figurations.

25 Joyce, *Ulysses*, ch. 11, 86, 149. Bloom does a similar kind of contiguous substitution with the name of Aaron Figatner while reading a sign: "Why do I always say Figather. Gathering figs, I think" (ch. 11, 149).

26 Jonathan D. Kramer, "New Temporalities in Music," *Critical Inquiry* 7 (Spring 1981), 550. I have in mind Roland Barthes' sense of the plurality of the "writerly," as opposed to the "readerly" text, or the text of easy consumption. See *S/Z*, pp. 4–5.

27 Joyce, *Ulysses*, ch. 11, 1, 98.

28 Ibid., ch. 11, 183, 306. What I am calling parodic continuity here might be one of the problems that a twelve-tone reading of "Sirens," such as Herman's, would have to take into account: that is, the linguistic and syntactic elements from the first part of the chapter do not necessarily reoccur in a way similar to their appearances later on. This does not accord with the principle of non-redundancy. As Rosen notes, a pitch must not sound as though "it had a second position [or function] in a series" (Rosen, *Schoenberg*, p. 83). As my reading above shows, Joyce's phrases offer very ambiguous "meanings" in the "basic set," which are not the same as their functions when next they appear in the chapter. The ambiguity of function or "meaning" of linguistic and syntactic units here suggests perhaps a more chromatic, yet still "tonal," sense of the plurality of function that any given unit may have in the linguistic, or musically tonal, composition.

29 Joyce, *Ulysses*, ch. 11, 350, 352. Marilyn French points out that of the three fundamental styles in "Sirens," "dialogue . . . Bloom's interior monologue . . . [and] narrational comment" (French, *Book as World*, p. 128), it is the last of these which is most pronounced.

30 See Rosen, *Schoenberg*, especially pp. 28–32, or all of chapter 2, on the generalized dissatisfaction with tonality and the increasing need felt by many composers for a revision of musical systems.

31 Joyce, *Ulysses*, ch. 11, 71, 76, 141, 169, 532, emphasis in original.

32 Ibid., ch. 11, 928, 1125, 1291, 83, 86, 85; see ch. 10, 606. Though "represented space" is probably a clear enough term for what I am pointing to here, I do have in mind Seymour Chatman's idea of "discourse space" which refers to "*the focus of spatial attention*. It is the framed area to which the implied audience's attention is directed by the discourse, that portion of the total story-space 'remarked' or closed in upon . . ." (Chatman, *Story and Discourse*, p. 102; see also p. 104).

33 Identity is an issue, especially (though not only) for Bloom throughout the book: remember his concern with the unknown man in the macintosh in "Hades;" the various roles, and genders he plays in "Circe;" or his misrepresentation in the *Telegraph* as "L. Boom" (ch. 16, 1260). As I mentioned earlier in connection with Pound, there is probably no way that language as written can really imitate the space of tonality.

34 Jackson I. Cope, "Sirens," *James Joyce's "Ulysses": Critical Essays*, eds. Clive Hart and David Hayman (Berkeley, CA: University of California Press, 1977), p. 226. Joyce, *Ulysses*, ch. 11, 146, 147, 148, 149.

35 Ibid., ch. 11, 151, 1086, 1088, 173, 178, 174, 180, 1003.

36 Ibid., ch. 11, 934, 938, 945. Rabaté, "The Silence of the Sirens," p. 87, 86. Rabaté will conclude that the trading here of the "imaginary" sound shows that the "real song of the Sirens is a song of silence" (p. 86). The emphasis on eyes and seeing has been marked in various ways before, especially as this visual thematics figures around Bloom. He is particularly interested, it seems, in miss Douce: "Bronze, listening, by the beerpull gazed far away. Soulfully. Doesn't half know I'm. Molly great dab at seeing anyone looking" (Joyce, *Ulysses*, ch. 11, 1046). The transference from look to gaze, or vice versa, is common in the episode. It is as though sensory activities trade off with one another.

In the same collection in which Rabaté's article appears, (Morris Beja, *et al.*, eds, *James Joyce: the Centennial Symposium* (Urbana, IL and Chicago, IL: U. of Illinois Press, 1986)), there are also several other significant pieces on "Sirens." Most important in relation to the above discussion, aside from Rabaté's, "The Silence of the Sirens," pp. 82–88, are André Topia's, "'Sirens': the Emblematic Variation," pp. 76–81; and Daniel Ferrer's, "Echo or Narcisuss?" pp. 70–75. Ferrer points out, that though "the formal element is capital in this chapter" it is, nevertheless, "upon this symbolic framework [that] a huge imaginary [in the Lacanian sense of identification and misidentification] construction rises." (p. 73). He notes too that the "infinite multiplication of this specular process proves that it is powerless to heal the narcissisitic wounds" (p. 74). Noting the various kinds of "symbolic conjunctions" that take place in terms of the transfer of sensory functions, André Topia notes that "[t]he fluid circulation of the musical substance seems to break all barriers and to include all senses in the activity of listening. The auditory function takes on such importance that it penetrates the bodies through all their openings" (p. 79).

37 Slavoj Žižek, "'I Hear You with My Eyes': or the Invisible Master," *Voice and Gaze as Love Objects*. SIC 1. eds. Renata Salecl and Slavoj Žižek (Durham, NC and London: Duke University Press, 1996), p. 103, 104.

38 Cope, "'Sirens'," p. 227. Joyce, *Ulysses*, ch. 11, 856, 895, 226, 599, 226, 201, emphasis in original; see also 508, 515. Richard Ellmann, in *Ulysses on the Liffey* (London: Faber and Faber, 1974), p. 107, notes the Martha–Douce–Molly connection, as does Cope, "'Sirens'," p. 227. Žižek, in a discussion unrelated to Joyce, also notes a kind of chiasmatic moment in the transfer between voice and gaze (p. 94). More pertinent to my argument perhaps is the transposition Žižek himself draws between between seeing and hearing and their relationship to truth: ". . . the founding illusion of the metaphysics of presence is not simply that of 'hearing oneself speaking,' but rather a kind of short circuit betwen 'hearing oneself speaking' and 'seeing oneself looking': a 'seeing oneself looking' *in the mode of 'hearing oneself speaking,'* a gaze that regains the immediacy of the vocal self-affection" ("I Hear You," p. 95, emphasis in the original). He reminds us that from Plato on, the basis of metaphysics has been based on "the predominance of *seeing*" (p. 95), but that "'metaphysics' itself stands for the illusion that, in the antagonistic relationship between 'seeing' and 'hearing,' it is possible to abolish the discord . . . that mediates between the two terms (*one hears things because one cannot see it all, and vice versa*) and to conflate them in a unique experience of 'seeing in the mode of hearing' . . ." (ellipsis at the end is in the original, but the emphasis is mine, p. 95). Bloom goes one further here and sees what *cannot* be heard.

39 Joyce, *Ulysses*, ch. 11, 774, 219, 224, 227, 229, 228, 302, 1067.

40 Ibid., ch. 3, 153; ch. 11, 1005; ch. 1, 207; ch. 11, 1098; ch. 8, 1075. Zack Bowen, *Musical Allusions in the Works of James Joyce: Early Poetry through "Ulysses"* (Albany, NY: State University of New York Press, 1974), p. 204. Bowen is referring to the entry of the tuner which is given in language similar to that of the song: "Tap. A youth entered a lonely Ormond hall" (Joyce, *Ulysses*, ch. 11, 1273). The line from the song, as quoted in Bowen, is "The youth enter'd an empty hall" (Bowen, *Allusions*, p. 196).

41 Joyce, *Ulysses*, ch. 11, 342. Stephen Heath, "Ambiviolences: Notes for Reading Joyce," *Post-structuralist Joyce: Essays from the French*, eds. Derek Attridge and Daniel Ferrer (Cambridge: Cambridge University Press, 1984), p. 40.

42 Roland Barthes, "The Grain of the Voice," *The Responsibility of Forms: Critical Essays on Music, Art, and Representation*, trans. Richard Howard (New York:

Hill and Wang, 1985), p. 269. Marc E. Blanchard, "The Sound of Songs: the Voice in the Text," *Hermeneutics and Deconstruction*, eds. Hugh J. Silverman and Don Ihde (Albany, NY: Sate University of New York Press, 1985), p. 130. Derek Attridge, as I noted earlier, points to a similar kind of interplay in his sense of the fusion between *langue* and *parole* in Joyce's use of lexical onomatopoeia. I take the term "public tonality" from Richard Norton's *Tonality in Western Culture: a Critical and Historical Perspective* (University Park, PA and London: Pennsylvania State University Press, 1984), where he suggests that it is through language that "consciousness purchases meaning from the subjective sphere of public tonality and turns it into an object for itself – my emotion, my feeling, my activity" (p. 175; see pp. 174–175).

43 Joyce, *Ulysses*, ch. 11, 291, 313.
44 Hugh Kenner, Ulysses (London: George Allen and Unwin, 1982), p. 89. Cope, "'Sirens'," p. 227. Joyce, *Ulysses*, ch. 11, 195.
45 Ibid., *Ulysses*, ch. 11, 320, 323.
46 Ibid., ch. 11, 89.
47 Barthes, "Grain," p. 268. Joyce, *Ulysses*, ch. 11, 337, 338, 336, 346, 226. The correct version of "The Shade of the Palm" is cited in Bowen, "Bronzegold," p. 252. Bowen points out that in the first stanza of the song, the speaker mentions "a maid keeping a tryst with me" (p. 251). The voice also asks: "How can I leave her alone . . .? How can I part from her . . .?" (pp. 251–252). Bowen suggests that the first stanza relates to Boylan and his coming meeting with Molly, while the second relates to Bloom with "its echoes of former days of love" (p. 252). The critical reading seems to sustain the absenting of miss Douce.
48 Joyce, *Ulysses*, ch. 11, 377, 368, 383, 409. Bowen quotes the phrase from the song as, "Fair one of Eden, look to the West for me!" (Bowen, "Bronzegold," p. 252).
49 Joyce, *Ulysses*, ch. 11, 396, 650. Bowen, "Bronzegold," p. 255.
50 Joyce, *Ulysses*, ch. 11, 573, 648, 639, 642. Bowen recaps the story of *La Sonnambula*: "Amina betrothed to Elvino, sleepwalks into another man's room at an inn, dreaming she is coming to Elvino . . . Elvino denounces . . . Amina, and his subsequent misery prompts the aria . . ." ("Bronzegold," pp. 264–265). Roland Barthes, *Mythologies*, trans. Annette Lavers (New York: Hill and Wang, 1972), p. 117.
51 Bowen, "Bronzegold," p. 266. Joyce, *Ulysses*, ch. 11, 668, 674, 680, 679, 677, 681, 709, 701.
52 Joyce, *Ulysses*, ch. 11, 705.
53 Ibid., ch. 11, 744. For the substitution of Bloom for Simon, see, for instance, Cope, "'Sirens'," p. 232. An interesting alternate reading of this moment of succession is Jeanne Perreault's suggestion that instead of seeing Bloom as "true" father to Stephen, Bloom is in fact his true mother. In "Male Maternity in *Ulysses*," *English Studies in Canada* 13 (1987), 304–314, she suggests that Bloom, like the Virgin Mary, is impregnated by means of the Holy Ghost: that is, by ear. With attention to the religious and mystical imagery

in the book, she goes on to trace the subtle progress of Bloom's gestation. Michael Hollington, "Svevo, Joyce and Modernist Time," *Modernism: 1890–1930*, eds. Malcolm Bradbury and James McFarlane (Harmondsworth: Penguin, 1981), p. 441.

54 Arthur Nestrovski, "Blindness and Inwit: James Joyce and the Sirens, a Reading of Chapter 11 of 'Ulysses'," *The Iowa Review* 18.1 (Winter 1988), 19. Joyce, *Ulysses*, ch. 11, 791, 793.

55 Joyce, *Ulysses*, ch. 11, 830, 836, 838, 839, 802.

56 Ibid., ch. 11, 860, 869, 868, 890, 892, 893, 904. Bloom seems to be associated with both bald Pat, hard of his hearing, and the blind piano tuner. Both Bloom and Pat are, in a sense, "waiters," and Bloom and the tuner are good listeners. The monosyllables that accompany Pat ("Bald deaf Pat brought quite flat pad ink," ch. 11, 847) are recapitulated in the "Tap" of the approaching tuner toward the end of the chapter. Bloom seems to wander between the extremes of blindness and good insight.

57 Joyce, *Ulysses*, ch. 11, 1112, 1101, 1092, 1091, 1110, 1122, 1134, 1194, 1187, 1270, 1281. The term "heroticized" comes from F. L. Radford's "King, Pope, and Hero-Martyr: *Ulysses* and the Nightmare of Irish History," *James Joyce Quarterly* 15.4 (Summer 1978), 287. Radford notes that the word comes from *Finnegans Wake*, and is a "parodic treatment of sentimental patriotism" (287) very like the kind we see during the playing of "The Croppy Boy."

58 Joyce, *Ulysses*, ch. 11, 1081, 1284, 1286, 1294.

5 GERTRUDE STEIN AND HER SAINTS

1 On Stein and cubism, see, for example, Linda T. Fitz, "Gertrude Stein and Picasso: the Language of Surfaces," *American-Literature* 45 (1973), 228–237; Marilyn Gaddis Rose, "Gertrude Stein and Cubist Narrative," *Modern Fiction Studies* 22 (1976–1977), 543–555; Marianne DeKoven, "Gertrude Stein and Modern Painting: Beyond Literary Cubism," *Contemporary Literature* 22.1 (Winter 1981), 81–95; Wendy Steiner, *Exact Resemblance to Exact Resemblance: the Literary Portraiture of Gertrude Stein* (New Haven, CT: Yale University Press, 1978), especially chapter four, "Literary Cubism: Limits of the Analogy;" Marjorie Perloff, *The Poetics of Indeterminacy: Rimbaud to Cage* (Princeton, NJ: Princeton University Press, 1981), chapter three, "Poetry as Word System: the Art of Gertrude Stein;" and Randa Dubnick, *The Structure of Obscurity: Gertrude Stein, Language, and Cubism* (Urbana, IL: University of Illinois Press, 1984). This list is by no means exhaustive. Jane Bowers, "The Writer in the Theater: Gertrude Stein's 'Four Saints in Three Acts'," *Critical Essays on Gertrude Stein*, ed. Michael J. Hoffman (Boston, MA: Hall, 1986), note 1, pp. 223–224). Gertrude Stein, "Plays,"in *Lectures in America*, introduction by Wendy Steiner (London: Virago, 1988), p. 117.

2 See Lisa Ruddick, *Reading Gertrude Stein: Body, Text, Gnosis* (Ithaca, NY: Cornell University Press, 1990); Harriet Scott Chessman, *The Public Is Invited to Dance: Representation, the Body, and Dialogue in Gertrude Stein* (Stanford,

CA: Stanford University Press, 1989); Marianne DeKoven, *A Different Language: Gertrude Stein's Experimental Writing* (Madison, WI: University of Wisconsin Press, 1983); see also Carolyn Burke, "Gertrude Stein, the Cone Sisters, and the Puzzle of Female Friendship," *Critical Inquiry*. 8.3 (Spring 1982), 543–564.

3 Chessman, for example, says that Stein's language is never "simply nonsignifying" (Chessman, *Public*, p. 4), but is a mixture of the "symbolic and the bodily" (p. 4). Though some critics disparage DeKoven's sense of Stein's experimentalism as emphasizing too strongly the play of signification (see, for example, Ruddick, *Reading Getrude Stein*, p. 7), DeKoven also feels the need for some reconciliation between patriarchal and antipatriarchal discourses (*A Different Language*, p. 22). Other critics attempt different solutions to the tension between meaning and obscurity in Stein: see Dubnick, *Structure of Obscurity*, Introduction; Ruddick, *Reading Gertrude Stein*, p. 7. Richard Bridgman, in *Gertrude Stein in Pieces* (New York: Oxford University Press, 1970) scolds Stein by saying that at times "aesthetic advances were overshadowed by autobiographical details" (p. 150). Others will search out the biographical for further domestic and erotic evidence to explain the writing: see for example, Catherine R. Stimpson, "The Mind, the Body and Gertrude Stein," *Critical Inquiry* 3.3 (Spring 1977), 489–506, and "The Somagrams of Gertrude Stein," *Poetics Today* 6.1–2 (1985), 67–80; Carolyn Burke, "Gertrude Stein, 543–564; Elizabeth Fifer, "Is Flesh Advisable? The Interior Theater of Gertrude Stein," *Signs* 4.3 (Spring 1979), 472–483; Pamela Hadas, "Spreading the Difference: One Way to Read Gertrude Stein's *Tender Buttons*," *Twentieth Century Literature*, 24.1 (Spring 1978), 57–75; Shari Benstock, *Women of the Left Bank: Paris, 1900–1940* (Austin, TX: University of Texas Press, 1986). Some who hold to a more indeterminate reading of Stein's work are Marjorie Perloff, *The Poetics of Indeterminacy*, chapter 3; DeKoven, *A Different Language*; Neil Schmitz, *Of Huck and Alice: Humorous Writing in American Literature* (Minneapolis, MN: University of Minnesota Press, 1983), chapters 6 and 7; Jayne L. Walker, *The Making of a Modernist: Gertrude Stein from "Three Lives" to "Tender Buttons"* (Amherst, MA: University of Massachusetts Press, 1984). Walker, *The Making of a Modernist*, p. xviii, is speaking in particular of Stein's work before and up to *Tender Buttons*. She claims that *Tender Buttons* is still a mimetic text (p. 134), though it is not merely some transcription of the Jamesian "stream-of-consciousness" (p. 134), nor is it some written imitation of painterly abstraction. She is opposing those who have accorded such great weight to the cubist/surrealist analogy with Stein's work, such as Michael J. Hoffman's *The Development of Abstractionism in the Writings of Gertrude Stein* (Philadelphia, PA: University of Pennsylvania Press, 1965), see especially chapters 5 and 6, and John Malcolm Brinnin's *The Third Rose: Gertrude Stein and Her World* (Boston, MA: Littlebrown, 1959). Walker claims that Stein is not merely imitating the painters, but rather investigating "the problem of representaion, redefined in terms of the distinctive resources of their medium" (pp. xxvi–xxvii).

Gertrude Stein, *Tender Buttons* (New York: Claire-Marie, 1914), p. 63. Pamala Hadas, "Spreading the Difference," p. 63.

4 Stein's own reflections on genre are rich and difficult. For instance, Stein claimed that *Tender Buttons* (1914) was poetry, but it is difficult, in terms of its linguistic procedures, to tell it apart from many of her plays of the twenties. In "Poetry and Grammar" she states that "having realized having completely realized that sentences are not emotional while paragraphs are, prose can be the essential balance that is made inside something that combines the sentence and the paragraph . . .," Stein, "Poetry and Grammar," *Lectures in America*, p. 229. Aside from this balance, Stein also notes that "vocabulary in respect to prose is less important than the parts of speech" (p. 230), whereas "[p]oetry has to do with vocabulary just as prose does not" (p. 230). Poetry requires an emphasis on and an *overcoming* of nouns: "in short to overcome them (nouns) by using them" (p. 228).

5 Stein, "Plays," p. 104.

6 Stein, "Composition as Explanation," *Look at Me Now and Here I Am: Writings and Lectures 1909–45*, ed. Patricia Meyerowitz, introduction by Elizabeth Sprigge (Harmondsworth: Penguin, 1971), p. 23. Elsewhere, Stein admits a fondness for pronouns, since, unlike nouns, they "cannot have adjectives go with them" ("Poetry and Grammar," *Lectures*, p. 213), and "they are not really the name of anything" (p. 213), and thus, "they already have a greater possibility of being something than if they were as a noun is the name of anything" (pp. 213–214).

7 Stein, "Composition," p. 21.

8 DeKoven, *A Different Language*, p. 24. Stein, *Picasso* (New York: Dover Publications, Inc., 1984), p. 11.

9 Stein did of course feel that a break with the nineteenth century had occurred, both with Cubism, and with the advent of her own work. In *Picasso* she says that the foundation of Cubism comes about in part because the nineteenth century had "exhausted its need of having a model, because the truth that the things seen with the eyes are the only real things . . . had lost its significance" (p. 10). In "Portraits and Repetition," Stein says that "[t]he newspapers are full of what anybody does and anybody knows what anybody does but the thing that is important is the intensity of anybody's existence" ("Portraits and Repetition," *Lectures*, p.182). Stein's distrust of causal narratives seems apparent even as early as the autobiographical *Q.E.D.* (1903), where there are no precedents, no histories of conduct, moral or otherwise, by which Adele and Helen, the two women protagonists, may enter into a successful intimacy. Stein could see that histories of continuity and progress, and the moral programs used to sustain notions of continuity, excluded her and left her few maps as woman, artist, lesbian, or any combination of these.

10 Bridgman, *Gertrude Stein in Pieces*, p. 186. Randa Dubnick too says of Stein's work generally that "she uses words as if they were new and had no history" (Dubnick, *The Structure of Obscurity*, p.xiv). For more on the resistance to the

linearity of writing, see Jacques Derrida, *Of Grammatology*, trans. Gayatri Chakravorty Spivak (Baltimore, MD: Johns Hopkins University Press, 1982), pp. 86–87. Jayne L. Walker suggests that it is Stein's ability to combine metaphorical substitutions within more or less conventional syntactic combinatory relations which allows her to expose the degree to which grammar itself may be responsible for creating the "real" (*The Making of a Modernist*, pp. 136, 142). Walker, in reference to *Tender Buttons*, points out that the syntax of the piece, as well as complex puns, repetitions – and we could add, rhymes, assonance, and alliterative devices too – operate in such a way as to "reinforce the prevailing structural principle of similarity" (p. 133), but without semantic equivalence (p. 133).

11 Stein, "Composition," pp. 22, 23.

12 Ibid., pp. 24, 25, 24.

13 Ibid., p. 24. *Narration: Four Lectures by Gertrude Stein*, introduction by Thornton Wilder (Chicago, IL: Chicago University Press, 1935), p.25. Stein goes on to say that "[a] great deal perhaps all of my writing of The Making of Americans was an effort to escape from this thing to escape from inevitably feeling that anything that everything had meaning as beginning and middle and ending" (p. 25). Stein, "Composition," pp. 29, 30. It should be noted that nowhere else does Stein use the terms "distribution," and "equilibration."

14 Stein, "Composition," pp. 30, 29.

15 Ibid. p. 25. Stein conflates the prolonged and the continuous present here, but, as Donald Sutherland suggests, there may be a significant difference between the two concepts: "a prolonged present assumes a situation or a theme and dwells on it and develops it or keeps it recurring . . . The continuous present would take each successive moment or passage as a completely new thing essentially . . .," Donald Sutherland, *Gertrude Stein: a Biography of her Work* (New Haven, CT: Yale University Press, 1951), pp. 51–52. Stein, "Portraits and Repetition," p. 167. Though Stein claims in "Composition" that she was, by the time of *Three Lives* already moving toward a continuous present ("Composition," p. 25), she is at the same, in such works as *A Long Gay Book* (1909–1912), "at the very height of her 'mixing and mingling and contrasting'" (Wendy Steiner, *Exact Resemblance*, p. 47). Steiner quotes here from *A Long Gay Book*, a work in which we are told that "[e]very one has in them a fundamental nature," Stein, *A Long Gay Book. Matisse, Picasso, and Gertrude Stein, with Two Shorter Stories* (Barton, NY: Something Else Press, 1972), p. 16, and that the book itself "is being a history of kinds of men and women, when they were babies and then children and then old ones" (p. 17). As Steiner points out, though, there is a discrepency between the focus on the present that Stein claims to be developing at this time and the attempt to capture the "fundamental nature," or as she calls it elsewhere, the "rhythm of a personality" ("The Gradual Making of 'The Making of Americans'," *Lectures in America*, p. 147) which requires continuity over time (Steiner, *Exact Resemblance*, p. 47). However, as I have been maintaining

above, Stein is attempting to transform the idea of "essence" to include the temporal; indeed, it seems that she is basing the very notion of essence upon temporality itself. *The Geographical History of America: or the Relation of Human Nature to the Human Mind*, introduction by Thornton Wilder (New York: Random House, 1936), p. 111. Stein's notion of identity (as opposed to entity) is, in her early work at least, close to that of William James' which also relies upon memory for the purposes of establishing resemblances and continuity. See William James, *The Principles of Psychology*. 2 vols, vol. 1 (New York: Dover Publications Inc., 1950), p. 334. James' concept of self-knowledge is an extension of his ideas on knowledge in general. James believed that there were two general kinds of knowledge: "knowledge about," and "acquaintance" (p. 259). There is a change in Stein's thinking about knowledge after *The Making of Americans* in which the basis for representation changes from knowledge about to acquaintance (Steiner, *Exact Resemblance*, p. 42). See James, *Principles*, vol. 1, p. 611; Betsy Alayne Ryan, *Gertrude Stein's Theatre of the Absolute* (Ann Arbor, MI: UMI Research Press, 1984), p. 20; and Stein, *The Making of Americans*, p. 151.

16 Stein, *Geographical History*, pp. 46, 137, 80, 51. Ryan, *Stein's Theatre of the Absolute*, p 25. In *The Making of Americans*, Stein refers to the "privilege," Stein, *The Making of Americans: Being a History of a Family's Progress* (New York: Something Else Press, 1972), p. 3, of being an American, "one whose tradition it has taken scarcely sixty years to create. We need only realise our parents, remember our grandparents and know ourselves and our history is complete" (p. 3). See also "Portraits and Repetition" in which Stein speaks of the present generation as one which "does not connect itself with anything" (Stein, "Portraits," p. 166). This, for Stein, makes it a particularly American generation.

17 Stein, "Plays," pp. 119, 121. Such a desire is also present in *Tender Buttons*. Elsewhere, Stein claims that at the time of *Tender Buttons* she "became more and more excited about how . . . words that make what I looked at be itself were always words that to me very exactly related themselves to that thing, . . . but as often as not had as I say nothing whatever to do with what any words would do that described that thing ("Portraits and Repetition," pp. 191–192). *What Happened*, quoted in "Plays," p. 205.

18 *Ladies Voices*, in *Geography and Plays*, introduction by Cyrena N. Pondrom (Madison, WI: University of Wisconsin Press, 1993), p. 203. Stein, "Plays," pp. 95, 93, 95, 102, 94, 109.

19 Stein, "Plays," p. 104. Stein, "Composition," pp. 104–105.

20 Stein, "Plays," p. 121.

21 Stein, *A List*, quoted in "Plays," pp. 124, 123.

22 *Say it with Flowers*, in *Operas and Plays*, foreword by James R. Mellow (Barrytown, NY: Station Hill Press, 1987), p. 332.

23 *Photograph*, in *Last Operas and Plays*. edited and with an Introduction by Carl Van Vechten (New York: Rinehart & Co., Inc., 1949), p. 152. *Paisieu*, in *Last Operas*, pp. 155, 157. Stein, *Doctor Faustus Lights the Lights*, in *Last Operas*, p. 95.

At one point in *Ida, a Novel* (1938), Andrew, Ida's husband, we are told, undergoes a name change to Ida. See Stein, *Ida, A Novel*. New York: Vintage, 1968, p. 94). Ida "twins" herself early in the novel and is known as Ida-Ida.

24 Stein, "Portraits and Repetition," p. 178. Stein, "Plays," pp. 129, 131. Stein was convinced that the plays should be played, and that they were actual, as opposed to closet, dramas. James R. Mellow, in his biography of Stein, quotes part of a letter from Stein to Mabel Dodge who was attempting to get Stein to publish the plays without waiting for production. Stein was firmly against it: "I do *not* want the plays published. They are to be kept to be played." See James R. Mellow, *Charmed Circle: Gertrude Stein & Company* (New York: Avon Books, 1974), p. 215. Stein's wish did not come true until the production of *Four Saints* in 1934. Her first published plays had, however, appeared in *Geography and Plays*, 1922.

25 Jean-François Lyotard, "The Sublime and the Avant-Garde," *The Lyotard Reader*, trans. Lisa Liebmann, ed. Andrew Benjamin with additions by Geoff Bennington and Maria Hobson (Oxford: Basil Blackwell Ltd., 1989), pp. 204, 197, 199.

26 Lyotard, "The Sublime," p. 199. Obviously, with my use of Lyotard here, I find some of the contemporary theorizations of postmodernity useful in coming to terms with Stein. The debate about Stein as modernist versus Stein as postmodernist is not new. See, for example, Neil Schmitz, "Gertrude Stein as Post-Modernist: the Rhetoric of *Tender Buttons*," *Journal of Modern Literature* (1974), 1203–1218; David Lodge, *The Modes of Modern Writing: Metaphor, Metonymy, and the Typology of Modern Literature* (London: Edward Arnold, 1977), p. 154; Walker, *The Making of a Modernist*, p. 163, note 18; and, more recently, Ellen E. Berry, *Curved Thought and Textual Wandering: Gertrude Stein's Postmodernism*, (Ann Arbor, MI: University of Michigan Press, 1992). It is the incorporation of chance into the writing of immediacy which in various ways runs from Mallarmé through Stein to John Cage. This is of course why Marjorie Perloff includes Stein with other writers on the periphery of modernism "proper" who are not really seeking another *grande récit* to replace those lost by Western culture. Instead, figures like Stein, John Cage, Rimbaud, and others try to produce new aesthetic practices of indeterminacy. See Perloff, *The Poetics of Indeterminacy*.

27 Maurice Grosser, Scenario, *Four Saints in Three Acts, An Opera*, piano-vocal score, by Gertrude Stein and Virgil Thomson (New York: G. Schirmer, 1948), p. iii.

28 Ibid. Virgil Thomson, *Virgil Thomson* (New York: A. A. Knopf, 1966), pp. 107, 106. Having seen Spanish altar decorations, I'm not sure that "naive" is at all accurate.

29 Virgil Thomson, *Four Saints in Three Acts*, sound recording, Orchestra of Our Time, Joel Thome, conductor, New York, Electra/Asylum/Nonesuch, 1982, 79035-2, liner notes.

30 Thomson, *Thomson*, p. 90. Thomson is here speaking specifically about his earlier settings of the Stein texts "Susie Asado," "Preciosilla," and *Capital*

Capitals. The Musical Scene is cited in Jane Bowers, "The Writer in the Theater," p. 213. Thomson often speaks in his late volume, *Music With Words: a Composer's View* (New Haven, CT: Yale University Press, 1989) of the meticulous exertions that both performers and composers must go through for the sake of emotional expression. See, for example, chapter 9 and p. 68, chapter 11.

31 Thomson, *Words*, pp. 51, 52. Thomson, *Thomson*, pp. 90, 105, 106.

32 Thomson, *Words*, pp. 17, 20, 85.

33 Marianne DeKoven says that the "music and the libretto are sympathetic in both structure and content, in form and in feeling" (DeKoven, *A Different Language*, p. 141). While I agree in a certain way, the kind of complementarity that DeKoven suggests here perhaps unifies the relationship between language and music in too conventional a fashion.

34 Bars 1–10 before *1*, 1–4 after *1*. From now on I will be quoting both words and music from the piano/vocal score of the opera: Gertrude Stein and Virgil Thomson, *Four Saints in Three Acts, An Opera*, Complete Vocal Score, scenario by Maurice Grosser (New York: G. Schirmer, 1948). I will note my citations by bar line in reference to the rehearsal numbers – the large numbers in the text given in squares, but which I will mark in *italics*: eg. *1*. There are 10 bars to every section in the score marked by a bold rehearsal number. Hence: Bars 1–10 before *1*, 1–4 after *1*. I will insert all references to the piano/vocal score within the body of my text.

35 Lawrence Kramer, *Music and Poetry, the Nineteenth Century and After* (Berkeley, CA: University of California Press, 1984), pp. 130, 131. Donald Sutherland mentions that both the saints and Stein capture an immediacy or a sense of being "fully present and alive to whatever [is] there" (Sutherland, *Gertrude Stein*, p. 127). The opera thus functions on "the very firm ground of absolute presence" (p. 130). Harry R. Garvin gives the opera narrative and symbolic significance going along completely with Maurice Grosser's and Thomson's transformation of the "Pigeons on the grass, alas" section as a vision of the Holy Ghost. See Harry R. Garvin, "Sound and Sense in *Four Saints in Three Acts*," *The Bucknell Review* 1 (December 1954), 3–5. The entire opera is thus about the "way two saints [Saint Ignatius and Saint Therese] achieve a spiritual life" (7). For Richard Bridgman Stein's theme is the "acceptance of the world as given. The invocation of a supernatural agency she found unnecessary" (Bridgman, *Gertrude Stein in Pieces*, p. 187). The predominance of what he calls "authorial statement and commentary" (p. 187) leads him to suggest that the opera is "an improvised piece that struggles along uncertainly ["Saint Therese something like that . . ." (Stein, 19 plus 9–10)], then suddenly picks up and sails confidently through to a positive conclusion" (p. 187). The focus on the self-referentiality of the libretto's language as a reflection of Stein's own human mind is to be found in many other critics such as Jane Bowers, "The Writer in the Theatre," p. 223; Norman Weinstein, *Gertrude Stein and the Literature of the Modern Consciousness* (New York: Ungar, 1970), p. 78; and Betsy Alayne Ryan, *Theatre of the Absolute*, pp. 103–104.

36 Bowers, "The Writer in the Theatre," pp. 221, 222, 221, 223, 221. DeKoven, *A Different Language*, p. 142; Weinstein, *Modern Consciousness*, p. 75. DeKoven claims that Stein's practice of using regular syntax with unusual selections, is part of her late twenties style, but in fact it is apparent in the much earlier *Tender Buttons*.

37 Thomson himself speaks of the way music can create "tension and release" (Thomson, *Thomson*, p.105), but the concept is hardly new. The most thorough discussion is in Leonard Meyer's *Emotion and Meaning in Music* (Chicago, IL: Chicago University Press,1956) in which he maintains that listeners with less musical training will hear emotionally, while those with more training will hear more technically. Both, however, will be able to appreciate the laws of "good continuation" present in good music, and be able to respond to them. Such laws can be heard as creating tension and release in "appropriate" ways which can both be technically explained and emotionally appreciated. Jane Bowers remarks in regard to this passage of *Four Saints* that "memory, which is normally a present evocation of a past event or entity, is used . . . with an apparent disregard for its temporal function . . ." (Bowers, "The Writer in the Theatre," p. 221).

38 David Harris, "The Original *Four Saints in Three Acts*," *The Drama Review*, 26.1 (Spring 1982), 101–130, offers the most definitive discussion of the original production. He notes how the "scenario developed for the 1934 production . . . was a vehicle for a specific subtextual interpretation of the libretto, a pretext by which the singers were able to do something more with the lyrics than to voice them as they would have done in an oratorio version" (115). He is referring specifically to the moment in Act 2 where St. Teresa 1, just after the "love scene" between the Commère and Compère, tastes wine and sings, "To ask how much of it is finished" (*112* plus 1). He is pointing out that the actual performance of the opera conflicts with interpretations, of the kind I offer above, where references might seem to apply to the opera itself instead of to some *action* the characters might be doing. I take this as a warning, but at the same time I do not see why, given Stein's kind of textual play, that the references could not have more than one application.

39 As Thomson notes, remarking upon the positive reception the first act received when played for friends: "I had wondered whether a piece so drenched in Anglican chant (running from Gilbert and Sullivan to Morning Prayer and back) could rise and sail" (Thomson, *Thomson*, p. 105). The chant sections are plain enough, and I have elaborated on them already.

40 Elizabeth Grosz's definition is succinct: "The imaginary is the order of identification with images. It is the order of dual, narcissistic relations with others . . ., of libidinal pleasure unregulated by law, and indistinguishably intra- and inter-psychical aggression." See Elizabeth Grosz, *Jacques Lacan: a Feminist Introduction* (London: Routledge, 1990), p. 43.

41 Again, I realize that I diverge from Lacan's ideas concerning the symbolic, especially in its relation to the acquisition of subjectivity through language and the necessity of the split within the subject. For more on the symbolic,

see Grosz, *Lacan*, pp. 72–73. Lawrence Kramer, *Classical Music and Postmodern Knowledge* (Berkeley, CA: University of California Press, 1995), p. 19. He is quoting from his own article, "Song and Story," *Nineteenth-Century Music* 15 (1992), 238; Kramer, *Postmodern Knowledge*, my emphasis p. 55. Grosser's stage direction, piano-vocal score, p. 23.

42 The tonic-dominant will change to tonic-subdominant in other keys, such as when the Commère returns in E♭ major after the introduction of St. Ignatius at *34* plus 7. St. Ignatius's first words are sung in G major, whereas the key everyone else is in at the moment is E♭.

43 Stein, "Plays," p. 130. Thomson spells the saint's name "Teresa," while Stein maintains the name as "Therese."

44 Ibid., pp. 131, 130, 131.

45 The libretto's inquiry here regarding Negroes does not, of course, respond to the fact that Thomson used in all of the performances with which he was involved only black performers. I will take this issue up at the end of the chapter.

46 For a very different reading of the gender relations in the opera, especially as these are organized by Maurice Grosser's scenario, see Meg Albrinck, "'How can a sister see Saint Therese suitably': Difficulties in Staging Gertrude Stein's *Four Saints in Three Acts*," *Women's Studies* 25 (1995). 1–20.

47 See, for example, Bowers, "The Writer in the Theatre," p. 222.

48 "The Negroes proved in every way rewarding . . . They moved, sang, spoke with grace and with alacrity, took on the roles without self-consciousness, as if they were the saints they said they were" (Thomson, *Thomson*, p. 239).

49 Speaking of the only element of the production which he claims never met with question, Thomson notes that "Negroes had not been much used for playing non-Negro roles. Today, though they are so used, even in opera, they are not used for their characteristic qualities, but in spite of them rather, as if one was not supposed to recognize their race. And operas, a few of them, have been choreographed. But they have been choreographed for white dancers, who tend always to look arch in the presence of song, and for white singers, who do not walk well and who stand around like lumps, rather than for Negroes, who can move boldly and who stand with style" (Thomson, *Thomson*, p. 242). The problem with such praise, of course, is the propensity it has to attribute racial traits to "nature," and not, perhaps, to Thomson's own constructed way of seeing. Scratch the surface here, and we are right back to the natural possession of rhythm "argument." Thomson, *Thomson*, p. 241. Richard Bridgman says that white reviewers were not impressed. He quotes from the *Newsweek* review of the original production in which the reviewer says that the "'diction left a good deal to be desired'" aside from Stein's own language (Bridgman, *Gertrude Stein in Pieces*, p. 181). In contrast, James R. Mellow reports that "[t]he superb diction of the Negroes was to be a leitmotiv in the reviews of the opera, both in its Hartford run and in its later month-long engagement at the Forty-Fourth Street Theatre in New York. Thomson's choice of the Negroe cast, the *New York Times*'s

reviewer reported, 'seemed amply to have justified itself last night'" (Mellow, *Charmed Circle*, p. 442). Mellow quotes too from a letter to Stein by Carl Van Vechten, in which he too states that the singers "'enunciated the text so clearly you could understand every word'" (quoted in Mellow, *Charmed Circle*, p. 442). Bridgman often seems to emphasize the negative when it comes to analyzing Stein's texts.

50 Bridgman, *Gertrude Stein in Pieces*, p. 181. Quoted in Kathleen Hoover and John Cage, *Virgil Thomson, His Life and Music* (Freeport, NY: Books for Libraries Press, 1959), p. 81. Quoted in Richard France, "Virgil Thomson/Gertrude Stein: a Correspondence," *Theatre History Studies* 6 (1986), 78.

51 Ibid. Compare the France version with the apparently self-censored version of this letter presented in Thomson's autobiography, *Thomson*, p. 231. For more on the attempts by African Americans to both use and resist the minstrel format, see Thomas L. Riis, *More than just Minstrel Shows: the Rise of Black Theatre at the Turn of the Century*, I.A.S.M. Monographs: 33. (New York: Brooklyn College, Institute for Studies in American Music, 1992). See the pictures included in Hoover and Cage's book on Thomson; also David Harris reproduces many pictures which show especially the bodies of dancers. See Harris, "The Original *Four Saints in Three Acts*," 116, 119, 126. Harris, "The Original *Four Saints in Three Acts*," 124, notes the importance of black performers on the dances in *Four Saints*. Another ambiguous statement by Thomson regarding blacks and music occurs in a review of Gershwin's "Porgy and Bess," in April 1946. Of Todd Duncan's black-face performance of Gershwin: "He [Thomson] has never been wholly comfortable in the presence of Negroes interpreting Negro life through the conventions of the white black-face stage. The whole procedure seems to him unbecoming. Gershwin's music, moreover, is neither Negroid nor in any sense primitive, and it always comes out more humane in a straightforward rendering," *The Art of Judging Music* (New York, Knopf, 1948), pp. 55–56. Somehow, Thomson's commendable critique seems to falter near the end here. He clearly understands that black-face comes out of a white, racist background, yet Gershwin needs defending from the potential Negro "primitiveness" – or is it the black-face conventions which are primitive? It isn't clear. Moreover, to say that there is nothing "Negroid" – if this means "primitive" – about Gershwin is true; but to say that there is nothing *black* – in the sense of being borrowed or appropriated from black music – is completely untrue.

52 In *Philosophy of Modern Music*, Adorno makes the interesting claim that modern music which still relies upon triadic harmony is now itself the truly dissonant music: "It is not simply that these sounds are antiquated and untimely, but that they are false. They no longer fulfill their function. . . . There are modern compositions which occasionally scatter tonal sounds in their context. It is precisely the triads which, in such context, are cacophonous and not the dissonances!" Theodor W. Adorno, *Philosophy of Modern*

Music, trans. Anne G. Mitchell and Wesley V. Blomster (London: Sheed and Ward, 1973), p. 34. Such a line of argument is of course central to Adorno's justification and explanation of Schoenberg's twelve-tone technique. He is here (almost playfully for Adorno) reversing the order of things; tonality is dissonance, chromatic twelve-tone technique is the necessity – the *historical* and revolutionary necessity – of truly modern music. Historically, it is a cacophonous and yet strangely consonant necessity. By this definition, Thomson's tonality would not only be retrogressive, but it would also be a clear attempt to reinstate the repressive powers of past musical practice: in effect an attempt at an oppressive and repressive technical and expressive mode. A cynical interpretation might lead us to conclude that Thomson was merely capitalizing on the vogue of the twenties and thirties for things Negro. Carl Van Vechten, who apparently introduced Grosser and Thomson to African-American theatre, was not only a supporter of Stein's, but also of many African-American writers and artists of the Harlem Renaissance, that burst of cultural energy which is going on in America during the whole period of *Four Saints*, from the writing of it, to its first production. Van Vechten was also considered "white America's guide through Harlem," David Levering Lewis, *When Harlem was in Vogue* (New York: Oxford University Press, 1989), p. 183, and had produced his own novel of African-American life in 1926, the infamous, *Nigger Heaven*. See Lewis, *When Harlem was in Vogue*, pp. 164–165 for more on the explosion of white interest, and tourism, in the Harlem of the twenties.

53 Eric Lott, *Love and Theft: Blackface Minstrelsy and the American Working Class* (New York: Oxford University Press, 1993), p. 6.

54 I have in mind here Fredric Jameson's discussion of Althusser in *The Political Unconscious*: "history is *not* a text, not a narrative, master or otherwise, but that, as an absent cause, it is inaccessible to us except in textual form, and . . . our approach to it and to the [Lacanian] Real itself necessarily passes through its prior textualization, its narrativization in the political unconscious," Fredric Jameson, *The Political Unconscious: Narrative as a Socially Symbolic Act* (Ithaca, NY: Cornell University Press, 1982), p. 35.

ENDINGS

1 Theodor W. Adorno, *Philosophy of Modern Music*, trans. Anne G. Mitchell and Wesley V. Blomster (London: Sheed and Ward, 1973), p. 33.

Works cited

Abrams, M. H. *The Mirror and the Lamp: Romantic Theory and the Critical Tradition.* London: Oxford University Press, 1953.

Adams, Stephen J. "Are the 'Cantos' a Fugue?" *University of Toronto Quarterly* 45.1 (Fall 1975). 67–74.

"Musical Neofism: Pound's Theory of Harmony in Context." *Mosaic* 13.2 (Winter 1980). 49–69.

Adorno, Theodor W. *Philosophy of Modern Music.* Trans. Anne G. Mitchell and Wesley V. Blomster. London: Sheed and Ward, 1973.

Albrinck, Meg. "'How can a sister see Saint Therese suitably': Difficulties in Staging Gertrude Stein's *Four Saints in Three Acts.*" *Women's Studies* 25 (1995). 1–22.

Arnold, Matthew. "The Function of Criticism at the Present Time." *The Complete Prose Works of Matthew Arnold.* Vol. III. Eds. R. H. Super, with Sister Thomas Marion Hoctor. Ann Arbor, MI: University of Michigan Press, 1962.

Aronson, Alex. *Music and the Novel: A Study in Twentieth-Century Fiction.* Totowa, NJ: Rowman and Littlefield, 1980.

Attridge, Derek. "Joyce's Lipspeech: Syntax and the Subject in 'Sirens.'" Eds. Morris Beja, *et al.*, 59–65. *James Joyce's: The Centennial Symposium.* Urbana, IL and Chicago, IL: University of Illinois Press 1986.

Peculiar Language: Literature as Difference from the Renaissance to James Joyce. Ithaca, NY: Cornell University Press, 1988.

Bacigalupo, Massimo. *The Forméd Trace: the Later Poetry of Ezra Pound.* New York: Columbia University Press, 1980.

Barthes, Roland. "The Grain of the Voice." *The Responsibility of Forms: Critical Essays on Music, Art, and Representation.* Trans. Richard Howard. New York: Hill and Wang 1985. 267–277.

"Introduction to the Structural Analysis of Narratives." *Image-Music-Text* Trans. Stephen Heath, 70–124. New York: Hill and Wang, 1977.

Mythologies, Trans. Annette Lavers. New York: Hill and Wang, 1972.

S/Z. Trans. Richard Howard. New York: Hill and Wang, 1975.

Writing Degree Zero. Trans. Annette Lavers and Colin Smith. New York: Hill and Wang, 1977.

Baudelaire, Charles. *Selected Poems.* Trans. Joanna Richardson. Harmondsworth: Penguin, 1975.

"The Painter of Modern Life." *Baudelaire: Selected Writings on Art and Artists*, Trans. P. E. Charvet, 390–435. Cambridge: Cambridge University Press 1971.

Beja, Morris. *Epiphany in the Modern Novel*. Seattle, WA: University of Washington Press, 1971.

Beja, Morris, *et al.*, eds., *James Joyce: the Centennial Symposium*. Urbana, IL and Chicago, IL: University of Chicago Press, 1986.

Bell, Michael. "Introduction: Modern Movements in Literature." *The Context of English Literature: 1900–1930*. Ed. Michael Bell. London: Methuen and Co., Ltd. 1980. 1–93.

Benstock, Shari. *Women of the Left Bank: Paris, 1900–1940*. Austin, TX: University of Texas Press, 1986.

Bernard, Suzanne. *Mallarmé et la musique*. Paris: Librairie Nizet, 1959.

Berry, Ellen E. *Curved Thought and Textual Wandering: Gertrude Stein's Postmodernism*. Ann Arbor, MI: University of Michigan Press, 1992.

Blanchard, Marc E. "The Sound of Songs: the Voice in the Text." *Hermeneutics and Deconstruction*. Eds. Hugh J. Silverman and Don Ihde. Albany, NY: State University of New York Press, 1985. 122–135.

Blanchot, Maurice. "Mallarmé and Literary Space." *The Sirens' Song: Selected Essays*, Trans. Sacha Rabinovitch. Ed. Gabriel Josipovici. Bloomington, IN: Indiana University Press, 1982. 110–120.

Bloom, Harold. "The Internalization of Quest Romance." *Romanticism and Consciousness: Essays in Criticism*. Ed. Harold Bloom, 3–24. New York: W. W. Norton and Co. 1970.

Selected Writings of Walter Pater. Edited with an introduction and notes by Harold Bloom. New York: Columbia University Press, 1974. vii–xxxi.

Borges, Jorge Luis. "Tlön, Uqbar, Orbis Tertius." *Labyrinths: Selected Stories and Other Writings*. Trans. James E. Irby. Eds. Donald A. Yates and James E. Irby, 3–18. New York: New Directions 1964.

Bowen, Zack. "The Bronzegold Sirensong: a Musical Analysis of the Sirens Episode in Joyce's 'Ulysses'." *Literary Monographs*. Vol. 1. Eds. Eric Rothstein and Thomas K. Dunseath. Milwaukee, WI: University of Wisconsin Press, 1967. 247–320.

Musical Allusions in the Works of James Joyce: Early Poetry through "Ulysses". Albany, NY: State University of New York Press, 1974.

Bowers, Jane. "The Writer in the Theater: Gertrude Stein's *Four Saints in Three Acts*." *Critical Essays on Gertrude Stein*. Ed. Michael J. Hoffman. Boston, MA: Hall, 1986. 210–225.

Bucknell, Brad. "Eliot's Impossible Music." *T. S. Eliot's Orchestra: Critical Essays on Poetry and Music*. Ed. John X. Cooper, *et al.* New York: Garland, 2000.

Budgen, Frank. *James Joyce and the Making of 'Ulysses'*. Bloomington, IN: Indiana University Press, 1960.

Bujic, Bojan, ed. *Music in European Thought: 1851–1912*. Cambridge: Cambridge University Press, 1988.

Burke, Carolyn. "Gertrude Stein, the Cone Sisters, and the Puzzle of Female Friendship." *Critical Inquiry* 8.3. (Spring 1982) 543–564.

Bridgman, Richard. *Gertrude Stein in Pieces*. New York: Oxford University Press, 1970.

Brinnin, John Malcolm. *The Third Rose: Gertrude Stein and Her World*. Boston, MA: Littlebrown, 1959.

Casillo, Robert. *The Genealogy of Demons: Anti-Semitism, Fascism, and the Myths of Ezra Pound*. Evanston, IL: Northwestern University Press, 1988.

Chamberlin, J. E. *Ripe was the Drowy Hour: the Age of Oscar Wilde*. New York: The Seabury Press, 1977.

Chatman, Seymour. *Story and Discourse: Narrative Structure in Fiction and Film*. Ithaca, NY: Cornell University Press, 1978.

Chessman, Harriet Scott. *The Public Is Invited to Dance: Representation, the Body, and Dialogue in Gertrude Stein*. Stanford, CA: Stanford University Press, 1989.

Clements, Patricia. *Baudelaire and the English Tradition*. Princeton: Princeton University Press, 1985.

Coffman, Stanley K. Jr. *Imagism: a Chapter for the History of Modern Poetry*. Norman, OK: University of Oklahoma Press, 1951.

Cole, David W. "Fugal Structure in the Sirens Episode of 'Ulysses.'" *Modern Fiction Studies* 19 (Summer 1973). 221–226.

Cookson, William, ed. *Ezra Pound: Selected Prose: 1909–1965*. Introduction by William Cookson. London: Faber and Faber, 1973.

Cope, Jackson I. "Sirens." *James Joyce's "Ulysses": Critical Essays*, Eds. Clive Hart and David Hayman. Berkeley, CA: University of California Press (1977). 217–242.

Coyle, Michael. *Ezra Pound, Popular Genres, and the Discourse of Culture*. University Park, PA: Pennsylvania State University Press, 1995.

Dahlhaus, Carl. *Esthetics of Music*. Trans. William W. Austin. Cambridge: Cambridge University Press, 1982.

　The Idea of Absolute Music. Trans. Roger Lustig. Chicago, IL: University of Chicago Press, 1989.

Daniel, Arnaut. "*Sols sui.*" *The Translations of Ezra Pound*. Trans. Ezra Pound. 178–181.

Davie, Cedric Thorpe. *Musical Structure and Design*. New York: Dover Publications, Inc., 1966.

Davie, Donald. "Critics Who Made Us: Ezra Pound." *Sewanee Review* 92 (July – September 1984). 421–432.

Davis, Kay. *Fugue and Frescoe: Structures in Pound's 'Cantos'*. Orono, Maine: The National Poetry Foundation, University of Maine, 1984.

Dayan Peter. *Mallarmé's "Divine Transportation": Real and Apparent Sources of Literary Value* (Oxford: Clarendon, 1986).

DeKoven, Marianne. *A Different Language: Gertrude Stein's Experimental Writing*. Madison, WI: University of Wisconsin Press, 1983.

　"Gertrude Stein and Modern Painting: Beyond Literary Cubism." *Contemporary Literature* 22.1 (Winter 1981). 81–95.

de Man, Paul. "Literary History and Literary Modernity." *Blindness and Insight: Essays in the Rhetoric of Contemporary Criticism*. Theory and History of

Literature VII Minneapolis, MN: University of Minnesota Press (1983). 142–165.

"Lyric and Modernity." *Blindness and Insight.* 166–186.

"The Rhetoric of Temporality." *Blindness and Insight.* 187–228.

Dennis, Helen M. "The Eleusian Mysteries as an Organizing Principle in 'The Pisan Cantos.'" *Paideuma* 10.2 (Fall 1982). 273–282.

Derrida, Jacques. "The Double Session." *Stéphane Mallarmé: Modern Critical Views.* Trans. Barbara Johnson. Ed. Harold Bloom. New York: Chelsea House Publishers, 1987. 80–86.

Of Grammatology. Trans. Gayatri Chakravorty Spivak. Baltimore, MD: Johns Hopkins University Press, 1982.

"Signature Event Context." *Margins of Philosophy.* Trans. Alan Bass. Chicago IL: University of Chicago Press, 1982, pp. 307–330.

Dubnick, Randa. *The Structure of Obscurity: Gertrude Stein, Language, and Cubism.* Urbana, IL: University of Illinois Press, 1984.

Dunn, Margaret M. "Eine Kleine Wortmusik: the Marriage of Poetry and Music in 'The Pisan Cantos.'" *Perspective on Contemporary Literature* 13 (1987). 101–109.

Eagleton, Terry. *The Ideology of the Aesthetic.* Oxford: Basil Blackwell Inc., 1990.

Edwards, John Hamilton and William W. Vasse. *Annotated Index to the 'Cantos' of Ezra Pound. I–XXXIV.* Berkeley, CA: University of California Press, 1957.

Eksteins, Modris. *Rites of Spring: the Great War and the Birth of the Modern Age.* Toronto: Lester and Orpen Dennys, 1989.

Eliot, T. S., ed. *Literary Essays of Ezra Pound.* Introduction by T. S. Eliot. London: Faber and Faber, 1954.

Ellmann, Richard. *James Joyce.* Rev. edn. New York: Oxford University Press, 1982.

Ulysses on the Liffey. London: Faber and Faber, 1974.

Fenollosa, Ernest. "The Chinese Written Character as a Medium for Poetry." *Prose Keys to Modern Poetry.* Ed. Karl Shapiro. New York: Harper and Row, 1962.

Ferrer, Daniel. "Echo or Narcissus?" *James Joyce: The Centennial Symposium.* Eds. Morris Beja, *et al.* 1986, 70–75.

Fifer, Elizabeth. "Is Flesh Advisable? The Interior Theater of Gertrude Stein." *Signs* 4.3 (Spring 1979). 472–483.

Fitts, Dudley. "Music Fit for the Odes." *The Hound and Horn* 4.2 (January–March 1931). 278–289.

Fitz, L. T. "Gertrude Stein and Picasso: the Language of Surfaces." *American Literature* 45 (1973). 228–237.

Fletcher, Ian. "Walter Pater." *Modern Critical Views: Walter Pater.* Edited with an introduction by Harold Bloom. New York: Chelsea House, 1985. 41–73.

France, Richard. "Virgil Thomson/Gertrude Stein: a Correspondence." *Theatre History Studies* 6 (1986). 72–86.

Frank, Joseph. *The Widening Gyre: Crisis and Mastery in Modern Literature.* New Brunswick, NJ: Rutgers University Press, 1963.

French, Marilyn. *The Book as World: James Joyce's "Ulysses."* Cambridge, MA: Harvard University Press, 1976.

Froula, Christine. *A Guide to Ezra Pound's Selected Poems.* New York: New Directions, 1982.

Garvin, Harry R. "Sound and Sense in *Four Saints in Three Acts.*" *The Bucknell Review* 1 (December 1954). 1–11.

Gilbert, Stuart. *James Joyce's 'Ulysses': a Critical Study.* New York: Viking, 1955.

Grosser, Maurice. Scenario. *Four Saints in Three Acts, An Opera.* By Gertrude Stein and Virgil Thomson. New York: G. Schirmer, 1948. iii-v.

Grosz, Elizabeth. *Jacques Lacan: a Feminist Introduction.* London: Routledge, 1990.

Grout, Donald Jay, with Claude V. Palisca. *A History of Western Music.* 3rd edn. New York: W. W. Norton and Company, 1980.

Hadas, Pamela. "Spreading the Difference: One Way to Read Gertrude Stein's *Tender Buttons.*" *Twentieth-Century Literature* 24.1 (Spring 1978). 57–75.

Hanslick, Eduard. *On the Musically Beautiful.* 8th edn. 1891. Trans. Geoffrey Payzant. Indianapolis, IN: Hackett Publishing Co., 1986.

Hardy, Ann. "A Fugal Analysis of the Sirens Episode in Joyce's 'Ulysses'." *Massachusetts Studies in English 2* (Spring 1970). 59–67.

Harris, David. "The Original *Four Saints in Three Acts.*" *The Drama-Review* 26.1 (93) (Spring 1982). 101–130.

Hartman, Elwood. *French Literary Wagnerism.* New York & London: Garland Publishing Inc., 1988.

Hassan, Ihab. "The Question of Postmodernism." *Bucknell Review* 25.2 (Fall 1977). 90–126.

Heath, Stephen. "Ambiviolences: Notes for Reading Joyce." *Post-structuralist Joyce: Essays from the French.* Eds. Derek Attridge and Daniel Ferrer. Cambridge: Cambridge University Press, 1984. 31–68.

Hegel, G. W. F. *Aesthetics: Lectures on Fine Art.* 2 vols. Trans. T. M. Knox. Oxford: Oxford University Press, 1975.

Herder, Johann Gottfried. *Kalligone. Music and Aesthetics in the Eighteenth and Early Nineteenth Centuries.* Peter le Huray and James Day. 1981. 253–257.

Herman, David. "'Sirens' after Schönberg." *James Joyce Quarterly* 31.4 (Summer 1994): 473–494.

Herr, Cheryl. *Joyce's Anatomy of Culture.* Urbana, IL and Chicago, IL: University of Illinois Press, 1986.

Hertz, David Michael. *The Tuning of the Word: the Musico-Literary Poetics of the Symbolist Movement.* Carbondale, IL and Edwardsville, IL: Southern Illinois University Press, 1987.

Hesse, Eva. "Klages in Canto LXXV/450: a Positive Identification." *Paideuma* 10:2 (Fall 1981). 295–296.

Hoffman, Daniel. *Poe Poe Poe Poe Poe Poe Poe Poe.* Garden City, NY: Doubleday and Co., Inc., 1972.

Hoffmann, E. T. A. "Beethoven's Instrumental Music." *Source Readings in Music History: the Romantic Era.* Ed. Strunk. 35–41.

Hoffman, Michael J., ed. *Critical Essays on Gertrude Stein.* Boston: Hall, 1986.

The Development of Abstractionism in the Writing of Gertrude Stein. Philadelphia, PA: University of Pennsylvania Press, 1966.

Hollington, Michael. "Svevo, Joyce and Modernist Time." *Modernism: 1890–1930.* Ed. Malcolm Bradbury and James McFarlane. Harmondsworth: Penguin, 1981. 430–442.

Hoover, Kathleen, and John Cage. *Virgil Thomson, his Life and Music.* Freeport, NY: Books for Libraries Press, 1959.

Horsley, Imogene. *Fugue: History and Practice.* New York: The Free Press, 1966.

Hough, Graham. *The Last Romantics.* London: Methuen; New York: Barnes and Noble, 1961.

Hughes, Glenn. *Imagism and the Imagists: a Study in Modern Poetry.* New York: The Humanities Press, 1960.

Hughes, Robert, dir. *Le Testament de François Villon* by Ezra Pound. Fantasy Records, 12001, 1973. Long-play record.

Hulme, T. E. "Romanticism and Classicism." *Speculations: Essays on Humanism and the Philosophy of Art.* 1924. Ed. Herbert Read. London: Routledge and Kegan Paul, 1987. 111–140.

Hutcheon, Linda. *A Poetics of Postmodernism: History, Theory, Fiction.* New York: Routledge, 1988.

Huyssen, Andreas. *After the Great Divide: Modernism, Mass Culture, Postmodernism.* Bloomington, IN and Indianapolis, IN: Indiana University Press, 1986.

Inman, Billie Andrew. "The Intellectual Context of Pater's 'Conclusion'." *Modern Critical Views: Walter Pater.* Ed. Harold Bloom. New York: Chelsea House, 1985. 131–149.

Iser, Wolfgang. *Walter Pater: the Aesthetic Moment.* Trans. David Henry Wilson. Cambridge: Cambridge University Press, 1987.

Jacobs, Robert L. *Wagner. The Master Musicians Series.* London: J. M. Dent & Sons, Ltd., 1980.

Jakobson, Roman. "Two Aspects of Language: Metaphor and Metonymy." *European Literary Theory and Practice: From Existential Phenomenology to Structuralism.* Ed. Vernon W. Gras. New York: Dell, 1973. 119–129.

James, William. *The Principles of Psychology.* 1890. 2 vols. Vol. 1. New York: Dover Publications Inc. 1950.

Jameson, Fredric. *The Political Unconscious: Narrative as a Socially Symbolic Act.* Ithaca, NY: Cornell University Press, 1982.

Joyce, James. *Letters of James Joyce.* Ed. Stuart Gilbert. New York: Viking, 1957.
Ulysses: a Critical and Synoptic Edition. 3 vols. Prepared by Hans Walter Gabler, et al. New York and London: Garland Publishing, Inc., 1984.

Kandinsky, Wassily. *Concerning the Spiritual in Art and Painting in Particular.* 1914. Trans. Michael Sadleir, Francis Golffing, et al. *The Documents of Art* V. New York: George Wittenborn, Inc., 1947.

Kant, Immanuel. *Critique of Judgement.* 1892. Trans. J. H. Bernard. New York: Hafner Publishing Co., 1951.

Kayman, Martin A. *The Modernism of Ezra Pound: the Science of Poetry.* London: Macmillan Press Ltd., 1986.

Kennan, Kent. *Counterpoint: Based on Eighteenth-Century Practice*. 2nd edn. New Jersey: Prentice-Hall, Inc., 1972.

Kenner, Hugh. *The Pound Era*. Berkeley, CA: University of California Press, 1971. *Ulysses*. London: George Allen and Unwin, 1982.

Kermode, Frank. "The Modern." *Modern Essays*. London: Collins, Fontana Books, 1971. 39–70.

Romantic Image. New York: Vintage Books, 1957.

Kivy, Peter. *Sound Sentiment: an Essay on the Musical Emotions, including the complete text of "The Corded Shell"*. Philadelphia: Temple University Press, 1989.

Korn, Marianne. *Ezra Pound: Purpose/Form/Meaning*. London: Middlesex Polytechnic Press; Pembridge Press, 1983.

Kramer, Jonathan D. "New Temporalities in Music." *Critical Inquiry* 7 (Spring 1981). 539–556.

Kramer, Lawrence. *Classical Music and Postmodern Knowledge*. Berkeley, CA: University of California Press, 1995.

Music and Poetry, the Nineteenth Century and After. Berkeley, CA: University of California Press, 1984.

"Song and Story." *Nineteenth-Century Music* 15 (1992). 238.

Langer, Susan K. *Philosophy in a New Key: a Study in the Symbolism of Reason, Rite, and Art*. 1957. 3rd edn. Cambridge, MA: Harvard University Press, 1980.

Laurence, Karen. *The Odyssey of Style in "Ulysses."* Baton Rouge, LA: Louisiana State University Press, 1982.

Lees, Heath. "The Introduction to 'Sirens' and the *Fuga Per Canonem*." *James Joyce Quarterly* 22.1 (Fall 1984). 39–54.

le Huray, Peter and James Day., eds. *Music and Aesthetics in the Eighteenth and Early-Nineteenth Centuries*. Cambridge: Cambridge University Press, 1981.

Lessing, Gotthold Ephraim. *Laocoön: an Essay on the Limits of Painting and Poetry*. 1766. Trans. with an introduction and notes by Edward Allen McCormick. Baltimore, MD: Johns Hopkins University Press, 1984.

Levenson, Michael H. *A Genealogy of Modernism: a Study of English Literary Doctrine 1908–1922*. Cambridge: Cambridge University Press, 1984.

Levin, Harry. *James Joyce: A Critical Introduction*. Rev. and augmented edn. New York: New Directions, 1960.

Levin, Lawrence. "The Sirens Episode as Music: Joyce's Experiment in Prose Polyphony." *James Joyce Quarterly* 3.1 (Fall 1965). 12–24.

Lewis, David Levering. *When Harlem was in Vogue*. New York: Oxford University Press, 1989.

Lewis, Paula Gilbert. *The Aesthetics of Stéphane Mallarmé in Relation to his Public* Cranbury, NJ: Associated University Presses, Inc.,1976.

Liszt, Franz. "Berlioz and His 'Harold' Symphony." *Source Readings in Music History: The Romantic Era*. Strunk. 107–133.

Litz, A. Walton. *The Art of James Joyce: Method and Design in "Ulysses" and "Finnegans Wake"*. London: Oxford University Press, 1964.

Lodge, David. *The Modes of Modern Writing: Metaphor, Metonymy, and the Typology of Modern Literature*. London: Edward Arnold, 1977.

Lott, Eric. *Love and Theft: Blackface Minstrelsy and the American Working Class*. New York: Oxford University Press, 1993.

Lyall, Larry. "Pound/Villon: 'Le Testament de Francois [sic] Villon'." *Paideuma* 2 (1973). 17–22.

Lyotard, Jean-François. "The Sublime and the Avant-Garde." *The Lyotard Reader*. Trans. Lisa Liebmann, ed. Andrew Benjamin with additions by Geoff Bennington and Maria Hobson. Oxford: Basil Blackwell Ltd., 1989.

Madou, Jean-Pol. "Langue, mythe, musique: Rousseau, Nietzsche, Mallarmé, Levi-Strauss." *Littérature et musique*. Ed. Raphaël Célis. Bruxelles: Publications des Facultés Universitaires Saint-Louis, 1982.

Mallarmé, Stéphane. *Oeuvres Completes*. Paris: Gallimard, 1945.

"The Book: a Spiritual Instrument." *Selected Prose Poems, Essays, and Letters*. Trans. Bradford Cook. Baltimore, MD: Johns Hopkins University Press, 1956. 24–29. necessarry

"Crisis in Poetry." *Selected Prose Poems, Essays, and Letters*. Trans. Bradford Cook. Balitmore, MD: Johns Hopkins University Press. 34–43.

Letter to Henri Cazalis, July, 1866. *Selected Prose Poems, Essays, and Letters*. Trans. Bradford Cook. Baltimore, MD: Johns Hopkins University Press, 1956. 89–90.

"Music and Literature." *Selected Prose Poems, Essays, and Letters*. 43–56.

"Mystery in Literature." *Selected Prose Poems, Essays, and Letters*. 29–34.

Preface. *Un Coup de dés jamais n'abolira le hasard. The Poems*. Trans. Keith Bosely, 209–212. Harmondsworth: Penguin, 1977.

"Richard Wagner, Reverie of a French Poet." *Selected Prose Poems, Essays, and Letters*. 72–78.

"Letter to Henri Cazalis, July, 1866." *Selected Prose Poems, Essays, and Lectures*. 89–90.

McDougal, Stuart Y. *Ezra Pound and the Troubadour Tradition*. Princeton, NJ: Princeton University Press, 1972.

McGrath, F. C. *The Sensible Spirit: Walter Pater and the Modernist Paradigm*. Tampa, FL: University of South Florida Press, 1986.

Meisel, Perry. *The Myth of the Modern: A Study in British Literature and Criticism after 1850*. New Haven, CT: Yale University Press, 1987.

Mellow, James R. *Charmed Circle: Gertrude Stein & Company*. New York: Avon Books, 1974.

Meyer, Leonard. *Emotion and Meaning in Music*. Chicago, IL: Chicago University Press, 1956.

Mitchell, W. J. T., ed. *The Language of Images*. Chicago, IL: Chicago University Press, 1980.

"Spatial Form in Literature." *The Language of Images*. Ed. Mitchell. 271–299.

Morgan, Robert P. "Musical Space/Musical Time." *The Language of Images*. Ed. Mitchell. 259–270.

Morris, R. O. *The Structure of Music: an Outline for Students*. London: Oxford University Press, 1935.

Nestrovski, Arthur. "Blindness and Inwit: James Joyce and the Sirens, a Reading of Chapter 11 of 'Ulysses'." *The Iowa Review* 18.1 (Winter 1988). 18–26.

Nicholls, Peter. *Modernisms: a Literary Guide*. Berkeley, CA: University of California Press, 1995.

Nietzsche, Frederich. *The Birth of Tragedy and the Case of Wagner*. Trans. Walter Kaufmann. New York: Vintage, 1967.

Norton, Richard. *Tonality in Western Culture: a Critical and Historical Perspective*. University Park, PA and London: Pennsylvania State University Press, 1984.

Pater, Walter. *Appreciations, with an Essay on Style*. 1889. Evanston, IL: Northwestern University Press, 1987.

   The Renaissance: Studies in Art and Poetry. 4th edn. 1893. Edited with an introduction by Adam Phillips. Oxford: Oxford University Press, 1986.

Payzant, Geoffrey. "Hanslick, Sams, Gay, and 'Tonend Bewegte Formen'." *Journal of Aesthetics and Art Criticism* 40.1 (Fall 1981): 41–48.

Pearlman, Daniel D. *The Barb of Time: on the Unity of Ezra Pound's 'Cantos'*. New York: Oxford University Press, 1969.

Pearson, Karl. *The Grammar of Science*. 1892. London: J. M. Dent and Sons Ltd., 1937.

Perelman, Bob. *The Trouble With Genius: Reading Pound, Joyce, Stein, and Zukofsky*. Berkeley, CA: University of California Press, 1994.

Perloff, Marjorie. *The Dance of the Intellect: Studies in the Poetry of the Pound Tradition*. Cambridge: Cambridge University Press, 1985. 33–73.

   The Poetics of Indeterminacy: Rimbaud to Cage. Princeton, NJ: Princeton University Press, 1981.

Perreault, Jeanne. "Male Maternity in *Ulysses*." *English Studies in Canada* 13 (1987). 304–314.

Pierrot, Jean. *The Decadent Imagination, 1880–1900*. Trans. Derek Coltman. Chicago, IL: University of Chicago Press, 1981.

Poe, Edgar Allan. "The Philosophy of Composition." *The Works of Edgar Allan Poe*. Biographical introduction by Hervey Allen. New York: P. F. Collier and Son Co., 1927. 812–820.

   "The Poetic Principle." *The Works of Edgar Allan Poe*. 766–780.

Pound, Ezra. *ABC of Economics*. *Selected Prose: 1909–1965*. Ed. Cookson,

   ABC of Reading. 1934. New York: New Directions, 1960.

   "A Retrospect." *Literary Essays of Ezra Pound*. Ed. Eliot. 3–14.

   "A Visiting Card." *Selected Prose: 1909–1965*. Ed. Cookson. 306–335.

   Antheil and the Treatise on Harmony. 1927. New York: Da Capo Press, 1968.

   The Cantos of Ezra Pound. New York: New Directions, 1970.

   "An Introduction to the Economic Nature of the United States." *Selected Prose: 1909–1965*. Ed. Cookson. 167–185.

   Ezra Pound and Music: The Complete Criticism. Edited with commentary by R. Murray Schafer. New York: New Directions, 1977.

   Gaudier-Brzeska: a Memoir. 1916. New York: New Directions, 1960.

   Guide to Kulchur. 1934. New York: New Directions, 1970.

"How to Read." *The Literary Essays of Ezra Pound.* Ed. Eliot. 15–40.

"I gather the limbs of Osiris." 1911–1912. *Selected Prose: 1909–1965.* Ed. Cookson. 19–43.

Introduction. *Cavalcanti Poems.* 1910. The Translations of Ezra Pound. Trans. Ezra Pound. 17–25.

The Letters of Ezra Pound: 1907–1941. Ed. D. D. Paige. London: Faber and Faber, 1951.

Literary Essays of Ezra Pound. Edited with an introduction by T. S. Eliot. London: Faber and Faber, 1954.

"Murder By Capital." *Selected Prose: 1909–1965.* Ed. Cookson. 227–232.

Selected Poems of Ezra Pound. New York: New Directions, 1956.

Selected Prose: 1909–1965. Edited with an introduction by William Cookson. London: Faber and Faber, 1973.

"The Serious Artist." *The Literary Essays of Ezra Pound.* Ed. T. S. Eliot. 41–57.

Le Testament de François Villon. Bienecke. Rare Book and Manuscript Library. New Haven, CT. YCAL MSS 43, Box 4, Folder 15. Dec. 31, 1923.

The Translations of Ezra Pound. Introduction by Hugh Kenner. New York: New Directions, 1970.

"Wyndham Lewis." *The Literary Essays of Ezra Pound.* Ed. T. S. Eliot. 423–430.

Pratt, Carroll C. *The Meaning of Music.* New York: McGraw-Hill, 1932.

Rabaté, Jean-Michel. "The Silence of the Sirens." *James Joyce: the Centennial Symposium.* Ed. Morris Beja, *et al.* 1986, 82–88.

Radford, F. L. "King, Pope, and Hero-Martyr: *Ulysses* and the Nightmare of Irish History." *James Joyce Quarterly* 15.4 (Summer 1978). 275–323.

Randel, Don Michael. *Harvard Concise Dictionary of Music.* Cambridge, MA: Belknap, Harvard University Press, 1978.

Riis, Thomas L. *More than just Minstrel Shows: the Rise of Black Musical Theatre at the Turn of the Century.* I.A.S.M. Monographs: 33. New York: Brooklyn College, Institute for Studies in American Music, 1992.

Ringbom, Sixten. *The Sounding Cosmos: a Study in the Spiritualism of Kandinsky and the Genesis of Abstract Painting.* Acta Academuae Aboensis. Ser. A. Vol. XXXVIII nr. 2. Abo: Abo Akademi, 1970.

Rose, Marilyn Gaddis. "Gertrude Stein and the Cubist Narrative." *Modern Fiction Studies* 22 (1976–1977). 543–555.

Robbe-Grillet, Alain. "From Realism to Reality." *For a New Novel: Essays on Fiction.* Trans. Richard Howard. New York: Grove, 1965. 157–168.

Rosen, Charles. *Arnold Schoenberg.* Princeton, NJ: Princeton University Press, 1975.

Ruddick, Lisa. *Reading Gertrude Stein: Body, Text, Gnosis.* Ithaca, NY: Cornell University Press, 1990.

Ryan, Betsy Alayne. *Gertrude Stein's Theatre of the Absolute.* Ann Arbor, MI: UMI Research Press, 1984.

Salecl, Renata, and Slavoj Žižek, ed. *Voice and Gaze as Love Objects.* SIC 1. Durham and London: Duke University Press, 1996.

Saussure, Ferdinand de. *Course in General Linguistics.* Trans. Wade Baskin. London: Collins, Fontana, 1974.

Schafer, R. Murray, ed. *Ezra Pound and Music: the Complete Criticism.* Commentary by R. Murray Schafer. New York: New Directions, 1977.

Ezra Pound and Music. Vol. 11. unpublished. National Library of Canada. File No.: 246–3–2–S1.

Schmitz, Neil. *Of Huck and Alice: Humorous Writing in American Literature.* Minneapolis, MN: University of Minnesota Press, 1983.

"Gertrude Stein as Post-Modernist: the Rhetoric of *Tender Buttons.*" *Journal of Modern Literature* 3.5 (July 1974). 1203–1218.

Schneidau, Herbert N. *Ezra Pound: the Image and the Real.* Baton Rouge, LA: Louisiana State University Press, 1969.

Schoenberg, Arnold. *Style and Idea: Selected Writings of Arnold Schoenberg.* Ed. Leonard Stein. Trans. Leo Black. London: Faber, 1975.

Schopenhauer, Arthur. *Die Welt als Wille und Vorstellung. Music and Aesthetics in the Eighteenth and Early-Nineteenth Centuries.* Eds. Peter le Huray and James Day. Cambridge: Cambridge University Press, 1981. 323–330.

Schwartz, Sanford. *The Matrix of Modernism: Pound, Eliot, and Early Twentieth-Century Thought.* Princeton, NJ: Princeton University Press, 1985.

Scott, Clive. "Symbolism, Decadence and Impressionism." *Modernism: 1890–1930.* Eds. Malcolm Bradbury and James McFarlane. Harmondsworth: Penguin, 1981. 206–227.

"The Seafarer." *The Translations of Ezra Pound.* Trans. by Ezra Pound. 207–209.

Shelley, Percy Bysshe. "A Defense of Poetry." 1821. *English Romantic Writers.* Ed. David Perkins. New York: Harcourt Brace Jovanovich, Inc., 1967. 1072–1087.

Sieburth, Richard. *Instigations: Ezra Pound and Remy de Gourmont.* Cambridge, MA: Harvard University Press, 1978.

Spender, Stephen. *The Struggle of the Modern.* London: Hamish Hamilton, 1963.

Staudt, Kathleen Henderson. "The Poetics of 'Black on White': Stéphane Mallarmé's 'Un Coup de dés'." *Ineffability: Naming the Unnameable from Dante to Beckett.* Eds. Peter S. Hawkins and Anne Howland Schotter. New York: AMS Press, Inc., 1984. 147–161.

Stead, C. K. *Pound, Yeats, Eliot and the Modernist Movement.* New Brunswick, NJ: Rutgers University Press, 1986.

Stein, Gertrude. *A Long Gay Book. Matisse, Picasso, and Gertrude Stein, with Two Shorter Stories.* Barton, NY: Something Else Press, 1972.

"Composition as Explanation." *Look at Me Now and Here I Am: Writings and Lectures 1909–1945.* Ed. Patricia Meyerowitz, Introduction by Elizabeth Sprigge. Harmondsworth: Penguin, 1971. 21–30.

Doctor Faustus Lights the Lights. Last Operas and Plays. 89–118.

Ida, A Novel. 1941. New York: Vintage, 1968.

The Geographical History of America: or the Relation of Human Nature to the Human Mind. Introduction by Thornton Wilder. New York: Random House, 1936.

Geography and Plays. Introduction by Cyrena N. Pondrom. Madison, WI: University of Wisconsin Press, 1993.

"The Gradual Making of the 'Making of Americans'." *Lectures in America,* 135–161.

Last Operas and Plays. Edited and with an introduction by Carl Van Vechten. New York: Rinehart & Co., Inc., 1949.

Lectures in America, 1935. Introduction by Wendy Steiner. London: Virago, 1988.

The Making of Americans: Being a History of a Family's Progress. New York: Something Else Press, 1972.

Narration: Four Lectures by Gertrude Stein. Introduction by Thornton Wilder. Chicago, IL: Chicago University Press, 1935.

Operas and Plays. 1932. Foreword by James R. Mellow. Barrytown, NY: Station Hill Press, 1987.

"Paisieu." *Last Operas and Plays*. 155–181.

"Photograph." *Last Operas and Plays*. 152–154.

Picasso. New York: Dover Publications, Inc., 1984.

"Plays." *Lectures in America*, 93–131.

"Poetry and Grammar." *Lectures in America*, 209–246.

"Portraits and Repetition." *Lectures in America*, 165–206.

"Say It With Flowers." *Operas and Plays*. 331–343.

Tender Buttons. New York: Claire-Marie, 1914.

Stein, Gertrude and Virgil Thomson. *Four Saints in Three Acts, An Opera*. Complete Vocal Score. Scenario by Maurice Grosser. New York: G. Schirmer, 1948.

Steiner, George. *Real Presences*. Chicago, IL: University of Chicago Press, 1989.

"Silence and the Poet." *Language and Silence: Essays on Language, Literature, and the Inhuman*. New York: Atheneum, 1982. 36–54.

Steiner, Wendy. *Exact Resemblance to Exact Resemblance: the Literary Portraiture of Gertrude Stein*. New Haven, CT: Yale University Press, 1978.

Stewart, Garrett. *Reading Voices: Literature and the Phonotext*. Berkeley, CA: University of California Press, 1990.

Stock, Noel. *The Life of Ezra Pound*. Expanded edition. San Francisco, CA: North Point Press, 1982.

Stimpson, Catherine R. "The Mind, the Body and Gertrude Stein." *Critical Inquiry* 3.3 (Spring 1977). 489–564.

"The Somagrams of Gertrude Stein." *Poetics Today* (1985) 6.1–2. 67–80.

Stravinsky, Igor. *Poetics of Music in the Form of Six Lessons*. Trans. Arthur Knodel and Ingolf Dahl. Cambridge, MA: Harvard University Press, 1942.

Strunk, Oliver, ed. *Source Readings in Music History: the Romantic Era*. 4 vols. New York: W. W. Norton, 1965.

Subotnik, Rose Rosengard. *Deconstructive Variations: Music and Reason in Western Society*. Minneapolis, MN: University of Minnesota Press, 1996.

Sultan, Stanley. "Sirens at the Ormond Bar: 'Ulysses'." *The University of Kansas City Review* 26.1 (October 1959). 83–92.

Surette, Leon. *A Light from Eleusis: a Study of Ezra Pound's Cantos*. Oxford: Clarendon Press, 1979.

Sutherland, Donald. *Gertrude Stein: a Biography of her Work*. New Haven, CT: Yale University Press, 1951.

Symons, Arthur. *The Symbolist Movement in Literature*. 1899. 2nd rev. edn. 1919. Introduction by Richard Ellmann. New York: E. P. Dutton and Co., Inc., 1958.

Sypher, Wylie. *The Loss of the Self in Modern Literature and Art*. New York: Vintage, 1962.

Terrell, Carroll F. *A Companion to the 'Cantos' of Ezra Pound*. 2 vols. Berkeley, CA: University of California Press, 1980–1984.

Thomas, Brook. *James Joyce's 'Ulysses': a Book of Many Happy Returns*. Baton Rouge, LA: Louisiana State University Press, 1982.

Thomson, Virgil. *The Art of Judging Music*. New York, Knopf, 1948.

Four Saints in Three Acts. Sound recording. Orchestra of Our Time. Joel Thome, conductor. New York: Electra/Asylum/Nonesuch, 1982. 79035–2.

Music With Words: a Composer's View. New Haven, CT: Yale University Press, 1989.

Virgil Thomson. New York: A. A. Knopf. 1966.

Topia, André. "'Sirens': the Emblematic Vibration." *James Joyce: the Centennial Symposium*. Ed. Morris Beja, *et al.* 76–81.

Trilling, Lionel. "On the Teaching of Modern Literature." *Beyond Culture: Essays in Literature and Learning*. New York: Viking Press, 1955. 3–30.

Tucker, John J. "Pound, Vorticism and the New Esthetic." *Mosaic* 16.4 (Fall 1983). 83–96.

Valéry, Paul. "A Foreword." *The Art of Poetry*. Trans. Denise Folliot. Ed. Jackson Matthews. Bollingen Series XLV. The Collected Works of Paul Valéry. Vol. VII. Princeton, NJ: Princeton University Press, 1958. 39–51.

van der Werf, Hendrik. *The Chansons of the Troubadours and Trouvères: a Study of the Melodies and Their Relation to the Poems*. Utrecht: A. Oosthoek's Uitgeversmaatschappij NV, 1972.

Villon, François. *The Testament. The Complete Works of François Villon*. Translated with a biography and notes by Anthony Bonner. Introduction by William Carlos Williams. New York: David McKay Co., Inc. 1960.

Wackenroder, Wilhelm Heinrich. *Phantasien über die Kunst für Freunde der Kunst. Music and Aesthetics in the Eighteenth and Early Nineteenth Centuries*. Eds. Peter le Huray and James Day. 249–250.

Wagner, Richard. "Beethoven." *Music in European Thought: 1851–1912*. Ed. Bojan Bujic. 65–75.

Wagner on Music and Drama. 1964. Trans. H. Ashton Ellis. Selected and arranged by Albert Goldman and Evert Sprinchorn. New York: Da Capo Press, Inc., 1988.

Walker, Jayne L. *The Making of a Modernist: Gertrude Stein from "Three Lives" to "Tender Buttons."* Amherst, MA: University of Massachusetts Press, 1984.

Weinstein, Norman. *Gertrude Stein and the Literature of the Modern Consciousness*. New York: Ungar, 1970.

White, Hayden. *Tropics of Discourse: Essays in Cultural Criticism*. Baltimore, MD: Johns Hopkins University Press, 1978.

Wilde, Oscar. The Preface. *The Picture of Dorian Gray.* 1891. Ed. Peter Ackroyd. Harmondsworth: Penguin, 1985. 21–22.

Williams, Carolyn. *Transfigured World: Walter Pater's Aesthetic Historicism.* Ithaca, NY: Cornell University Press, 1989.

Williams, Ralph Vaughan. "Fugue." *Grove's Dictionary of Music and Musicians.* Ed. Eric Blom. 5th edn. Vol. III. London: Macmillan; New York: St. Martin's Press, 1954. 513–521.

Wilson, Edmund. *Axel's Castle: a Study in the Imaginative Literature of 1870–1930.* New York: Charles Scribner's Sons, 1931.

Winn, James Anderson. *Unsuspected Eloquence: A History of the Relations between Poetry and Music.* New Haven, CT: Yale University Press, 1981.

Woolf, Virginia. "Mr. Bennett and Mrs. Brown." 1924. *The Captain's Death Bed, and Other Essays.* London: Hogarth Press, 1950. 90–111.

Wordsworth, William. "Preface to the Second Edition of the Lyrical Ballads." 1800. *English Romantic Writers.* Ed. David Perkins. New York: Harcourt Brace Jovanovich, Inc., 1967. 320–331.

Worringer, Wilhelm. *Abstraction and Empathy: a Contribution to the Psychology of Style.* 1908. Trans. Michael Bullock. New York: International Universities Press, 1953.

Yeats, W. B. "A Packet for Ezra Pound." *A Vision.* 1937. London: Macmillan; Papermac, 1989. 1–30.

"Introduction." *The Oxford Book of Modern Verse: 1892–1935.* Chosen by W. B. Yeats. Oxford: Oxford University Press, 1936. vxlii.

Žižek, Slavoj. "I Hear You with My Eyes": or the Invisible Master." *Voice and Gaze as Love Objects.* SIC 1. Eds. Renata Salecl and Slavoj Žižek. Durham, NC and London: Duke University Press, 1996. 90–126.

Zukovsky, Louis. "The Cantos of Ezra Pound." *The Criterion* 10.40 (April 1931): 424–440.

Index

Note that numbers in italics refer to illustrations.